PHYSICS
Matters
THIRD EDITION

PHYSICS
Matters
THIRD EDITION

NICK ENGLAND

Hodder & Stoughton
A MEMBER OF THE HODDER HEADLINE GROUP

The publishers would like to thank the following individuals, institutions and companies for permission to reproduce photographs in this book. Every effort has been made to trace ownership of copyright. The publishers are happy to make arrangements with any copyright holder whom it has not been possible to contact.

ActionPlus page 4, 16 (bottom), 25, 26 (left), 30, 34, 36, 39, 40 (bottom), 48, 50, 102 (top), 155, 287; Airfotos Limited page 168; AKG London page 88; Associated Press KEYSTONE page 18 (left); Bettmann/Corbis 2 (top); Black and Decker page 267; Celestial Image Co. page 63; Anup Shah/BBC Natural History Unit page 213; Bruce Coleman Collection page 1, 26, 55 (right), 148, 192; Corbis page 311; Corel Corporation page 215; Henry Diltz/Corbis page 297; Kevin Fleming/Corbis page 229; Fujitsu page 305; Philip Harris Education Images page 173 (right), 277, 289, 303; Jean Heguy/Corbis page 110; Andrew Lambert page 260, 262, 264; Barbara Berkowitz/Life File page 230, Joseph Green/Life File page 140, Mike Maidment/Life File page 106 (top), Barry Mayes/Life File page 102 (bottom), Nigel Sitwell/Life File page 141, Flora Torrance/Life File page 127, Andrew Ward/Life File page 105, 106 (top), 124, 161,162, 124 (top), 190 (top), 219, Emma Lee/Life File page 125, John Woodhouse/Life File page 100, Life File Photo Library page 18 (top), 108 (right); Robert Maass/Corbis page 327; The National Grid Company Plc page 276; PA Photos page 28, Polaroid page 183 (top and bottom); Quadrant/ Simon Everett page 270; Reuters New Media Inc./Corbis page 300; Science & Society Picture Library page 2 (left), 121.186 (top); Alex Bartel/Science Photo Library page 139, Tim Beddow/Science Photo Library page 328, Martin Bond/ Science Photo Library page 97, 236, Dale Boyer/Science Photo Library page 178 (right), Dr Tony Brain/Science Photo Library page 304, Jean-Loup Charmet/Science Photo Library page 222 (top), Deep Light Productions/ Science Photo Library page 207, Luke Dodd/Science Photo Library page 79, Martin Dohrn/Science Photo Library page 165, 234, Science Photo Library page 31, George East/Science Photo Library page 200, Simon Fraser/Science Photo Library page 199, 248, Francois Gohier/Science Photo Library page 76, Carlos Goldin/Science Photo Library page 171, GJLP/CNRI/Science Photo Library page 261, Klaus Guldbrandsen/Science Photo Library page 328 (bottom), David A. Hardy/Science Photo Library page 72 (right), Tony & Daphne Hallas/Science Photo Library page 73 (left), Chris Knapton/Science Photo Library page 231, Lick Observatory/Science Photo Library page 81, Chris Madeley/Science Photo Library page 68, Will & Deni Mcintyre/Science Photo Library page 186 (bottom), John Meade/Science Photo Library page 112 (bottom), Peter Menzel/Science Photo Library page 222 (bottom), Mount Stromlo and Siding Sprong Observatories/Science Photo Library page 80, Nasa/Science Photo Library page 75, 78, 82 (top), 82 (bottom), 84 (left), 85 (top), 85 (bottom), 87, 95, 178 (left), 257, Novosti/Science Photo Library page 324, David Nunuk/Science Photo Library page 69, David Parker/Science Photo Library page 320, Alfred Pasieka/Science Photo Library page 258, Max-Planck-Institut fur Physik und Astrophysik/Science Photo Library page 81 (left), Philippe Plailly/Science Photo Library page 119, Science Source/Science Photo Library page 120, Hubert Raguet/Eurelios/Science Photo Library page 181, Maximilian Stock Ltd/Science Photo Library page 53, 73, Andrew Syred/ Science Photo Library page 285, US Air Force/Science Library Photo page 312, US Department of Energy/Science Photo Library page 313, 326, US Geological Survey/Science Photo Library page 84 (right), Gary Watson/Science Photo Library page 244, Charles D. Winters/Science Photo Library page 108 (left), Frank Zullo/Science Photo Library page 72 (left); Science Photo Library page 316, 321; Colin Taylor Productions page 108 (right); Third Eye Images/ Corbis 112 (top); Volvo page 40 (top), 41; Tim Wright/Corbis 40 (bottom)

The illustrations were drawn by Peters & Zabransky Limited

We are grateful to WJEC, Edexcel and OCR for permission to reproduce specimen GCSE questions.

Orders: please contact Bookpoint Ltd, 130 Milton Park, Abingdon, Oxon OX14 4SB. Telephone: (44) 01235 827720, Fax: (44) 01235 400454. Lines are open from 9.00 – 6.00, Monday to Saturday, with a 24 hour message answering service. Email address: orders@bookpoint.co.uk

British Library Cataloguing in Publication Data
A catalogue record for this title is available from The British Library
ISBN 0 340 79054 7

First published 1989, 2nd edition 1995, 3rd edition 2001
Impression number   10 9 8 7 6 5 4 3 2
Year   2007 2006 2005 2004 2003 2002 2001

Cover photo from Julian Baum/Science Photo Library
Typeset by Fakenham Photosetting Ltd
Printed in Italy for Hodder & Stoughton Educational, a division of Hodder Headline Ltd, 338 Euston Road, London NW1 3BH.

Preface

The first edition of *Physics Matters* was written in 1989 to meet the demands of the newly introduced GCSE courses. The purpose then was to make the book lively, interesting and relevant to the world around us. The third edition has the same aims, but has been updated to take account of recent syllabus changes. This edition is suitable for students taking Double Award science and for students who are studying Physics as a separate science.

The major feature of the new edition is the inclusion of more questions in the double page spreads, as well as more than 20 extra exam-style question pages. This edition also features a whole host of websites, providing a great deal of useful core and background information. Due to the transient nature of the World Wide Web, teachers are advised to check as to the existence and content of any web addresses before incorporating them into a lesson. Exercises which could have applications to IT are marked as such throughout, and text which may be useful as part of the 'Ideas and Evidence' section of the new GCSEs are highlighted with the following icon:

I am particularly grateful to the following people who have helped me prepare this edition: Stephen Halder and Elisabeth Tribe at Hodder & Stoughton; Paul Barrett and David Harrison for friendship, advice and teaching me how to teach; and Sue England for her forbearance, encouragement and secretarial skills.

Nick England
Ryde School
Isle of Wight
2001

Contents

Forces

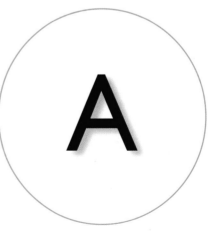

If this spider had made her web from steel with a similar thickness, it would probably break when a fly hit it

By the end of this section you should:

- be able to define and understand density
- understand and name different forces
- know the difference between stress and pressure
- understand Hooke's Law
- know about turning forces and simple levers
- be aware of the centre of gravity
- understand Archimedes' principle
- know the difference between a vector and a scalar

A

1 Density

Concorde was made from aluminium to give it a low density and high strength

Material	Density (kg/m³)
gold	19 300
mercury	13 600
lead	11 400
steel	8000
titanium	4500
aluminium	2700
glass	2500
water	1000
cork	200
air	1.3 } at standard
hydrogen	0.09 } temperature and pressure

Table 1

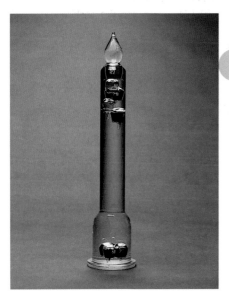

Galileo's thermometer (see question 2)

	Steel	Glass fibre
relative strength	40 000	50 000
density (kg/m³)	8 000	2 000
$\dfrac{\text{strength}}{\text{density}}$	5	25

Table 2

A tree obviously weighs more than a nail. Sometimes, you hear people say 'steel is heavier than wood'. What they mean is this: a piece of steel is heavier than a piece of wood with the same volume.

To compare the heaviness of materials we use the idea of **density**. Density can be calculated using this equation:

$$\text{density} = \frac{\text{mass}}{\text{volume}} \quad \text{or} \quad d = \frac{m}{V}$$

Density is usually measured in units of kg/m³. Some typical values of density are in Table 1.

Using density in engineering

Knowing the density of materials is very important to an engineer. This allows her to calculate the mass of building materials.

Example. What is the mass of a steel girder which is 10 m long, 0.1 m high and 0.1 m wide?

$$\text{The volume of the girder} = 10 \text{ m} \times 0.1 \text{ m} \times 0.1 \text{ m}$$
$$= 0.1 \text{ m}^3$$
$$d = \frac{m}{V}$$
$$\text{So } m = d \times V$$
$$= 8000 \text{ kg/m}^3 \times 0.1 \text{ m}^3$$
$$= 800 \text{ kg}$$

Steel is a very common building material because it is so strong. Despite this, in aeroplane construction aluminium and titanium are used because they have low densities. It is important to make an aeroplane as light as possible.

Glass fibre is one of the most important modern building materials. It is made by strengthening plastic with glass fibres. Table 2 allows us to compare steel and glass fibre. Glass fibre is actually a little stronger than mild steel. This means a larger force is needed to break it. Glass fibre has a much lower density than steel. This makes it ideal for building small boats. Unfortunately glass fibre cannot be used for very large boats because it bends too much.·

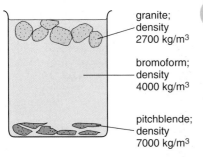

granite;
density
2700 kg/m³

bromoform;
density
4000 kg/m³

pitchblende;
density
7000 kg/m³

Figure 1

Density of rocks

Rocks near the surface of the Earth, such as granite, have densities of about 2700 kg/m³. Volcanic rocks have higher densities. This is because the lava that is thrown out of volcanoes comes from deep below the Earth's surface, where the density is higher.

The density of an object determines whether it sinks or floats. Cork floats on water, steel sinks. Cork is less dense than water, steel is more dense than water. An object only floats on a liquid if it is less dense than the liquid.

Geologists use this idea to separate out minerals. Pitchblende, a valuable material because it contains uranium, is usually found in granite rocks. Granite and pitchblende can be separated because of their different densities. The mixture of the two is crushed up. Then it is all put into bromoform (tribromomethane), a dense, toxic and carcinogenic liquid. The pitchblende sinks but the lighter granite floats (Figure 1).

Homework Questions

1 A student wrote the following sentence in an exam paper; read it and correct any mistakes you see.
'A cork floats in a pond because it is lighter than water; a stone sinks because it is too heavy to float in any liquid.'

2 Look at the photograph of Galileo's Thermometer. The density of water changes as it warms up; each float has a slightly different mass, so we can measure the temperature. As the temperature rises, do floats rise or sink?

3 (a) Explain why aluminium and titanium are used to build aeroplanes.
(b) In Table 2, the last row is headed 'strength/density'. Explain why this is an important ratio.

4 Copy Table 3 and fill in any gaps.

5 Carole is a geologist. She wants to work out the density of rock. First she weighs the rock, then she puts it into a beaker of water to work out its volume.

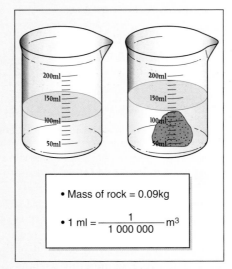

• Mass of rock = 0.09kg

• 1 ml = $\dfrac{1}{1\,000\,000}$ m³

(a) Use the diagrams to calculate the rock's volume. Give your answer in m³. (The markings on the beaker are all in ml.)
(b) Now calculate the rock's density in kg/m³.

6 Use Table 1 to calculate the volume of:
(a) 1000 kg of aluminium,
(b) 100 kg of cork.

7 White dwarf stars are extremely dense. They have a density of about 100 million kg/m³. If you had a matchbox full of material from a white dwarf, what would its mass be? (Hint: A matchbox has a volume of about 0.00005 m³.)

Table 3

Material	Volume (m³)	Mass (kg)	Density (kg/m³)
Osmium	0.02	450	
Lithium	0.000 02	0.01	
Titanium	0.5		4500
Water		3000	1000
Alcohol		3200	800
Radium	0.35		5000

Forces Near and Far

A force is a push or, as in this case, a pull

What is a force?

A force is a push or a pull. Whenever you push or pull something you are exerting a force on it. The forces that you exert can cause three things:

- **You can change the shape of an object**. You can stretch or squash a spring. You can bend or break a ruler.
- **You can change the speed of an object**. You can increase the speed of a ball when you throw it. You decrease its speed when you catch it.
- **A force can also change the direction in which something is travelling**. We use a steering wheel to turn a car.

The forces described so far are what we call **contact forces**. Your hand touches something to exert a force. There are also **non-contact forces**. Gravitational, magnetic and electric forces are non-contact forces. These forces can act over large distances without two objects touching. The Earth pulls you down whether or not your feet are on the ground. Although the Earth is 150 million km away from the Sun, the Sun's gravitational pull keeps us in orbit around it. Magnets also exert forces on each other without coming into contact.

The size of forces

- The pull of gravity on a fly = 0.001 N
- The pull of gravity on an apple = 1 N
- The frictional force slowing a rolling football = 2 N
- The force required to squash an egg = 50 N
- The pull of gravity on you = 500 N
- Tension in a rope, towing a car = 1000 N
- The frictional force exerted by the brakes of a car = 5000 N
- The push from the engines of a rocket = 1 000 000 N
- 1000 N = 1 kN (kilonewton)
- 1 000 000 = 1 MN (mega newton)

The unit we use to measure force is the **newton**, (**N**). The box in the margin will help you to get the feel of the size of several forces.

A force is a **vector** quantity; this means that it has both a size and a direction. We show forces by drawing an arrow in the direction of the force, and next to it we write its size, remembering to show the unit of force, N. Figure 1 shows Annabel's weight, which pulls her downwards; Figure 2 shows the tension in a rope which is pulling a car forwards.

600N

Figure 1

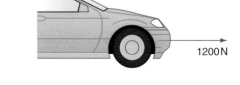

1200 N

Figure 2

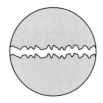

Figure 3 *How two surfaces appear when seen through a powerful microscope.*

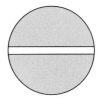

Figure 4 *Reducing friction*
(a) If the surfaces are highly polished, friction is less.

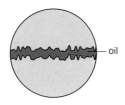

oil

(b) A layer of oil between two surfaces acts as a cushion to stop the edges catching.

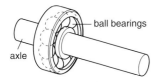

ball bearings
axle

(c) Steel balls reduce friction by allowing surfaces to roll over each other.

Some important forces

Weight is the name that we give to the pull of gravity on an object. Near the Earth's surface the pull of gravity is 10 N on each kilogram. We say that the Earth's gravitational field strength is 10 N/kg.
Example. What is your weight if your body has a mass of 50 kg?

$$weight = pull\ of\ gravity$$
$$= 50\ kg \times 10\ N/kg$$
$$= 500\ N$$

Tension is the name given to a force which acts through a stretched rope; when two teams pull on a rope it is under tension. When something is squashed it comes under forces of **compression**; the pillars of a building are under compression.

Friction is the contact force that slows down moving things. Friction can also prevent stationary things from starting to move when other forces act on them. Figure 3 helps you to understand why frictional forces occur. No surface is perfectly smooth. If you look at a surface through a powerful microscope you will be able to see that it has many rough spikes and edges. When two surfaces move past each other these rough spikes catch onto each other and slow down the motion.

Friction is often a nuisance because the rubbing between two surfaces turns kinetic (motion) energy into heat. Some ways of reducing friction are shown in Figure 4. Sometimes, though, friction is useful. Brakes work by using friction to slow down cars. Also, when you walk, the frictional forces between your foot and the floor push you forward.

Homework Questions

1 (a) Give three examples of forces which are pulls, and three examples which are pushes.
(b) For each of the forces above, state an approximate value for the size of the force.
(c) Draw a diagram to show the size and direction of the force.
2 How big is the weight of
(i) a 2 kg bag of sugar
(ii) a 1000 kg car?
3 (a) Explain how a wheel acts to reduce friction.
(b) There is a frictional force between a bicycle wheel and its axle. Explain two ways in which frictional forces are reduced.

4 In the following diagrams some forces are shown acting on some objects. In each case explain the effect which the forces produce.

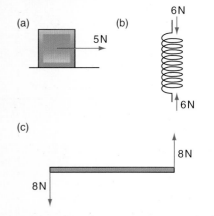

You always choose a sharp knife when you want to chop up meat or vegetables ready for cooking. A sharp knife has a very thin edge to the blade. This means that the force which you apply is concentrated into a very small area. We say that the pressure under the blade is large.

$$\text{pressure} = \frac{\text{force}}{\text{area}} \quad \text{or} \quad P = \frac{F}{A}$$

The unit of pressure is **N/m²** or **pascal** (**Pa**); $1 \ \text{N/m}^2 = 1 \ \text{Pa}$.

Pressure points

The photograph shows a physics teacher lying on a bed of nails. How can he lie there without hurting himself? You all know that nails are sharp and will make a hole in you if you tread on one. The teacher has spread his body out, so that it is supported by a lot of nails. The area of nails supporting him is large enough for it not to hurt (too much!).

What point is he trying to make here? (Don't try this at home!)

When an engineer, designs the foundations of a bridge she must think about pressure. In the example shown in Figure 1, the bridge will sink into the soil if it causes a pressure greater than 80 kN/m² (80 000 N/m²). What minimum area must the foundations have to stop this happening?

The bridge has a weight of 1.2 MN, so each pillar will support 0.6 MN (600 000 N).

$$P = \frac{F}{A}$$
$$\text{So} \quad A = \frac{F}{P}$$
$$= \frac{0.6 \ \text{MN}}{80 \ \text{kN/m}^2} = \frac{600\,000 \ \text{N}}{80\,000 \ \text{N/m}^2} = 7.5 \ \text{m}^2$$

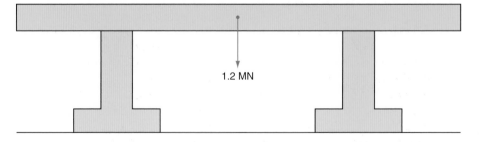

1.2 MN

Figure 1

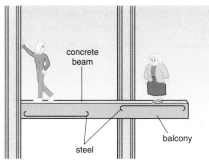

Figure 2

Material	Crushing pressure MN/m²	Breaking stress MN/m²
concrete	70	1
cast iron	70	10
steel	400	200

Table 1

Crushing pressure and breaking stress

Engineers also have to think about the pressure that a material can withstand without breaking; this is called the **crushing pressure**. A lot of modern buildings are made out of concrete, which is cheap and easy to produce. Concrete is very strong when it is compressed (squashed) but weak when it is stretched. When materials are stretched we say that they are **under stress**, or tension. We define stress like this:

$$\text{stress} = \frac{\text{stretching force}}{\text{area}}$$

So stress is rather like pressure, but it stretches something rather than squashing it.

If a concrete beam is going to be stretched (under tension) in a building it is strengthened with steel bars. As you can see from Table 1, steel is far stronger than concrete under tension. A breaking stress of 200 MN/m² means that a steel bar of area 1 m² could support 200 MN before breaking.

Homework Questions

1 (a) Explain why in some buildings people are not allowed to wear stiletto heels.
(b) How does a drawing pin take advantage of high pressure at one end and low pressure at the other end?
(c) Give two examples in sport or other activities in which something is used to reduce pressure.
(d) Give two examples of a device which is used to increase pressure.

2 (a) Make a copy of Figure 2 and show which parts of the beam are under tension, and which are under compression (being squashed).
(b) Explain the positioning of the steel bars.

3 (a) When a pressure of 4.5 N/mm² is applied to your skin it hurts. Each nail in the bed opposite has a point with an area of 1.5 mm². How much weight can the teacher put on each nail without being hurt?
(b) The teacher's weight is 690 N. How many nails (at least) should he put in the bed?
(c) Explain why he must be very careful getting on and off the bed.

4 (a) Use the information in Table 1 and Figure 1 to work out the smallest area which the concrete pillars can have if they are to hold up the bridge safely.
(b) The chief engineer advises you to build the bridge with pillars five times the area you have just calculated. Why?

5 Opposite you can see Boris, Vladimir and Leonid. Boris is twice as tall, twice as long and twice as wide as Vladimir, but they have the same density.
(a) How many times more massive than Vladimir is Boris?
(b) The area of Boris's paw is greater than the area of Vladimir's paw. By how many times is it bigger?
(c) Is the pressure bigger under Boris's paws or under Vladimir's paws? By what factor does the pressure differ under the two cats' paws?
(d) Leonid the lion is a distant cousin to Boris. Lions, as you know, are much bigger than domestic cats. Can you use the

result of part (c) to explain why a lion's legs are proportionately thicker than a cat's?

Boris (cat)

Vladimir (kitten)

Leonid (lion)

Pressure in Liquids

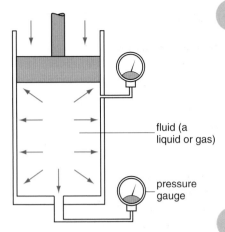

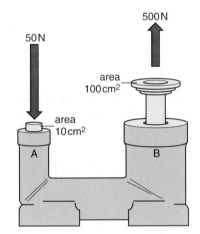

Figure 1 *The pressure in a fluid acts equally in all directions*

Figure 2 *The principle of a hydraulic jack*

Transmitting pressures

When you hit a nail with a hammer the pressure is transmitted downwards to the point. This happens only because the nail is rigid.

When a ruler is used to push a lot of marbles lying on a table, they do not all move along the direction of the push. Some of the marbles give others a sideways push. The marbles are behaving like a fluid.

In Figure 1 you can see a cylinder of fluid which has been squashed by pushing a piston down. The pressure increases everywhere in the fluid, not just next to piston. The fluid is made up of lots of tiny particles, which act like marbles, to transmit the pressure to all points.

Hydraulic machines

We often use liquids to transmit pressures. Liquids can change shape, but they hardly change their volume when compressed. Figure 2 shows how a hydraulic jack works.

A force of 50 N presses down on the surface above A. The extra pressure that this force produces in the oil is:

$$P = \frac{F}{A}$$

$$= \frac{50 \text{ N}}{10 \text{ cm}^2} \qquad = 5 \text{ N/cm}^2$$

The same pressure is passed through the liquid to B. So the upwards force that the surface B can provide is:

$$F = P \times A$$

$$= 5 \text{ N/cm}^2 \times 100 \text{ cm}^2 = 500 \text{ N}$$

With this machine you can lift a load of 500 N, by applying a force of only 50 N. Figure 3 shows another use of hydraulics.

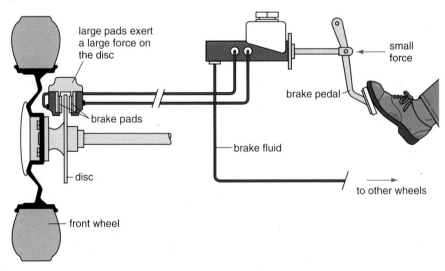

Figure 3 *Cars use a hydraulic braking system. The foot exerts a small force on the brake pedal. The pressure created by this force is transmitted by the brake fluid to the brake pads. The brake pads have a large area and exert a large force on the wheel disc. The same pressure can be transmitted to all four wheels.*

Increase of pressure with depth

The pressure below the surface of a liquid depends on three things:

- **depth**, h
- **density**, d
- the **pull of gravity** per kilogram, g (g = 10 N/kg)

The pressure that acts on a diver depends on the weight of water above him. As he goes deeper the weight of water on him increases, so the pressure also increases.

The diver feels a bigger pressure under 10 m of sea water than under 10 m of fresh water. Sea water has a higher density than fresh water.

The strength of the gravitational pull on the diver affects the force that the water exerts on the diver. The Earth gives a downwards pull of 10 N per kilogram.

To calculate the pressure P under a liquid you can use this formula:

$$P = g \times h \times d$$

The units of these quantities in the equation are: P, N/m²; g, N/kg; h, m; d, kg/m³.

The manometer

Figure 4 shows how you can use a **manometer** to measure the pressure of a gas supply. The two points X and Y are at the same level in the liquid. This means that the pressures at X and Y are the same.

Pressure at X = gas supply pressure.
Pressure at Y = atmospheric pressure + pressure due to 27.2 cm of water.

So the gas supply pressure is greater than atmospheric pressure, by an amount equal to the pressure due to a column of water 27.2 cm high. We say that the extra pressure (above atmospheric pressure) of the gas supply is '27.2 cm of water'.

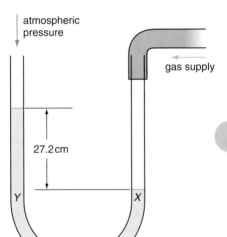

Figure 4 *A manometer*

Homework Questions

1 This question refers to the gas supply in Figure 4.
(a) One day you notice that the difference in height between the water levels at X and Y has increased to 30.2 cm. Explain what has happened.
(b) The water is replaced by oil. Use the information in the table to explain what will happen to the difference in height now.

Liquid	Density (kg/m³)
Water	1000
Oil	800

2 Sometimes, after a road accident, the Fire Brigade uses inflated air bags to lift a vehicle, to free passengers who have become trapped. Explain how such bags can lift a large load easily.

3 (a) Use the equation above and the table in question 1 to calculate the pressure acting on a diver at depths of (i) 10 m, (ii) 30 m.
(The atmosphere exerts a pressure of 100 000 N/m² at the surface.)
(b) Calculate the force exerted by the sea's pressure on the diver's mask at a depth of 30 m. (His mask has an area of 0.02 m².)
(c) Explain why the diver's mask is in no danger of breaking under this pressure.

4 The diagram opposite shows the principle of a hydraulic jack. Two cylinders are connected by a reservoir of oil. A 200 N weight resting on piston A, can be used to lift a larger load on piston B.
(a) Calculate the extra pressure at x, due to the 200 N weight.
(b) Explain why the pressure at y is the same as the pressure at x.
(c) Why would the jack not work if the oil were replaced by a gas?
(d) Calculate the size of the load, W, which can be lifted.
(e) If you need to lift W by 0.5 m, how far do you need to move piston A?

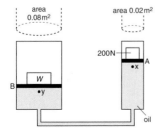

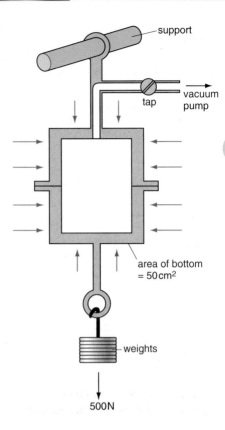

Figure 1 *You can measure atmospheric pressure using this apparatus*

A simple experiment can show you the action of atmospheric pressure. A vacuum pump is used to remove the air from a metal can. Soon after the pump is switched on, the can collapses. This shows that:

● Atmospheric pressure acts in all directions.
● Atmospheric pressure is very large.

The size of atmospheric pressure

Figure 1 shows a hollow metal cylinder, which comes apart in two pieces. When the air is pumped out of it, a large force is needed to pull the two halves apart. You can measure the size of this force, by attaching weights to the bottom half of the cylinder.

Example. You might find that a total mass of 50 kg is needed to pull the halves apart. When this happens, the pressure from the weight of the 50 kg balances atmospheric pressure.

So atmospheric pressure, $P = \dfrac{F}{A}$

$$= \frac{500 \text{ N}}{50 \text{ cm}^2}$$

$$= \begin{array}{l} 10 \text{ N/cm}^2 \textit{ or } 100\,000 \text{ N/m}^2 \text{ (Pa)} \\ (\text{since } 1 \text{ m}^2 = 10\,000 \text{ cm}^2) \end{array}$$

This is a very large pressure. The atmosphere exerts a force of about 100 000 N (the weight of 100 large men) on the outside of a window (area about 1 m²). The window does not break, because air inside the house pushes back with a force the same size.

Using atmospheric pressure

Piles which anchor the foundations of buildings are usually knocked into the ground by a large pile driver. However, circular or ring piles can be driven into the ground by atmospheric pressure (Figure 2). The idea is to place a dome over the top of the piles. Then a vacuum pump takes the air out of the space under the dome. There is now a large pressure difference between the inside and outside, which pushes the piles into the ground.

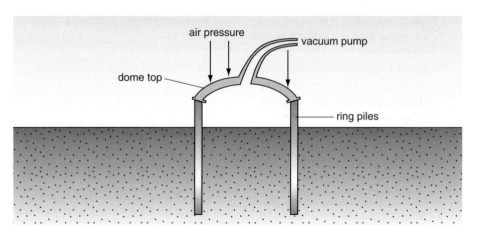

Figure 2 *Driving in piles with air pressure*

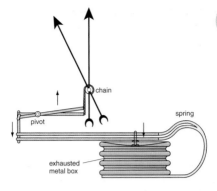

Figure 3 *An aneroid barometer. The expansion of the metal box, when the pressure drops, causes the movement of a pointer.*

Measuring atmospheric pressure

Instruments that measure atmospheric pressure are called **barometers** (see Figures 3 and 4). The most accurate type is the mercury barometer (Figure 4). The pressure at the points x and y is the same. So the pressure due to 760 mm of mercury, Hg, is equal to the atmospheric pressure. This is the average pressure of the atmosphere, written as: 760 mm Hg.

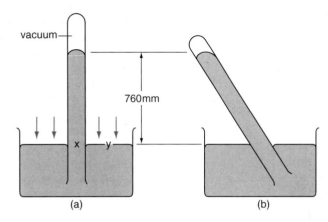

Figure 4 *A mercury barometer. The average atmospheric pressure is 760 mm of mercury. It does not matter if the barometer is tilted, as the vertical height of the mercury column stays the same.*

Homework Questions

1 Describe two experiments which show that atmospheric pressure is very large.

2 Explain why atmospheric pressure is less at the top of a mountain, in comparison with sea level.

3 (a) When you drink through a straw, what forces the liquid upwards?
   (b) If you climbed to the top of Mount Everest, where atmospheric pressure is 300 mm Hg, would you find it easier to drink through a straw?

4 This question is about driving piles in using atmospheric pressure (Figure 2).
   (a) Use the diagram and scale to check that the area of the top of the dome is about 12 m².
   (b) Use your answer to work out

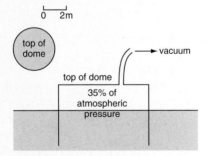

the force with which the atmosphere pushes down on the dome top. (Atmospheric pressure is 100 000 Pa.)
   (c) The pile sinks into the ground when the air pressure is reduced to 35% of atmospheric pressure. What force then pushes upwards on the dome?

   (d) What is the maximum load which can be allowed to rest on these piles?
   (e) The atmosphere also acts on the sides of the dome. Why do you not need to include this effect in your calculations?

5 You take the apparatus shown in Figure 1 to the planet Zeta where the pull of gravity is 25 N on each kilogram. When you evacuate the apparatus, as described opposite, you find that a mass of 40 kg is needed to pull apart the two halves of the cylinder.
   (a) How big is the pull of gravity on the 40 kg mass?
   (b) Calculate the atmospheric pressure on Zeta.

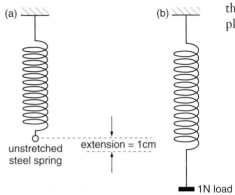

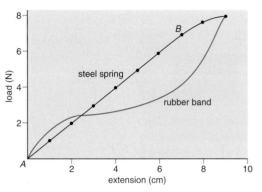

Figure 1 shows a simple experiment to investigate the behaviour of a spring. The spring stretches when a load is hung on the end of it. The increase in length of the spring is called its **extension**. You can enter values in a spreadsheet and then plot a graph of load against extension on a computer.

Figure 1

Figure 2

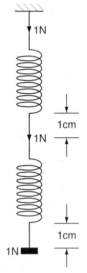

(a) The total extension is 2 cm

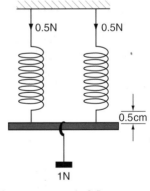

(b) Each spring extends 0.5 cm

Figure 3

You will find that it produces a straight line such as *AB* in Figure 2. This shows that the extension is proportional to the load. A material that behaves in this way is said to obey Hooke's Law:

> Extension is proportional to the load

At point *B* the spring has reached its **elastic limit**. Hooke's Law is no longer obeyed. Over the region *AB* of the graph the spring shows elastic behaviour. This means that when the load is removed from the spring, it returns to its original length and shape.

However, if a load of more than 7 N (beyond point *B*) is applied to this spring, it changes its shape permanently. When the load is removed it does not return to its original shape. This is called **plastic deformation**. When you bounce a hard rubber ball it deforms **elastically**. How do you think Plasticine deforms?

Only some materials obey Hooke's Law. You can see from Figure 2 that a rubber band certainly does not.

Figure 3 shows what happens when a load is put onto two springs. When you put two springs in series each one is pulled by the force of 1 N. Each spring is extended by 1 cm, and the total extension is now 2 cm (Figure 3a). When springs are put in parallel (side by side) each one supports half of the load. Each spring only extends by 0.5 cm (Figure 3b).

Building materials

Any engineer needs to understand the properties of the materials which are used to build a house or a bridge. Figure 4a shows a laboratory sample of steel with a load applied, and Figure 4b shows how it deformed under tension. When the tensile force reached 1800 N, the sample deformed plastically – it changed shape irreversibly.

On the same graph (Figure 4b), you can see how an identically shaped sample of cast iron behaved. The iron broke suddenly when the stretching force reached 1100 N. Cast iron is a **brittle** material; this means that it breaks without first bending or stretching out of shape.

In some ways iron and steel are quite similar. They are both *strong* materials, needing a large force to break them; they are also both *stiff* materials because a large force only causes a small change in shape. However, because iron is brittle it is not safe for building large structures. At the end of the nineteenth century, the

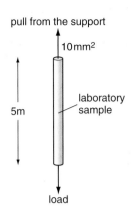

Figure 4(a)

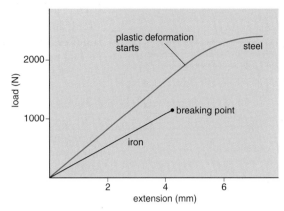

Figure 4(b) *The load/extension graph for steel and iron samples*

Tay Bridge (built of iron) collapsed, plunging a train with its passengers into the river below. Had the bridge been made of steel, it might have buckled, but brittle fracture would not have occurred with such catastrophic effect.

Homework Questions

1. In diagram A, a 2 N weight extends the spring by 4 cm. In each case, B, C and D, calculate the weight hanging on the springs; all the springs are identical.

2. Use the diagram below to help you work out the size of the force which will cause this steel girder to deform plastically.

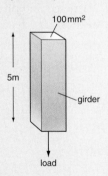

3. (a) Draw diagrams to show the forces acting on a steel girder which is: (i) under tension, (ii) under compression.
   (b) The diagram shows forces acting on a rod; what effect will these *shearing* forces have on it?

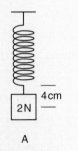

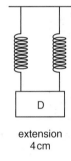

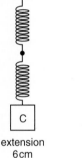

Diagram A

4. Figure 2, in the text, shows the force extension graphs for a rubber band and a spring. Use this graph to work out
   (i) the extension caused by a force of 3N when the band and spring are in series
   (ii) the force needed to produce a 4 cm extension when they are in parallel.

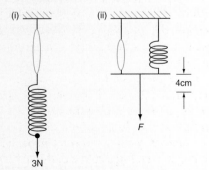

5. The table below shows how a spring extends when increasing loads are hung on it.
   (a) Plot a graph of extension (*y*-axis) against load (*x*-axis).
   (b) Up to what load does this spring obey Hooke's Law?
   (c) What has happened to the spring after a load of 5.0 N has been put on it?

Load (N)	Extension (cm)
0	0
1.0	2.0
2.0	4.0
3.0	6.0
4.0	8.0
5.0	11.0
6.0	15.0

7 Turning Forces

Figure 1

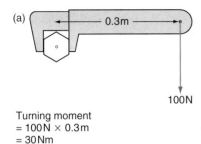

(a)

0.3m

100N

Turning moment
= 100 N × 0.3 m
= 30 Nm

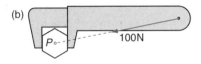

(b)

P

100N

A force acting through the nut has no turning moment.

If you have ever tried changing the wheel on a car, you will know that you are not strong enough to undo the nuts with your fingers. You need a spanner to get a larger turning effect. A tight nut will need a long spanner and a large force.

The size of the turning effect of a force about a point is called a **turning moment**.

$$\text{Turning moment} = \text{force} \times \begin{array}{l}\text{perpendicular distance of}\\\text{the force from the point}\end{array}$$

Perpendicular means 'at right angles'. Figure 1 shows you why this distance is important. If you push the spanner towards the nut (Figure 1b) you get no turning force at all.

The same idea applies to lifting heavy loads with a mobile crane (Figure 2). If the turning effect of the load is too large the crane will tip over. So, inside his cab, the crane operator has a table to tell him the greatest load that the crane can lift for a particular working radius.

Table 1 shows you how this works. For example, the crane can lift a load of 60 tonnes safely with a **working radius** of 16 m. If the crane is working at a radius of 32 m, it can only lift 30 tonnes. You get the same turning effect by doubling the working radius and lifting half the load.

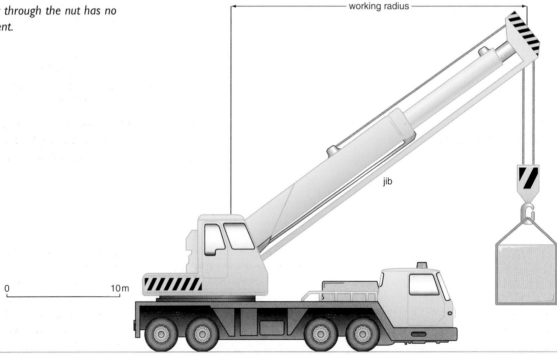

Figure 2 *A mobile crane*

Working radius (m)	Maximum safe load (tonnes)	load × radius (tonne × m)
12	80	960
16	60	960
20	48	960
24	40	960
28	34	960
32	30	960
36	27	960

Table 1 **A load table for a crane operator**

Balancing

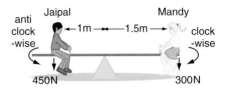

Figure 3 *How is the see-saw balanced?*

In Figure 3 you can see Jaipal and Mandy sitting on the see-saw, which is balanced. It balances because Jaipal's turning moment is balanced exactly by Mandy's turning moment in the opposite direction.

Jaipal's anticlockwise turning moment = 450 N × 1.0 m
= 450 Nm

Mandy's clockwise turning moment = 300 N × 1.5 m
= 450 Nm

The see-saw is in **equilibrium**.

In equilibrium:

● The sum of the anticlockwise moments = The sum of the clockwise moments
● The forces in any direction must balance to produce no resultant force.

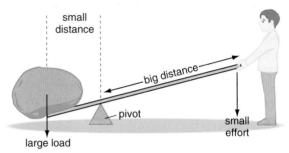

Figure 4 *A simple lever. The rock can be lifted when its turning effect is balanced by the turning effect of the man's push. With a long lever a small effort can lift a large load.*

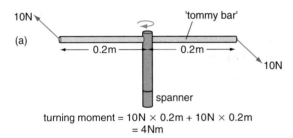

turning moment = 10N × 0.2m + 10N × 0.2m
= 4Nm

Figure 5 *When two equal forces act to produce a turning effect, they are called a couple. A couple causes a rotational effect, but the resultant force on the bar is zero.*

Homework Questions

1 (a) When you cannot undo a tight screw, you use a screwdriver with a large handle. Explain why.
(b) Explain why door handles are not put near hinges.
(c) Where do you have to put the spare penny to balance the ruler?

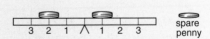

2 Look at the crane in Figure 2.
(a) What is meant by working radius?
(b) Use the scale in Figure 2 to calculate the working radius of the crane.

(c) Use the data in Table 1 to calculate the greatest load that the crane can lift safely in this position.
(d) Laura, a student engineer, makes this comment: 'You can see from the driver's table that the crane can lift 960 tonnes, when the working radius is 1 m.' Do you agree with her?

3 Alice, 225 N, and Dominic, 360 N, join Jaipal and Mandy at the park.
(a) Jaipal stays 1 m from the pivot, and Mandy gets off the see-saw. Where does Alice sit to balance Jaipal? Where would Dominic have to sit?
(b) Mandy sits 1.2 m from the

pivot, where does Dominic sit to balance her?
(c) Alice sits 2 m from the pivot, and Dominic 1.25 m, both on the same side. Where does Jaipal sit to balance the see-saw now?

4 What turning moment about the nut does this 200 N force have?

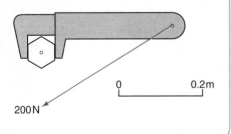

Centre of gravity

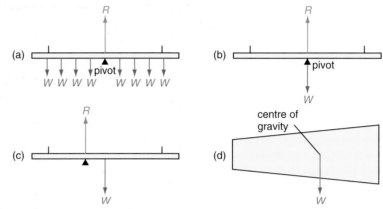

Figure 1

This rocking toy is stable because its centre of gravity is below the pivot

Figure 1(a) shows a see-saw that is balanced about its midpoint. Gravity has the same turning effect on the right-hand side of the see-saw, as it has on the left-hand side. The resultant turning effect is zero.

The action of the weight of the see-saw is the same as a single force, W, which acts downwards through the pivot (Figure 1(b)). This force has no turning moment about the pivot. As the see-saw is stationary, the pivot must exert an upwards force R on it, which is equal to W.

When the see-saw is not pivoted about its midpoint, the weight will act to turn it (Figure 1(c)).

The point that the weight acts through is called the **centre of gravity**. The centre of gravity of the see-saw lies at its midpoint because it has a regular shape. In Figure 1(d) the centre of gravity lies nearer the thick end of the shape.

Jumping higher

When you stand up straight your centre of gravity lies inside your body. But in some positions you can get your centre of gravity outside your body.

This idea is most important for pole vaulters and high jumpers (Figure 2(a)). Suppose a high jumper's legs can provide enough energy to lift her centre of gravity to a height 2 m above the ground. If she can make her centre of gravity pass under the bar, she can clear a bar higher than 2 m (Figure 2(b)).

Why do Fosbury-floppers usually win?

Figure 2 *(a) Centre of gravity inside the body*

(b) Centre of gravity outside the body

Equilibrium, stability and toppling

Something is in equilibrium when both the resultant force and resultant turning moment on it are zero. We talk about three different kinds of equilibrium, depending on what happens to the object when it is given a small push.

- A football on a flat piece of ground is in **neutral equilibrium**. When given a gentle kick, the ball rolls, keeping its centre of gravity at the same height.
- A tall thin radio mast is in **unstable equilibrium**. It is balanced with its centre of gravity above its base. However, a small push (from the wind) will move its centre of gravity downwards. To prevent toppling the mast is stabilised with support wires.
- A car is in **stable equilibrium** (Figure 3(a)). When the car is tilted the centre of gravity is lifted, (b). In this position the action of the weight keeps the car on the road. In (c) the centre of gravity lies above the wheels; the car is in a position of unstable equilibrium. If the car tips further (d), the weight now provides a turning moment to topple the car. Cars are more stable if they have a low centre of gravity and a wide wheel base.

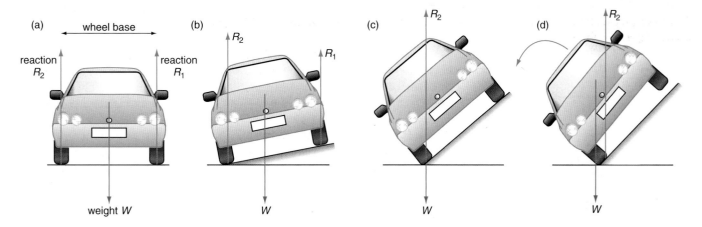

Figure 3

Homework Questions

1 You are in the business of manufacturing lager glasses. You want to make your profits as big as possible, so you decide to produce a very unstable glass, which will get knocked over very easily. Then people will have to buy more glasses. Discuss which shape of glass will be most suitable for your purpose.

   (a)　　　(b)　　　(c)

2 (a) Explain why people are allowed to stand on the lower deck of a double decker bus, but not on the higher one.
   (b) Explain three features which give Formula 1 cars great stability.

3 Look at the information in the diagram and work out where the centre of gravity of the retort stand is; its weight is 9 N.

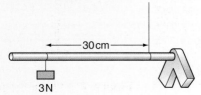

4 The diagram shows a steering wheel. Copy it and add arrows to show the forces which act on it when (i) two hands exert a force of 5 N each to turn it; (ii) one hand turns it with a force of 10 N (hint: there is a second force).

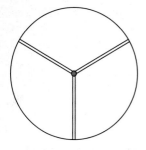

9 Floating

The salt water in the Dead Sea is denser than the water in other seas. This makes you float higher so that it is easier to just lie back than to swim!

Archimedes' Principle applies to objects in the air as well. This hot-air balloon has the same weight as the air which the balloon has displaced

You may be able to lie on your back and float in a swimming pool. There are two forces which are acting on you. Your weight acts downwards and the water provides an upwards push, called an upthrust. Without this upthrust you would sink. Water provides this upthrust because the pressure of water underneath you is greater than the pressure on top.

Figure 1 shows how you can measure the size of an upthrust. The metal block has a weight of 3.0 N (Figure 1(a)). When it is lowered into the displacement can, the balance reading falls from 3.0 N to 2.0 N (Figure 1(b)). This means that the water provides an upthrust of 1.0 N on the block. When the block is submerged some water is displaced. In this case, the weight of water displaced is 1.0 N.

The upthrust on an object when all or part of it is submerged in a fluid is equal to the weight of water displaced. This is **Archimedes' Principle**.

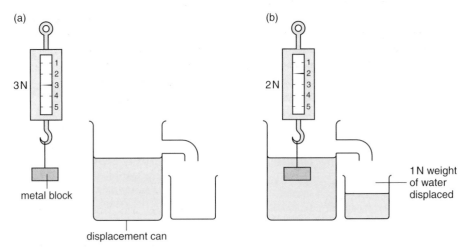

Figure 1

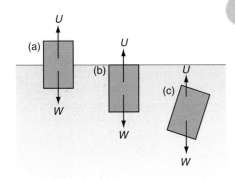

floating *U = W*   sinking *W > U*

Figure 2

Floating

Figure 2 shows two blocks of wood of different densities, which are floating. Since these blocks are in equilibrium there can be no resultant force acting on them. This means that the upthrust from the fluid is equal to the weight of the wood.

So when something floats, the weight of the object equals the weight of fluid displaced.

In Figure 2(a) the block of wood floats with only half of its volume submerged. What is its density?

$$\text{weight of wood } = \text{ weight of water displaced}$$

$$\text{so, mass of wood } = \text{ mass of water displaced}$$

$$\text{the volume of wood } = 2 \times \text{ volume of water displaced.}$$

This means that, in comparison with water, the wood has the same mass, but has twice the volume. Its density is therefore half that of water, so it is 500 kg/m³.

In Figure 2(b) the density of the wood is the same as that of water. The wood will float if its density is the same or less than that of water. It will sink if its density is greater (Figure 2(c)).

When you are describing the size of a ship it is usual to talk about its **displacement**. A ship that has a displacement of 100 000 tonnes, displaces that amount of water. This means that the ship's mass is also 100 000 tonnes. If the ship takes on board 10 000 tonnes of cargo it must displace a total of 110 000 tonnes of water to float.

Homework Questions

1 When a merchant ship is loaded in a port, it should not be allowed to sink below the level marked on *The Plimsoll Line*. The diagram shows safe loading levels for such a line: WNA winter North Atlantic; W, winter; S, summer; T, tropics; F, freshwater; TF, tropical freshwater.
(a) Why is the safety line higher in freshwater?
(b) Why does a ship float higher in winter than in summer?

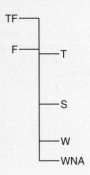

2 When an underwater diver breathes in he begins to rise; when he breathes out he begins to sink. Explain these observations.

3 A long cylinder hangs from a spring balance. As the cylinder is lowered into some water, measurements are taken from the spring balance, for different values of *d*, (see diagram and table opposite).
(a) Plot a graph of the balance reading (*y*-axis) against the distance *d* (*x*-axis).
(b) Use your graph to work out the length of the cylinder.
(c) What is the weight of the cylinder?
(d) When the cylinder is fully submerged what upthrust acts on it?
(e) Work out the density of the cylinder. (Density of water = 1000 kg/m³).

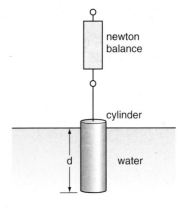

Distance, d (cm)	Force on balance (N)
0	51
10	46
20	41
30	36
40	32
50	32
60	32

Vectors and scalars

If you want to move a chair you have to give it a push. The direction in which the chair moves depends on the direction of your push. A large push gets the chair moving quickly; so both the direction and size of the force are important.

Force is an example of a vector quantity. Vector quantities have both size and direction. Other examples of vectors are: velocity (the wind blows at 50 km/h from the North); displacement (a car travels 20 km due East). A quantity which has only size is a scalar. Some examples of scalar quantities are: mass (3 kg of potatoes); temperature (20 °C); energy (100 joules).

Drawing forces

In previous sections you met the idea of forces such as weight, friction and tension. Because these forces have both size and direction, we represented them by an arrow to show the direction in which the force acts. Next to the arrow we write how large the force is, remembering to add its unit, newton (N).

Figure 1 shows two examples of forces acting on Michael: (a) his weight (the pull of gravity on him) is 600 N; (b) a rope with a tension of 150 N pulls him forwards.

It is usual for more than one force to act on something. Then we must show all the forces acting. When Michael is pulled by the rope (Figure 1(b)), his weight acts on him, and the floor supports him too – if the floor did not exert an upwards force on him equal to his weight, he would be falling downwards. The force is called the floor's **reaction force**, **R**. The floor will also exert a frictional force on him, in the opposite direction to that in which he is moving. All these forces are shown together in Figure 2.

Adding forces

When two forces act in the same direction, they add up to give a larger **resultant** or **net** force. In Figure 3, for example, two people each push the car with a force of 300 N. The resultant force acting on the car is now 600 N.

If forces act in opposite directions they may cancel each other out. In Figure 2 Michael's which weight pulls him downwards, is cancelled by the upwards force

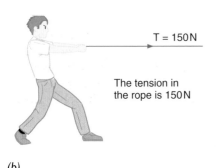

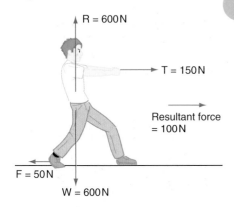

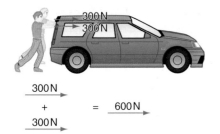

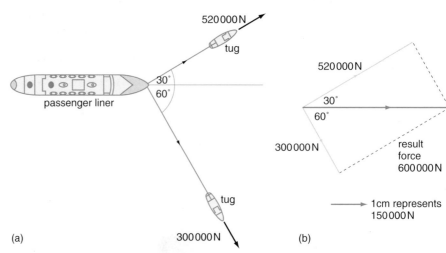

Figure 4

Figure 3

| 10N
| 10N

Figure 5 *(a)*

from the floor. The resultant force is zero; 600 N – 600 N. We say that these forces are balanced.

Michael therefore stays on the floor. There are other forces which act on Michael; the pull from the rope to the right is 150 N, but the frictional force to the left is 50 N. The resultant force on Michael is therefore 150 N – 50 N = 100 N, to the right.

In Figure 4, you can see two tugs pulling a passenger liner into port. To work out the resultant force on the liner it is necessary to make a scale drawing. We shall choose 1 cm to represent a force of 200 000 N. The forces from the two tugs are then drawn to the right length in the right direction as shown in Figure 4(b). (These are the blue lines.) Then two further (black broken) lines are drawn to complete the **parallelogram of forces**. The resultant force is the diagonal line across this parallelogram. You can see that the resultant force is 600 000 N straight ahead, because the length of the vector is 3 cm.

Forces – a summary

The purpose of this paragraph is to summarise what you should now know about the effects of forces. When balanced forces act on an object they can squash or stretch that object, or cause it to turn, as in Figure 5. However, if the forces are unbalanced (as they are in Figure 2) then that object will begin to move, or change its state of motion. This last important idea is covered in the next section of the book.

(b)

Homework Questions

1 A fisherman has caught a large fish and has to use two balances to weigh it. Look at the diagram to calculate its weight.

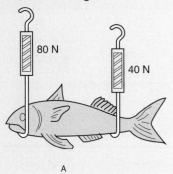

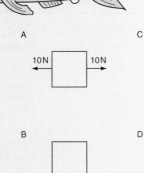

2 A golf ball is hit off its tee, 200 m down the fairway. Draw diagrams to show all the forces acting on the ball:
   (a) when the ball rests on the tee
   (b) while the club strikes the ball on the tee
   (c) as the ball is in flight.

3 (a) The diagrams below show all the forces acting on a box. In each case, describe what effect these forces have on the box.
   (b) For the diagrams A, B, C, D and

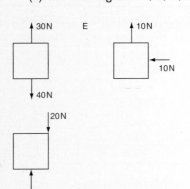

E state the size of the resultant force in each case.

4 Frank's weight is 800 N, and his bike's weight is 2500 N. What upwards force is exerted by the road on his rear wheel?

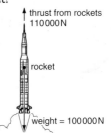

1100 N 2500 N 800 N

5 What is the resultant force on this rocket?

↑ thrust from rockets
110 000 N

rocket

weight = 100 000 N

SECTION A: Questions

1 The diagram shows two forcemeters, A and B. Each meter has a weight of 1 N. What is the reading on A?

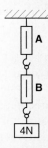

2 Make a copy of each of these drawings. Mark in the centre of gravity of each object.

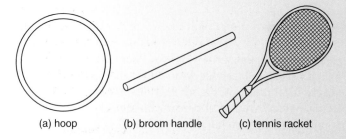

(a) hoop   (b) broom handle   (c) tennis racket

3 In the diagram below, each of the springs is identical. A load of 3 N stretches the springs 3 cm, until the top plate rests firmly on two fixed plates.
(a) Explain how this device can be used to measure both small and large loads accurately. Where in the

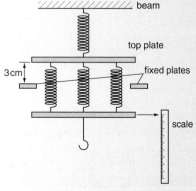

home might you use such a device?
(b) Sketch a graph to show how the movement of the bottom plate changes for loads from 0–12 N. Label the axes carefully.

4 Popeye is blowing into the sail in his boat to push it forwards. Is this possible?

5 The table below shows the properties of some materials used in the manufacturing and building industries. When choosing a material for a particular job, you need to consider the stiffness, strength and density of the material. You need to be aware of the cost too.
(a) Explain why concrete, brick and wood are often used for building houses.
(b) Explain what is meant by **stiffness**.

Why is the $\dfrac{\text{stiffness}}{\text{density}}$ ratio important?

(c) **Strength** is a measure of what load can be placed on 1 m² of a material before it crumbles or breaks.

Why is the $\dfrac{\text{strength}}{\text{density}}$ ratio important?

(d) Explain why steel is used for building bridges, but aluminium is used to build aircraft.
(e) GRP (fibre glass) can be used to build small boats, and even small minesweepers for the Navy.
(i) Why is it useful to make minesweepers from GRP?
(ii) Why are large ships not made from GRP?
(f) Turbine blades for aircraft engines need to be strong, stiff and light. Which material in the table would you choose for making the blades?

Material	Relative stiffness	Relative strength*	Density (kg/m³)	Stiffness Density	Strength Density	Cost per tonne (pounds)
Steel	21 000	40 000	7800	2.7	5.1	100
Aluminium	7300	27 000	2700	2.7	10	400
Wood	1400	2700	500	2.8	5.4	30
Concrete	1500	4000	2500	0.6	1.6	6
Brick	2100	5500	3000	0.7	1.8	10
GRP	2000	50 000	2000	1	25	70
CFRP	20 000	100 000	2000	10	50	1700

*These strengths are for when the materials are under compression.
GRP: Glass Reinforced Plastic (fibre glass).   CFRP: Carbon Fibre Reinforced Plastic.

6 Below, you can see two wells. Oil, salt water and natural gas are trapped by oil-proof layers of rock.

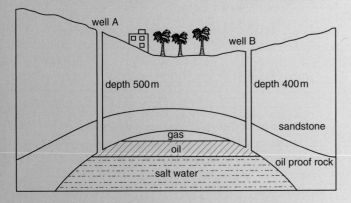

(a) (i) Why is the salt water lying below the oil?
(ii) Why is the natural gas lying above the oil?
(b) When well A is drilled, oil shoots 10 m above the ground. When well B is drilled, oil shoots much higher above the ground. Explain why oil shoots much higher from well B.
(c) As the oil escapes from the wells, what happens to (i) the volume of the natural gas; (ii) the pressure of the natural gas?
(d) After a few months, oil can still be obtained from well A but it has to be pumped out. Explain why the oil does not shoot out by itself.

EDEXCEL (ULEAC)

7 (a) State clearly *two* conditions necessary for a body to be in equilibrium.
(b) The diagram shows a mousetrap. The idea is that as the mouse walks towards the cheese he tips the plank up and then falls conveniently near to Boris the cat. Go through the following calculations to see how far along the plank the mouse can go before it tips up.
(i) Calculate the turning moment of the counter balance about the pivot.
(ii) The weight of the plank may be taken to act through the 50 cm mark. Calculate the turning moment of the cheese and the plank together.
(iii) Use your answers to (i) and (ii) to find where the mouse will overbalance the trap.
(c) Use the information in the diagram to calculate the upwards force that the pivot exerts on the plank, just as the 'trap' overbalances.

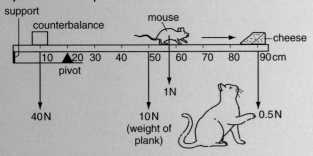

8 Bristol airport lies about 150 km due west of Heathrow airport.

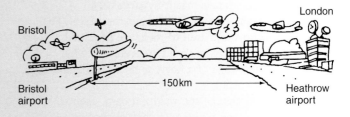

(a) On a windless day a light aircraft sets off from Heathrow to Bristol. The plane flies at 250 km/h. How long does it take to get there?
(b) On the return journey, a strong wind blows due north. The wind speed is 50 km/h. If the pilot sets off to fly east to Heathrow, in which direction will he end up going? Draw a diagram to illustrate your answer.
(c) He corrects his course so that he actually flies eastwards. In which direction must he point the plane? How long does his journey take? (You might find it useful to make a scale drawing.)

9 Mike is a physicist who likes to weigh himself in unusual ways. He knows that atmospheric pressure (100 000 N/m²) supports a column of mercury 75 cm high. He has attached a hot water bottle to a mercury manometer. When he stands on it the mercury moves as shown.

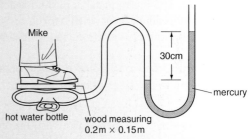

(a) What extra pressure does Mike cause?
(b) What is the area of the wood that Mike stands on?
(c) Now work out Mike's weight. What is his mass in kg?
Unfortunately the bottle burst just as Mike was reading the height of the mercury. So, he has devised another method of weighing himself. He has borrowed a Newton balance that can measure weights up to 500 N. The diagram shows his next weighing experiment.

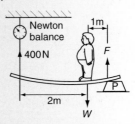

(d) Use the diagram to work out Mike's weight.

(e) How big is the force *F*?

10 (a) (i) State what is meant by **pressure**.

(ii) A suitable unit for pressure is the pascal (Pa). State another unit used to measure pressure.

(b) Explain briefly, in terms of pressure, why:

(i) the sharp edge of a knife, and not the blunt edge, is used for cutting,

(ii) the thickness of the wall of a dam, used to store water, is greater at the base than at the top,

(iii) a tin can collapses when the air is removed from it,

(iv) aneroid barometers may be used as altimeters in aircraft.

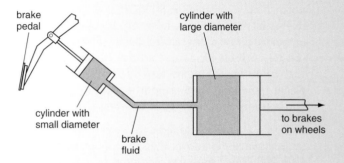

brake pedal

cylinder with large diameter

cylinder with small diameter

brake fluid

to brakes on wheels

(c) Here is a simple type of hydraulic braking system: The areas of cross-section of the small cylinder and large cylinder are 0.0004 m² and 0.0024 m² respectively. The brake pedal is pushed against the piston in the small cylinder with a force of 90 N.

(i) Determine the pressure exerted on the brake fluid.

(ii) Determine the force exerted by the brake fluid on the piston in the large cylinder.

11 Colonel Carruthers has been murdered at Campbell Castle. Inspector Grappler of the Yard has been sent to investigate. He finds old Carruthers dead in the library. Outside the library window there are some footprints in the flower bed (exhibit A). This is an important clue; the inspector realises that he can estimate the suspect's height. Inspector Grappler carries out an experiment in the flower bed. He uses a wooden square (exhibit B) and some weights. He piles the weights onto the square and measures how far the square sinks into the flower bed. His results are in the table.

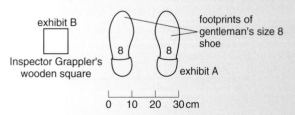

exhibit B

□

Inspector Grappler's wooden square

footprints of gentleman's size 8 shoe

8   8

exhibit A

0   10   20   30 cm

Mass of the inspector's weights (kg)	Depth of the hole made by the square (mm)
5	7
10	14
15	20
20	25
25	30

(a) Work out the area of the suspect's shoes.

(b) Inspector Grappler measured that the shoes had sunk 23 mm into the flower bed. Use the data in the table and your answer to part (a) to make an estimate of the suspect's mass.

(c) Exhibit C shows roughly how the height of a man depends on his mass. Exhibit D shows roughly how a man's shoe size depends on his height. Use these graphs to make an informed guess of the suspect's height.

(d) Of Colonel Carruthers' servants, which one do you suspect?

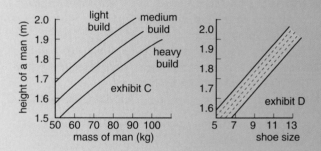

height of a man (m)

2.0
1.9
1.8
1.7
1.6
1.5

light build   medium build

heavy build

exhibit C

50 60 70 80 90 100
mass of man (kg)

2.0
1.9
1.8
1.7
1.6

exhibit D

5   7   9   11 13
shoe size

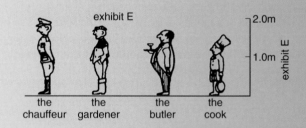

exhibit E

2.0m

1.0m

exhibit E

the chauffeur   the gardener   the butler   the cook

Forces in Motion

When moving in a straight line at a constant speed, balanced forces must act on this surfer

By the end of this section you should:

- be able to calculate average speed
- know the difference between speed and velocity
- be able to calculate acceleration
- understand how ticker tapes can be used to measure acceleration
- know Newton's three laws of motion
- know what the acceleration due to gravity is, and understand the term 'terminal velocity'
- know about car safety
- be able to interpret distance-time and velocity-time graphs
- know what the centripetal force is
- be able to calculate changes in momentum and know about the principle of conservation of momentum
- understand how rockets and jets work
- know about fluid flow and Bernoulli's principle

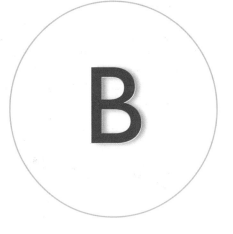

B

How Fast Do Things Move?

Marion Jones won the gold medal for the women's 100 metres at the Sydney Olympics in 2000. She covered the distance in 10.75 seconds; what was her average speed?

Moving object	Speed (m/s)
glacier (Rhonegletsher)	0.000001
snail	0.0005
human walking	2
human sprinter	10
express train	60
Concorde	600
Earth moving round the Sun	30 000
light and radio waves	300 000 000

This snail would take nearly two and a half days to go 100 metres!

When you travel in a fast car you finish your journey in a short time. When you travel in a slow car your journey takes longer. If the speed of a car is 100 kilometres per hour (100 km/h) it will travel a distance of 100 kilometres in one hour. We can write a formula connecting distance, speed and time.

$$\text{average speed} = \frac{\text{distance travelled}}{\text{time taken}} = \frac{d}{t}$$

We write average speed because the speed of the car may change a little during the journey. When you travel along a motorway your speed does not remain exactly the same. You slow down when you get stuck behind a lorry and speed up when you pull out to overtake a car.

Example. At top speed a guided-missile destroyer travels 170 km in three hours. What is its average speed in m/s?

$$\text{average speed} = \frac{d}{t}$$

$$= \frac{170 \times 1000 \text{ m}}{3 \times 3600 \text{ s}}$$

$$= 16 \text{ m/s}$$

remember 1 km = 1000 m;
1 hour = (60 × 60 s) = 3600 s

www

http://www.mcasco.com/ ploutln.html

Velocity

It is not just the speed which is important when you go on a journey. The direction matters as well. Figure 1 shows three possible routes taken by a helicopter leaving London. The helicopter travels at 300 km/h. So in one hour the helicopter can reach Liverpool, Paris or Brussels depending on which direction it travels in.

When we want to talk about a direction as well as a speed we use the word **velocity**. For example, when the helicopter flies towards Liverpool, we can say that its velocity is 300 km/h, on a compass bearing of 330°. Velocity is a vector, speed is a scalar (see page 20).

Time-tabling railway trains

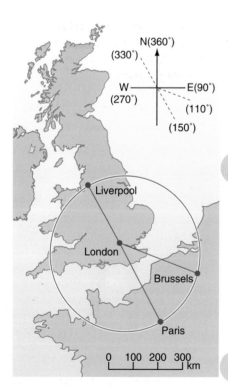

Figure 1

You have probably sat on a slow train in a railway station wondering why the train was taking so long to start. As likely as not you would have been waiting for an express train to overtake you. There is often only one line between railway stations. The trains must be time-tabled so that the faster express trains can overtake a slower train which has stopped at a station.

A passenger train planning officer has to make sure that a slow train going from Reading to Chippenham does not get in the way of the London to Cardiff express train. The slow train travels at an average speed of 70 km/h and the express train at an average speed of 120 km/h.

Plotting a graph of the distance travelled by these trains against time helps to solve the problem. You can see from Figure 2 what happens if both trains leave their stations at 0900 h. The slow train travels the 70 km to Swindon, and the faster train travels from London to Swindon, in the same time. You can also see from the graph that there is a slow train to Newport leaving Bristol Parkway at 1015 h that is going to get in the way of the express train.

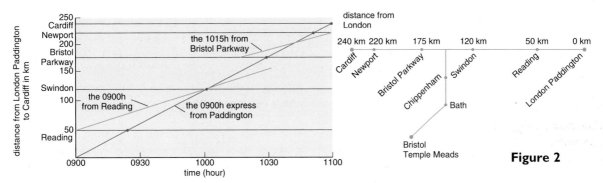

Figure 2

Homework Questions

1 The table below shows average speeds and times recorded by top athletes in several track events. Copy and complete the table.

2 Sketch a graph of distance travelled (y-axis) against time (x-axis) for a train coming into a station. The train stops for a while at the station and then starts again.

3 This question refers to the train time-tabling shown in Figure 2.
(a) How can you tell from the graph that the express train travels faster than the other two?
(b) At what time does the express train reach Bristol Parkway?

(c) At what time should the 1015 h from Bristol leave so that it meets the express train at Newport?

4 Ravi, Paul and Tina enter a 30 km road race. The graph (right) shows Ravi's and Paul's progress through the race.
(a) Which runner ran at a constant speed? Explain your answer.
(b) What was Paul's average speed for the 30 km run?

Tina was one hour late starting the race. During the race she ran at a constant speed of 15 km/h.
(c) Copy the graph and add to it a line to show how Tina ran.
(d) How far had Tina run when she overtook Paul?

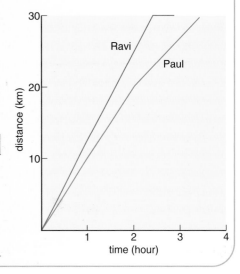

Event	Average speed (m/s)	Time
100 m		10 s
200 m	10.3	
400 m	8.9	
	7.1	3 m 30 s
10 000 m		29 m 10 s
	5.7	2 h 8 m 2 s

When a car is speeding up, we say it is *accelerating*. When it is slowing down we say it is *decelerating*. A deceleration can be thought of as a negative acceleration.

You may be interested in driving a sports car which can accelerate quickly away from traffic lights when they turn green. A car which accelerates rapidly reaches a high speed in a short time. For example, a sports car speeds up to 45 km/h in 5 seconds. A truck speeds up to 45 km/h in 10 seconds. We say the acceleration of the car is twice as big as the truck's acceleration.

You can work out the acceleration of the car or truck using the formula:

$$\text{acceleration} = \frac{\text{change of velocity}}{\text{time}}$$

$$\text{acceleration of sports car} = \frac{45 \text{ km/h}}{5 \text{ s}}$$

$$= 9 \text{ km/h per second}$$

$$\text{acceleration of truck} = \frac{45 \text{ km/h}}{10 \text{ s}}$$

$$= 4.5 \text{ km/h per second}$$

We usually measure velocity in metres per second. This means that acceleration is usually measured in **m/s per second.** What is the acceleration of our sports car in m/s per second?

$$45 \text{ km/h} = \frac{45\,000 \text{ m}}{3600 \text{ s}} = 12.5 \text{ m/s}$$

$$\text{So acceleration} = \frac{\text{change of velocity}}{\text{time}}$$

$$= \frac{12.5 \text{ m/s}}{5 \text{ s}} = 2.5 \text{ m/s per second}$$

or

$$2.5 \text{ m/s}^2 \text{ (metres per second squared)}$$

This car has been in a major accident. A fast moving, massive object like a car experiences a very large force when it decelerates rapidly. The force is large enough to crumple the roof.

Velocity/time graphs

You have already seen that distance/time graphs can be helpful when looking at problems involving moving cars or trains. It can also be helpful to plot graphs of velocity against time.

Figure 1 shows the velocity of a cyclist as she cycled through a town. The following things happened in her journey.
(1) For the first 20 seconds, as she came into the town, she travelled at a constant velocity.
(2) Then she started to cycle up a hill, so she slowed down.
(3) At the top of the hill she came to some traffic lights. She had to wait for them to change.
(4) When the traffic lights changed to green she accelerated away.

The slope of a velocity/time graph is useful, because it shows how quickly the cyclist changes velocity. If the slope is steep, she is changing velocity (accelerating or decelerating) quickly.

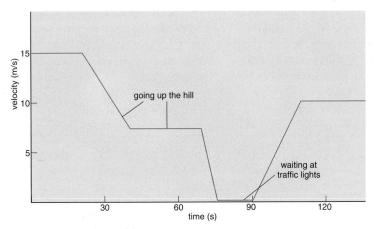

Figure 1

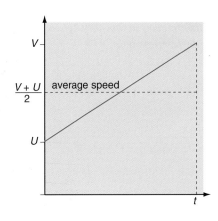

Figure 2

Equations for motion

Figure 2 shows a velocity time graph for something which accelerates from an initial speed, *u*, reaching a final speed, *v*, in a time, *t*. There are two useful equations which can be derived from this graph.

$$\text{acceleration} = \frac{v - u}{t} \qquad \text{average speed} = \frac{u + v}{2}$$

The average speed is halfway between the starting speed and the finishing speed.

Homework Questions

1 This question refers to the graph in Figure 1.
(a) What was the cyclist's velocity after 60 s?
(b) How long did she have to wait at the traffic lights?
(c) Which was larger, her deceleration as she stopped at the traffic lights, or her acceleration when she started again? Explain your answer.
2 Below, Table 1 shows how the speed, in km/h, of Jean Alesi's Formula 1 racing car changes, as he accelerates away from the starting

grid at the beginning of the Brazilian Grand Prix.
(a) Plot a graph of speed (*y*-axis) against time (*x*-axis).
(b) Use your graph to estimate the acceleration of the car in km/h per second at: (i) 16 s, (ii) 1 s.
3 Copy Table 2 below and fill in the missing values.
4 In America drag cars are designed to cover distances of 400 m in about 6 seconds. During this time the cars accelerate very rapidly from a standing start. At the end of

6 seconds, a drag car reaches a speed of 150 m/s.
(a) What is the drag car's average speed?
(b) What is its average acceleration?
5 Describe the motion in the following two cases:

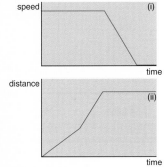

Table 1

speed (km/h)	0	35	70	130	175	205	230	250	260	260
time (s)	0	1	2	4	6	8	10	12	14	16

	Starting speed (m/s)	Final speed (m/s)	Time taken (s)	Acceleration (m/s²)
Cheetah	0	30	5	6
Second stage of a rocket	450	750	100	
Aircraft taking off	0		30	2
Car crash	30	0		−150

Table 2

Athletes use photographs like this one to analyse their motion so that they can improve their performance

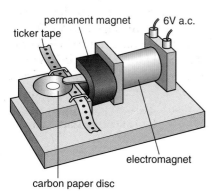

Figure 1

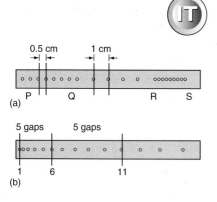

Figure 2

A trainer who wants to know how well one of his athletes is running stands at the side of the track with a stopwatch in his hand. By timing the athlete over a set distance, the trainer knows how fast he is running. But this only tells the trainer an average speed. If he wants to learn more, he needs to look at the athlete's movements over very short time intervals. The best way to look at something that is moving is to film it. This is what sports scientists do to check on an athlete. By looking at each frame of film the scientists can see if the athlete is wasting any effort in his running action.

Another way to look at motion is to use multiflash photography. On the next page you can see a photograph of a golfer hitting a ball. In this technique the golfer swings his club in a darkened room, while a lamp flashes on and off at regular intervals. When the images of the club are close together, the club is moving slowly. When the images are far apart, it is moving quickly.

Ticker timer

Nowadays changing speeds and accelerations can be measured directly using light gates, data loggers and computers. However, motion is still studied using the **ticker timer**, because it collects data in a clear way, which can be usefully analysed (Figure 1). A ticker timer has a small hammer that vibrates up and down 50 times per second. The hammer hits a piece of carbon paper which leaves a mark on a length of tape.

Figure 2 shows you two tapes which have been pulled through the timer. You can see that the dots are close together over the region *PQ*. Then the dots get further apart, so the object moved faster over *QR*. Then the movement slowed down again over the last part of the tape, *RS*. Since the timer produces 50 dots per second, the time between dots is $\frac{1}{50}$ s or 0.02 s. So we can work out the speed:

$$\text{speed} = \frac{\text{distance between dots}}{\text{time between dots}}$$

Between *P* and *Q*, speed $= \dfrac{0.5 \text{ cm}}{0.02 \text{ s}}$

$= 25 \text{ cm/s } or \text{ } 0.25 \text{ m/s}$

In tape B the dots get further and further apart, so the object attached to this tape was accelerating all the time.

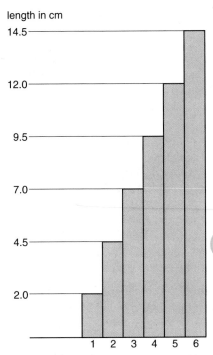

length in cm

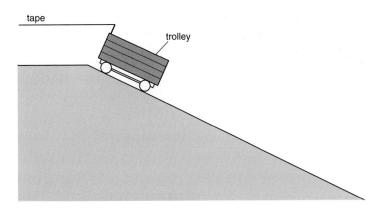

Figure 3

Figure 4 *Each length of tape shows the movement of the trolley over 0.1 s*

Measuring acceleration

Figure 3 shows how you might measure the acceleration of a trolley moving down a slope. When you have let the trolley go down the slope the tape stuck to it will look a bit like tape (b) in Figure 2. It is helpful to cut up the tape into 5-tick lengths. You do this by cutting through the first dot, then the sixth and eleventh and so on. Each length of tape is the distance travelled by the trolley in $\frac{1}{10}$ s (5 spaces between dots means $5 \times \frac{1}{50}$ seconds). You can then use your pieces of tape to make a graph and see how the trolley moved. If your pieces of tape form a straight line then the acceleration was constant (see Figure 4).

Cutting up your tape like this is like plotting a graph of speed against time; the steeper the slope the greater the acceleration.

Homework Questions

1 Work out the speed of the tape in Figure 2(a) in: (i) the region QR, (ii) the region RS.

2 (a) How can you tell from Figure 4 that the trolley accelerated down the slope at a constant rate?
(b) Work out the average speed of the trolley in: (i) interval 4, (ii) interval 6.
(c) What is the time between the middle of interval 4 and the middle of interval 6?
(d) Now use your results from parts (b) and (c) to calculate the acceleration of the trolley.

3 (a) Examine the photograph of the golfer. Where is the club moving fastest? Explain your answer.
(b) The time interval between each flash was about 0.03 s. Use this information and the scale to calculate (i) the speed of the club on impact with the ball and (ii) the initial speed of the ball.

(c) Use the increasing gap size between successive positions of the club to estimate the club's acceleration on its downward swing.

4 The graph shows how the velocity of a jet aircraft increases as it takes off from the deck of an aircraft carrier.
Calculate its acceleration (i) during the first second; (ii) between 3 and 4 seconds.

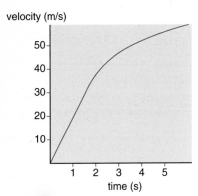

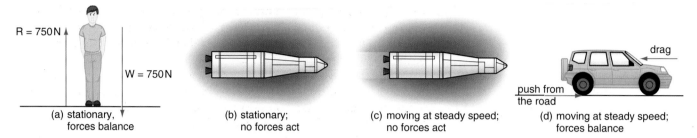

(a) stationary, forces balance

R = 750N

W = 750N

(b) stationary; no forces act

(c) moving at steady speed; no forces act

(d) moving at steady speed; forces balance

drag

push from the road

Figure 1

Newton's first law: balanced forces

Newton's first law of motion states that when no unbalanced force acts on an object, its state of motion will be unchanged. Either a body remains at rest, or it carries on moving in a straight line at a constant velocity.

In Figure 1 there are four examples, which illustrate Newton's first law.

(a) A person is standing still. There are two forces acting on him: the pull of gravity (his weight) is 750 N; the reaction from the ground is 750 N. These forces balance and he stays still.

(b) A spacecraft, *Explorer*, is stationary in space, so far away from the Sun and planets, that we can ignore the pull of gravity. There are no forces on *Explorer* and it stays still.

(c) The next diagram looks remarkably similar to the previous one. In this case *Explorer* is moving at a constant speed in outer space, where we can ignore any gravitational pull. In space no resistive or frictional forces act to stop motion, so *Explorer* carries on moving forever. Once something has kinetic energy, that energy will only be transferred to another form when work is done by resistive forces.

(d) Applying Newton's first law becomes more complicated on Earth because frictional forces act. In this last example, a car moves at a constant speed along a level road. Its weight is balanced by the reaction from the road, but the forces acting horizontally balance too. There is a forwards push on the wheels, which is balanced by air resistance and friction; when forces balance, the car moves at a constant velocity in a straight line. It is necessary to have the engine running so that it can do work against these resistive forces.

Newton's second law: unbalanced forces

You have just learnt that when balanced forces act there is no change to the motion of a body. When unbalanced forces act on something, then the state of motion changes. An unbalanced force causes acceleration; the body on which the

force on Explorer

(a) acceleration of Explorer

drag

(b) a car decelerates

Figure 2

force acts might speed up, slow down, or change direction. A larger unbalanced force causes a larger acceleration; this is part of Newton's second law of motion – a full version of this law is given in the next section. Examples of speeding up and slowing down are given in Figure 2.

(a) *Explorer* has turned on its rocket. There is now a force pushing the spacecraft forward and its speed increases. The stored chemical energy in the fuel is turned into the kinetic energy of the moving spacecraft, and thermal energy.

(b) The driver of the car has seen the traffic slowing down ahead of him. He takes his foot off the accelerator; no forward force acts on the car now, but air resistance continues to act. An unbalanced force acts to slow the car down.

Newton's third law

Newton's third law of motion states that: to every force there is an equal and opposite force. This law sounds easy to apply, but it requires clear thinking. First, it is important to appreciate that the pair of forces mentioned in the law act on different bodies. Some examples are given in Figure 3.

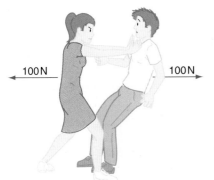

100 N   100 N

(a) each person experiences the same force when contact is made

force on foot

force on ground

(b) a foot pushes the ground backwards; the ground pushes the foot forwards

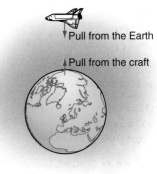

Pull from the Earth

Pull from the craft

(c) there is an equal and opposite gravitational pull on the craft and on the Earth

Figure 3

www

http://www.marshall.tstc.edu/
pages/applied/mom5.htm

(a) If I push you with a force of 100 N, you push me back with a force of 100 N in the opposite direction.

(b) When you walk, you push the ground backwards; the ground pushes you forwards.

(c) A spacecraft returning to Earth is pulled downwards by Earth's gravity; the spacecraft exerts an equal and opposite gravitational pull on the Earth. This means that as the spacecraft moves, the Earth moves too. But the Earth is so big that it only moves a tiny amount – far too little for us to notice.

Taking the plunge

When you go for a swim you need all three of Newton's laws of motion to explain how you get from one end of the pool to the other. Figure 4 shows a swimmer at three stages of swimming a length.

(a) At the beginning of the length, the swimmer pushes the water; the water pushes her forwards. An unbalanced force acts on the swimmer and she accelerates.

(b) In the middle of the length, the forwards push from the water is balanced by resistive forces on the swimmer. She moves at a constant speed.

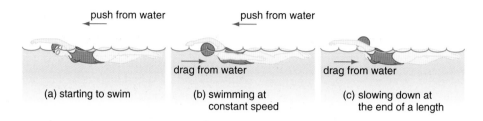

(a) starting to swim

(b) swimming at
constant speed

(c) slowing down at
the end of a length

Figure 4

(c) At the end of the length, she stops swimming and drag forces slow her down.

In the paragraphs above drag forces were mentioned. When something moves through water or air, a resistive force acts on the moving object. This force is small when the speed is low, but drag (or water resistance) increases as the speed increases. For the swimmer, in (a) the drag force is small so she accelerates whereas in (b) she is moving quickly and the drag force is larger and balances the forwards push; this is why she cannot go any faster. You can learn more about drag forces in units B6 and B13.

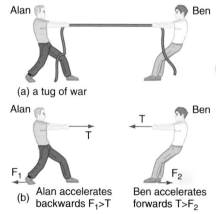

(a) a tug of war

(b) Alan accelerates backwards $F_1 > T$

Ben accelerates forwards $T > F_2$

Figure 5

Tug of War

In Figure 5(a) you can see two people engaged in a tug of war. From Newton's third law we know that the force which Alan exerts on Ben must be exactly the same size as, but in the opposite direction to the force which Ben exerts on Alan.

To understand why Alan wins and Ben loses we must draw **free body diagrams** for each person, Figure 5(b). Each person pushes on the ground, and the ground pushes him back. Alan is stronger than Ben and pushes the ground harder than Ben. Alan accelerates backwards because $F_1 > T$; Ben accelerates forwards because $T > F_2$. Each has an unbalanced force acting on him. However, they exert the same force on each other.

Homework Questions

1. (a) A car gets stuck on some ice on a road. Explain why the car might have difficulty starting on ice.
(b) A sprinter fixes blocks into the ground to help him get a good start. Explain how these assist him.

2. You leave a parcel on the seat of a car. When you brake suddenly, the parcel falls onto the floor. Explain why.

3. You start to freewheel down a hill with a shallow gradient.
(a) What force starts you moving down the hill?
(b) You reach a constant speed. Draw a sketch to show the forces acting on you. Comment on the size of the forces.

4. You catch a fast moving ball. You have to apply a force of 200 N to stop it.
(a) How big is the force the ball exerts on you?
(b) Draw a diagram of the hands and the ball side by side to show (i) the force on the ball (ii) the force on your hands.

5. The diagram shows the direction of a force on a model car. Which of the following is a possible state of motion for the car? Explain your answers.
(a) Staying at rest.
(b) Beginning to move backwards.
(c) Moving backwards at a constant speed.

(d) Slowing down while moving forwards.

6. Draw all the forces which act on a plane (i) just after take off (ii) while flying at a constant speed at a constant height.

7. You do a 'bungee' jump off a high bridge. Draw the forces which act on you (i) at the top of the jump and (ii) at the bottom of the jump, just before you bounce up again.

5 Force, Mass and Acceleration

The large force produced by a powerful engine acts on a small mass to give this racing car a large acceleration

When an unbalanced force acts on a car it will accelerate. What affects how large the acceleration is? If you have ever had a car with a flat battery then you will have given the car a push to start. When one person tries to push a car alone then the acceleration of the car is very slow. It takes a long time for the car to increase its speed. When three people give the car a push, it accelerates much more rapidly.

$$\text{acceleration} \propto \text{force}$$

You also know from everyday experience that large massive objects are difficult to set in motion. When you throw a ball you can accelerate your arm more quickly if the ball has a small mass. You can throw a cricket ball much faster than you can put a shot. A shotput has a mass of about 7 kg and the force that your arm can apply cannot accelerate it as rapidly as a cricket ball.

The acceleration is inversely proportional to the mass:

$$\text{acceleration} \propto \frac{1}{\text{mass}}$$

It is difficult to get large things moving, but it is also very difficult to stop large things when they are moving. The world's largest ship is the *Seawise Giant*; it is 460 m long and has a mass of about 560 000 tonnes. Once a ship like this is moving the captain has to allow about 10 km for the ship to slow down.

Newton's second law of motion

With some careful experiments in the laboratory, you can see how the size of the acceleration is connected to the size of the force. Figure 1(a) shows the idea. A trolley placed on a table is accelerated by pulling it with an elastic cord. This is stretched so that it always remains the length of the trolley. The acceleration of the trolley is measured by attaching a piece of ticker tape to the back of the trolley.

The first experiment is to increase the force acting on one trolley, by using extra elastic cords in parallel with the first one. You can see how our ticker tape graphs get steeper as the force increases. This means the acceleration is getting bigger. A 1 kg trolley accelerates at a rate of 1 m/s² for a force of 1 N; 2 m/s² for a force of 2 N; and 3 m/s² for a force of 3 N.

In the second experiment (Figure 1(b)), you change the mass of the trolley but you pull with the same force. As the mass increases the ticker tape graphs become less steep. This means the acceleration is getting less. For a force of 1 N acting on a 1 kg trolley the acceleration is 1 m/s², for a 2 kg trolley the acceleration is ½ m/s², for a 3 kg trolley the acceleration is ⅓ m/s². For each of the experiments in Figure 1, you can see that the following equation is true:

$$\text{Force} = \text{mass} \times \text{acceleration}$$

This is **Newton's second law of motion**. This equation lets us define the newton in this way: *A force of 1 N will accelerate a mass of 1 kg at a rate of 1 m/s².*

Two points should be noted about the use of this equation. First you must make sure that the mass is converted to kilograms, the acceleration to m/s²; then the force will be in newtons. Secondly, the force is the resultant or unbalanced force; remember if two forces balance there is no acceleration.

http://www.learner.org/exhibits/parkphysics/coaster.html

http://www.newton.org.uk/

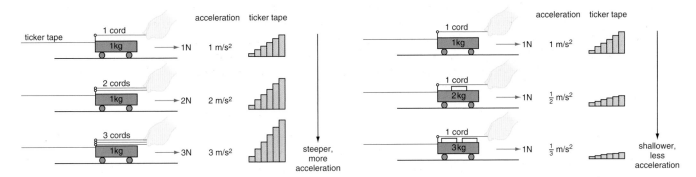

Figure 1 (a) Experiment 1
Keep the mass constant and change the force

Figure 1 (b) Experiment 2
Keep the force constant and change the mass

Example. A sledge has a mass of 10 kg. A boy pulls it with a force of 20 N. What is its acceleration?

$$F = m \times a$$

So

$$a = \frac{F}{m} = \frac{20\text{ N}}{10\text{ kg}} = 2\text{m/s}^2$$

Defining Mass

Sometimes mass is defined as the amount of matter in a body. However, Newton's second law of motion allows a better and more exact definition to be made. In Figure 1(b) you can see that a more massive trolley accelerates more slowly than a lighter trolley for the same applied force. Massive objects have an inbuilt 'reluctance' to start moving; this is called **inertia** (from the Latin for laziness).

Mass is defined as a numerical measure of inertia.

Homework Questions

1 Trains accelerate very slowly out of stations. Why is their acceleration very much slower than that of a car?

2 The manufacturers of Formula 1 racing cars try to make them as light as possible. Why do you think they do that?

3 This question refers to the experiments described in Figure 1.
(a) How many cords are needed to accelerate a trolley of mass 4 kg at a rate of 0.5 m/s²?
(b) What acceleration is produced by four cords acting on a trolley of mass 3 kg?
(c) The trolley in this experiment has frictional forces acting on it.

What effect does friction have on your results?
(d) What can you do to help compensate for friction?

4 A driver travelling on the motorway at 30 m/s takes her foot off the accelerator and slows down to 27 m/s in 6 s.
(a) Calculate the size of her deceleration.
(b) The mass of the car is 1000 kg. Calculate the size of the air resistance and frictional forces that are acting on the car.
(c) What driving force must act on the wheels for the car to maintain a steady speed of 30 m/s?
(d) What is the car's forward

acceleration, at a speed of 30 m/s, when the driving force on the wheels is 650 N?

5 You are in a spacecraft in a region where there is no gravitational pull. You have two biscuit tins, one of which has no biscuits (because you have eaten them) and the other is full. How can you tell which is full, without opening the lid?

6 (a) What acceleration is produced in a mass of 3 kg which experiences a resultant force of 15 N?
(b) What is the mass of an object which experiences an acceleration of 4 m/s² when a resultant force of 10 N acts on it?

6 Free Fall

When you drop something it accelerates downwards, moving faster and faster, until it hits the ground. There is a story that Galileo used the leaning tower of Pisa to demonstrate the effect of gravitational acceleration. He dropped a large iron cannon ball and a small one. Both balls reached the ground at the same time. They accelerated at the same rate of about 10 m/s^2.

Weight and mass

The size of the Earth's gravitational pull on an object is proportional to its mass. The Earth pulls a 1 kg mass with a force of 10 N and a 2 kg mass with a force of 20 N. We say that the strength of the **Earth's gravitational field**, g, is 10 N/kg.

The **weight**, W, of an object is the force that gravity exerts on it, which is equal to the object's mass × the pull of gravity on each kilogram.

$$W = mg$$

http://www.marshall.tstc.edu/
pages/applied/mom4.htm

The value of g is roughly the same everywhere on the Earth, but away from the Earth it has different values. The Moon is smaller than the Earth and pulls things towards it less strongly. On the Moon's surface the value of g is 1.6 N/kg. In space, far away from all planets, there are no gravitational pulls, so g is zero, and therefore everything is weightless.

Example. What is the weight of a 70 kg man on the Moon?

$$W = mg$$
$$= 70 \text{ kg} \times 1.6 \text{ N/kg}$$
$$= 112 \text{ N}$$

The size of g also gives us the **gravitational acceleration**, because:

$$\text{acceleration} = \frac{\text{force}}{\text{mass}} \quad or \quad g = \frac{W}{m}$$

Parachuting

You have read earlier that everything accelerates towards the ground at the same rate. But that is only true if the effects of air resistance are small. If you drop a feather you know that it will flutter slowly towards the ground. That is because the size of the air resistance on the feather is only slightly less than the downwards pull of gravity.

The size of the air resistance on an object depends on the area of the object and its speed:

● the larger the area, the larger the air resistance
● the larger the speed, the larger the air resistance.

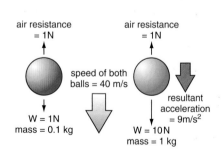

Figure I *At this instant both balls have a speed of 40 m/s. At this speed the weight of the red ball is balanced by air resistance, but the heavier blue ball is still accelerating*

Figure 1 shows the effect of air resistance on two balls, which are the same size and shape, but the red ball has a mass of 0.1 kg and the blue ball a mass of 1 kg. The balls are moving at the same speed, so the air resistance is the same, 1 N, on each. The pull of gravity on the red ball is balanced by air resistance, so it now moves at a constant speed. The red ball will not go any faster and we say it has reached **terminal velocity**. For the blue ball, however, the pull of gravity is greater than the air resistance so it continues to accelerate.

Figure 2 shows how the speed of a sky diver changes as she falls towards the ground. The graph has five distinct parts:
(1) *OA*. She accelerates at about 10 m/s^2 just after leaving the aeroplane.

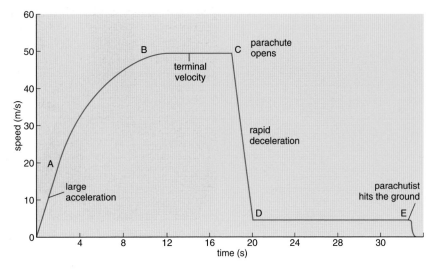

Figure 2 *Speed/time graph for a parachutist*

The sky diver has reached his terminal velocity. He is in a streamlined position. How could he slow down?

(2) *AB*. The effects of air resistance mean that her acceleration gets less as there is now a force acting in the opposite direction to her weight.

(3) *BC*. The air resistance force is the same as her weight. She now moves at a constant speed because the resultant force acting on her is zero.

(4) *CD*. She opens her parachute at *C*. There is now a very large air resistance force so she decelerates rapidly.

(5) *DE*. The air resistance force on her parachute is the same size as her weight, so she moves with a constant speed until she hits the ground at *E*.

Homework Questions

1 A student wrote 'my weight is 67 kg'. What is wrong with this statement, and what do you think his weight really is?

2 A hammer has a mass of 1 kg. What is its weight (i) on Earth (ii) on the Moon (iii) in outer space?

3 Explain this observation: 'when a sheet of paper is dropped it flutters down to the ground, but when the same sheet of paper is screwed up into a ball it accelerates rapidly downwards when dropped'.

4 Refer to Figure 1, and explain the following.
(a) Why does the red ball fall at a constant speed?
(b) Why does the blue ball fall with an acceleration of 9 m/s²?

5 This question refers to the speed/time graph in Figure 2.
(a) What was the speed of the sky diver when she hit the ground?

(b) Why is her acceleration over the part *AB* less than it was at the beginning of her fall?
(c) Use the graph to estimate roughly how far she fell during her dive. Was it nearer 100 m, 1000 m, or 10 000 m?

6 The graph (right) shows how the force of air resistance on our sky diver's parachute changes with her speed of fall.
(a) How big is the resistive force acting on her if she is travelling at a constant speed of 5 m/s?
(b) Explain why your answer to part (a) must be the same size as her weight.
(c) Use the graph to predict the terminal velocity of the following people using the same parachute: (i) a boy of weight 400 N, (ii) a man of weight 1000 N.
(d) Make a copy of the graph and

add to it a sketch to show how you think the air resistance force would vary on a parachute with twice the area of the one used by our sky diver.
(e) Why do parachutists bend their legs on landing?

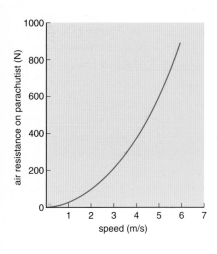

Most of the energy of an impact in a car crash is absorbed by the crumple zones. This photograph shows the front crumple zones on a Volvo

Car crashes

In the last unit you read about a parachutist who landed on the ground travelling at 5 m/s. This may not sound like a very high speed but it is quite fast enough for a parachutist to suffer an injury such as a broken ankle. You hit the ground at the same speed when you jump down from a garden wall. To avoid injuring themselves, parachutists are taught to bend their knees on landing. This helps them to decelerate more slowly, because their decrease in speed takes longer. When the deceleration is less, the force acting on the parachutist's legs is less. Now there is a better chance of avoiding injury.

So, when a rapid deceleration occurs a large force acts to cause it. This idea is most important when designing cars with safety in mind. The photograph above shows a typical family saloon car. In the centre of the car is a rigid passenger cell which is designed not to buckle in a crash. However, the front and back of the car are designed to crumple on impact. These structures, which in an accident cause the deceleration to be reduced, are called the **crumple zones**. This is because of the time taken for the front of the car to crumple. This works in the same way as bending your legs on landing on the ground.

Another factor that has helped road safety is the wearing of seat belts (Figure 1). The photograph below shows what happens to a passenger when he is involved in an accident, but is wearing a seat belt. If he is not wearing a seat belt

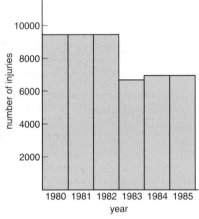

Figure 1 *The number of serious injuries to front-seat passengers and drivers in cars and light vans in Great Britain. In January 1983 it became compulsory to wear seat belts in the front seats. The number of passengers and drivers wearing seat belts rose from 45% to 95%. The statistics speak for themselves. Will you drive a car without a seat belt?*

Wearing a seat belt could save your life in an accident. Only dummies forget to put their seat belts on.

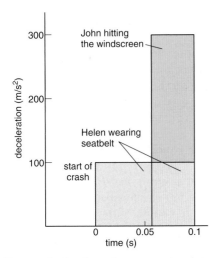

Figure 2 *Graph to show approximate decelerations in a car crash*

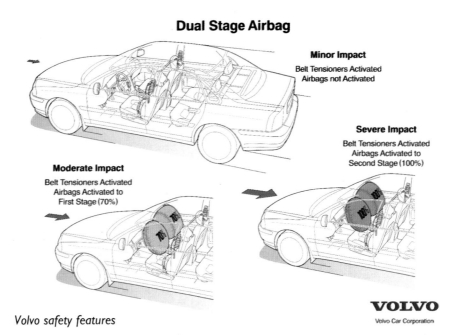

Volvo safety features

VOLVO
Volvo Car Corporation

then when the car stops suddenly he carries on moving because there is no force acting on him. The first thing he hits is the windscreen. He now experiences a large decelerating force which could fracture his skull. Glass from the window will also cut his face very badly.

Figure 2 shows the deceleration of two passengers in a car crash; Helen was wearing a seat belt and John was not. Helen decelerated over a period of 0.1 s. During this time the front end of the car was crumpling up. John was not wearing a seat belt, so he did not take advantage of the time provided by the crumple zone. Instead he carried on moving until he hit the windscreen; his deceleration was then much faster and the force acting on his head was very large indeed. John was killed; Helen survived.

Car safety features

Thirty years ago car manufacturers were concerned to design and sell high performance cars; safety features were sometimes neglected. Nowadays, all car manufacturers wish to provide a car which gives its passengers the greatest possible protection in the event of a crash.

Statistics provided by the Department of Transport show how effective modern car design has been in reducing incidences of serious injuries. Although the number of car journeys has increased immensely since 1980, the number of passengers killed or seriously injured in 2000 was about 60% of the number in that category in the early 1980s.

The photograph above shows some safety features developed by Volvo. You have already read about strong passenger cages, seat belts and crumple zones. Additionally this car has an airbag system which inflates according to the size of the impact.

Homework Questions

1 Explain why it is a good idea to wear your safety belt in a car. Why is it safer for the driver if the back seat passengers are also strapped in?

2 (a) Explain, using ideas involving forces and acceleration, how crumple zones help to protect passengers during car crashes.
(b) Are crumple zones effective if passengers are not wearing seat belts? Explain your answer.

3 Look at all three photographs and choose three safety features. For each of these features explain carefully, using scientific terms, how they help to protect the passenger.

4 This question refers to John and Helen's car crash. John's mass was 80 kg and Helen's was 60 kg.
(a) Use Figure 2 to calculate the force that was acting on each of them to slow them down during the crash.
(b) How can you tell from the graphs that before the collision they were travelling at 10 m/s?
(c) Use the information to draw speed/time graphs for Helen and John during the crash.

(d) Helen was driving and was responsible for the crash. The police found that she had a large amount of alcohol in her blood. What measures should be taken to stop people from drinking and driving?

5 In 1981, 1863 pedestrians were killed on British roads; in 2000 that number had been reduced to 906. What measures have been introduced over the last twenty years to make our roads safer for pedestrians?

8   Equations of Motion

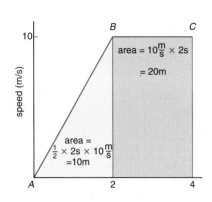

Figure 1 *The speed/time graph of a sprinter*

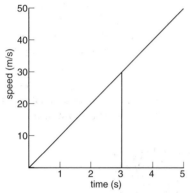

Figure 2 *The speed/time graph for a falling ball*

Time (s)	Speed (m/s)	Distance fallen = ½ speed × time (m)
0	0	0
1	10	5
2	20	20
3	30	45
4	40	80
5	50	125

Table 1 *Distance fallen as a function of time. Check that the distance fallen = ½ × 10 × t^2 (t = time). Can you explain why this formula works?*

Velocity/time graphs

When a sprinter runs a 100 m race, she does not reach her top speed as soon as the starting pistol is fired. She takes a few seconds to accelerate from rest up to her top speed. Figure 1 shows this in the form of a speed/time graph. From Figure 1 you can see that she took 2 seconds to accelerate up to 10 m/s. So her acceleration is 5 m/s², which is the gradient of the graph.

> The gradient of a velocity/time graph equals the acceleration

You can also use the same graph to calculate the distance that she has run. It is easy to work out the distance travelled once she has reached a constant speed of 10 m/s. She runs 10 m each second, so over the region *BC* of the graph she runs a distance of 10 m/s × 2 s = 20 m, which is the **area** under that part of the graph.

> The area under a velocity/time graph equals the distance travelled

We can check this formula for the first 2 seconds of her race. The distance travelled in that time is equal to the area of the triangle under the line *AB*.

$$\text{Area of triangle} = \tfrac{1}{2} \text{ base} \times \text{height}$$
$$= \tfrac{1}{2} \times 2 \text{ s} \times 10 \text{ m/s}$$
$$= 10 \text{ m}$$

We would have found the same answer if we had used the formula:

> Distance = average speed × time.

The average speed over the first 2 seconds is 5 m/s, halfway between 0 and 10 m/s

$$\text{So } d = \text{average speed} \times \text{time}$$
$$= 5 \text{ m/s} \times 2 \text{ s}$$
$$= 10 \text{ m}$$

Falling

When an object is allowed to fall freely towards the ground, it accelerates at a rate of 10 m/s². Provided wind resistance is very small in comparison with the object's weight, this acceleration remains constant. Figure 2 shows the speed/time graph for a falling ball; each second its speed increases by 10 m/s. The distance the ball has fallen after 3 seconds, for example, may be calculated from the area under the graph.

$$d = \tfrac{1}{2} \times 30 \text{ m/s} \times 3 \text{ s}$$
$$= 45 \text{ m}$$

Table 1 shows the distance travelled in intervals of 1 second. Check the calculations for yourself. Figure 3 shows the position of the ball during the first 3 seconds, after it is released.

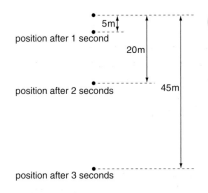

position after 1 second
5m

position after 2 seconds
20m
45m

position after 3 seconds

Figure 3 *The ball travels further as it travels faster, so the gaps between the ball's position grow each second*

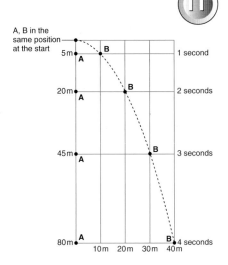

A, B in the same position at the start
5m
20m
45m
80m
1 second
2 seconds
3 seconds
4 seconds
10m 20m 30m 40m

Figure 4 *Note that both balls fall the same distance in the same time. B moves at a constant speed sideways. B falls in a parabolic path*

Falling sideways

What happens to the ball if it is thrown sideways off the edge of a cliff with a speed of 10 m/s? Provided air resistance can again be ignored, the problem is not too difficult. We can treat the downwards and sideways motions of the ball separately.

- Downwards motion: the ball is acted on by the pull of gravity, so it accelerates as before, falling 5 m after 1 second, 20 m after 2 seconds, etc.
- Sideways motion: since air resistance is very small, no force acts sideways on the ball. Therefore it moves sideways with a constant speed of 10 m/s (Newton's first law). After 1 second it has travelled sideways 10 m, after 2 seconds 20 m, etc.

Figure 4 shows the positions, in intervals of 1 second, of a ball (A) dropped off the edge of the cliff, and a ball (B) thrown sideways with a speed of 10 m/s. The balls are released at the same instant. B falls in a **parabolic path** – it moves sideways at a constant speed, while accelerating downwards at a constant rate. Any object that is hit, launched or thrown on Earth will follow a parabolic path. Figure 5 is a computer simulation of a multiflash photograph of two balls launched in the laboratory. The balls are illuminated by a stroboscope, so that their positions are shown every 0.1 seconds. The balls were launched at different angles and speeds, and the two paths were superimposed on the same film.

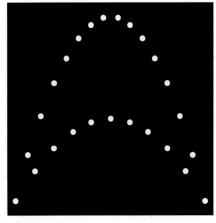

Figure 5

Homework Questions

1 Copy Figure 4 carefully onto graph paper.
   (a) Mark carefully where ball B will be after 2.5 seconds.
   (b) Draw the path B would follow if thrown sideways at only 5 m/s.

2 On the Moon the gravitational acceleration is 1.6 m/s². A stone is dropped from a cliff; how far does it fall in 6 seconds?

3 This question is about the photograph in Figure 5. Explain your answers carefully.
   (a) Which ball was travelling faster just after it was released?
   (b) Which ball was travelling faster at the top of its path?
   (c) Each ball travelled the same horizontal distance, 3 m, this is called the ball's range.

Using the fact that the time between flashes was 0.1 s, calculate the horizontal speed of each ball.
   (d) Make a sketch of the upper path from Figure 5. Add to it a second path of a ball, which is launched with the same upwards speed but twice the sideways speed. What is the range of this ball?

The purpose of these two pages is to give you some practice in applying your knowledge. A summary of important laws and formulas are below.

- Average speed $= \dfrac{\text{distance}}{\text{time}}$

- Acceleration $= \dfrac{\text{change of velocity}}{\text{time}}$

- Average speed $= \dfrac{u + v}{2}$ (where u = starting speed and v = final speed)

- The gradient of a distance-time graph is the speed.
- The area under a velocity-time graph is the distance travelled.
- The gradient of a velocity-time graph is the acceleration.
- Newton's first law: if balanced forces act on an object, it remains at rest or moves with constant speed in a straight line.
- Newton's second law: resultant force = mass × acceleration.
- Newton's third law: if body A exerts a force, F, on body B; body B exerts Force F on body A, in the opposite direction.

Motion

1 Edward sets off from the country to drive into town. The first half of his journey is quick, but then he hits traffic and proceeds more slowly.
(a) In the first hour Edward travels a distance of 40 km. Calculate his average speed.
(b) In the next half hour Edward travels a distance of 5 km. Calculate his average speed for the second part of the journey.
(c) Now calculate Edward's average speed for the whole journey.

2 (a) A car is travelling at 25 m/s. The driver takes his foot off the accelerator and slows down. His deceleration is 2 m/s². How long does it take him to reach a speed of 15 m/s².
(b) The car speeds up again reaching a speed of 30 m/s in 10 s. What was its acceleration?

3 A fly can take off and reach a speed of 3 m/s in a time of 60 milliseconds. What is its acceleration?

4 Frances goes for a cycle ride. There are four stages to her day out.
    (i) Cycling away from home at a speed of 20 km/h for 1 hour.
    (ii) Cycling uphill for ½ hour at a speed of 10 km/h.
    (iii) Resting for lunch for ½ hour.
    (iv) Cycling home, by another route, at a constant speed of 15 km/h, a distance of 25 km.
(a) Draw a distance-time graph to show how the distance travelled changes with time.
(b) Show on the graph where Frances travelled the fastest, and the time taken for each part of the journey.

5 Figure 1 shows a distance-time graph of how Anthony moved over 6 seconds. Draw a velocity-time graph for his movement over that period.

6 Figure 2 shows a velocity-time graph for an athlete running a short race.
(a) Calculate:
    (i) the acceleration over the region AB.
    (ii) the acceleration over the region CD.
(b) The athlete finished the race after 8 s.
    (i) Calculate the race distance.
    (ii) Calculate her average speed for the race.

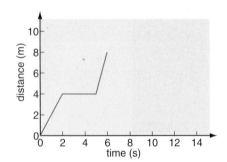

Figure 1

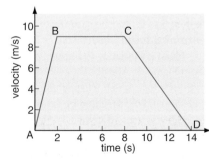

Figure 2

7 Sketch graphs to show how the *velocity* changes for each of the distance-time graphs shown in Figure 3.

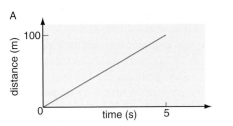
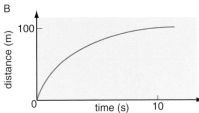

Figure 3

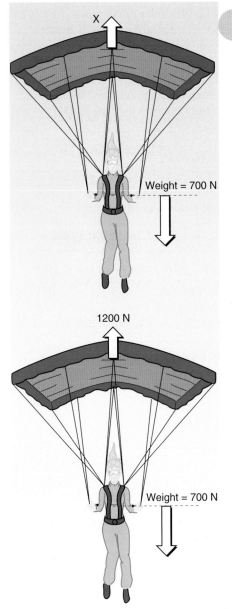

Figure 5

Forces

These questions test your understanding of Newton's Laws. One common problem arises with the use of Newton's second law. You need to remember that when things accelerate, it is the *resultant* force which causes the acceleration.

Example
A Saturn V rocket (Figure 4) of mass 3 000 000 kg, takes off; its rockets provide a thrust of 33 000 000 N. What is the rocket's acceleration?

There are two forces acting; the thrust upwards and the weight downwards, which is 3 000 000 kg × 10 N/kg or 30 000 000 N.

$$\text{So acceleration} = \frac{\text{resultant force}}{\text{mass}}$$

$$= \frac{33\ 000\ 000\ \text{N} - 30\ 000\ 000\ \text{N}}{3\ 000\ 000\ \text{kg}}$$

$$= 1\ \text{m/s}^2$$

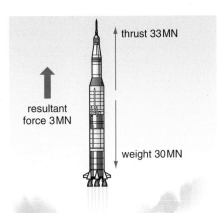

Figure 4

8 (a) Angela is a skydiver. In Figure 5a she is falling at a constant speed. How big is the drag force, X, acting on her parachute?
(b) In Figure 5b, Angela has just opened her parachute after diving at high speed. Describe how her motion is changing.

9 You are in outer space, and you are worried that your crew are looking thin. How are you going to work out their mass in a weightless environment? Describe an experiment to calculate an astronaut's mass, using a chair, a large spring balance, a stop clock and a tape measure.

10 Andrew is cycling at 5 m/s, and in 5 seconds increases his speed to 7 m/s.
(a) Calculate his acceleration.
(b) The mass of Andrew and his bicycle is 50 kg. The push forwards from the road on the bicycle is 30 N. Calculate the size of wind resistance, R, acting on him (Figure 6). Assume he has the acceleration calculated in part (a).

11 Greg test drives his new car. He accelerates rapidly until he reaches a speed of 20 m/s. The mass of the car (with him in it) is 750 kg. Figure 7 shows how his speed changes.
(a) Calculate his acceleration over the first 4 seconds.
(b) Work out the force acting on the car to accelerate it.
(c) Greg invites three friends (total mass 250 kg) into his car to demonstrate its rapid acceleration. Copy Figure 7, and show how the car accelerates over the first 4 seconds. (Label the graph clearly.)

12 This question is about the take off of a lunar landing craft. Use the data provided: mass of craft 20 000 kg; thrust from engines on craft 52 000 N; Moon's gravitational field strength 1.6 N/kg.
(a) What is the craft's weight?
(b) At take off, calculate the net force on the craft.
(c) Calculate the acceleration of the craft at take off.
(d) How fast will the craft be travelling after 30 seconds?
(e) How far above the Moon's surface will the spacecraft be after 30 seconds?
(f) Give two reasons why the craft will actually have travelled slightly further than you estimate.
(g) Why could this spacecraft not take off from the surface of the Earth?

13 (a) After take off a Saturn V rocket burns 14 000 kg of fuel per second. How much mass has the rocket lost after 2 minutes?
(b) What is the mass of the rocket after 2 minutes? (Saturn V had a mass of 3 000 000 kg before take off.)
(c) Now calculate the acceleration of the rocket after 2 minutes. The thrust from the engines is 33 million N.

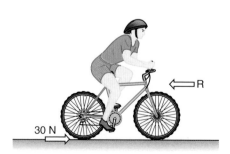

Figure 6

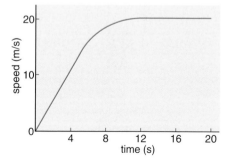

Figure 7

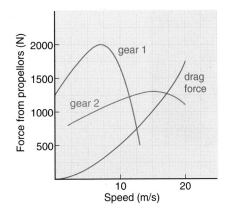

Figure 8

14 The graph in Figure 8 shows information about the performance of a high speed power boat. It has two gears and you can see how the thrust available from the propellers depends on the speed of the boat. Also shown on the graph is how the drag force depends on the speed. The mass of the power boat with its occupants is 500 kg.
  (a) What is the boat's top speed in (i) first gear (ii) second gear? Explain how you arrived at your answer.
  (b) Calculate the boat's acceleration (i) in first gear, when the speed is close to zero (ii) in first gear travelling at 7 m/s.
  (c) Discuss how a power boat is designed to maximise its speed.

15 A skier, mass 70kg, sets off from rest down a slope. He is accelerated down the slope with a 'diluted' gravitational pull of 350N.
  (a) Explain why the gravitational force is 'diluted'.
  (b) Calculate the skier's initial acceleration.
  (c) How fast is he travelling after 10 seconds?
  (d) How far has he travelled in that time?
  Although he continues down the same gradient of slope, the skier reaches a maximum constant speed of 30m/s.
  (e) Explain why the skier reaches this maximum speed.
  (f) What is the size of the drag force acting on the skier at this speed?
  (g) Suggest three changes to his posture or equipment which the skier could make to enable him to go even faster.

10 Moving in Circles

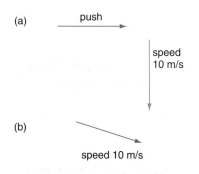

An Argentinian player tries to push a French winger into touch

In the photograph you can see a rugby international between Argentina and France in progress. France's right wing has the ball and is running to score a try by the corner flag. However, the Argentinian winger is running across to stop him, and he succeeds by giving the French winger a push. The sideways push does not slow him down but it changes the direction that he is running in. He is forced out of play, and France fails to score a try.

This account of rugby players demonstrates an important idea. So far, when you have seen forces acting on moving objects, the forces have caused something to speed up or slow down. However, if a force is applied at right angles to the direction of motion then there is no change of speed, but the direction of the motion is changed (Figure 1).

Earlier you met acceleration and you used the equation:

$$\text{acceleration} = \frac{\text{change of velocity}}{\text{time}}$$

When we use the word **velocity** we need to state the direction of motion as well as the speed. The rugby player changes his velocity but does not alter his speed. So it is possible to have an acceleration without changing speed. This is a very difficult idea to understand, but makes sense if you think about this: the player was pushed, and you know that pushes cause acceleration ($F = ma$).

Figure 1
(a) Before the push
(b) After the push the direction in which the man runs is changed. There is no change of speed, but there is a change of velocity

Circular motion

You can fasten a conker to a string and whirl it around your head in a horizontal circle. The conker moves at a constant speed, but its direction is always changing. The velocity of the conker is changing so it must be accelerating. The pull of the string is the force which accelerates the conker. The direction of this force is always at right angles to the motion of the conker. It is towards the centre of the circular path. It is called **centripetal force** (Figure 2).

There are many examples of centripetal forces making things move in a circular path. When a gymnast does her exercise on the asymmetric bars, her arms provide the centripetal force which is necessary to keep her moving in a circular path. When she dismounts, the gymnast lets go of the bar, and she keeps moving along the direction in which she was travelling at the moment of release.

A satellite in orbit around the Earth provides an interesting example of a centripetal force in action. The Earth's gravitational pull acts on the satellite to keep it in its circular path.

A spin-dryer is an example of a machine which works using the principle of centripetal force – or rather the lack of it. As clothes are spun at a high speed, they need a large force to keep them in their circular path; this is provided by the dryer's drum. However, the rotating drum has holes in it, through which the water

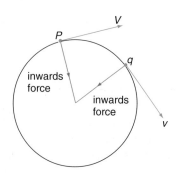

Figure 2 Conker on a string moving around a horizontal circle at constant speed

48

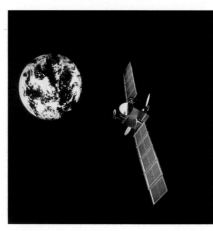

Satellites rely on the centripetal force to keep them in orbit

http://www.mcasco.com/
p1cmot.html

Homework Questions

1 Explain carefully how it is possible for something to accelerate but not change its speed.

2 The diagram below shows a ball attached to a string going around a circle.
   (a) Copy the diagram and mark the direction of the force on the ball at A.
   (b) When it gets to B the string breaks. In which direction does the ball move?

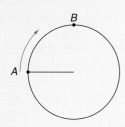

3 You are in a train which goes round a bend at high speed. An orange, which is on the table in front of you, rolls off the edge. Explain this observation.

can pass. The holes do not provide a centripetal force, so the water carries on moving in a straight line.

Calculating the size of centripetal force

There are three factors which affect the size of the centripetal force acting on an object moving in a circular path. More force is needed if:

● the mass is increased
● the speed is increased
● the radius of the path gets smaller.

You feel a greater force acting on you in a car which travels quickly round a sharp bend. The size of the centripetal force which must act on an object to keep it in its circular path can be calculated using the formula:

$$F = \frac{mv^2}{r}$$

where m is the mass of the object, v its speed and r the radius of the path. When you compare this with the formula $F = ma$, you can see that the centripetal acceleration is given by

$$a = \frac{v^2}{r}$$

Example
What gravitational pull does the Earth exert on a satellite of mass 120 kg, with an orbital speed of 7600 m/s in an orbit 7000 km from the Earth's centre?
   The Earth's gravitational pull provides the necessary centripetal force.

$$F = \frac{mv^2}{r}$$

$$= \frac{120 \times (7600)^2}{7\,000\,000} \quad \text{(NB } r \text{ must be measured in m)}$$

$$= 990 \text{ N}$$

4 A satellite which is in orbit is always accelerating towards the Earth. How can the satellite accelerate towards the Earth, but not crash into the ground?

5 Use the data from the example above.
   (a) Calculate the centripetal acceleration of the satellite using the equation $a = \frac{v^2}{r}$
   (b) Knowing that the weight (gravitational pull) of the satellite is 990 N, and its mass is 120 kg, calculate the value of the gravitational field strength, g, at this height.

   (c) Knowing that the circumference of a circle, c, can be calculated using the formula $c = 2\pi r$, calculate the time taken for the satellite to complete one orbit; its speed is 7600 m/s.
   (d) Another satellite is in an orbit of radius 21 000 km. At this height the Earth only exerts a force of 110 N.
   (i) Explain why the pull on the satellite is smaller than before.
   (ii) Calculate its new orbital speed.
   (iii) Calculate the time of orbit at this height.

Momentum

Momentum is defined as the product of mass × velocity. We measure it in units of kilogram metres per second (kg m/s).

$$\text{momentum} = m \times v$$

Velocity is a vector quantity, so momentum is too. We must give a direction when we talk about momentum (see Figure 1). Momentum is very useful when we meet problems involving collisions or explosions. There is always as much momentum after a collision as there is before it.

3 m/s → 3kg

momentum
= −3kg × 3 m/s
= −9kg m/s

4 m/s → 2kg

momentum
= +2kg × 4 m/s
= +8kg m/s

Figure 1 *In this diagram we have given anything moving to the right positive momentum, and anything moving to the left negative momentum*

Why does a gun recoil when it is fired?

Impulse

When a force, F, pushes a mass, m, we can work out the acceleration using:

$$F = ma$$

But the acceleration, $a = \dfrac{v - u}{t}$

where v is the final velocity, u is the starting velocity and t is the time taken for the velocity to change. The second equation can be substituted into the first to give:

$$F = \frac{m(v - u)}{t}$$

$$\text{or } Ft = mv - mu$$

Ft is called an **impulse** and has units of newton seconds. In words the equation can be expressed as:

$$\text{impulse} = \text{change of momentum}$$

So to cause a change of momentum of 100 kg m/s, for example, we must apply an impulse of 100 Ns. We could apply a force of 100 N for 1 s, or 1 N for 100 s. Each causes the same change of momentum.

Conservation of momentum

In Section B4 you met Newton's third law. This law says that when one body pushes against a second body, the second body pushes back with an equal and opposite force. Using this idea we can work out what happens in collisions.

Figure 2 shows two ice hockey players chasing after the puck. The blue player pushes the red player with his stick. The size of the push is 400 N and it lasts for 0.4 s. How fast are the players moving after the push? Since Ft = change of momentum, the red player's momentum increases by 400 N × 0.4 s = 160 Ns. We can calculate his increase in velocity using:

$$\text{increase in momentum} = \text{mass} \times \text{increase in velocity}$$

$$\text{So } 160 \text{ Ns} = 80 \text{ kg} \times \text{increase in velocity}$$

$$\text{increase in velocity} = 2 \text{ m/s}$$

This means the red player moves with a velocity of 5 m/s after the push. While the stick was touching the red player, there was also a push back on the blue

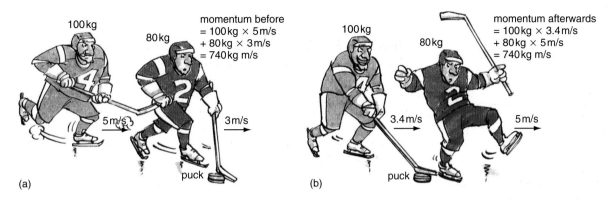

Figure 2

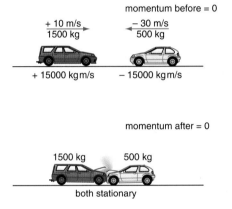

Figure 3

player. The same force of 400 N acted on the blue player for 0.4 s. So his momentum decreased by 160 Ns.

$$\text{His decrease in velocity} = \frac{\text{decrease in momentum}}{\text{mass}}$$

$$= \frac{160\,\text{Ns}}{100\,\text{kg}}$$

$$= 1.6\,\text{m/s}.$$

His final velocity = 5 m/s − 1.6 m/s = 3.4 m/s.

The momentum of one player increases by 160 Ns, the momentum of the second player decreases by 160 Ns. So the total change in momentum was zero. This leads to an important law:

> The momentum before a collision *always* equals the momentum after the collision.

This is known as the **principle of conservation of momentum**. Figure 3 shows another example: you can see that momentum is conserved.

Homework Questions

1 (a) Explain why momentum can be measured in units of kg m/s or Ns.
   (b) What change of momentum is caused by an impulse of 2 Ns?
2 What is the momentum of a runner of mass 70 kg running at 10 m/s?
3 In each of the following experiments, shown in the diagram, the two trollies collide and stick together, Work out the speeds of the trollies after their collisions.

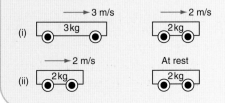

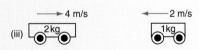

4 In Figure 3 two cars collided head on; each driver had a mass of 70 kg.
   (a) Calculate the change of momentum for each driver.
   (b) The cars stopped in 0.25 s. Calculate the average force that acted on each driver.
   (c) Explain which driver is likely to be more seriously injured.
5 A field gun of mass 1000 kg, which is free to move, fires a shell of mass 10 kg at a speed of 200 m/s.
   (a) What is the momentum of the shell after firing?

(b) What is the momentum of the gun just after firing?
   (c) Calculate the recoil velocity of the gun.
   (d) Why do you think very large guns are mounted on railway trucks?
6 Use the principle of momentum conservation to explain the following:
   (a) a gun recoils when fired,
   (b) you can swim through water.

Every time you go swimming you demonstrate Newton's third law. As you move your arms and legs through the water, you push the water backwards. But the water pushes you forwards.

The same idea applies to an aeroplane in flight powered by a propeller (Figure 1). The propeller accelerates air backwards, but the air exerts an equal forwards force on the aircraft. As you will see below, rockets and jet engines use the same principle.

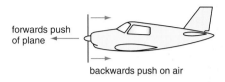
forwards push of plane
backwards push on air

Figure 1 *The forces acting on an aeroplane powered by a propeller*

Rockets

A propeller takes advantage of air resistance. If air did not exert a force on us as we move through it, a propeller would not work. This is why an ordinary aeroplane cannot fly in space, where there is no air for its propellers to push against. The simplest way to demonstrate the action of a rocket is with an air-filled balloon. If you blow up a balloon and then let it go, it whizzes around the room. It would also whizz around in space where there is no air, because the balloon gets its forwards push from the escaping air, You can explain this by using the principle of conservation of momentum. Before you let go of the balloon, the momentum of the balloon and air is nothing. Once the air is allowed to escape from the balloon the *total* momentum is still zero, but the balloon has forwards momentum and the air has backwards momentum (Figure 2).

Figure 3 shows a simple design for a rocket. The rocket carries with it fuel, such as kerosene, and liquid oxygen (oxygen is needed for the fuel to burn). These are mixed and burnt in the combustion chamber. High pressure gases are then forced out backwards through the nozzle at speeds of about 2000 m/s.

Figure 2
(a) No momentum

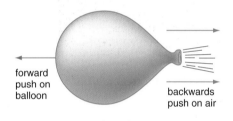
forward push on balloon
backwards push on air

(b) Balloon has momentum to the left
Air has momentum to the right
Total momentum is still zero

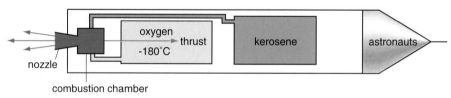
nozzle — combustion chamber — oxygen -180°C — thrust — kerosene — astronauts

Figure 3 *A simple rocket*

Jets

Figure 4 shows a simplified diagram of the sort of **jet turbine engine** which is found on an aeroplane. At the front of the engine a compressor sucks in air, acting rather like a propeller, but the air is compressed and as a result it becomes very hot. Some of the heated air then goes through into the combustion chamber and is mixed with the fuel (kerosene). The fuel burns and causes a great increase in the pressure of the gases. The hot gases are then forced out at high speed through the exhaust nozzle. The escaping gases provide a forward thrust on the engine.

The engine needs to be started with an electric motor to rotate the compressor, but once the engine is running some of the energy from the exhaust gases is used to drive a turbine. The turbine is mounted on the same shaft as the compressor so air can now be sucked in without the help of an electric motor.

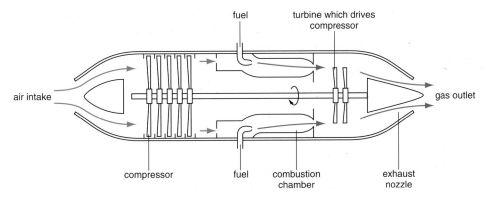

combustion
chamber

Figure 4 *The jet turbine engine*

This is a large jet engine. You can clearly see the turbines

Homework Questions

1 (a) Explain carefully how a rocket works.
(b) An aeroplane powered by jet engines cannot fly in space, but a rocket can. Why?

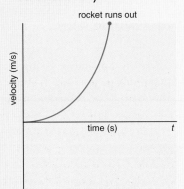

2 Above you can see a velocity/time graph for a firework rocket. The graph stops at the moment the firework stops burning. A positive velocity on this graph means the rocket is moving upwards.

(a) How can you tell from the graph that the acceleration of the rocket is increasing?
(b) Why does the acceleration rise? (Hint: What happens to the mass of the rocket as it burns?)
(c) Copy the graph and sketch how the velocity changes until the rocket hits the ground.

3 The diagram shows a home-made water-powered trolley. The idea is that you fill the tank up with water, and allow it to flow out of the back.
(a) Explain why the trolley starts to move forwards.
(b) At the start of an experiment the trolley is at rest; its mass is 3 kg, including 2 kg of water. When water is allowed to flow out of the back, it flows at a rate of 0.05 kg/s with a speed of 3.0 m/s. Calculate the backwards momentum of the water which flows out of the trolley

in the first two seconds.
(c) How much forwards momentum has the trolley gained in this time?
(d) Now calculate the approximate forwards speed of the trolley. (You may ignore the mass loss of the water.)
(e) Calculate the trolley's initial acceleration.
(f) The trolley's acceleration changes as the water level drops; discuss two factors which affect the size of its acceleration.

13 Fluid Flow

Something which flows is given the name **fluid**: usually we would associate this name with a liquid or a gas. You are used to pouring liquid into a glass, and you feel air flow in the form of a wind. Sometimes solids can act as a fluid; an avalanche is an example of 'solid flow'.

Viscosity

Fluids do not flow of their own accord. There needs to be a difference in pressure (called a pressure gradient) to cause the flow. A difference in temperature between places on the Earth's surface creates pressure differences, and then winds blow. Water flows down mountain sides and onwards to the sea, driven by the pull of gravity which creates the pressure gradient.

Without a pressure gradient a fluid stops flowing, because there are frictional forces which act on the fluid. This is well illustrated by looking at the flow of water in a river (Figure 1). Frictional forces cause the water on the river bed or near the river bank to move very slowly. The fastest flow of water occurs at the surface in the middle of the river. However, the water at the top also experiences frictional forces from the layers of water next to it. In winter when rainfall has been heavy, the river flows faster; there is a greater pressure of water, but a deeper river experiences less drag as more of the water is further from the river bed.

We give the name **viscosity** to describe a fluid's resistance to flow. Some fluids, such as treacle, are very viscous and flow slowly; water is less viscous than treacle. The viscosity of a fluid depends on the strength of inter-molecular bonding. Molecules in water, for example, are held together by attractive forces between neighbouring hydrogen and oxygen atoms (Figure 2). At higher temperatures the molecules have more energy and more of these bonds are broken; the fluid flows more easily and has a lower viscosity.

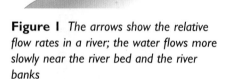

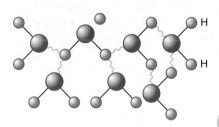

Figure 1 *The arrows show the relative flow rates in a river; the water flows more slowly near the river bed and the river banks*

Figure 2 *Attractive forces between an oxygen atom in one molecule and a hydrogen atom in another molecule provides viscous drag in water*

Flow through pipes

Figure 3 shows apparatus which can be used to investigate which factors affect the rate of flow of water through different pipes or tubes. To make it a fair test, water is collected in the time that it takes the level to drop from A to B.

- The flow rate is large if the cross-sectional area of the tube is large.
- The flow rate is small if the tube is long.

The effect of pressure can also be investigated using this apparatus. Using the one tube, the markers A and B can be moved up and down the flask. A greater depth of water, creates a greater pressure difference across the tube, and water flows faster.

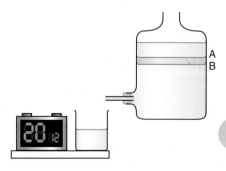

Figure 3

Streamlined and turbulent flow

When water flows slowly down a tube the flow is usually steady or **streamlined**; the direction of water flow is parallel to the tube walls at all points (Figure 4a). When the flow is **turbulent** the resistance to flow is larger than when the flow is streamlined (Figure 4b).

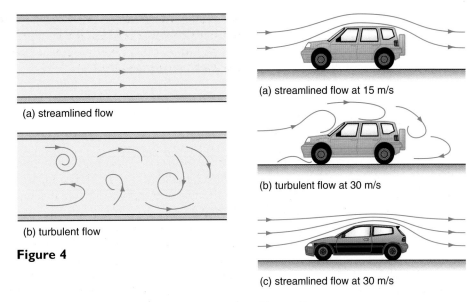

(a) streamlined flow

(b) turbulent flow

Figure 4

(a) streamlined flow at 15 m/s

(b) turbulent flow at 30 m/s

(c) streamlined flow at 30 m/s

Figure 5

Reducing drag

The idea of streamlined flow is very important when it comes to designing vehicles. The factors which affect the air resistance or drag on a vehicle are the speed, the cross-sectional area and shape. The drag rises as the speed or area of a vehicle rises. However, at a certain **critical speed** the flow becomes turbulent and the drag rises further. By choosing a well streamlined shape, turbulent flow occurs at a higher speed (Figure 5). We see sleek, streamlined shapes in fast trains, boats, cars and aeroplanes.

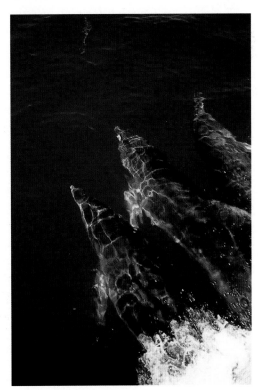

The streamlined shape of these dolphins allows them to move through water easily

Bernoulli's Principle

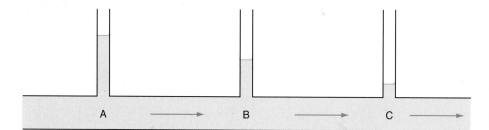

Figure 6

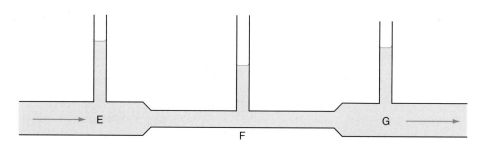

Figure 7

Figure 6 shows water passing down a tube of uniform diameter. The pressure is measured at three points, A, B and C with manometers; you can see that the pressure drops steadily down the tube. Pressure can be thought of as potential or stored energy in a fluid. A rocket, for example, is propelled by the force of escaping high pressure gases. The pressure in the water drops from A to C, because work is done against frictional forces. Figure 7 shows a different effect. The tube has a constriction at F. Now the pressure at F is much lower than at E, but rises again as the flow continues to G. The volume of water flowing each second, is the same at E as it is at F. However, because the tube is thinner at F, the water is moving faster. In terms of energy transfer, potential energy at E (high pressure) has been used to accelerate the water to a higher speed at F, so that it has more kinetic energy, but it now has less potential energy and so a lower pressure. The water slows in going from F to G, so kinetic energy is transferred back to potential energy and the pressure rises again.

Bernoulli's Principle states that when a fluid's speed increases, its pressure decreases; when the speed decreases, the fluid's pressure increases.

Applications of Bernoulli's Principle

You can demonstrate Bernoulli's principle very easily by holding out a piece of paper as shown in Figure 8. You then blow hard over the top of it, and the paper rises. The pressure in the fast moving air on top of the paper, is less than the pressure in the static air below; the difference in pressure causes the paper to rise.

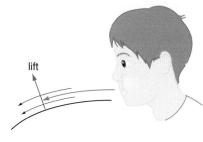

lift

Figure 8

Flying

The lift produced by an aeroplane wing relies on Bernoulli's Principle, Figure 9. The wing is curved so that the air has further to travel over the top of it. The streamlines join up again at the rear of the wing, so the air travels faster over the

http://explorescience.com/activities/activity_list.cfm?categoryID=10

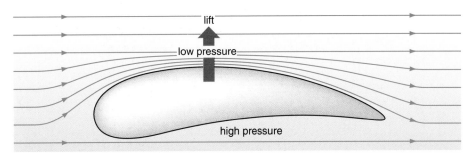

Figure 9 *This wing experiences lift; the air pressure below the wing is greater than that above*

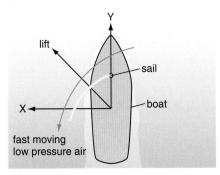

Figure 10 *This diagram shows the direction of lift on a yacht's sail*

top of the wing. The faster moving air experiences a drop in pressure, so the wing is pushed upwards by the pressure difference.

Sailing

A sail on a yacht also acts like an aeroplane wing to give the sail 'lift'. When a yacht sails into the wind, air travels more quickly round the outside of the sail than inside. Part of this lift force, Y, pushes the yacht forwards, Figure 10. The other component X, tends to push the boat sideways; this sideways push is resisted by the yacht's keel and by steering with the rudder.

Homework Questions

1 (a) Explain how you would use the apparatus shown in Figure 3 to compare the viscosity of two liquids.
(b) Liquid flows more quickly through a short, wide pipe, than it does through a long narrow one. Explain why.

2 When an object falls through air, it accelerates initially, but after a while reaches a 'terminal velocity'.
(a) What is meant by a terminal velocity?
(b) Why does a falling object accelerate at low speeds, but not exceed the terminal velocity?

3 Why do car manufacturers design streamlined models?

4 This question refers to Bernoulli's Principle.
(a) Why must the volume flow rate be the same at points E and F in Figure 7?

(b) Explain why the pressure of a fast moving fluid is less than the pressure in the same liquid flowing slowly.
(c) A yellow line is drawn near to the edge of platforms on railway stations, and we are advised to keep behind it. What hazard could a high speed train present to someone too close to it?
(d) The diagram shows a paint sprayer. How does the fast moving stream of air pull the paint out of the tin?

5 Pressure has units of N/m²; this unit can also be expressed as J/m³. Prove this statement and hence explain why pressure may be thought of as potential energy per m³.

6 Give three examples of Bernoulli's principle which can be found in everyday life.

SECTION B: Questions

1 This graph of velocity against time represents the motion of a cyclist.

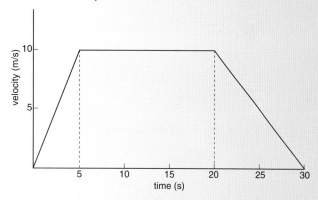

(a) Calculate her deceleration in the last 10 seconds of the journey.
(b) Calculate the distance that she travelled during the journey.

2 (a) Use the information in the table below to draw a graph of distance travelled, y-axis, against time x-axis.
(b) Use the graph to find
(i) for how long the cyclist was **not** moving,
(ii) the distance travelled between 80s and 140s.

WJEC

3

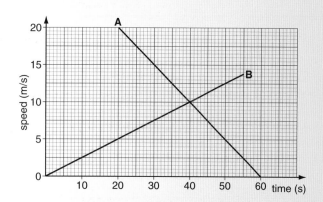

The motion of two cars, **A** and **B** is shown on the speed – time graph above.
(a) Describe fully the motion of **A**.
(b) Find
(i) the time when both cars travelled at the same speed,
(ii) the difference in speed between the two cars at 20 s.

WJEC

4 Ruth takes a motor bike for a short test drive. Here is the speed-time graph for the drive.

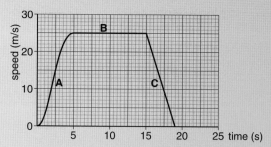

(a) The graph has three sections, labelled **A**, **B** and **C**. In which section is
(i) Ruth accelerating to top speed?
(ii) Ruth slowing down and stopping?
(iii) the counter force equal to the driving force?
(b) (i) Write down the formula linking speed, distance and time.
(ii) Ruth travels at top speed for 10 s. Calculate how far she goes in that time.

(c) Charlotte's motor bike has a less powerful engine than Ruth's. Charlotte takes her bike on the same test drive as Ruth.

Charlotte takes the bike to its top speed as quickly as possible. After ten seconds at top speed, Charlotte applies the brakes.

Copy Ruth's graph, and sketch a speed-time graph for Charlotte's test drive on the same graph.

(d) The next day Charlotte repeats the test drive after some rain. What difference will rain make to the speed-time graph of the test drive? Explain your answer.

OCR

5 A sky diver, whose weight is 800 N, jumps out of an aeroplane. After he has been falling for some time he is travelling at a constant speed. How big is the force of air resistance acting on him: is it (a) 800 N, (b) greater than 800 N, or (c) less than 800 N?

6 Ravi and Sarah are very good friends. But unfortunately they live 10 km apart. However, at 7 pm every evening they set out to meet each other; Ravi walks at 6 km/h and Sarah walks at 4 km/h. Ravi has a dog called Rover who always goes out with him. Rover thinks they must be mad to walk so far every night. However, he likes a good run. So as soon as he leaves Ravi's house he runs at 12 km/h until he

Table for question 2

distance (m)	0	100	200	300	400	400	400	500	600	700	800
time (s)	0	7.5	15	22.5	30	40	60	80	100	120	140

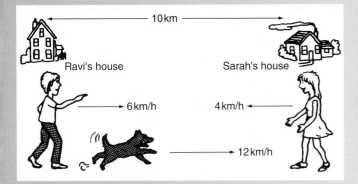

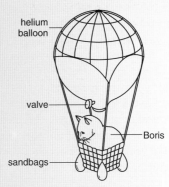

meets Sarah. As soon as he meets Sarah he turns round until he meets Ravi. Rover runs backwards and forwards between Ravi and Sarah until they meet. How far has Rover run when they meet?

7 Greig has worked out a new way to measure his mass. He is in a trolley that accelerates down a slope when released. Use the data below to answer these questions.

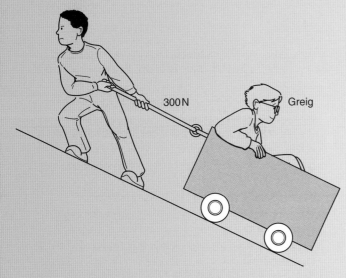

- It takes 300 N to hold Greig stationary on the slope.
- When released Greig travels 36 m in 6 s.
- Mass of the trolley = 32 kg.

(a) What is Greig's average speed over the 36 m?
(b) Assuming he accelerates at a steady rate, what is his final speed after travelling 36 m?
(c) Now work out his acceleration.
(d) Calculate Greig's mass.

8 Archimedes' Principle states that 'if a body is wholly or partially immersed in a fluid then the upthrust is equal to the weight of fluid displaced'.
- Total mass of sandbags + Boris + basket = 24 kg
- Volume of balloon = 30 m³
- Density of air at sea level ≈ 1.2 kg/m³
- Density of helium in balloon ≈ 0.2 kg/m³

(a) What is the force due to gravity on the balloon and its contents? (Include the helium.)
(b) What upthrust is there on the balloon?
(c) What is Boris's initial acceleration upwards?
(d) Assuming this acceleration is constant how far will he have travelled after 2 seconds?
The graph shows how the density of air varies with height above sea level.

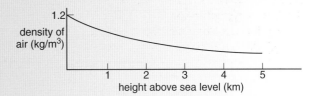

(e) Deduce from the graph how high Boris will rise.
(f) What must he do to go higher?
(g) How could he get down again?

9 Sara drops a stone off the edge of a cliff. It takes 2 s to reach the bottom.
(a) Calculate the speed of the stone just before it reaches the ground.
(b) Calculate the stone's average speed.
(c) Calculate the height of the cliff.

10 The diagram shows an accelerometer, which can be used to test the performance of a train. Springs can exert a force on a mass, *M*. The scale shows the size and direction of the resultant force. When the train is at rest the reading on the scale is zero.

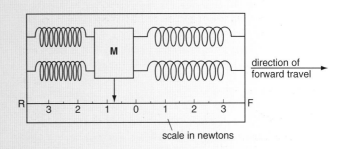

(a) What will the reading on the scale be when the train has been travelling at a steady speed for some time? Explain your answer.

(b) When the train accelerates forwards, the mass moves towards the end marked R. Explain why.

(c) Calculate the acceleration shown in the diagram (the mass of M is 0.5 kg).

(d) The train brakes suddenly and the deceleration is 3 m/s². What is the reading on the scale now?

(e) How would you adapt this accelerometer to measure greater accelerations?

11 The diagrams show the forces acting on a car of mass 800 kg when its speed changes from 20 m/s to 25 m/s.

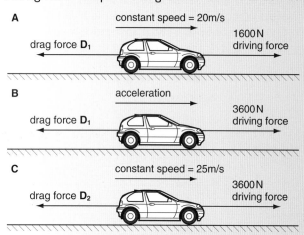

Diagram **A** shows the forces acting when the car travels at a constant speed of 20 m/s.

Diagram **B** shows the instant when a new driving force of 3600 N is applied.

Diagram **C** shows the forces acting when the car travels at a new constant speed of 25 m/s.

(a) Write down the size of
 (i) drag force **D**$_1$,
 (ii) the resultant force on the car in **B**,
 (iii) drag force **D**$_2$.
(b) (i) Write down, **in words**, an equation connecting acceleration, mass and force.
 (ii) Calculate the initial acceleration of the car in **B**. [The mass of the car = 800 kg.]
(c) (i) Explain why the resultant force and the acceleration of the car between stages **B** and **C** will gradually fall to zero.
 (ii) What is the average resultant force between stages **B** and **C**?

WJEC

12 The diagram shows an experiment which is designed to calculate the acceleration due to gravity, g. A small ball bearing is allowed to fall past four 'light gates'. The time at which the ball bearing passes

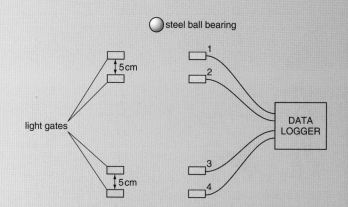

through each light gate is recorded by a data logger. The times recorded for such an experiment are shown in the table; the times are in milliseconds (ms).

Light gate	Time (ms)
1	0
2	25
3	310
4	320

The gates are arranged in two pairs. The separation of the gates in each pair is 5 cm, as shown in the diagram.

(a) Work out the average speed of the ball bearing as it falls past gates 1 and 2.

(b) Work out the average speed of the ball bearing as it falls past gates 3 and 4.

(c) Work out the acceleration of the ball bearing as it falls. Explain your working carefully.

(d) Explain how a light gate works.

(e) The same experiment can also be done by attaching a ticker tape to a heavy ball. Explain two advantages that the light gates have over the ticker tape method.

13 This question is about the performance of the Montego 2.0 HL, manufactured by the Rover company. Examine the data shown provided by the manufacturers. Graph A is a velocity/time graph, showing how the velocity of the car changes as it accelerates through the gears. This was obtained by attaching a data logger to the speedometer. Graph B shows the available force at the wheels, for different gears and speeds. The total resistive force acting on the car is also shown.

(a) The manufacturers claim that the Montego can cover 400 m, starting from rest, in under 20 seconds. Use the velocity/time graph to show this is correct.

(b) Use the velocity/time graph to calculate the acceleration between times of 1 s and 3 s. (The region AB of the graph.)

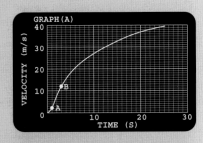

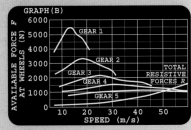

(c) Use Graph B to work out the maximum possible acceleration of the car, in first gear. The mass of the Montego is 1000 kg.
(d) Explain why the car's acceleration is less in the higher gears.
(e) Which gear would you drive in to obtain the maximum acceleration from a speed of 20 m/s?
(f) Use Graph B to show that the car's maximum speed is 48 m/s. In which gear is this speed reached?

14 When a bomber releases a load of bombs they fall freely under the action of gravity. The table below gives positions of the bombs at 2 s intervals.
(a) Plot a graph of the height of the bombs above the ground (y-axis) against the distance travelled horizontally (x-axis).
(b) How fast is the plane travelling?
(c) Use the graph to predict the position of the bombs after:
(i) 6 s, (ii) 20 s.
(d) The bomber now flies on a mission at a height of 1500 m at the same speed. How far away from the target must the bombs be released if they are going to hit? Use your graph to help you answer this.
(e) Another bomber flies at a speed of 200 m/s at the same height. Draw a second graph, using the same axes as before, to show the position of bombs that fall from this plane.

15 The diagram below shows an alpha particle colliding head on with a stationary proton in a cloud chamber. Before the collision the alpha particle has a speed of 10^7 m/s. After the collision its speed is 0.6×10^7 m/s. The mass of the alpha particle is 4 times that of the proton. Calculate the speed of the proton after the collision.

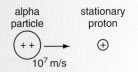

Before the collision

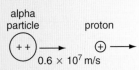

After the collision

16 A hot-air balloon is tied to the ground by two ropes to stop it from taking off. The diagram shows the forces acting on the balloon.

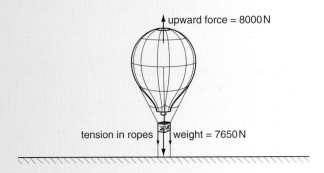

The ropes are untied and the balloon starts to move upwards.
(a) Calculate the size of the unbalanced force acting on the balloon. State the direction of this force.
(b) The mass of the balloon is 765 kg. Calculate the initial acceleration of the balloon.
(c) Explain how the acceleration of the balloon changes during the first ten seconds of its flight.

Table for question 14

		0	2	4	6	8	10	12	14	16	18	20
						Time(s)						
height above the ground (m)		2000	1980	1920		1680	1500	1280	1020	720	380	
distance travelled horizontally (m)		0	600	1200		2400	3000	3600	4200	4800	5400	

(d) When the balloon is still accelerating, the balloonist throws some bags of sand over the side. Explain how this affects the acceleration of the balloon.

17 For this question these equations may be useful.

$$v = u + at$$
$$s = ut + \frac{1}{2} at^2$$

The diagram shows the Shuttle spacecraft as it is launched into space.

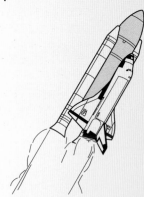

During the first eight minutes of the launch the average acceleration of the Shuttle is 17.5 m/s².
(a) Calculate the speed of the Shuttle after the first 8 minutes. You **must** show how you work out your answer.
(b) Calculate how far the Shuttle travels in the first 8 minutes. You **must** show how you work out your answer.
(c) In fact the acceleration of the Shuttle is increasing. Suggest a reason for this and explain your answer.

OCR

18 The diagram shows an astronaut and a space telescope. He is stationary relative to the telescope. He is about to use the thrusters on his backpack to move towards the telescope.

(a) He switches on the thrusters.
In a short burst, 0.020 kg of gas is ejected backwards at 300 m/s.

(i) Calculate the momentum gained by the gas. Use the equation below. You **must** show how you work out your answer.

momentum = mass × velocity

(ii) What is the momentum gained by the fully equipped astronaut in this time? Explain your answer.
(iii) The thrusters give the astronaut a velocity of 0.06 m/s towards the telescope. Calculate the mass of the fully equipped astronaut. You **must** show how you work out your answer.

(b) The astronaut arrives at the telescope. He uses a long spanner to undo a nut. On Earth he can do this easily. In space it is more difficult.

Use your ideas about forces to explain why.

OCR

19 The diagram below shows some of the forces acting on a car of mass 1200 kg.

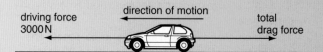

(a) State the size of the total drag force when the car is travelling at constant speed.

(b) The driving force is increased to 4800 N.
(i) Find the resultant force on the car at this instant.
(ii) Write down, **in words**, the equation connecting mass, force and acceleration.
(iii) Calculate the initial acceleration of the car.

(c) Explain why the car will eventually reach a new higher constant speed.

WJEC

20 During a journey through space, to make a velocity correction, a rocket must increase its emission of exhaust gases.

(a) Explain how this causes an increase in velocity of the rocket.

(b) The rocket has a mass of 20000 kg and fires 6 kg of burnt fuel out of its engines as hot gases travelling at 10000 m/s.

Use the equation momentum (kg m/s) = mass (kg) × velocity (m/s) to calculate the change in
(i) momentum of the hot gases,
(ii) momentum of the rocket,
(iii) velocity of the rocket.

WJEC

The Earth in Space

True-colour image of the Vela supernova remnant in the constellation Vela. The thin strands are the remains of a star which underwent a supernova explosion around 11 000 light years ago. The remnant lies about 1000 light years from Earth, and covers an area almost 10 Moon widths across. At the centre of this gas shell is pulsar 0833-45, a rapidly spinning neutron star, believed to be the remains of the original star.

By the end of this section you should:

- be able to name all the planets in the solar system, and know about their internal structure
- understand why we have four seasons
- know why the stars, planets and the Moon appear to change positions in the night sky
- know that a system of stars grouped together is called a galaxy
- know that the Earth is part of a galaxy called the Milky Way, and that there are many other galaxies in the universe

- understand the consequences of Newton's Law of Gravitation
- know what comets, meteors and asteroids are
- be able to name different types of stars, and know how they produce energy
- know how our view of the Earth's place in the universe has changed with time
- be able to define cosmology, and know what the Big Bang theory is

The Solar System

The brightest thing that you can see in the sky is our **Sun**. The Sun is a star which provides all the heat and light that we need to live. The Earth is a **planet** which moves around the Sun. Altogether, there are nine planets which move round the Sun in curved paths. These paths are called **orbits**. The Earth is the third planet out from the Sun. Planets do not produce their own light like the Sun; we can see planets at night because they *reflect* the Sun's light. The Sun and its nine planets are known as the **solar system**. The word 'solar' means 'belonging to the sun'. Some of the planets have moons that move around them. The Earth has only one moon.

The four planets nearest to the Sun, including Earth, have hard, solid and rocky surfaces. The planet closest to the sun is **Mercury**. This has a cratered surface that looks like our Moon's surface. During its day, Mercury is baking hot. Even lead would melt on its surface. Mercury travels quickly round the Sun, taking 88 days to complete one orbit.

Venus lies between Mercury and the Earth. It has a thick atmosphere; its clouds are made from burning hot sulphuric acid. Nothing could survive on its hot, poisonous surface.

Mars is the last of the rocky planets. It is a lot colder than the Earth because it is further away from the Sun. Like the Earth, it has large polar icecaps, which can be seen through a telescope. At some stage in the past, Mars had active volcanoes. The largest is called Olympus Mons. It towers 25 km above the surrounding land, this is more that 2½ times the height of Mount Everest above sea level. As continents move on the Earth, mountains grow. The Himalayas are growing now at about the same rate as your fingernails. Mountains may still be growing on Mars.

Beyond the orbit of Mars, are four giant planets: **Jupiter**, **Saturn**, **Uranus** and **Neptune**. Each of these is much larger than the four inner planets (Figure 1). In Figure 2, you can see that these four giant planets move in orbits that are far away from the Sun. Each of these planets is made from gas. If you landed on one of these planets, you would sink into it.

The largest planet is Jupiter, which has a diameter 11 times bigger than that of the Earth. More than 1000 Earths would be needed to fill Jupiter's enormous volume. The swirling clouds in Jupiter's atmosphere blow around at hurricane wind speeds of 200 miles per hour. Jupiter has 14 moons which orbit around it. Four of these are about the same size as our Moon. The innermost of these four large moons is called Io; when Voyager 1 flew by Io in 1979, it photographed active volcanoes. Saturn is best known for its beautiful rings.

The planet furthest from the Sun is Pluto; it is smaller than our Moon. It is a frozen and dead world. Its temperature is 240°C below freezing. From its cold surface, the Sun would look like a bright star, not the provider of life giving light and warmth that we know it.

http://freespace.virginnet.co.uk/solar.system/index.html

http://www.eia.brad.ac.uk/btl/

http://www.bbc.co.uk/planets/solarguide.shtml

http://zebu.uoregon.edu/galaxy.html

http://www.jpl.nasa.gov/basics/

http://amazing-space.stsci.edu/

http://www.nasa.gov/

http://www.deepspace.ucsb.edu/ia/index.htm

http://www.star.le.ac.uk/edu/solar/homepage.html

http://szyzyg.arm.ac.uk/~spm/neo_map.html

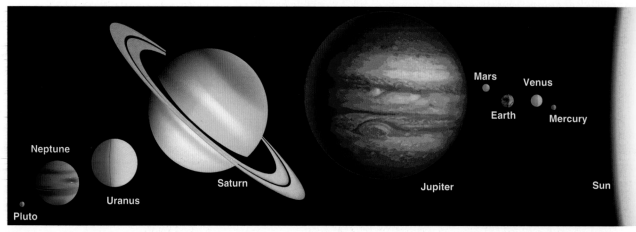

Figure 1 *The relative sizes of the Sun and its planets. (Figure 2 shows the positions of the planets relative to one another)*

Planet	Diameter of planet	Average distance of planet from the Sun	Time taken to go round the Sun	Number of moons	Average temperature on sunny side
Mercury	4900 km	58 million km	88 days	0	350°C
Venus	12 000 km	108 million km	225 days	0	480°C
Earth	12 800 km	150 million km	365¼ days	1	20°C
Mars	6800 km	228 million km	687 days	2	0°C
Jupiter	143 000 km	780 million km	12 years	14	−150°C
Saturn	120 000 km	1430 million km	29 years	24	−190°C
Uranus	52 000 km	2800 million km	84 years	15	−220°C
Neptune	49 000 km	4500 million km	165 years	3	−240°C
Pluto	3000 km	5900 million km	248 years	1	−240°C

Table 1 Facts about the planets

Facts about the Sun:
diameter 1 400 000 km;
surface temperature 6000°C

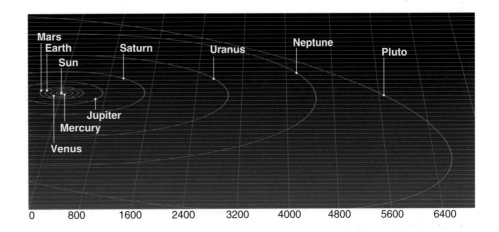

Figure 2 The orbits of the planets around the Sun. The four inner planets are very close to the Sun; the gaps between the outer planets are very large

Homework Questions

1 Using Table 1:
(a) Which is the largest planet?
(b) Which planet has a temperature closest to that of our Earth?
(c) Which planet takes just under two years to go round the Sun?
(d) Are the temperatures of the planets related to their distance from the Sun? Why is Venus hotter than Mercury?
(e) Is there any pattern in the number of moons which planets have? Try and explain any pattern that you find.
(f) Which planets will go round the Sun more than once in your lifetime?

2 (a) Here is something active to do. You can make a model of the solar system. The scale of your solar system should be 1 m for 20 million kilometres. Use Table 1 to calculate how far each planet needs to be placed from the Sun. Now go outside and make your model – you will need a lot of space!
(b) Now work out where the nearest star system, Alpha Centauri, should be placed on your model. Should it be in the next street, the next town or where?

(Alpha Centauri is 6000 times further away from the Sun than Pluto is.)

3 Try and answer these questions about the solar system. You may need to go to a library or use the Internet to find the answers.
(a) Where is the Sea of Tranquillity?
(b) Which planet has a red spot?
(c) What are Oberon and Titania?
(d) What are 'asteroids'?
(e) Which planet has the shortest day?
(f) How many planets have rings around them?

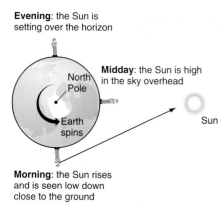

Evening: the Sun is setting over the horizon

Midday: the Sun is high in the sky overhead

North Pole

Earth spins

Sun

Morning: the Sun rises and is seen low down close to the ground

Figure 1

The Earth spins around on its axis. It rotates once in about 24 hours. This is why we have days and nights. When we face the Sun it is day; and when we cannot see the Sun it is night. At night we can see stars. The stars are there all the time, but the sky is too bright for us to see them during the day.

Because the Earth spins, the Sun, Moon and stars seem to move across the sky. Figure 1 shows the Earth as you would see it from above the North Pole. Professor Chandrasekhar lives on the Equator. You can see from Figure 1 that the Professor sees the Sun close to the ground in the morning and evening, but that it is overhead at midday.

The Earth moves around the Sun in an approximately circular orbit. The closest the Earth gets to the Sun is 147 million kilometres; the furthest is 152 million kilometres. The Earth takes 365¼ days to complete its path round the Sun. This is why we have 365 days in our calendar. Every four years, we have a **leap year** with an extra day to make up for the ¼ day lost every year.

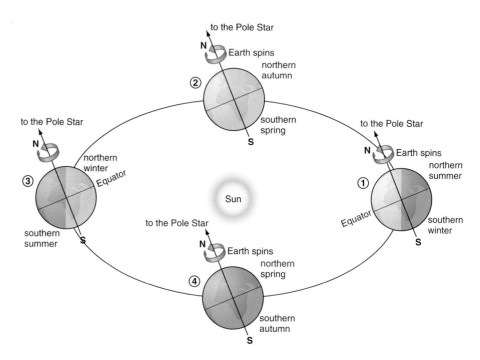

Figure 2 *Earth's path around the Sun*

Figure 2 shows the Earth's yearly path. The Earth spins around an axis which goes through the North and South Poles. All the time, the North Pole points towards the pole star (Polaris). The Earth's axis is tilted as shown in Figure 3. This tilt gives the Earth its seasons. In the middle of our summer the northern half of the Earth is tipped towards the Sun by an angle of 23½° (position (1) in Figure 2). At this time, the south of the Earth is tipped away from the Sun. Because the north is tipped towards the Sun it is hotter, so it is summer in the north. But the south is tipped away, so it is cold and winter in the south. Six months later, the Earth has reached position (3). The north is tipped away from the Sun, and the south is tipped towards the Sun. It is now winter in the north, and summer in the south. In the spring and autumn, the northern and southern halves of the Earth get equal amounts of sunshine.

The tilt of the Earth's axis also causes the length of our days to change. In

Winter

Summer

Figure 4 *In winter, the Sun is low in the sky and shadows are long. In summer, the Sun is high in the sky and so shadows are shorter*

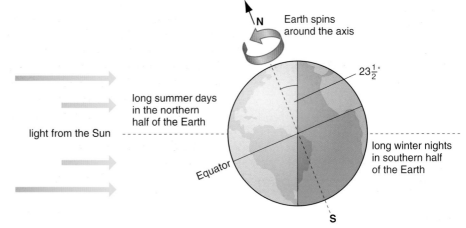

long summer days in the northern half of the Earth

light from the Sun

Earth spins around the axis

$23\frac{1}{2}°$

long winter nights in southern half of the Earth

Equator

Figure 3

Figure 3, you can see that it is summer in the north. Look at the half of the Earth north of the equator; more of it is in sunlight than in darkness. This makes our summer days long. More of the south is in darkness, so it has long winter nights. In the northern summer, the North Pole always sees the Sun, so it has 24 hours of daylight each day. But in the winter, the North Pole has no daylight at all. The equator has days which are 12 hours long all through the year. If you live in Kenya, the Sun rises at 6 am every morning and sets at 6 pm; there is very little twilight. If you live in Oslo, you will get 20 hours of sunlight in the summer, but only four hours of sunlight in winter.

Homework Questions

1 With the help of diagrams explain the following:
(a) Why we have summer and winter seasons.
(b) Why days are longer in our summer.
(c) Why people who live inside the Arctic circle see the sun at midnight in June.
(d) Why each day on the equator is 12 hours long.
(e) What sort of seasons do you get on the equator?

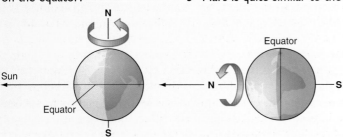

2 Imagine what it would be like on the Earth if it was tilted at a different angle. In the left diagram below, the Earth does not tilt at all.
(a) What happens then? Do we have different seasons? Do our days change in length?
(b) In the right diagram below, the North Pole is facing the Sun. Explain what our days and seasons would be like now.

3 Mars is quite similar to the Earth, its axis of rotation is tilted towards the sun by an angle of 24°, and its day is 24½ hours long.

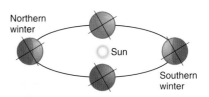

Northern winter

Sun

Southern winter

The diagram above shows Mars' orbit round the Sun. In southern winter it is 250 million km away from the Sun, but only 200 million km from the Sun in northern winter. Describe how the seasons on Mars differ from ours. Is a northern winter on Mars colder than a southern winter?

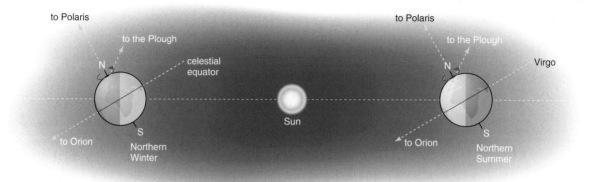

Figure 1

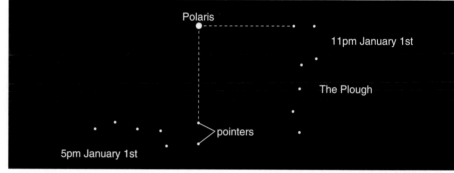

Figure 2 *Computer simulation of the movement of the stars*

We live in an enormous universe which contains millions of stars, planets and moons. In the daytime the sky is dominated by the Sun, the star which the Earth orbits around. At night time you can easily see lots of stars and the Moon; with more skill you can also see some planets. The purpose of these pages, is to explain what you might see on any night, and why you do not see the same stars all year round.

Figure 1 shows the position of the Earth in space; the north pole tilts towards the Sun in the northern summer and away from the Sun in the northern winter. The Earth rotates every 24 hours around an axis which points towards the Pole Star (or Polaris). Because of this daily rotation of the Earth, the stars appear to rotate each night. For example, Figure 2 shows the position of the plough at 5 pm in January; six hours later (11 pm) the Earth has completed a quarter of a rotation, so the plough has rotated through an angle of 90°. If you want to find the Pole Star, you can follow the line or the 'pointers' to help you locate it.

The Plough is a group of stars (constellation) which is 'circumpolar'; this means it lies close to the Pole Star. These stars are visible from Britain every night of the year. Stars which are close to the Celestial Equator (Figure 1) are not visible all year round. Orion is a constellation which is visible from Britain in winter, but is on the wrong side of the Earth to be visible in summer. On the other hand, the constellation of Virgo is visible in our summer but not in winter.

http://www-spof.gsfc.nasa.gov/
stargaze/Sintro.htm
http://tycho.usno.navy.mil/
vphase.html

The changing Moon

Our nearest neighbour in space is the Moon. The shape of the Moon always seems to be changing. The position of the Moon in the sky also changes from day to day.

Phases of the Moon: early in the month the Moon is a waxing crescent

Phases of the Moon: as the month goes on the Moon becomes a waxing gibbous

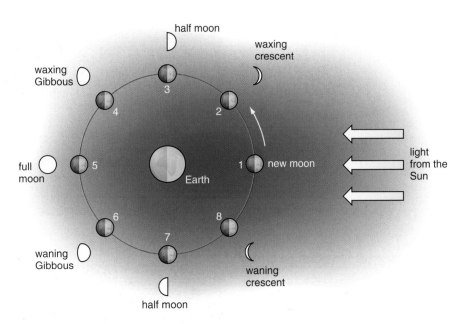

Figure 3 *Phases of the Moon*

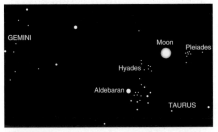

Figure 4 *Looking south on December 5 at 11 pm*

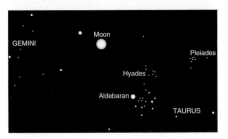

Figure 5 *Looking south on December 6 at 11 pm*

The Moon moves around the Earth once a month. This is shown in Figure 3. The diagram shows the Moon in eight different places or **phases**. It takes the Moon about 3½ days to move from one position to the next. The Sun shines on the Moon and lights up half of it. In position 1, we cannot see the bright side of the Moon. This is a **new moon** which is very difficult to see. In position 3, we see a **half moon**, since we can see equal amounts of the dark and bright sides of the Moon. When the Moon is in position 5, we see all of the bright sides of it. This is a **full moon**.

During the first half of the month, the Moon grows from a crescent to a half, to a gibbous and finally, to a full moon. While the Moon is growing, we say it is **waxing**. In the second half of the month, it is **waning**. During this time it shrinks back to a new moon.

As the Moon moves round us, we see it close to different stars each night. Figure 4 shows the view south one night in December. The Moon is near the bright group of stars, the Pleiades. The next night (Figure 5) the Moon has moved towards the constellation of Gemini.

Homework Questions

1 Draw a diagram to help explain why the Moon appears in different parts of the sky each night.

2 Look at Figure 3 and use it to explain
(i) why a full moon rises at sunset,
(ii) why a half moon reaches its highest point in the sky at dawn or sunset.

3 (a) Why do we never see the Moon near the Plough?
(b) What is meant by a circumpolar star?

4 Figure 4 shows the Moon near to the Pleiades on 5 December. Draw diagrams to show how the Moon and its neighbouring stars looked on the same day when viewed from (i) the Equator and (ii) Australia.

5 (a) Copy Figure 2 and draw the position of the Plough at (i) 7 pm on 1 January (ii) 2 am on 2 January.
(b) On the same diagram mark the position of the Plough at 11 pm on 1 July (half a year later).

6 Explain carefully, with the aid of appropriate diagrams why we see different stars during different seasons.

4 | Moving Planets

www

http://www.physics.nwu.edu/
ugrad/vpl/mechanics/planets.
html

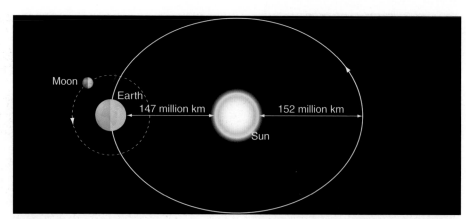

Figure 1 *The Earth moves in an elliptical orbit round the Sun. The Moon moves around the Earth*

The Earth moves round the Sun in a curved path. The shape of this path is an **ellipse**. The ellipse is a bit like a squashed circle. Figure 1 shows how the Earth and Moon move together round the Sun. All the planets move in elliptical paths around the Sun. They all move in the same direction, as shown in Figure 2. The planets near the Sun move faster than those further away. In Figure 2 you are looking down on the solar system from above. If you could look at it from the side (Figure 3), you would see all the planets in nearly the same plane. This is called **the plane of the ecliptic**. Our Moon also lies in the same plane. This means that you can quite often see the Moon close to some planets in the sky.

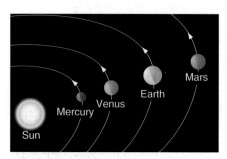

Figure 2 *All planets rotate around the Sun in the same direction*

Figure 3 *All planets lie very close to the same plane. Will all planets always be on the same side of the Sun?*

In ancient Greece, the word 'planet' meant 'wanderer'. The planets were given their name because they appear to wander around the sky. The Earth moves round the Sun once a year. In January, we are always in the same position so we see the same stars at night each year. The stars are so far away that they do not appear to move at all, even over thousands of years. Each January we see the bright star Aldebaran high in the sky. From 2000 to 2003, Saturn could be seen clearly on January evenings close to Aldebaran. But Saturn moves slowly round the Sun taking about 30 years to go once round (Figure 4). During 2001 and 2002 Saturn moved slowly past Aldebaran (Figure 5).

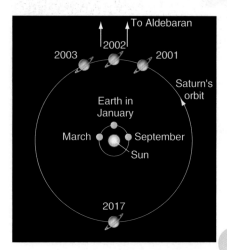

Figure 4 *As Saturn moves slowly round the Sun, we see it move against the stars*

Yearly motion

Figure 5 shows Saturn's passage through the stars over a period of several years. However, by looking at Saturn's position at the same time each year, the effect of the Earth's motion has been ignored. When you look at a planet every month or so, you see a more complicated motion.

Figure 6 shows how Mars moved past the Spica in early 1999. Notice that Mars moved to the left for most of the time; but between April and June it moved backwards, through a **retrograde loop**. This loop occurs because the Earth, which orbits the Sun faster than Mars, overtakes Mars at this point.

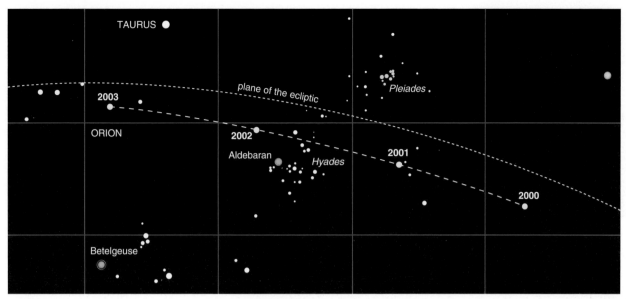

Figure 5 *This is how Saturn moved over a period of 4 years*

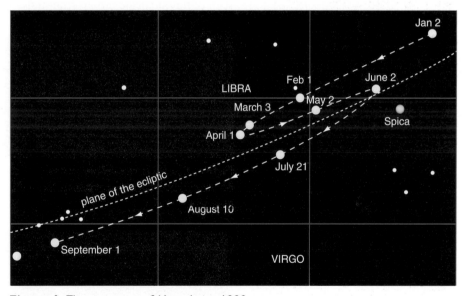

Figure 6 *The movement of Mars during 1999*

Homework Questions

1 (a) Look at the star map in Figure 5. Approximately where will you see Saturn in 2032? (Remember Saturn takes about 30 years to go round the Sun.)
   (b) Explain why it will be very difficult to see Saturn in January 2017. In which month will it be best to see Saturn in 2017?

2 If you look at Jupiter or Saturn through a telescope, you can see a large planet with clear markings. If you look at Pluto through a telescope it looks like a star – a small point of light. Pluto was discovered in 1930. How did astronomers know that Pluto is a planet and not a fixed star?

3 (a) Make a copy of Figure 4. Draw lines from Earth positions 1, 2 and 3 to Saturn's position in 2002. Use your diagram to explain why Saturn appears to go through a retrograde loop every year.
   (b) Explain why Mars appears to move more rapidly than Saturn.

4 In Figures 2 and 3 of the last section (page 69) you can see the Moon near Aldebaran: Saturn is near the same star in 2002. Explain why Saturn and the Moon appear in the same part of the sky.

5 | Beyond the Solar System

From the Earth, we see the stars of our galaxy as the Milky Way

Look at the sky on a dark night. How many stars do you think you can see? All of these stars are great distances away from us. We measure distances to stars in **light years**. A light year is the distance that light travels in one year. This is about 10 million million kilometres. The brightest star in the sky (after the Sun) is Sirius. It is also one of the nearest, but light takes nine years to reach us from Sirius. Light takes only six hours to reach Pluto from the Sun. This makes our solar system look very small.

Try to look at the sky on a clear night through binoculars or a small telescope. You will be able to see even more stars. You may be able to see the Milky Way. Many of the stars in the Milky Way have their own solar systems.

Clusters of millions of stars like the Milky Way are called galaxies. The Sun is one of the stars in the Milky Way (Figure 1). The Milky Way has about 100 000 million stars in it. If you could see our galaxy from the side, it would look like two fried eggs stuck back to back (Figure 1a); it is long and thin except for a bulge in the middle. If you could see the galaxy from the top it would look like a giant whirlpool with great spiral arms (Figure 1b). In fact, the galaxy does spin round. Our Sun takes about 220 million years to go once round the centre of the galaxy. In your lifetime, the pattern of stars that you see each night will not appear to change. But over thousands of years the pattern will change as our Sun moves through the galaxy. Our ancestors who lived 100 000 years ago would have seen different constellations from those we can see today.

Figure 1 *(a) Side view of our galaxy*　　　　*(b) Top view of our galaxy*
An artist's impression of our galaxy, the Milky Way. The red circle shows the approximate position of our Sun.

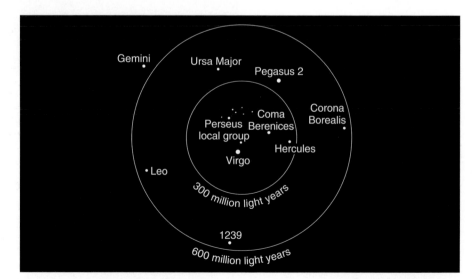

Figure 2 *This map shows groups of galaxies close to our local group. The most distant galaxies in the universe are 15 000 million light years away from us. In this map, a large dot means that the group of galaxies contains more than 50 galaxies*

This spiral galaxy lies around 12 million light years away

About 10 000 million years ago there were no galaxies at all, and the universe was full of hydrogen and helium gas. **Gravity** is a force which acts over enormous distances, even over thousands of millions of light years. Groups of galaxies were formed when gravity gradually pulled large volumes of gas together. After the galaxies were formed, stars were formed inside the galaxies. Look at Figure 2. This shows a map of groups of galaxies. Our local group is in the middle. There are about 20 galaxies in our local group. Some groups of galaxies have as many as 1000 galaxies in them. There are about 10 000 million galaxies in the universe.

The Virgo cluster of galaxies lies 50 million light years away from us. It consists of about 1000 galaxies spread across 10 million light years.

Homework Questions

1 Explain what is meant by each of the following terms.
(a) moon, (b) planet, (c) star, (d) galaxy, (e) group of galaxies, (f) universe

2 Our Sun is about 4600 million years old. Use the information in the text to calculate the number of times the Sun has rotated round the galaxy. Humans have existed on the earth for about 50 000 years; how many times round the galaxy has the Sun rotated in that time?

3 Voyager 1 was launched in September 1977 and passed Saturn in November 1980. It travelled about 1400 million km to Saturn.
(a) Work out its average speed in millions of kilometres per year.

(b) The nearest star to us after the Sun is Proxima Centauri, 4 light years away, in the Alpha Centauri star system. Use the information that light travels at 0.3 million km/s to calculate the distance to Proxima Centauri in millions of kilometres.
(c) Estimate how long Voyager would take to reach Proxima Centauri travelling at the speed calculated in part (a).
(d) Comment on the likelihood of our finding extraterrestrial life.

4 Use the information in the text to estimate the number of stars in the Universe.

5 Imagine that a spacecraft could be launched at the speed of light. How long would it take to reach the

following heavenly bodies? Select your answer from the list below.
(i)   the star Sirius
(ii) Jupiter
(iii) the Andromeda Galaxy
(iv) the far side of the Milky Way
(v)   the Sun
(vi) Pluto
(vii) the cluster of galaxies in Hercules (Figure 2)

Possible answers:
10 000 years   9 years
2 million years   8 minutes
70 000 years   1 minute
2 seconds   5 hours
60 000 million years
40 minutes
260 million light years

6 Gravitation

Newton's law of gravity

In the 100 years before Isaac Newton was born, astronomers had carefully observed the motion of planets and the positions of stars. From these measurements, the astronomers worked out that the Sun is the centre of our solar system, and that the planets move in orbits around it. But nobody understood what kept the planets moving along their paths.

In 1665, the great plague swept across England. Cambridge University was closed and all the students, including Newton, were sent home. It was then, stranded in Lincolnshire, that Newton worked out his Law of Gravity. He suddenly realised that the Earth's gravitational pull does more than keep our feet on the ground. It reaches out, beyond the highest mountains, and into the depths of space. The Earth's pull stretches 400 000 km across space, and keeps the Moon moving around us.

Newton said that any two masses in the universe attract each other with a gravitational pull. The size of this force is given by:

$$F = \frac{GM_1M_2}{R^2}$$

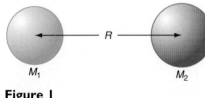

Figure I

F is the force (in newtons) between two masses, M_1 and M_2 (in kg). These masses might be planets for example. R is the distance between the centre of these masses (in m), see Figure 1. G ('big gee') is the universal constant of gravitation; its value is 6.7×10^{-11} Nm²/kg². The pull is too weak to be noticeable between two people. It is only when one of the masses is the size of a planet that we can feel the force of gravity.

Newton's equation shows us that the Earth's pull gets weaker the further out into space we go (Figure 2). What is the Earth's pull on the Moon? The Moon is 60 times further from the centre of the Earth than we are. For us, the pull is 10 N/kg – each kg experiences a pull of 10 N. In the equation, if R gets 60 times bigger, $1/R^2$ gets 60^2, or 3600, times smaller. So the Earth exerts a pull of 10/3600 N on each kg of the moon; that is about 0.003 N/kg.

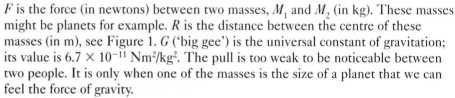

Figure 2 *The Earth's pull gets weaker further away, but it is strong enough to keep the Moon in orbit around us*

Orbits

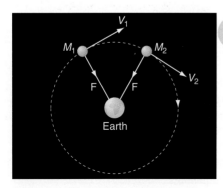

Figure 3 *The Earth's pull changes the velocity of the Moon from v_1 to v_2*

Figure 3 shows the Moon's orbit round the Earth; in position M_1, the moon is moving along the direction v_1. Without any force acting on it, the Moon would continue to move in that direction. But the Earth is always pulling the Moon towards it. This pull is at right-angles to the Moon's motion. The pull does not speed the Moon up; the pull deflects the Moon away from a straight path, into a curved path. At M_2, the Moon has a new velocity v_2. The Earth's pull changes this velocity again. The Earth pulls on the Moon all the way round its orbit.

The Moon has stayed in orbit for billions of years. As it goes round the Earth it does not lose any energy. There are no frictional forces in space to slow it down.

Voyager I took this photograph of Jupiter in 1979 when only 20 million km away. Two Jovian moons are visible in the foreground, Io to the left and Europa to the right. Newton used his theory to explain that all stars and planets have their own gravitational pulls. Jupiter keeps its Moons in orbit and the Sun keeps Jupiter in orbit.

The Earth's force on the Moon does not change its speed, because it acts at right-angles to its motion. (See Unit D1; no work is done when the push is at right-angles to the motion.)

Tides

The gravitational pull of the Moon on the ocean causes our **tides**. We get two high tides a day. The Earth-Moon system rotates about a centre of gravity (or **barycentre**) at B (Figure 4). This is inside the Earth but not at its centre. At A, there is a high tide because the Moon pulls more strongly on the water closer to it. At C there is also a high tide. At C the Moon pulls the water less strongly. As the water rotates around B it piles up; this is because the Moon's pull is not strong enough to keep it in a smaller circular path.

The Sun also exerts a tidal pull on our seas, but about half as much as the Moon. Twice a month, the Sun and Moon line up to produce a large tidal pull. We then get **spring tides**. When the Sun and Moon pull at right-angles to each other, the high tides are smaller, These are called **neap tides** (Figure 5). Other factors, such as strong winds, also affect the height of tides.

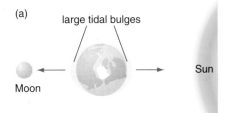

(a)

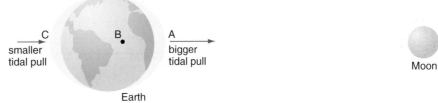

Figure 4 *The tidal pulls are exaggerated here; the height of the tides is only a few metres*

(b)

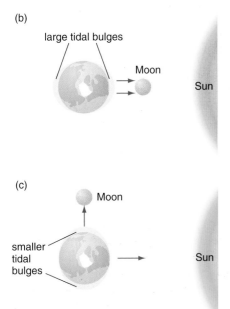

(c)

Figure 5 *Spring tides occur at (a) full Moons and (b) new Moons. Neap tides occur when the Sun and the Moon pull at right angles to each other (c).*

Homework Questions

1 (a) Draw a diagram to show the Earth in orbit around the Sun.
   (b) Mark the direction of the force which acts on the Earth to keep it in orbit. What is the name of this force?
   (c) This force causes the Earth to accelerate. In which direction is this acceleration?
   (d) The Earth does not speed up in its orbit due to this force. Explain why, even though the Earth is accelerating, it does not speed up.
2 Why do planets stay in orbit for so long without running out of energy?
3 Jupiter is 325 times as massive as the Earth, and Jupiter is five times further away from the Sun than we are. Calculate the ratio of the Sun's pull on Jupiter to the Sun's pull on the Earth.
4 On 21 March, the morning high tide at Plymouth was at 0818 hours. On 22 March, the morning high tide was at 0900 hours. Can you explain why? (Hint: the Moon takes about 29 days to go around us.)
5 Draw careful diagrams to explain why neap tides and spring tides occur.

7 | Comets, Meteors, Asteroids

We think that our solar system formed some 4500 million years ago (see Section C9). As the Sun grew at the centre of the system, planets and moons were made as the force of gravity pulled many fragments of rocks together. Even after the passage of this great length of time, there remains a large number of pieces of rock in orbit around the sun.

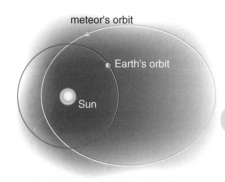

Figure I

Meteors

Meteors are small rock particles whose elliptical orbit crosses the Earth's orbital path (Figure 1). At the same times each year, we see 'showers' of meteors. The small particles enter the Earth's atmosphere travelling at great speeds (20 000 m/s); we see them as streaks of light as they burn up. Sometimes larger fragments of rock hit the ground; these are called meteorites. When you look at the Moon through a telescope, its cratered surface shows plenty of evidence of early meteor bombardment. The Earth, too, would have been cratered with meteor impacts when it formed, but millions of years of weathering has removed the craters. A large crater in the Arizona desert is thought to be only about 20 000 years old.

This crater in the Arizona desert is thought to have been formed by a meteor impact about 20 000 years ago. It is 200 m deep and 800 m wide.

Asteroids and comets

Mars is the outermost of four small rocky planets, and Jupiter is the innermost of four gaseous giant planets (Figure 2). There is a large gap between these two planets in which thousands of lumps of rock orbit; some of these measure as

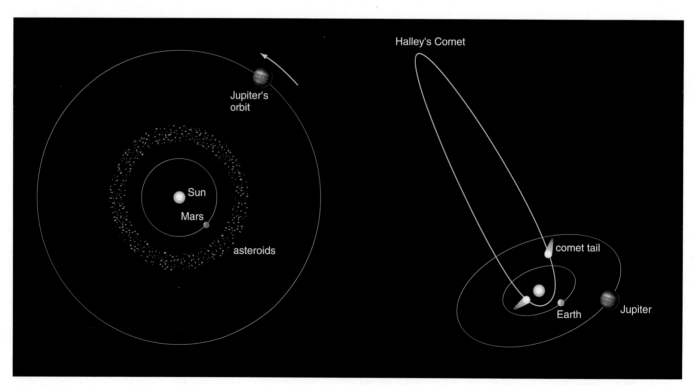

Figure 2   **Figure 3**

much as 700 km across. They are known as asteroids, planetoids or minor planets. The larger ones are given names; Ceres, Pallas, Juno, Vesta.

Comets, like asteroids, are rocks which orbit the Sun. However, comets have very elongated elliptical orbits (Figure 3). We think that at the edge of the solar system there is a cloud of such comets. Occasionally, one is disturbed in its orbit so that it falls inwards towards the Sun. We notice a comet as it gets close to the Earth and Sun. Heat from the Sun melts ice contained in the rocks. The Sun emits a stream of charged particles called the Solar wind. This wind blows the melted ice away from the Sun, producing the comet's tail; the tail always points away from the sun. Nearly everything in the solar system orbits in the plane of the ecliptic (the plane containing the Earth and Sun); comets are an exception as they orbit in any plane.

Elliptical orbits

If a planet orbits the Sun in a circular orbit, it moves at a constant speed. In Figure 4(a) you can see that the Sun's gravitational pull is always at right angles to the planet's path. No work is done by such a force; the force causes the planet to change direction but its speed is unaltered.

However, a comet or asteroid in an elliptical orbit does not move at a constant speed. In Figure 4(b) the gravitational pull of the Sun on a comet at A is not at right angles to its path. The force does two things: it deflects the comet towards the Sun and speeds it up. At C the pull of the Sun slows the comet down again. At D the comet has low kinetic energy but high potential energy; as the comet falls towards the sun it increases its kinetic energy to a maximum at B, and decreases its potential energy.

Although comets change their speed and distance away from the sun, it is possible to predict their time of orbit. Kepler's third law of planetary motion states that:

$$\frac{(\text{Average radius of Orbit})^3}{(\text{Time of orbit})^2} = \text{a constant}$$

For an ellipse the average radius is half of the major axis, the distance BD/2 in Figure 4(b).

Figure 5 shows the relationship between the radius of orbit and time of orbit for several planets and asteroids. Try plotting this graph on your school computer.

(a)

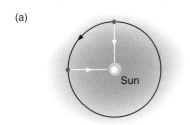

(b)

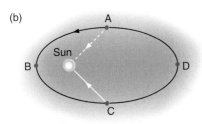

Figure 4

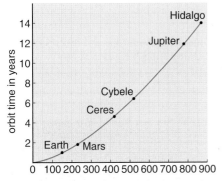

Figure 5 *Average distance from the Sun (millions of km)*

Homework Questions

1 Why are there craters on the Moon, but very few on the Earth?

2 Explain why we might see a comet near the Pole Star, but we would never see a planet in that part of the sky.

3 Explain how a comet's tail forms, and why the tail always points away from the Sun.

4 (a) Make a sketch to show the path of a comet.
(b) Mark on the sketch the place where it is travelling most slowly. Why is it travelling slowly at that point?
(c) Where is the pull of the Sun greatest on the comet?
(d) Where is the comet accelerating at its greatest rate? Show the direction of the acceleration.

5 The comet Shoemaker-Levy 5 has an orbital period of 8.7 years. Use Figure 5 to calculate its average distance from the Sun.

6 Halley's comet takes 76 years to orbit the Sun. Use Kepler's Law to calculate its average distance from the sun in Astronomical Units (AU). 1 AU is the average distance of the Earth from the Sun.

7 Use the information in Figure 5 to compare the orbital speed of Jupiter with the orbital speed of the Earth.

Making a Star

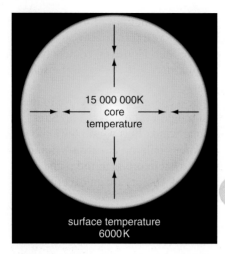

15 000 000K
core
temperature

surface temperature
6000K

Figure I *A star is a battle ground. The forces of gravity try to collapse a star, but these inward forces are balanced by the enormous outward pressure exerted by the hot core. The pressure at the centre of the star is about 500 million times bigger than the Earth's atmospheric pressure*

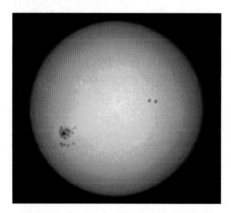

Sunspots. The dark colour associated with sunspots is due to their temperature being lower than surrounding surface of the Sun. It is thought that localised magnetic fields inhibit convection processes which brings hot material to the surface.

Like all stars, our Sun was formed from a giant cloud of gas. The photograph opposite shows part of the **Orion nebula**, where stars are being formed now. The Orion nebula is made mostly from hydrogen gas. The density of the gas is very low – about 100 million million times less dense than water. However, over millions of years, gravity acts to condense the gas into a smaller volume. This warms the gas up. As the gas atoms fall towards each other they speed up; potential energy is turned into kinetic energy. When the atoms collide, their large kinetic energy is turned into heat energy. Eventually, the temperature at the centre of the ball of gas reaches 15 million K and a star is born (Figure 1).

Nuclear fusion

Once the inside of a star reaches a temperature of about 15 million K, nuclear fusion starts. Like the cloud of gas which made it, a star is made mostly of hydrogen. At very high temperatures the hydrogen atoms are ripped apart, leaving only protons and electrons inside the star. At low temperatures two protons cannot collide because their charges repel each other. But at the very high temperatures inside stars, two protons have enough energy to overcome this repulsion. When two protons collide they can join or fuse together. By this process of fusion, protons join to form helium nuclei (Figure 2). The fusion of nuclei releases a lot of energy. This is how stars produce their heat and light.

Our Sun is halfway through its life of 10 thousand million years. Throughout its life, the Sun has burnt fairly constantly. Life has evolved on our planet, because the temperature has been steady. However it seems possible that, from time to time, the Sun's output of energy might change by a very small amount. In the second half of the seventeenth century, the climate was very harsh. The Thames froze over during winter. It is possible that the Ice Ages were caused by a decline in solar power output.

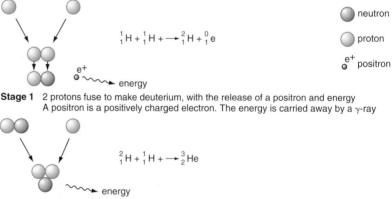

neutron

proton

e^+_0 positron

$^1_1H + ^1_1H + \longrightarrow ^2_1H + ^0_1e$

e^+

energy

Stage 1 2 protons fuse to make deuterium, with the release of a positron and energy
A positron is a positively charged electron. The energy is carried away by a γ-ray

$^2_1H + ^1_1H + \longrightarrow ^3_2He$

energy

Stage 2 Deuterium fuses with a proton to form Helium-3, with a further release of energy

$^3_2He + ^3_2He + \longrightarrow ^4_2He + ^1_1H + ^1_1H$

energy

Stage 3 The process is completed when two Helium-3 nuclei fuse to make Helium-4

Figure 2 *Nuclear fusion in the Sun*

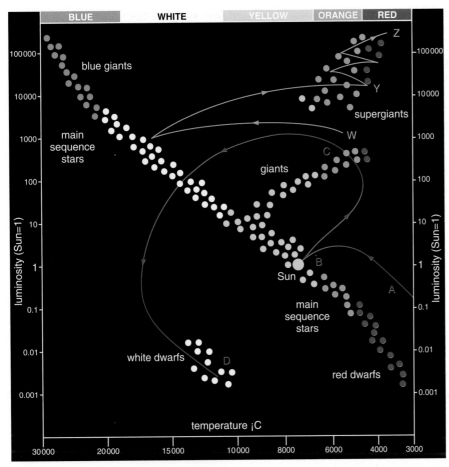

Figure 3 *The Hertzsprung-Russell diagram*

Figure 4 *Stars come in all sizes*

Betelgeuse - a red supergiant
(500 Sun diameters)

Rigel - a blue giant (10 Sun diameters)

Sun - a yellow dwarf

Sirius B - a white dwarf
(0.03 Sun diameters)

The Hertzsprung-Russell diagram

When you look at the sky at night, you can see stars with many different colours. These stars also have a wide range of brightness. The first astronomers to realise that the brightness of a star was related to its colour were Ejnar Hertzsprung and Henry Russell. They introduced the idea of plotting a graph of the brightness or luminosity of a star against the star's colour. Figure 3 shows such a graph, which is called a Hertzsprung–Russell diagram. Each point represents a star.

Most stars are grouped along a band stretching from the top left to the lower right of the diagram. This band is called the main sequence. The Sun occurs roughly in the middle of the main sequence. The most striking feature of the diagram is that the brightest and hottest stars are blue or white, and the dullest and coldest stars are red. Russell and Hertzsprung also discovered that there are very bright orange and red stars; these are giants and supergiants, which form a separate branch at an angle to the main sequence. Besides these stars there are also some white dwarf stars. The Hertzsprung–Russell diagram shown here gives a slightly distorted picture of the relative numbers of different types of star. You might have got the impression that the sky is full of giant stars. In fact, the Sun is larger than most stars. Only 5% of stars are bigger than the Sun and only 0.05% of stars are giants. However, giants are easy to see at great distances, because they outshine by far all other stars. The relatively small number of stars larger than our Sun provide over 95% of a galaxy's light output. You can see this clearly in the photograph of the galaxy NGC 253. This galaxy lies about 10 million light years

Spiral Galaxy NGC 253. In this photograph you can pick out red and blue giants which outshine other stars in the galaxy

http://www.rdrop.com/users/green/school/index.htm

The Jewel Box. This cluster is renowned for the contrast in colour between its brightest star, Kappa Crucis, a red supergiant, and the other bright stars, which are blue and white supergiants. These stars are thought to be about 80 000 times brighter than the Sun! The cluster lies about 7500 light years from Earth.

away from us, yet you can clearly pick out blue and red supergiants which shine like beacons. Figure 4 shows the wide variety of star sizes.

Star lifetimes

The red line on the Hertzsprung–Russell diagram shows the evolutionary path of the Sun. At A it is collapsing out of a huge cloud of gas. B is its present position on the main sequence. The Sun has already been a main sequence star for about 4.6 thousand million years; it is about half way through its life. During its lifetime, a main sequence star converts hydrogen to helium by the process of thermonuclear fusion (see page 78). The main sequence lifetime of a star depends on two factors: the mass and luminosity (or brightness) of the star. If a star is very bright it uses its hydrogen up very quickly, and a more massive star has more hydrogen for the fusion process. To take an example, look at Table 1. A blue giant 15 times as massive as the Sun is 15 000 times as bright. This means it is using hydrogen 15 000 times as rapidly as the Sun, but it has 15 times as much to provide. Its lifetime, therefore is 15/15 000 × the Sun's lifetime, which is only 10 million years. At the other extreme, a red dwarf glows very dimly, but lives for 2000 times longer than the Sun.

Mass of star (Sun =1)	15	10	5	3	2	1	0.5	0.2
Lifetime of star (thousand millions of years)	0.01	0.02		0.23	0.7	10		2000
Luminosity of star (Sun = 1)	15 000	5000	700	130		1	0.1	0.001

Table 1 *The life time of main sequence stars*

Eventually, the Sun's hydrogen will run out. Without the high pressure in its core, maintained by nuclear fusion, it will collapse. This collapse will warm the Sun's core further to a temperature of 100 million K. At this temperature helium nuclei fuse to make heavier elements such as oxygen and carbon. The Sun will swell up into a red giant with a diameter 100 times bigger than now. Its increase in size will be accompanied by a huge increase in brightness. The Sun will live only briefly as a red giant – some 10 million years or so. Because the lifetime of a giant is much less than that of a main sequence star, there are fewer of them to be seen. The Sun will end its life as a white dwarf, before cooling down like a dying fire.

Novas, Supernovas and Black Holes

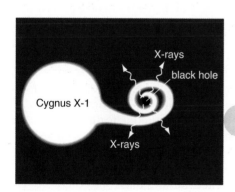

Figure 5 *Cygnus X-1 is a massive hot star, which is pulled around by a massive but invisible dark companion. The companion is as heavy as four suns. The companion is thought to be a black hole, which sucks matter out of its neighbouring star. As matter falls into the black hole, X-rays are emitted*

The green line on the Hertzsprung-Russell diagram shows the evolutionary path of a star 1000 times brighter than the Sun. It settles on to the main sequence for about 100 million years. When its hydrogen runs out it expands, but now into a supergiant. These supergiants pass through a series of expansions and contractions growing brighter at every stage. Finally, these stars blow themselves apart. Some are seen as **novas** – bright new stars. Others become **supernovas**, when a star is completely destroyed. A supernova is so bright that it can outshine an entire galaxy of 100 thousand million stars. Some supernovas leave behind very dense **neutron stars**, which spin rapidly emitting pulses of radiation; these stars are also known as **pulsars**.

Some stars die in a dramatic way. Stars which are about four times as massive as the Sun collapse so rapidly at the end of their lives that they turn into **black holes**. The gravitational pull of a black hole is so strong that not even light can escape from it (Figure 5).

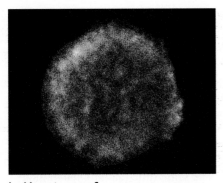

An X-ray image of a supernova remnant. This supernova was observed by Tycho Brahe in 1572. Material is still travelling away from the supernova at a speed of about 11 000 km/second

This star ended its life as a nova, briefly flaring up (left, in the centre) before fading away to insignificance

Homework Questions

1 (a) Explain carefully how stars are formed.
   (b) What causes the centre of a star to warm up when it forms?

2 (a) Explain what is meant by nuclear fusion.
   (b) Why can nuclear fusion only occur at high temperatures?
   (c) What is deuterium?
   (d) Why is a star less massive at the end of its life than it was when it was formed?

3 (a) How do black holes form?
   (b) What is a supernova? How does it get its name?

4 In the text a blue giant is described as living for 'only' ten million years. Why is this time thought of as short for a star?

5 Look at the table of data about some stars. Then answer the questions that follow.

   (a) Is there a connection between the brightness of a star and its temperature?
   (b) Is there a connection between the brightness of a star and its diameter?
   (c) Can you work out which star is a red giant?
   (d) Can you work out which star is a white dwarf?
   (e) Can you work out which star is a blue giant?

6 (a) Explain what is meant by a Hertzsprung–Russell diagram. Describe its main features.
   (b) What is a main sequence star?

7 Only 5% of all stars are brighter than the Sun. Use the table of lifetimes and luminosities to explain why there are fewer bright stars than there are dull stars.

8 (a) The lifetime, T, of a main sequence star (in thousand millions of years) can be calculated using the formula:

   $$T = \frac{10M}{L}$$

   M is the star's mass relative to the Sun, and L is the star's luminosity relative to the Sun: i.e. for the Sun $M = 1$, $L = 1$.
   Explain why the lifetime is proportional to the star's mass, and inversely proportional to the star's luminosity.
   (b) Use the formula to fill in the gaps in Table 1 on page 80.
   (c) The brightest known star is S-Doradus in the Magellan Clouds. It is thought to be about 1 million times brighter than our Sun and 50 times as massive. Explain why there are so few stars as bright as this.

Star	Temperature at surface (°C)	Diameter relative to Sun	Mass relative to Sun	Brightness relative to Sun
Antares	3100	300	15	2500
Rigel	30 000	10	30	25 000
B-Centauri	19 000	6	4	4000
Vega	10 600	2.6	3	40
Sun	5800	1	1	1
61 Cygni	3900	0.7	0.5	0.1
Sirius B	9000	0.03	1	0.002

The planets: their development and composition

Most scientific theories are developed as a result of experiment or observation. There are a few theories about the development of the solar system. However, they are quite speculative because we cannot easily observe other solar systems forming. Astronomers think that about one third of all stars have planets, but only recently has the Hubble Telescope photographed a star with planets. Figure 1 shows a popular theory for the development of the solar system. The planets, Sun and moons are thought to have developed at the same time (about 4500 million years ago) out of a large gaseous cloud.

http://seds.lpl.arizona.edu/billa/tnp/

Europa is an icy moon of Jupiter, and this photograph shows how the surface has been folded into a complex series of ridges and faults. Scientists believe that there may be oceans beneath the icy surface, and conditions there may be suitable to support some primitive life forms. No-one knows for sure right now – but could Europa hold alien life-forms?

1 4500 million years ago a shock wave, in a spiral arm of our galaxy, triggered the collapse of a gas cloud. This developed into a doughnut shape, which flattened out

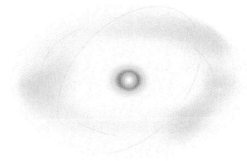

2 Enough hydrogen gathered in the centre for fusion to start in the Sun. Solid particles began to strike each other and stick together

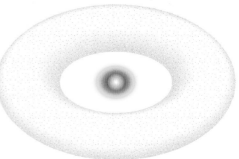

This photograph of Saturn was taken by Voyager 1 in 1980 from a distance of 11 million miles. You can see the moons Tethys (outer top left), Enceladus (inner top left) and Mimas (bottom right) in orbit around Saturn. Saturn is famous for its majestic rings which have an estimated width of 10 000 km. To give a sense of scale, the Earth has a diameter of 12 800 km…

3 Eventually, as the small particles continued to coalesce, just a few large planets and moons were left. Most of the gas and dust in the solar system became attached to a planet, or was removed by a strong solar wind. After millions of years, the gravitational attraction between the planets tended to pull their orbits into the same plane.

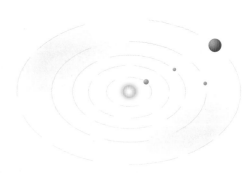

Figure 1

The Sun is made mostly from hydrogen and helium, but there are traces of other elements too. The composition of the planets can be split into three classes, depending on their volatility: **rocky**, **icy** and **gaseous**. Rocks are mostly iron, and oxides and silicates of magnesium, calcium and aluminium. There are, however, many other elements present in all planets, but in less abundance. The gases present in planets are mostly hydrogen and helium, then oxygen, nitrogen, ammonia, carbon dioxide and methane. Water ice is the commonest icy material, but there are also solid and liquid gases to be found. For example, the polar caps on Mars are thought to contain a lot of solid carbon dioxide; the atmosphere of Jupiter contains water and ammonia ice.

The composition of a planet depends very much on its position in the solar system. The planets close to the Sun have a very different composition to those further away. Table 1 summarises the composition of the planets, and Figure 2 their internal structures.

You should realise that there remains considerable doubt over the planets' exact structure and composition. The four inner planets are rocky. The four large giant planets have rocky and icy cores, but have large amounts of gas in their

Planet	Mass relative to Earth	Radius (Earth = 1)	Relative density (water = 1)	Distance from Sun in AU†	% Rocks	% Ice	% Gas	Main gases in atmosphere
Mercury	0.06	0.38	5.4	0.39	nearly all	–	–	none
Venus	0.82	0.95	5.2	0.72	nearly all	–	some in atmosphere	CO_2
Earth	1	1	5.5	1	nearly all	water in oceans, ice at poles	some in atmosphere	N_2, O_2
Mars	0.11	0.53	3.9	1.5	nearly all	ice at poles	some in atmosphere	CO_2
Jupiter	318	11.2	1.3	5.2		10% rock/ice	90%	H_2, He
Saturn	95	9.4	0.7	9.5		30% rock/ice	70%	H_2, He
Uranus	14.6	4.1	1.2	19.1		70% rock/ice	30%	H_2, He, CH_4
Neptune	17.2	3.9	1.7	30.1		70% rock/ice	30%	H_2, He, CH_4
Pluto	0.1?	0.4?	?	39.4		mostly rock/ice	?	none?

Table 1

† 1 Astronomical Unit of AU is the average Earth–Sun distance.
O_2 oxygen, N_2 nitrogen, CH_4 methane, CO_2 carbon dioxide.

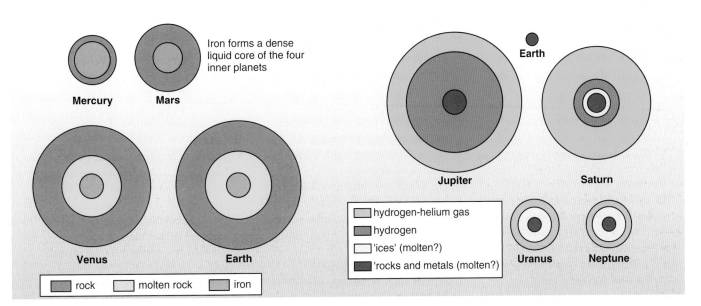

Figure 2 *Internal structure of the planets*

outer parts. The moons of Earth and Mars are rocky. The moons of the outer planets usually contain a considerable proportion of ice as well as rock. A possible explanation for the composition of the planets is as follows. In its early stages, the Sun was a lot hotter than it is now. The Sun lost a lot of material as a strong solar wind, which removed most of the gas from the inner planets.

Early in the life of the solar system, there were millions of small rocks still whizzing around. Some are still in orbit around the Sun, but most have collided with planets or moons. Mercury, Mars and many moons show the 'impact craters' caused by these rocks. Many of these craters are thought to be 4000 million years old, nearly as old as the solar system. The action of the Earth's atmosphere has eroded away craters. On the Moon and Mars, lava flows from volcanoes have covered over some craters, leaving flat plains. The volcanoes on Mars show that the planet was recently geologically active. Although there is no active volcano on the Moon, seismometers left there by the Apollo astronauts have detected small **moonquakes**, and Io and Europa, two moons of Jupiter, are very active. Both are squeezed by Jupiter's strong gravitational field as they orbit, which generates a lot of heat. On Io, this heat results in many active volcanoes. On Europa, recent ice flows from beneath the surface have covered up the craters.

Viking orbiter image of the giant extinct volcano Olympus Mons, on the surface of Mars. Olympus Mons is the largest volcano in the solar system.

Io is a moon of Jupiter, and as the most active body in the solar system is dotted with volcanoes, some of which are visible in this photograph

Homework Questions

1 (a) In the second paragraph, the words *volatility* and *abundance* are used. What do these words mean?
(b) Explain why theories about the formation of the solar system are 'speculative'.

2 Mars has craters on its surface, but few craters are seen near volcanoes. Explain why.

3 Use the information in Table 1 and Figure 2 to answer these questions.
(a) Why are the four inner planets denser than the outer planets?
(b) What makes Neptune more dense than Saturn?
(c) Jupiter contains a larger

proportion of gas than Saturn, yet Jupiter is denser than Saturn. Account for this in terms of the planets' masses.
(d) Mars and Mercury are nearly the same size, yet Mercury is denser. Account for this in terms of their compositions.
(e) Which two planets are (i) the most similar, (ii) the most dissimilar?

4 Go to the library, do some research and write a short article on one of the following:
(a) the moons of Jupiter,
(b) the rings of Saturn,
(c) Uranus and Neptune,

(d) the atmosphere of Venus,
(e) Mars,
(f) rills and craters on the Moon,
(g) Mercury,
(h) the composition of Jupiter and Saturn.

5 The Hubble Space Telescope (HST) has produced better photographs of stars than any previous Earth-bound telescope.
(a) Explain what advantage the HST has over other telescopes.
(b) How might the HST be used to gather evidence about the formation of planetary systems?

10 Sun, Stand Still!

Earth at the centre

Look at Figure 1. This shows how Pythagoras thought the Earth fitted into space in about 500 BC. He realised (correctly) that the Earth is a sphere. His model (incorrectly) places the Earth at the centre of the universe. The Earth was thought to be surrounded by several **crystal spheres** which carried the heavenly bodies. The outer **celestial** sphere carried the stars. To explain the motion of the stars, Pythagoras said that this sphere rotated once every 24 hours around a stationary Earth. The inner spheres rotated at slightly slower speeds. This allowed Pythagoras to explain the motion of the Moon, Sun and planets reasonably well.

The Moon was formed 4600 million years ago at which time its surface was made of molten rock. There was a large number of meteors whizzing around in space then. The Moon was bombarded by some of these meteors, which caused the cratered surface we see today

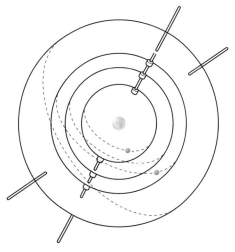

Figure 1 *In 500 BC, the Greek philosophers thought heavenly bodies rotated round the Earth on crystal spheres. The stars are on the outer sphere*

Pythagoras could not explain why some planets appear to make strange loops. Look at Figure 2. This shows how Jupiter appeared to move past the stars in 2001–2.

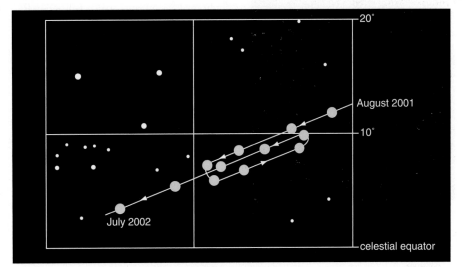

Jupiter's red spot has been a feature of its atmosphere for well over a hundred years. The spot is surrounded by swirling clouds blown around by winds of hurricane strength, with speeds in excess of 300 km per hour

Figure 2 *This simulation shows Jupiter's retrograde loop during 2001 and 2002. Jupiter's position is marked at intervals of one month*

Ptolemy (120 AD) produced another model to account for this motion (Figure 3). The arm EA rotates around the Earth every 12 years (in Jupiter's case). The arm AJ rotates around A once a year. The combined motion gives a looping movement. This model was only a calculating machine. It predicted very accurately the positions of planets, but there was no scientific evidence to back up the reality of the model.

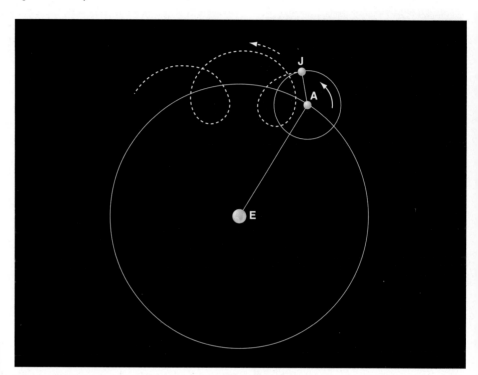

Figure 3 *Ptolemy explained the loops of planets with this construction of 'epicycles'*

Nicholas Copernicus (1473–1543)

Nicholas Copernicus was a scholarly Polish monk. He divided his time between church duties and studying astronomy. He believed that the universe was a divine creation, but he thought that God's arrangement of the planets would be a simple one. Copernicus took a bold step, against the teaching of the previous 2000 years. He produced a new model, with a stationary Sun placed at the centre. The Earth and other planets rotate around the Sun. Copernicus explained the motion of the Moon by saying it rotates around the Earth. The daily motion of the stars is explained by the Earth rotating on its axis every 24 hours. It is the Earth that spins round, not the celestial sphere of stars. Copernicus also measured carefully the planets' orbits. He worked out that Mercury and Venus move in orbits closer to the Sun than the Earth; Mars, Jupiter and Saturn are farther away from the Sun. This theory was very simple and also produced the following successful explanations.

- Copernicus could explain the looping paths of the planets: a loop is caused by a combination of the Earth moving round the Sun, together with the planet moving in a larger orbit more slowly round the Sun (Figure 4).
- With the new theory, it was possible to explain why Mars and Venus change in brightness. In Figure 5, Mars appears brighter when it is close to us in position M_1, but duller when it is further away in position M_2.
- Copernicus also predicted that, if our eyesight were better, we should see phases of Venus and Mercury just as we can see the Moon's phases.

apparent position of Jupiter in the sky

Jupiter's orbit

Earth's orbit

Figure 4 *Over a year, Jupiter appears to move through the star pattern. As the Earth overtakes Jupiter, it seems to go backwards*

The atmosphere of Venus is mainly made from poisonous sulphuric acid clouds

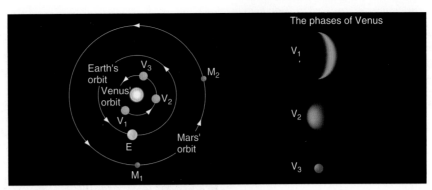

Figure 5 *This is how Copernicus thought Mars, Earth and Venus orbited the Sun. The shapes to the right of the diagram show the phases of Venus at positions V_1, V_2 and V_3, when viewed from E*

Galileo Galilei

In 1610, Galileo used a new invention, the telescope, to look at the skies. By projecting an image of the Sun, he discovered **sunspots**. He also saw craters on the Moon and rings around Saturn. He looked at Venus over a period of time, and saw the phases that Copernicus predicted.

When Galileo turned his telescope to Jupiter, he saw what looked like stars close to it. But each night the number and position of the 'stars' changed.

He realised that he was seeing four moons in orbit around Jupiter. He could observe their movement over a few hours. This was a miniature solar system which he could see. Jupiter stood in the middle as the moons went round it, just as planets rotate about a stationary Sun.

Galileo became a champion of the Copernicus system. He became an outspoken critic of the church's teaching because the church maintained that the Earth and the human race were the centre of God's creation. Eventually, fearing torture or execution, Galileo promised to stop teaching or believing the idea that the Sun stood still.

Homework Questions

1 How did the ancient Greeks' model of the Universe differ from our ideas today?

2 (a) Copernicus produced a new model for our solar system. What was it?
(b) A new theory needs **evidence** to help prove it. Explain carefully, using diagrams, how the following pieces of evidence helped support Copernicus' theory:
(i) The retrograde loops of planets.

(ii) The changing brightness of Mars.
(iii) The phases of Venus.
(iv) The moons of Jupiter.
(c) Can you think of more evidence to support Copernicus?

3 Choose another theory or law. Was the theory based on experimental observation, or was the theory invented first? You might choose a law such as Ohm's Law, Hooke's Law, or one of Newton's Laws of Motion.

Michelangelo's The Creation of Adam, *which decorates the Sistine Chapel in Rome, was painted in 1511 or 1512. How do our views about the creation of the human race differ from those of Michelangelo's generation?*

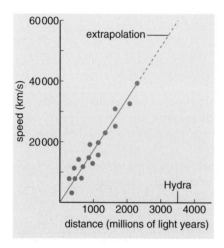

Figure 1 *The speed of the galaxies is proportional to their distance away from us, according to Hubble's results*

The galaxy is found in this constellation	Distance of galaxy (millions of light years*)	Speed of galaxy (km/s)
Virgo	72	1200
Perseus	400	
Ursa Major		15 000
Corona Borealis	1200	20 000
Bootes	2400	40 000
Hydra		60 000

* 1 light year = 10 million million (10^{13}) km. This is the distance light travels in one year.

Table 1

Most of us at an early age start asking questions like 'Where did I come from?' And, when we know the answer to that question, we ask 'Who made the Earth?' This second question is one that has puzzled the human race since the earliest days of civilisation. The ancient Greeks and Romans believed that the Earth was made by three gods: Aether (light), Hemera (day) and Eros (love). Most modern religions have similar creation stories: at some moment in the past a divine being created the Earth, Sun, Moon and stars. Animals and, later, humans were put on the Earth. According to the account in the Book of Genesis in the Bible, this took six days. Modern science too has a story of creation to tell, but it stretches over 15 000 million years.

The big bang

By 1930, astronomers realised that our Sun is part of an enormous galaxy of stars. They also discovered that there are millions of other galaxies in the universe. By looking carefully at the light sent out by galaxies, Edwin Hubble (1889–1953) noticed that it had been shifted towards the red end of the spectrum. This told him that the galaxies were moving away from us. Table 1 shows the distances of galaxies in various constellations and their calculated speeds.

Hubble's data suggest that the speed of a galaxy is proportional to its distance away from us (Figure 1). The galaxies in Bootes are twice as far away as those in Corona Borealis; the speed of a galaxy in Bootes is twice as fast as the speed of a galaxy in Corona Borealis. From this law, Hubble could make predictions. By extending the graph (extrapolation) he calculated the distance of far off galaxies; for example, Hydra's measured speed is 60 000 km/s, so it must be about 3600 million light years away.

Hubble's work led to an amazing result. In all directions, galaxies are flying away from us; the further away they are, the faster they go. Billions of years ago, the galaxies must have been a lot closer together. Even further back in time, all the galaxies were in the same place. This led to the idea that the universe originated with an enormous cosmic explosion – the **Big Bang**. About 15 000 million years ago, all of the matter in the visible universe exploded out of a point smaller than a pin head. Physicists call this point a singularity. Ever since, matter has been flying outwards away from the explosion.

Evidence for the big bang theory

When a fire engine rushes past you with its siren blaring, you hear an example of the **Doppler effect**; as the engine approaches the note is of a higher pitch than normal, and as it goes away it is lower than normal. Figure 2 helps to explain why. In Figure 2(a) a source of sound, S, is stationary: the waves spread out symmetrically in all directions. People standing at A and B hear the same note. In Figure 2(b) the source is moving to the left. The waves are distorted as a result of this motion, bunching up to the left and spreading out to the right. A person standing at C hears more waves per second than a person at D, because the waves are closer together. So C hears a higher pitch and D hears a lower pitch than normal.

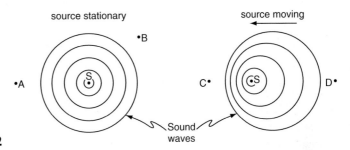

Figure 2

A similar Doppler effect happens with light if a source is moving very quickly; if the source is going away from us the wavelength of the light increases or shifts towards the red end of the spectrum. This is known as the **red shift**. The faster the source moves the greater the shift. Hubble discovered that distant galaxies showed a red shift (Figure 3). The more distant galaxies show a greater red shift and so are travelling faster away from us.

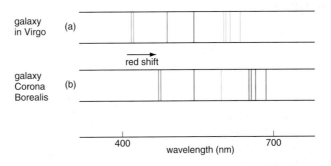

Figure 3 *(a) shows a line spectrum emitted by a galaxy in Virgo. Notice how the same pattern of lines is seen in the light emitted from the Corona Borealis galaxy. (b) However, the Corona Borealis galaxy is moving away faster and the pattern has a greater red shift*

Further evidence for the big bang theory was provided by Penzias and Wilson (1965) who discovered **cosmic background radiation**. The whole universe emits radiation which is thought to be a distant echo of the big bang.

Cosmology

Cosmology is the science that tries to explain the origins of the Universe. Another theory that briefly held sway was the **steady state theory**, produced by Hoyle 1948. In this theory, it was stated that matter was continuously being created in an expanding universe. A consequence of this theory is that all galaxies would look the same. However, this theory is no longer accepted. Quasars which are a

(a) 15 billion years ago: the moment of creation. The universe explodes outwards from a tiny point

(b) 1 billion years after the 'big bang', the universe is expanding rapidly but galaxies are beginning to form

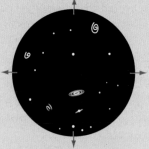

(c) 10 billion years after the 'big bang' galaxies have formed. Our solar system forms in one of them. The universe is expanding less rapidly now. There is gravitational attraction between all galaxies, which tries to pull them all back together. So the galaxies are slowing down. Perhaps eventually all the galaxies will start to fall back towards each other . . .

Figure 4

very great distance from us are thought to be galaxies at an early stage of that evolution. Now most cosmologists believe the big bang theory.

Minutes after the big bang, the universe was full of only the elementary particles that make up our atoms: electrons, protons and neutrons, together with a lot of radiation. After millions of years (Figure 4) gravity started pulling matter together in large clumps. After a billion (1000 million) years, galaxies were forming. In these galaxies stars began to form. About 10 billion years after the big bang, our Sun and Earth were formed from the remnants of a supernova explosion. In the next 4½ billion years life evolved on the Earth. Eventually, 50 000 years ago, modern man and woman arrived.

Cosmologists have suggested what our universe might have been like right back in the dawn of time. But nobody can explain why there was a big bang. The whole universe was made in an instant, which is even more amazing than other creation stories. Cosmology has neither proved nor disproved the existence of God; the ultimate mystery remains unsolved. Where did the universe come from?

.... and the end?

You have just read about the origin of the universe, so we might ask 'How will it end?' We can use quite simple ideas to speculate about various possibilities. In Figure 4(c) you can see galaxies moving away from others. We only know of one force which acts on a galaxy – the pull of gravity due to all the other galaxies. If the gravitational pull is strong enough it might stop the galaxies moving away from each other, and pull them back together, so that at some stage in the distant future there might be a 'big crunch' as all the matter in the universe collides at one point. On the other hand, if the galaxies have enough kinetic energy, they may carry on moving forever. The third possibility is that the universe is so finely balanced that it will expand to a stationary state, where the galaxies are so far apart that they exert negligible gravitational forces on each other.

Figure 5 shows how the size of the universe would vary with time, for each of the three possibilities.

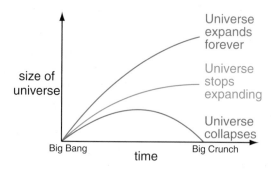

Figure 5

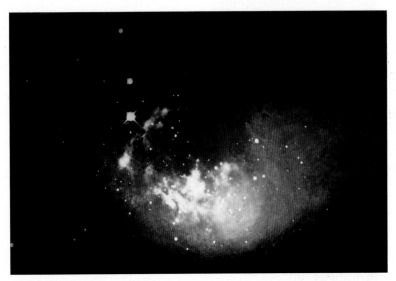

The Big Bang Theory says that all the matter in the entire universe originated from a single point

Homework Questions

1 (a) Look at Table 1. Work out the speed of the galaxies in Perseus.
   (b) Quasars are some of the brightest, but most distant objects in the universe. They are very small, but hundreds of times brighter than a galaxy. They are thought to be galaxies which are forming. But we see them as they were a long time ago, because they are so distant. Such a quasar travels away from us at 200 000 km/s. How far away is it?

2 Galaxies are moving away from us, but they are slowing down. Explain why.

3 Hubble's constant H, is defined by the equation:
   $$v = HR$$
   v is the speed of recession of a galaxy and R is its distance away from us.
   (a) Use Figure 1 to calculate Hubble's constant. Express your answer in (i) km/s per million light year, (ii) s^{-1}. (1 light-year $= 10^{13}$ km
   (b) Use your answer to (a) part (ii) to show that the age of the universe must be thousands of millions of years. [Hint: the time the universe has been expanding for is approximately $\frac{1}{H} = \frac{R}{v}$]

4 Outline two pieces of evidence which support the Big Bang Theory. (This question should be answered at some length, with diagrams to help; in a GCSE exam this might be worth 6 or 8 marks, so you need to make several good points.)

5 (a) The light emitted from stars in distant galaxies is observed to be **red shifted**. What is meant by red shift?
   (b) Explain what causes red shift.
   (c) What type of shift would be observed in light from stars travelling towards us?
   (d) Galaxies in the constellations of Ursa Major are observed to be moving away from us with a speed of 15 000 km/s. Use Figure 1 to calculate how far away from us these galaxies are.
   (e) How many years would it take light to travel this distance?
   (f) Light travels at a speed of 300 000 km/s; at what fraction of the speed of light are the galaxies in Ursa Major moving away from us?
   (g) Assuming that all the matter in the Universe started in one place, use your answers above to calculate how long it has taken for our galaxy

and the galaxies in Ursa Major to reach this separation. (Assume the galaxies move at a constant speed.)
   (h) What is the significance of this value?

6 (a) Although galaxies are moving away from us, they are slowing down. Explain why.
   (b) Figure 5 shows three possible outcomes for the Universe. Use energy considerations to explain whether the Universe will expand forever, or collapse again.
   (c) Suppose we live in a Universe which is going to collapse. Use Figure 5 to explain why your estimate for the age of the Universe in question 3(b) is going to be too large.

7 A fire engine emits a note of frequency 1000 Hz from its siren. When it is moving away from you at a speed of 20 m/s you hear a note of frequency 940 Hz.
   (a) Explain why you hear this change of pitch.
   (b) What frequency will you hear when the fire engine travels
   (i) towards you at 20 m/s,
   (ii) away from you at 30 m/s?

SECTION C: Questions

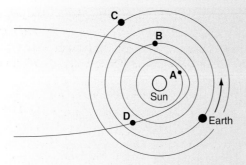

1 The diagram shows the orbits of some bodies around the Sun. The arrow shows the direction of the Earth's orbit.
  (a) Choosing from **A**, **B**, **C** and **D**, state which body is
     (i) a comet
     (ii) Venus
  (b) In which direction does A move round the Sun? Illustrate your answer with a diagram.
  (c) (i) Describe the shape of the orbit of **D**.
     (ii) Name the force which keeps **D** in its orbit.
                                                      WJEC

2 (a) Astronomers use the term *Milky Way* to describe part of the universe. What is the *Milky Way*?
  (b) The table below gives information about some planets in the solar system.

Planet	Average surface temperature (°C)	Time to orbit the Sun (years)	Diameter of the planet (km)
Jupiter	−150	12	143360
Uranus	−210	84	51200
Saturn	−180	29	120320

     (i) Which of the above planets is nearest to the Sun
     (ii) Use information from the table to give **two** reasons for your answer to (b)(i).
                                                      WJEC

3 (a) Jupiter is the largest planet in the Solar System. It is thought to consist mainly of hydrogen and helium. Explain why the density of Jupiter is less than that of the Earth.
  (b) The next table compares some features of Jupiter and Earth.

Feature	Earth	Jupiter
average surface temperature in °C	20	−150
magnetic field	strong	very strong
density in g/cm^3	5.5	1.3
time to rotate on axis in hours	24	10
time to orbit the Sun in years	1	11.9
mean orbital speed in millions of km/hour	0.11	0.05
surface gravitational field strength in N/kg	10	23

     (i) Which feature suggests that the core of Jupiter might contain iron?
     (ii) Explain why Jupiter takes much longer than the Earth to orbit the Sun.
     (iii) Suggest why the temperature at the surface of Jupiter is less than that at the surface of the Earth.
  (c) Jupiter has several moons. One of them, Io, is about the size of the Earth's moon. There is volcanic activity on Io. Conditions on Io differ from those on the Earth's moon.
     Suggest TWO differences.
  (d) A probe entered Jupiter's atmosphere. The probe was fitted with a parachute to reduce its speed as it entered the atmosphere.
     The probe sent back information about the atmosphere for over an hour before it was destroyed.
     (i) Suggest why the probe was destroyed as it fell through the atmosphere.
     (ii) Explain how the parachute prolonged the 'life' of the probe as it fell.
                                                      Edexcel

4 (a) The table below contains data about the Earth and Saturn.

	Earth	Saturn
Distance from Sun million km	150	1427
Average temperature	20 °C	−180 °C
Surface gravitational field strength	9.8 N/kg	8.9 N/kg
Time to rotate on axis	24 hours	22 hours
Time to orbit Sun	1 year	29.5 years
Density	5.5 g/cm^3	0.7 g/cm^3

  Use the data in the table to answer the questions.
     (i) How long is a day on Saturn?
     (ii) Suggest why Saturn is colder than the Earth.
     (iii) Give ONE reason why astronomers think that Saturn is composed mainly of gases.
     (iv) A space probe lands on Saturn's surface. How will the weight of the probe on Saturn compare with its weight on Earth?

(b) In October 1997 the spacecraft Cassini left Earth on a seven year journey to Saturn. The diagram below shows the path that Cassini was expected to follow on its journey.
  (i) Write down TWO changes in Cassini's motion as it approaches Jupiter.
  (ii) What causes these changes in Cassini's motion?

Edexcel

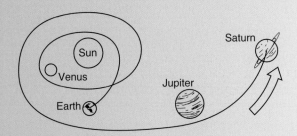

5 Barnard's Star is one of the closest stars to us, at a distance of 6 light years. Careful observation of this star (over some years) shows that it wobbles. The wobble can be explained by the presence of two large planets, which exert a gravitational pull on the star. It is also thought that Vega, a young star, might have planets too. At the moment, very little information has been gathered about other solar systems because Earth-based telescopes have not been able to see planets. It is hoped that, in the future, the Hubble space telescope might show us planets near other stars.
Table 1 provides some hypothetical information about planets and their stars, gathered by such a telescope. In this question you are asked to speculate about the conditions on these planets. You might find Table 2 and sections C1 and C9 helpful.

(a) How could an alien astronomer, looking at our Sun, detect that it has a solar system? How long would it take this astronomer to be sure?
(b) Why will a telescope on a spacecraft be better than one of the same size on Earth?
(c) Assuming that other solar systems might be similar to ours, suggest which planets in Table 1 might be rocky and which might contain a large proportion of ice and gas (see unit C9.)
(d) Describe what conditions might be like on the surfaces of (i) Vega's innermost planet, and (ii) Barnard's Star's outerplanet.
(e) The relative heating effects of stars on the surfaces of planets can be compared using the formula: $H = L/R^2$, where H is the average energy arriving each second on 1 m^2 of a planet's surface, L is the luminosity of the star, and R is the distance between star and planet in AU. For example, for the Earth, $L = 1$, $R = 1$, and so $H = 1$.
Show that H is 1/8 for the second planet of Ophiuchi A. (This means this planet will be a lot colder than the Earth.)
(f) Use the idea in part (e) to investigate which planet will be nearest to the Earth's temperature and which planet will be nearest to Jupiter's temperature.
(g) Which star system is most likely to support intelligent life? Explain your answer.

Planet	Distance from Sun (AU)	Temperature in day (°C)
Mercury	0.4	350
Earth	1	20
Jupiter	5	−150
Neptune	30	−240

Table 2 *The solar system*

Star name	Star luminosity (Sun = 1)	Star temperature (K)	Star mass (Sun = 1)	Estimated age of star system (millions of years)	PLANET 1 Mass (Earth = 1)	PLANET 1 Distance from star (AU)*	PLANET 2 Mass (Earth = 1)	PLANET 2 Distance from star (AU)*	PLANET 3 Mass (Earth = 1)	PLANET 3 Distance from star (AU)*
Barnard's Star	0.0004	2800	0.1	14 000	80	4	150	7	unknown	unknown
Ophiuchi A	0.5	4900	0.9	10 000	unknown	1	3	2	100	8
Alpha Centauri A	1.1	5750	1.1	5000	3	2.5	20	5	70	12
Allenby 247	2.1	5900	1.2	4000	2	1.5	150	7	20	30
Procyon	5.2	6300	1.2	4000	4	2	2	3	15	25
Vega	40	10 600	3	500	1	10	6	200	40	

*AU = 1 Astronomical unit = Earth–Sun distance

Table 1

6 The diagram shows the passage of the Moon across the Earth's shadow on January 21, 2000. You can answer the questions which follow using the information in the diagram and your knowledge and understanding of Astronomy. (UT means Universal Time; this is the Astronomer's term for GMT or Greenwich Mean Time.)

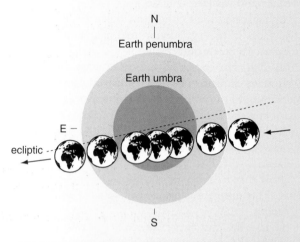

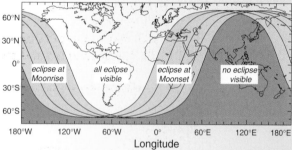

(a) What causes a lunar eclipse?

(b) What was the duration of the full lunar eclipse?

(c) Draw a diagram to explain how a lunar eclipse might last longer. Estimate how much longer an eclipse might last.

(d) The ecliptic is the plane in which the Sun and Earth lie. Explain why an eclipse path always crosses this plane.

(e) The map of the Earth shows where the eclipse was visible. Draw a clear diagram to explain the following points.

    (i) The eclipse was visible in America, but not in Australia.

    (ii) The eclipse was visible at nearly all places inside the Arctic Circle, but not inside the Antarctic Circle.

7 The (imaginary) planet Zeta Minus rotates around its star Zuben. Zeta Minus is a twin planet of the Earth, and Zuben is a star just like our Sun. Zuben orbits

around a larger star called Bokonon. Use the data and the diagram to answer these questions.

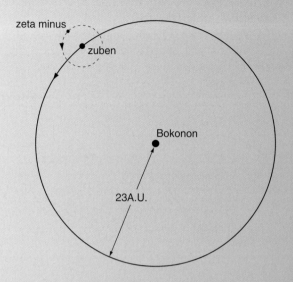

Data
- 1 AU = Earth–Sun distance
- Bokonon–Zuben distance = 23 AU
- Zuben–Zeta Minus distance = 1 AU
- Day length on Zeta Minus = 24 hrs
- Zeta Minus rotates around Zuben once a year
- Zuben rotates around Bokonon once ever 43 years
- Zeta Minus rotates on an axis which is tilted to the Zeta Minus/Zuben plane by 15° – rather less than the tilt of the Earth's axis.
- Bokonon is 25 times brighter than Zuben (as seen from Earth)
- Zeta Minus on average receives 5% of its energy from Bokonon and 95% from Zuben
- Bokonon is 4 times as massive as Zuben

(a) Bokonon is 25 time brighter than Zuben, yet Bokonon provides Zeta Minus with a lot less energy. Explain why.

(b) Describe the variations in season and climate which inhabitants of Zeta Minus experience.

(c) In the Zetean language, there are two words for 'night'. The words have a slightly different meaning. Explain what these meanings are.

(d) Bokonon and Zuben are about 50 light years from Earth. Make a sketch to show the observed motion of the two stars over a period of 43 years.

8 Examine carefully the photograph of the Moon on the next page. Suggest an explanation in terms of geological activity, for the features you can see.

9 This question sets out to explain the term *geostationary orbit* which is where a satellite appears to be stationary above a point on the Earth's equator.

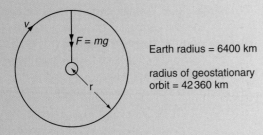

Earth radius = 6400 km

radius of geostationary orbit = 42360 km

(a) Explain why a satellite can only be stationary above the equator.

(b) Why does such a satellite take about 24 hours to complete one orbit?

(c) Use the data in the diagram and the equation $v = 2\pi r/T$ to calculate the speed of the satellite (in metres per second).
When a satellite moves in a circular path, a force is needed to pull it towards the centre of the Earth; this force is the satellite's weight, $W = mg$.

(d) Show that the radius of the satellite's orbit is 6.6 times bigger than the Earth's radius.

(e) The Earth's gravitational field strength is 9.8 N/kg at its surface. Explain why the field strength at the height of the satellite's orbit is $9.8 \times (1/6.6)^2$ N/kg. Calculate this value.

(f) Calculate the weight of a 100 kg geostationary satellite.

(g) For anything moving in a circular path, there must be a necessary centripetal force directed towards the centre. For an object of mass m, speed v in a path of radius r, the size of this force is given by: $F = mv^2/r$
Calculate the size of this force for a geostationary satellite of mass 100 kg. Comment on your answer.

10 (a) The table below gives information about the way in which the Earth's gravitational field varies with distance from the centre of the Earth.

g (N/kg)	6.28	2.45	1.09	0.61	0.39	0.27
$r \times 10^6$ (m)	8.00	12.8	19.2	25.6	32.0	38.4

(i) Use the data in the table to plot a graph of gravitational field strength against distance from the centre of the Earth.

(ii) Use your graph to estimate the gravitational field strength at the Earth's surface. The radius of the Earth is 6400 km.

(iii) The Earth's gravitational field strength can be calculated from

$$g = \frac{\text{constant}}{r^2}$$

where r is the distance from the Earth's centre.
Use the relationship and the graph to calculate a value for the constant. State the units for the constant.

(iv) The Moon in 380000 km from the centre of the Earth.
Calculate the strength of the Earth's gravitational field at the Moon.

(b) The diagram shows a satellite in geostationary orbit around the Earth. The diagram is not drawn to scale.

(i) Copy the diagram and add arrows to show:

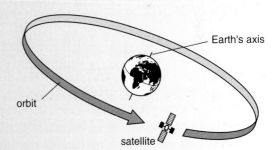

1. the resultant force acting on the satellite;
2. the direction of the velocity of the satellite in the position shown.

(ii) The speed of the satellite is 3100 m/s and it has a time period of 24 hours. Use this information to find the radius of orbit.

(iii) Calculate the centripetal acceleration of the satellite in this orbit.

(iv) Use your graph from part (a) to find the value of the Earth's gravitational field strength at the radius calculated in part (b)(ii). Comment on your answer.

Edexcel

11 Over the last million years, it is thought that there have been five Ice Ages. These have been dated by geologists. Diagram (1) shows the calculated variation in the Earth's temperature over this time. This question asks you to consider some theories for the cause of Ice Ages.

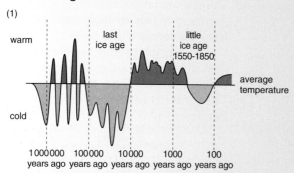

(1)

Diagram (2) shows the fluctuation in the number of sunspots observed since 1610. Sunspot activity can be seen to vary in a regular cycle. It is possible that the Sun is a little hotter when there are lots of spots. This has little effect on our climate over a short period. However, it is suggested that the absence of spots over a long period might cause the Earth to cool. In diagram (2), you can see a period of about 100 years, 'the **Maunder minimum**', when a few observations of sunspots were recorded.

(a) Use diagram (2) to calculate the average period of the sunspot cycle.

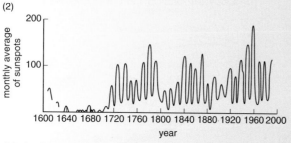

(2)

(b) Is there enough evidence to link the little Ice Age with a decrease in solar activity? (During the little Ice Age the Earth suffered very severe winters; people were able to skate on the Thames regularly.)

(c) Do you think it is reasonable to link the main Ice Ages with a decrease in solar activity?

(d) Other theories for Ice Ages include these:
- Volcanic eruptions have filled the atmosphere with dust.
- As the Sun rotates around the galaxy, it occasionally passes through regions of dust and gas.
- Variations in the Earth's tilt and orbit have caused cooling.
- Meteorite collisions with the Earth.

Comment on each of these theories, explaining how each might account for the Ice Ages.

12 Stars form from large clouds of gas and dust.

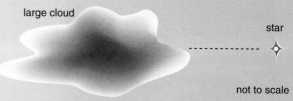

not to scale

(a) Use words from this list to copy and complete the sentences.

> **attracts   decreases   electricity**
>
> **gravity   increases   magnetism   repels**

Each particle in the cloud _____ every other particle by a force called _____. This force accelerates the particles, so their speed _____. Therefore the diameter of the cloud _____ and the kinetic energy of the particles _____.

(b) When the cloud is small enough and hot enough, a fusion reaction starts.
   (i) Describe the **fusion reaction**.
   (ii) The fusion reaction stops the cloud from collapsing. Explain why.

(c) Eventually the fusion reaction stops. Describe what might happen to the star.

OCR

13 The Earth has a mass about 18 times that of Mercury; Earth is three times further away from the Sun than Mercury. Use Newton's law of gravitation (page 74) to compare the Sun's pull on each.

14 (a) Copy the table. Add an extra column and work out their orbital speeds in million km per year.

Planet	Average distance from planet (million km)	Time to go round Sun (years)
Mercury	58	0.24
Venus	108	0.62
Earth	150	1.0
Mars	228	1.88
Jupiter	780	11.9
Saturn	1430	29.5
Uranus	2800	84
Neptune	4500	165
Pluto	5900	248

(b) Show that Mercury travels round the Sun with a speed ten times bigger than Pluto's.

(c) Is there any pattern connecting the speed of a planet and its distance from the Sun?

(d) Two satellites orbit the Earth. Metosat is in a lower orbit than Skysat; which one is travelling more quickly?

Energy and Power

Drax power station in Yorkshire. The plumes from this coal-fired power station are illuminated by the station's own lighting. The wide cooling towers to the right are releasing water vapour into the atmosphere, which is harmless. The thin combustion tower to the left is fitted with flue gas desulphurisation equipment, to reduce the pollution that escapes into the atmosphere due to the burning of coal. Power stations like this one operate 24 hours a day, 365 days a year to provide us with heating, lighting and all the other benefits that electricity brings.

By the end of this section you should:

- be able to define work
- understand that energy is used to do work
- know some different energy forms, and know how one form can be transferred to another
- understand that energy is always conserved
- be able to define power
- know how force multipliers work
- be able to define efficiency
- understand that electricity can be produced in many different ways, be able to appreciate the differences between them and know the difference between renewable and non-renewable fuels

D

1

What is Work?

Tony works in a supermarket. His job is to fill up shelves when they are empty. When Tony lifts up tins to put on the shelves he is doing some work. The amount of work Tony does depends on how far he lifts the tins and how heavy they are.

We define work like this:

$$\text{Work done} = \text{force} \times \text{distance} = F \times d$$

Work is measured in **joules** (J). 1 joule of work is done when a force of 1 newton moves something through a distance of 1 metre, in the direction of the applied force.

$$1J = 1\,N \times 1\,m$$

Example. How much work does Tony do when he lifts a tin with a weight of 20 N through a height of 0.5 m?

$$
\begin{aligned}
W &= F \times d \\
&= 20\,N \times 0.5\,m \\
&= 10J
\end{aligned}
$$

Tony does the same amount of work when he lifts a tin with a weight of 10 N through 1 m.

Figure 1

Does a force always do work?

Does a force always do work? The answer is no! In Figure 1 Martin is helping Salim and Teresa to give the car a push start. Teresa and Salim are pushing from behind; Martin is pushing from the side. Teresa and Salim are doing some work because they are pushing in the right direction to get the car moving. Martin is doing nothing useful to get the car moving. Martin does no work because he is pushing at right angles to the direction of movement.

In Figure 2 Samantha is doing some weight training. She is holding two weights, but she is not lifting them. She becomes tired, because her muscles use energy, but she is not doing any work, because the weights are not moving. To do work you have to move something, for instance lifting a load or pushing a car.

Finding the fuel

When you want a job done you have to pay for it. This is because you have to buy fuel. This provides **energy** for the job to be done. The supermarket manager has to pay Tony to do his work. The most important thing that Tony buys with his money is food. Food gives him the energy to do his work.

Figure 3 shows a crane at work on a building site. The crane runs on diesel fuel. Table 1 shows the amount of diesel used for some jobs. You can see that the amount of diesel used is proportional to the amount of work done lifting a load.

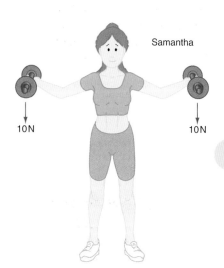

Figure 2

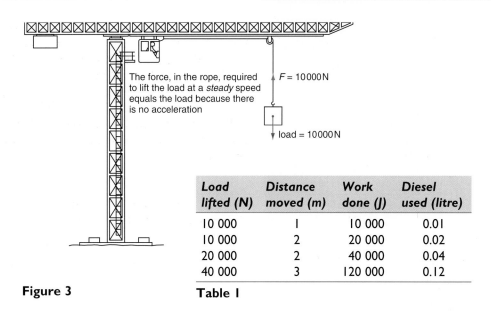

The force, in the rope, required to lift the load at a *steady* speed equals the load because there is no acceleration

$F = 10000\,N$

load = 10000 N

Load lifted (N)	Distance moved (m)	Work done (J)	Diesel used (litre)
10 000	1	10 000	0.01
10 000	2	20 000	0.02
20 000	2	40 000	0.04
40 000	3	120 000	0.12

Figure 3

Table I

Homework Questions

1 In which of the following cases is work being done?
(a) A magnetic force holds a magnet on a steel door.
(b) You pedal a cycle along a road.
(c) A pulley is used to lift up a load.
(d) You hold a 2 kg weight, but without moving it.

2 Calculate the work done in each case below.
(a) You lift a 20 N weight through a height of 2 m.
(b) You drag a 40 kg mass 8 m along a floor using a pull of 80 N.

3 Table 2 below shows some more jobs done by the crane in Figure 3. Copy the table and fill in the missing values.

4 Joel is on the Moon in his spacesuit. His mass (and the suit) is 80 kg. The gravitational field strength on the Moon is 1.6 N/kg.
(a) What is Joel's weight?
(b) Joel now climbs 30 m up a ladder into his space craft. How much work does he do?

5 Mr Hendrix runs a passenger ferry service in the West Indies. He has three ships, which are all the same. Sometimes he has problems with

the bottoms of the ships, when barnacles stick to them. This increases the drag on the ships, and they use more fuel than usual.
(a) Explain why a larger drag makes the ships use more fuel.
(b) Table 3 below shows the amount of fuel used by Mr Hendrix's three ships, on recent journeys. Which one has barnacles on her bottom?
(c) (i) Calculate how much fuel is used per km travelled for each boat.
(ii) The drag force on the *Caribbean Princess* is 50 000 N. How large is the drag force on *Windward Beauty* and on *Island Queen*?

Load lifted (N)	Distance moved (m)	Work done (J)	Fuel used (litre)
5000	2		0.01
10 000	4		
	10	40 000	
6000			0.06
	5		0.1
25 000		90 000	

Table 2

Boat	Journey	Distance (km)	Fuel used (litre)
Island Queen	Vieux Fort–Bridgetown	175	1050
Windward Beauty	Plymouth–Kingstown	220	1100
Caribbean Princess	Bridgetown–St. George's	255	1275

Table 3

2

Energy

This ride in a theme-park demonstrates one way to transfer potential energy to kinetic energy ...

http://www.geocities.com/
Athens/Aegean/8438/
menuenergy.html

http://home.earthlink.net/
~dmocarski/chapters/chapter5
/ch5page.htm

What is energy?

You have to put fuel into a machine to make it work. We say that the fuel has got some **energy**. For example, 1 litre of petrol has 40 million joules (MJ) of energy stored in it. This means that the greatest amount of work which we can get out of 1 litre of petrol is 40 MJ. Notice that work and energy are both measured in joules.

Energy can be used to do work

Different types of energy

We cannot make energy and we cannot lose energy. This means that once we have got some energy we always have it. But energy often changes from one form to another. This is called the principle of conservation of energy. Several different types of energy are listed below:

- **Chemical energy**. Food has chemical energy stored in it, which is released by chemical reaction inside our bodies. Food provides energy to keep us warm and to do work. The stored energy in petrol is released when it is burnt inside a car's engine. (Burning is a chemical reaction.)
- **Gravitational potential energy**. When a rock is at the top of a hill, it has some stored energy. This sounds odd, because a rock at the top of a hill looks the same as a rock at the bottom of the hill. But when the rock is sent rolling down the hill, it can do some work. Water stored in a high-level dam helps us to produce electrical energy. The water has the potential to do work.
- **Kinetic energy** is the name given to the energy of motion. All moving objects have kinetic energy. A moving hammer has kinetic energy; it can do the job of knocking in a nail.
- **Heat energy**. When something is hot it possesses heat energy.
- **Strain energy**. If you have ever used a bow, you will know that you have to pull hard on the string before you can fire the arrow. You have done work to pull the string. The bow is now strained, and it stores some energy. The strain energy is used to give the arrow kinetic energy.
- When a battery makes a current flow, **electrical energy** has been produced.
- You will also meet **nuclear**, **sound** and **light energy** later in the book.

Energy transfers

Chemical energy in Wally's muscles allows him to do work to pull up the box (Figure 1). This work gives the box potential energy. When Wally slips, the potential energy turns into kinetic energy. When the box hits the ground the kinetic energy turns into heat energy, and sound energy.

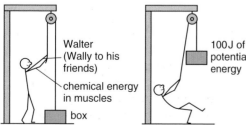
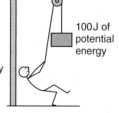
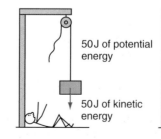
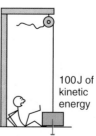
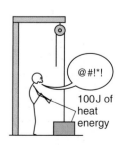

Walter (Wally to his friends)
chemical energy in muscles
box

100J of potential energy

50J of potential energy
50J of kinetic energy

100J of kinetic energy

@#!*!
100J of heat energy

Figure 1

Homework Questions

1 In the question below state clearly all the energy transfers which occur. Do not just write the forms of energy, explain precisely where the energy is at each stage.
   (a) A golfer hits a ball down the fairway.
   (b) An electric motor lifts a load.
   (c) A firework rocket flies into the air and explodes.
   (d) A car brakes and comes to a halt without skidding.
   (e) A car brakes and skids to a halt.

2 In the diagram below a ball falls to the ground. Near the ball, in positions A to E are marked some values of its kinetic energy and potential energy. Copy the diagram and fill in the missing values (you may ignore wind resistance.)

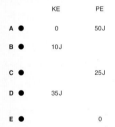

	KE	PE
A ●	0	50J
B ●	10J	
C ●		25J
D ●	35J	
E ●		0

3 Three people give a car a push start; each person applies a force of 200 N to the car and they push for a distance of 50 m.
   (a) What is the maximum value of the kinetic energy which the car can have, assuming that all their efforts have been turned into kinetic energy?
   (b) Why is the kinetic energy likely to be less than the value calculated in part (a)?

4 Explain what is meant by the Principle of Conservation of Energy.

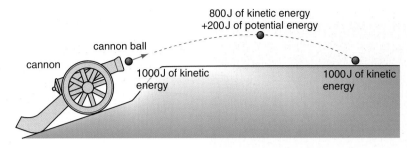

Figure 2

In Figure 2 you can see how kinetic energy can be turned into potential energy, then back to kinetic energy again.

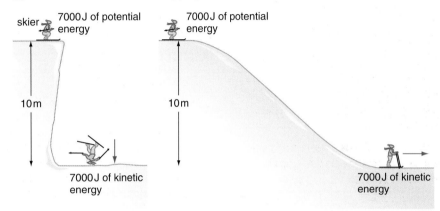

Figure 3

In Figure 3 a skier falls through a height of 10 m. He ends up with the same kinetic energy whether he falls straight down or accelerates more smoothly down the slope. In each case he loses the same potential energy.

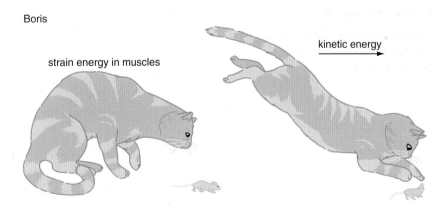

Figure 4

In Figure 4 Boris the cat is catching his supper. Chemical energy is used to create strain energy in Boris' muscles. This strain energy is converted to kinetic energy when Boris pounces on the mouse.

Some energy transfers are more complicated than the ones described above. For example, this is what happens when a car is driven: chemical energy in petrol is transferred to heat, sound and kinetic energy in the pistons and engine. The kinetic energy in the pistons is transferred to the body of the car to do work against drag and frictional forces. This work transfers energy to heat.

3

Calculating the Energy

Potential energy

How much work is done in lifting 110 kg through 2 m?

When a weight-lifter lifts his weights he does some work. This work increases the gravitational potential energy (PE) of the weights. The mass on the bar is now *m*. How much work does he do when he lifts the bar a height *h*? (*m* is in kilograms and *h* is in metres.) The pull of gravity on the bar (its weight) is *m* × *g*. We call the pull of gravity on each kilogram *g*; this is 10 N/kg.

$$\text{Work done} = F \times d$$
$$= mgh$$

The work done is equal to the increase in potential energy.

$$\text{Potential energy} = mgh$$

Kinetic energy

Can you estimate the total kinetic energy of the vehicles in this photograph?

The kinetic energy of a moving object is given by the formula:

$$\text{kinetic energy} = \tfrac{1}{2} mv^2$$

m is the mass of the object in kg, and *v* is its velocity in m/s.

This formula is very important for working out the stopping distance of a moving car. When cars are travelling very quickly, they need a large distance to stop in. The table below shows the stopping distances for a car travelling at different speeds. Next time you are travelling down the motorway at 40 m/s (90 mph) remember that your car needs about 120 m to stop in.

When a driver sees a hazard, there is a small delay between taking his foot off the accelerator and putting it on the brake. In this time the car moves forward at its original speed. This is the *thinking distance*, which is proportional to the car's speed. When the brakes are applied, work is done by the braking force to take away the car's kinetic energy. Since the car's kinetic energy depends on v^2, the *braking distance* also depends on v^2. This means that when the car's speed doubles from 10 m/s to 20 m/s, the braking distance increases by a factor of 4.

Speed (m/s)	Thinking distance (m)	Braking distance (m)	Total stopping distance (m)
10	6	6	12
20	12	24	36
30	18	54	72
40	24	96	120

Table 1 *The faster the car travels, the greater the distance it needs to stop.*

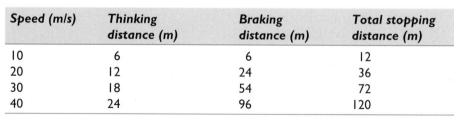

www

http://www.batesville.k12.in.us/Physics/PhyNet/Mechanics/Energy/EnergyIntro.html

Strain energy

When a spring is stretched it stores strain energy. This energy can be obtained from the spring when it is released, provided that it has not been stretched past its elastic limit.

Figure 1 shows a force/extension graph for a spring. How much energy is stored when the spring is stretched 0.1 m?

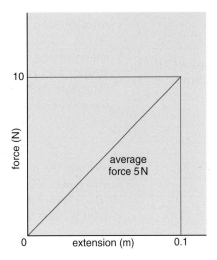

Figure 1

Energy stored = work done in stretching the spring

= average force × distance

= 5 N × 0.1 m

= 0.5 J

When the spring is stretched the force pulling it changes, so we have to average the force.

Converting kinetic energy to potential energy

Sean throws a ball into the air with an upwards speed of 20 m/s. How high will it go? Using the principle that energy is conserved, we can say: the kinetic energy of the ball as it leaves Sean's arm, $\frac{1}{2}mv^2$, turns into potential energy, mgh, at its highest point.

So $\frac{1}{2}mv^2 = mgh$

$$h = \frac{v^2}{2g} = \frac{(20 \text{ m/s})^2}{20 \text{ m/s}^2} = 20 \text{ m}$$

Homework Questions

1 A charging rhinoceros moves at a speed of 15 m/s, and its mass is 750 kg. What is its kinetic energy?

2 A car of mass 1000 kg does an emergency stop when it is travelling at 15 m/s; it stops in a distance of 20 m.
(a) Calculate the change in kinetic energy for the car.
(b) Calculate the force which acts to slow it down.
(c) On another day the car is travelling at 30 m/s; if the brakes exert the same force, what distance will the car stop in now?
(d) If the car is heavily loaded it has a mass of 1250 kg. What distance

will it stop in when it is travelling at 30 m/s?
(e) What will happen to your braking distance if:
(i) the road is icy,
(ii) you are going downhill?

3 Figure 1 shows a graph of force against extension for a spring. The same spring is extended to 0.05 m.
(a) Calculate the force required to cause this extension.
(b) Calculate the energy stored in the spring now.

4 A car of mass 750 kg slows down from 30 m/s to 15 m/s over a distance of 50 m.
(a) What is its change in kinetic

energy?
(b) What is the average braking force that acts on it?

5 What is the thinking time of the driver whose thinking distances are shown in Table 1?

6 A catapult stores 10 J of strain energy when it is fully stretched. It is used to fire a marble of mass 0.02 kg straight up into the air.
(a) Calculate how high the marble rises.
(b) How fast is the marble moving when it is 30 m above the ground? (Ignore any affects due to air resistance.)

4 Power

http://www.glenbrook.k12.il.
us/gbssci/phys/phys.html

Alice and David are lifting some bricks. They each lift 20 bricks through a height of 5 m. This means that they do the same amount of work, However, David is large and powerful and he lifts all of his bricks in one go. Alice who is rather smaller, lifts her bricks one at a time. We use the word powerful to describe someone who can do the work quickly. **Power** is the rate of doing work or converting energy.

$$\text{Power} = \frac{\text{work done or energy converted}}{\text{time taken}}$$

From the equation above you can see that power is measured in J/s. But we give power its own unit called the **watt**. 1 watt is equal to a rate of working of 1 J/s. Power ratings can be very large; then we use the units of kW (kilowatt or 1000 W) and MW (megawatt or 1 000 000 W).

Body power

Alice measures her personal power output by running up a flight of steps. She takes 8.4 s to run up a flight of steps. Her mass is 14 kg. What power does she develop? She has done some work to lift her weight of 140 N through a height of 6 m.

$$\text{Work done} = \text{force} \times \text{distance}$$

$$= 140 \text{ N} \times 6 \text{ m} = 840 \text{ J}$$

$$\text{power} = \frac{\text{work done}}{\text{time}}$$

$$= \frac{840 \text{ J}}{8.4 \text{ s}} = 100 \text{ W}$$

Alice is converting energy at about the same rate as an electric light bulb.

Power of an express train

The photograph on the next page shows a Eurostar express train approaching the station at a steady speed. When the train moves at a constant speed, the driving force from the wheels is exactly balanced by opposing frictional forces. These opposing forces are caused by friction in the axles of the wheels and by wind resistance. So the train does work against these frictional forces.

How much power does the train have to produce when it is running at 20 m/s?

$$\text{Power} = \frac{\text{work done}}{\text{time}} = \frac{\text{force} \times \text{distance}}{\text{time}}$$

$$= F \times \frac{d}{t}$$

So the power developed is equal to the driving force × the distance travelled per second. But the distance travelled per second is the speed, v.

$$\text{Power} = F \times v$$

The resistive force on the train travelling at 20 m/s can be found from Figure 1.

$$\text{Power} = 8 \text{ kN} \times 20 \text{ m/s}$$
$$= 8000 \text{ N} \times 20 \text{ m/s}$$
$$= 160\,000 \text{ W}$$
$$\text{or } 160 \text{ kW}$$

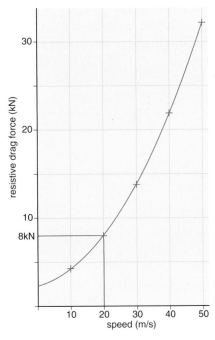

Figure 1 *Graph to show the resistive force acting on a Eurostar as the speed increases*

This engine can provide 2 megawatts to drive the train at full speed

Homework Questions

1 What is the unit of power?

2 David runs up the same flight of steps as Alice, 6 m high, in a time of 6 seconds. His mass is 100 kg. Calculate his power. How many times more powerful is he than Alice, whose power is 100 W?

3 A weightlifter lifts 280 kg above his head. In the last part of the lift he raises the bar through 1.0 m in 1.5 s.
(a) How much work does he do?
(b) How much power does he develop?

4 (a) Use the graph to estimate the resistive drag force on a Eurostar train when it is travelling at:
(i) 40 m/s, (ii) 50 m/s.
(b) Show that the power that the engine produces to pull the train at 40 m/s is 880 kW.
(c) Calculate the power the engine produces when the train runs at 55 m/s.

5 (a) Use the formula $W = F \times d$ to calculate the work done against resistive forces when the train goes on a 200 km journey travelling at (i) 20 m/s (ii) 40 m/s. Give your answers in MJ.
(b) Now explain why, in 1973, when there was a temporary shortage of petrol, the government imposed a speed limit of 50 mph on all roads.

6 Here is part of an answer written by a student to explain the motion of a cricket ball. She has made some mistakes. Rewrite what she has written, explaining and correcting her errors.
'When a batsman hits a cricket ball he gives it a certain force. As the ball rolls over the grass this force is used up and eventually the ball stops. All the power that the batsman used in hitting the ball ends up as heat.'

7 Read this extract from a magazine article: *The hind legs of a locust are extremely powerful. The insect takes off with a speed of 3 m/s. The jump is fast and occurs in a time of 25 milliseconds. The locust's mass is about 2.5 g.*
Use the information to answer problems set below.
(a) Calculate the locust's average acceleration during take off. (25 milliseconds = 0.025 s.)
(b) Now work out the average force exerted by the locust's hind legs (remember to turn the mass into kg.)
(c) The locust's legs extend by 5 cm (0.05 m) during its jump. Calculate the work done by its legs.
(d) How much power does the locust develop in its muscles?
(e) Calculate the power/mass ratio for the locust and compare this with David's power/mass ratio (from question 2).

Force multipliers

Some machines are clever devices that multiply forces for us. They help us to lift up loads that we are not strong enough to lift up directly. But do they multiply energy for us as well; do we get more energy out of the machine than we put in?

Figure 1 shows the principle of the **lever**, a simple machine. A 300 N downwards force acts 1 m to the left of the pivot. This force is balanced by a force of 100 N, that acts downwards at a distance of 3 m to the right of the pivot:

$$300 \text{ N} \times 1 \text{ m} = 100 \text{ N} \times 3 \text{ m}$$

So we can lift a load of 300 N by applying a force (effort) of only 100 N. The work done in lifting the load through 0.5 m is

$$300 \text{ N} \times 0.5 \text{ m} = 150 \text{ J}$$

The work done by the person applying the effort is

$$100 \text{ N} \times 1.5 \text{ m} = 150 \text{ J}.$$

Energy is conserved, so we cannot get more out than we put in.

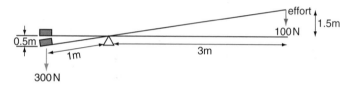

Figure 1 *The principle of the lever*

An **inclined plane** is another example of a common machine. Figure 2 shows a man rolling a barrel up to the top of the slope. The work he would do in lifting the barrel straight up through a height of 1m is 1000 N × 1 m = 1000 J. By rolling the barrel along the slope the effect of gravity is reduced. This way the man will avoid serious damage to his back. We can work out what force needs to be applied to the barrel.

$$\text{Work} = F \times d; \text{ work done} = 1000 \text{ J}; \text{ distance} = 5 \text{ m}.$$

$$1000 \text{ J} = F \times 5 \text{ m}$$

$$F = \frac{1000 \text{ J}}{5 \text{ m}} = 200 \text{ N}$$

A **pulley system**, another simple machine, is shown in Figure 3. The load is 600 N and the lower pulley block is supported by two ropes. So if the tension in the rope is 300 N the load will be supported. The man can lift the load by applying a smaller effort, but he does not win from the energy point of view. If he lifts his load 1 m, each of the supporting ropes is shortened by 1 m, so he pulls the rope through 2 m. He applies half the force, but pulls through twice the distance, thereby doing the same work as if he had lifted the load straight up.

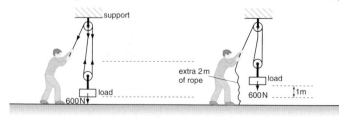

Figure 3 *A pulley system*

A car jack can multiply a force about 20 times

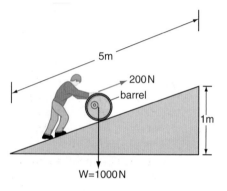

Figure 2 *An inclined plane*

Stonehenge was built using huge rocks from over a hundred miles away. This was thousands of years ago! How do you think the rocks were moved? Do you think force multipliers were used?

Gears

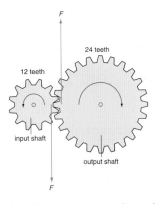

Figure 4 *Where the gear teeth touch, equal and opposite forces act*
Couple on input shaft = F × r
Couple on output shaft = F × 2r = 2F × r

The machines that we have looked at so far increase forces; **gears** will increase (or decrease) couples (see page 15). Figure 4 shows two gear wheels in contact; the input shaft has to be turned twice to make the output shaft turn once. However, the couple from the output shaft is twice as big as that applied to the input shaft.

The bicycle is an example of a machine that is a distance multiplier. The force needed to push a bicycle along a road is small. So a cyclist applies a large force on the pedals, but moves his feet a small distance in one rotation of the pedals. This work is converted into a small force acting to push the bicycle forward, but the distance that the wheel rotates in one revolution is a lot more than the pedals' rotation. So the bicycle has increased the distance the cyclist has moved – that is the idea, to get there faster (Figure 5).

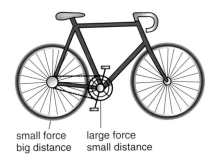

small force   large force
big distance   small distance

Figure 5 *A distance multiplier*

Homework Questions

1 (a) Why is it useful to have machines to multiply forces for us?
   (b) Can a machine save us energy? Explain your answer.

2 A screwdriver is used
   (i) to tighten up screws,
   (ii) to lift the lid of a paint tin.
   Explain how the screwdriver acts as a machine in each example above.

3 For each of the pulley systems below, calculate:
   (a) the distance moved by the effort force, if the load is lifted up by 0.5 m,
   (b) the work done to lift each load 0.5 m,
   (c) the work done by each effort force, when the load is lifted 0.5 m.
   (d) Explain why the work done by the effort is greater than the work done on the load.

4 Soraya is pedalling her bicycle along level ground (see diagram below).

   • distance moved by the pedal in one rotation = 0.94 m
   • circumference of wheel = 1.88 m

   (a) How many times does the wheel turn for each rotation of the pedals?
   (b) How far does the bicycle move for one rotation of the pedals?
   (c) How much work does Soraya do in one rotation of her pedals?
   (d) All the work Soraya does is used to push her along the road. Calculate *F*.
   (e) Soraya turns her pedals twice per second. Calculate (i) the speed of the bicycle (ii) the power her legs produce.

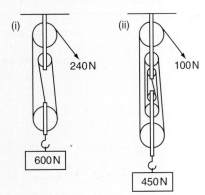

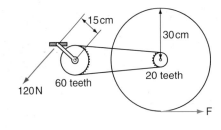

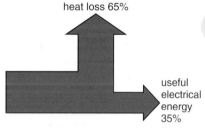

(a) How energy is used in a power station. The efficiency is 35%

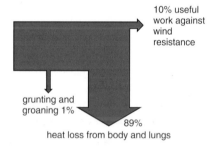

(b) How an athlete's energy is used. The efficiency is 10%

Figure 1

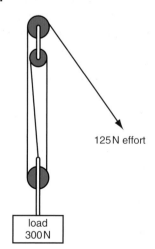

load 300 N

Figure 2

Unwanted heat

In the last unit we met some machines. It was assumed that we got as much work out of these machines as we put in. However, this is not usually true. Energy must be conserved, but it is often converted to a form that we do not want. The photographs above are examples of hot machines. The power station is producing electrical energy from chemical energy. The light bulb is producing light energy from electrical energy. But in both cases heat energy is produced too. Figure 1 illustrates the energy conversions for a power station and an athlete.

This leads us to the idea of **efficiency**, which is defined like this:

$$\text{Efficiency} = \frac{\text{useful energy (or work) out of machine}}{\text{energy (or work) put into a machine}}$$

$$\textit{or } \text{Efficiency} = \frac{\text{power out}}{\text{power in}}$$

Example. Figure 2 shows a pulley system being used to lift a load. What is its efficiency?

If the load moves 1 m, the effort rope will have to be pulled 3 m.

$$\text{Efficiency} = \frac{\text{work done on load}}{\text{work done by effort}}$$

$$= \frac{300 \text{ N} \times 1 \text{ m}}{125 \text{ N} \times 3 \text{ m}}$$

$$= 0.8 \text{ or } 80\%$$

We can express efficiency either as a fraction or as a percentage.
The main causes for unwanted energy losses in the pulley system are:

- we are lifting the lower pulley block
- there are frictional forces on the pulley axles which produce heat.

Human efficiency

We get our energy from food by the process of **respiration**. During respiration, food reacts with oxygen in our bodies forming carbon dioxide and water. We obtain the oxygen when we breathe in, and when we breathe out we get rid of the carbon dioxide formed during respiration.
When we take exercise we breathe faster. This means we get more oxygen to provide the mechanical energy. But the process is inefficient and our muscles make lots of heat too.

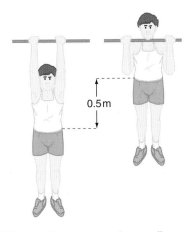

Figure 3 *A gymnast doing pull-ups*

Station	Date	Efficiency
Battersea A	1933	16%
Drax	1975	37%

Table 1

Figure 3 shows a gymnast doing pull-ups in the gym. While he does this his body uses 30 000 J of energy every minute. In one minute the gymnast does 20 pull-ups, before stopping to rest. Each pull-up was through a height of 0.5 m, his weight is 750 N; what is his efficiency?

$$\text{Work out} = 20 \times 750 \text{ N} \times 0.5 \text{ m}$$
$$= 7500 \text{ J}$$
$$\text{Efficiency} = \frac{\text{work out}}{\text{work in}}$$
$$= \frac{7500 \text{ J}}{30\,000 \text{ J}} = 0.25 \text{ or } 25\%$$

Table 1 shows the efficiencies of two power stations. You can see that the efficiencies have improved over the years. But will we ever be able to do better than 37%? Surely we ought to be able to make a power station nearly 100% efficient? The answer is no. We are producing electricity (an ordered form of energy) from heat, which is associated with the disordered movement of molecules. Creating order is far harder than creating disorder, so the production of electricity will always be inefficient.

Producing electricity in a coal-fired power station is an example of an irreversible process. Most processes are irreversible, because the **entropy** of molecules always increases. Entropy is a measure of the disorder or randomness of molecular motion.

Homework Questions

1 (a) Explain what is meant by efficiency, when describing a machine.
(b) People and cars are two examples of inefficient machines; how do they waste energy?
(c) Give a further example of an inefficient machine, and one which is nearly 100% efficient.

2 (a) A filament light bulb uses 60 W of electrical power, and produces 2 W of light energy. Calculate its efficiency. How does it waste energy?
(b) A high efficiency long-life bulb, has an efficiency of 18%, and uses 11 W of power from the mains. Show that it gives out approximately as much light as the filament bulb.

3 The diagram shows a wheel and axle. A load of 600 N is lifted a distance of 1 m by an effort of 200 N.
(a) How far does the effort force move to lift the load up 1 m? (Hint: look at the radius of each part of the machine.)

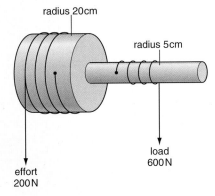

(b) How much work is done on the load?
(c) How much work is done by the effort?
(d) What is the efficiency of the machine?

4 In this question you are required to select breakfast to provide you with the energy for a morning; you are not allowed any snacks between meals!
(a) First choose breakfast from the table below to provide your energy requirement for a quiet morning when you are not active; boys will need approximately 2000 kJ, girls

1500 kJ. (The exact values do depend on your weight and metabolic rate.)
(b) Now choose a breakfast for an active morning: boys will need about 2500 kJ, and girls about 1800 kJ.
(c) Why might somebody put on weight if they switch from an active job to an office job?
(d) Use the information in part (a) to estimate how much energy each second you give out as heat when you are sitting still, assuming breakfast provides your energy requirement for 5 hours.

Food	Energy value (kJ)
Apple	250
Cereal (30 g)	450
Cereal (50 g)	750
Slice of toast, Butter, jam	600
Egg	400
Bacon slice	700
Sausage	600
Tea with sugar	100

Electrical Energy Production

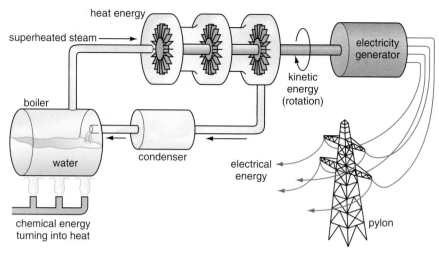

Figure 1 *The principle of a power station*

This is a 600 megawatt generator inside the coal-fired Drax power station. Superheated steam is used to drive the generator

Figure 1 shows the principle behind the production of electrical energy in a power station. Many power stations use coal as their source of energy. When coal is burnt its stored chemical energy is released as heat energy. This heat energy boils water at high pressure to make superheated steam at temperatures of about 700°C. The kinetic energy in the superheated steam is used to drive **turbines**. These are connected to the electricity generator's large coils, which rotate inside a strong magnetic field (see Unit J8).

You can see in Figure 2 a chart showing how energy is used in this process. There is a lot of heat lost in the power station. The electrical energy itself is also converted to heat energy in factories and houses.

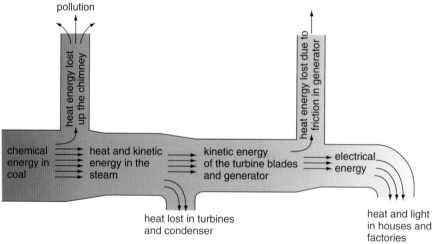

Figure 2

http://www.purchon.com/
physics/energy.htm#chemical

There are two problems that arise from the production of electricity that worry a lot of people.

Pollution. Burning coal makes the gases carbon dioxide and sulphur dioxide. These pollute the atmosphere. When sulphur dioxide dissolves in water, an acidic solution is formed containing sulphuric acid.

Water + sulphur dioxide → sulphuric acid

So when sulphur dioxide gets into rain, the rain becomes acidic. We call this **acid rain**. Acid rain damages stonework in buildings. It is thought that acid rain is also killing trees in Scandinavia. It is likely that sulphur dioxide produced in Britain is blown across to Scandinavia by the prevailing south-westerly winds.

2 **Global warming.** Heat energy is always produced when we make electrical energy. People worry that we will warm the Earth up, as we increase our use of electrical energy. This warming is caused by (1) the extra heat from power stations, factories and homes; (2) extra carbon dioxide in the atmosphere trapping heat in, so that the Earth's temperature will rise slowly. This phenomenon is called the **greenhouse effect**. An **increase in the Earth's temperature** could have very serious consequences. An increase of 1°C or 2°C to the Earth's average temperature would probably melt a large amount of ice from the polar ice caps. Although we get great benefits from electrical energy, we have to consider its effect on the environment. If we are not careful we will damage the world that we live in.

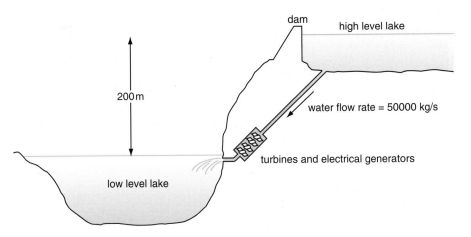

Figure 3 A pumped storage power station

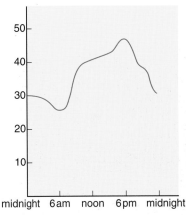

Figure 4 The typical use of electrical energy on a winter's day in Britain

Homework Questions

1 (a) What is smog? (Look in a library or on the Internet if you don't know). Why is it usually found in large cities?
(b) Why do large cities have smokeless zones?

2 (a) What is acid rain?
(b) How is acid rain formed?
(c) What effects does acid rain have on the environment?
(d) What would you do to reduce the problems caused by acid rain?

3 Give a detailed account of the energy changes which occur to generate electricity in a coal-fired power station.

4 Figure 3 (above) shows the layout of a pumped storage power station. Water from the high level lake

produces electrical energy by flowing through the turbine generators. These are placed just above the low level lake. When there is a low demand for electricity, the generators are driven in reverse to pump water back into the high level lake. This means there will be enough water to generate electricity again, when demand is high.
(a) Why is this sort of power station useful to electricity companies?
(b) Would this pumped storage power station pollute the atmosphere when it generates electricity?
(c) Where does the energy come

from to pump the water back up the hill again?
(d) What energy changes occur as water flows from the high level lake to the low level lake?
(e) Calculate the loss of potential energy of the water in 1 second. (Use the information in Figure 3.)
(f) The turbines are 60% efficient. Calculate the electrical power output of this station. Give your answer in MW.
(g) For the next two questions, look at Figure 4. At what times of day will the pumped storage power station be producing electricity?
(h) Explain the shape of the graph in Figure 4. Why does it reach a maximum at about 6 pm?

A large city might use 10^{14}J of energy in one day. You need to burn 10 000 tonnes of coal to provide this amount of energy. The Sun is the major energy source for the Earth. The Sun provides heat and light to make our lives possible, as well as providing energy for the growth of foods that we eat. Fossil fuels, which we burn, originally derived their energy from the Sun too.

Fossil fuels

At the moment the world faces an energy crisis. This may seem surprising; you have learnt that energy cannot be lost. The problem is that we are burning fuels like coal, oil and gas. These fuels produce electricity, warm our houses and provide energy for transport. The end product of these fuels is heat energy. We cannot recapture the heat and turn it back into coal or oil. These fuels are known as **non-renewable energy sources**. Once we have burnt them they have gone forever.

Coal, oil and gas are known as *fossil fuels*. They are the remains of plants and animals that lived some hundreds of millions of years ago. Supplies of these fuels are limited. We use coal mainly for the production of electrical energy. If we go on using coal at its present rate, it will last us for about another 300 years.

We get petrol from oil. So this energy source is vital for running cars and aeroplanes. At our present rate of use, oil will last us about 50 years. Gas will last for about the same time.

In the early 1970s, Britain started to drill for oil in the North Sea. Although supplies still exist there, they are becoming depleted and more expensive to extract. The price of oil continues to rise; the shortage of fossil fuels is a problem which will have to be faced in our lifetime. It is important that we use fossil fuels carefully, and we must also look for other sources of energy.

A large wind farm. Each wind turbine has three blades and can produce a power of up to 3 megawatts. Such a large farm could replace a coal-fired power station.

Other energy sources

- **Nuclear power** is being used more and more to generate electricity. France generates 95% of its electrical energy using nuclear power. The nuclear fuel which is used is uranium. This is also a non-renewable energy source. But nuclear power could provide our energy for a few thousand years. Nuclear power worries people because of the radioactive waste that is produced. This is discussed further in Section L.

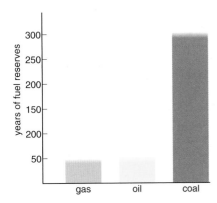

Figure 1 *How long will our fossil fuels last?*

Homework Questions

1　Explain the difference between a renewable and a non-renewable fuel.

2　(a) Why are air fares likely to be extremely expensive in 50 years' time?
(b) Government ministers talk of introducing 'Green Taxes'. What are they, and do you agree that they should be introduced?
(c) Why is petrol wasted if a car accelerates or brakes rapidly?

3　Explain carefully the energy transfers which occur to produce a fossil fuel; remember to explain where the energy came from in the first place.

4　(a) Discuss briefly the advantages we enjoy from using electricity as a source of energy.
(b) Discuss the disadvantages we face as a result of electricity production. You might consider the effects on the atmosphere, hazards, the aesthetic impact on the environment, and possible effects on wildlife which projects such as the Severn Barrage might have.

Some further sources of energy are described below; these are **renewable energy sources**. In these cases we extract energy from the environment and these energy sources will always be available to us.

● **Biomass** is the name we use when talking about plants in the sense that we can extract energy from them. The most common way of extracting energy from biomass is to cut down a tree and burn it. Trees are a renewable energy source so long as forests are looked after properly. Unfortunately, in Africa, Asia and South America trees are being cut down far faster than they are being replanted. It is thought that cutting down large forests has changed our climate by reducing rainfall in some parts of the world.

In some countries vegetable oils are already in use to drive farm machinery. So the world's biomass may be used in future to power our cars.

● **Tidal power.** Figure 2 shows a map of the Severn estuary, which is a suitable position for a tidal barrage. The idea is that water flows in through the sluice gates at A at high tide. At low tide water flows out through the turbogenerators at B. We are using the potential energy of the water to generate electrical energy. If the Severn estuary barrage is built it will produce about 7000 MW of power.

● **Hydroelectric power** is widely used in Scandinavia, where a lot of water flows down the mountains from melted snow. The principle is the same as tidal power: the potential energy of the water is used to generate electrical energy.

● **Wind power.** Energy from the wind can also be used to generate electricity. The photograph opposite shows a wind farm.

● **Geothermal power.** Energy can be obtained from a hot spring. As the water in the spring boils, the steam formed is used to drive electrical turbines. In China, warm water (50°C) is pumped directly into factories and houses to provide central heating.

● **Solar power** can be used directly to warm up water in panels in the roofs of houses. Energy from the sun can also be used to generate electricity using photocells. A lot of us now use solar-powered calculators.

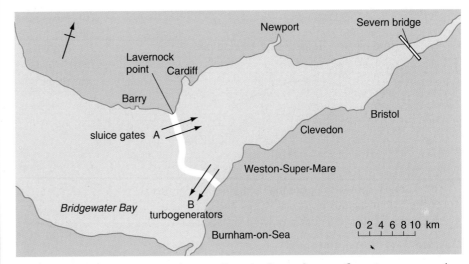

Figure 2 *The Severn Barrage. A report from the Severn Barrage Committee suggested that it was technically feasible to build the barrage. At the time of the report (1981) the cost was estimated at £7.5 billion. The barrage would be able to produce 7000 MW of power. This amounts to about 6% of the national need*

SECTION D: Questions

1   In the following cases explain *carefully* the energy changes or transfers which occur. Do not first write something like 'potential to kinetic', be specific; where is the energy? Is the energy given to another object?
    (a) You pluck a guitar string, and your friend hears a sound.
    (b) You fire a marble with a catapult, and accidentally break a window.
    (c) You throw a ball vertically upwards.
    (d) You kick a football along the ground, it comes to a halt.
    (e) Energy is transferred from the Sun, to warm you up while sunbathing.
    (f) You accelerate a car, then bring it to rest using the brakes.
    (g) A firework rocket takes off, explodes and falls back to the ground.

2   The diagram shows a section of track near a railway station. The track at the station is slightly higher than the rest of the track. What advantage does this give? Explain your answer in terms of energy changes.

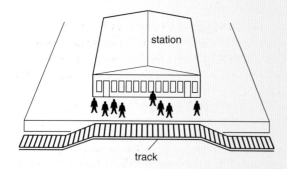

3   The diagram shows the path of a cannon ball.

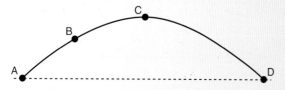

    (a) Where is it travelling most slowly?
    (b) Table 1 shows the potential and kinetic energies of the ball in various positions. Copy and complete the table. (You can ignore any wind resistance.)

Position	Potential energy (J)	Kinetic energy (J)
A	0	1000
B	200	
C		600
D		

4   Which of the following forces are doing work?
    (a) A magnetic force holding a magnet onto a steel door.
    (b) A force driving a car forward.
    (c) A weight-lifter holding a weight stationary.
    (d) A paper weight holding down a pile of paper.
    (e) A crane applying a force to lift a load.
    (f) The pull of gravity holding a satellite in a circular orbit around the Earth.

5   Three physics students decide to compare the force of wind resistance on their cars. They decide to carry out a fair test to see how far each car can travel, at a constant speed of 70 km per hour, using only 5 litres of petrol. The table shows their results.

Car	Distance travelled (km)
Renault Clio	75
Astra 1.3 l	70
Volvo 440	50

    (a) Which car do you think is the most streamlined?
    (b) Compare the resistive forces on the Renault and Volvo, when they travel at 70 km per hour.
    (c) Their teacher tells them it is not really a fair test. What factors have they forgotten?

6   An electric winch is used to pull a coal truck up an inclined plane.
    (a) How much useful work is done in lifting the load through 15 m?
    The winch uses a 6 kW electrical supply, and pulls the truck up the slope at a rate of 5 m/s.
    (b) How long does it take to pull the truck up the slope?
    (c) How much work is done by the winch?
    (d) Calculate the efficiency of the machine. Where do you think unwanted energy transfers occur?

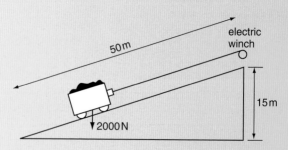

7   Pete and Wesley are two muscle men. Stephen is not as strong, but he has devised a machine to beat Pete and Wesley in a trial of strength. Explain how Stephen can win.

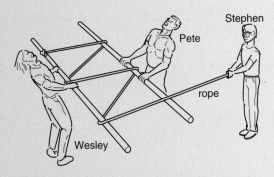

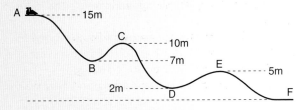

9 You can see the profile of a fairground ride in the diagram. A car leaves point A and arrives later at point F. The mass of the car, including occupants, is 200 kg.

(a) Calculate the car's potential energy at each of the points A to F.
(b) Now calculate the car's speed at each of the points B to F. Assume its speed was very small at A.

10 (a) Explain the energy transfers that occur when a car stops, without skidding, when the brakes are applied.
(b) What energy transfers occur when a car does skid?

11 An electric motor on a building site lifts a load of bricks through a height of 5 m. The weight of the bricks is 800 N.
(a) Calculate the work done on the load.
(b) It took 16 s to raise the load through 5 m. Calculate the power output of the motor.
(c) The motor is only 30% efficient. Calculate the power input to the motor.
(d) Explain why the motor is inefficient.

8 Look at the pulley system.

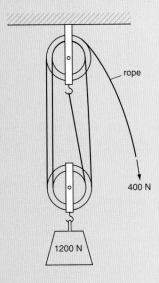

Calculate:
(a) its mechanical advantage
(b) velocity ratio
(c) the work done on the load when it is lifted 0.5 m.
(d) the work done by the *effort* when the load is lifted 0.5 m.
(e) the efficiency of this pulley system.

12 *Voyager I* was launched on 5 September 1977. After a journey of nearly two years it reached Jupiter. On 30 January 1979 *Voyager I* was 35.1 million km away from Jupiter. The data below show how *Voyager* approached Jupiter during the next month until passing close by Jupiter on 5 March. The times

	Distance from Jupiter's centre R (millions of km)	Velocity v (m/s)	Time from 00.00 h GMT Jan 30 1979 days	hours	Date
1	35.10	10 900	0	00	Jan 30
1A	34.71	10 904	0	10	
2	28.08	11 000	7	10	Feb 6
2A	27.68	11 006	7	20	
3	21.06	11 135	14	18	Feb 13
3A	20.66	11 145	15	4	
4	14.04	11 402	21	23	Feb 20
4A	13.88	11 411	22	3	
5	7.02	12 165	28	21	Feb 27
5A	6.93	12 184	28	23	
6	3.51	13 564	32	1	Mar 3
6A	3.46	13 601	32	2	
7	2.81	14 212	32	15	Mar 5
7A	2.76	14 271	32	16	

recorded are from 0.00 h GMT on 30 January 1979.

During all of the approach to Jupiter, the motors on *Voyager* were turned off. So the only force acting on *Voyager* was the gravitational pull of Jupiter.

(a) Explain why *Voyager's* speed increased as it approached Jupiter.

(b) Work out the acceleration of *Voyager* between points: (i) 1 and 1A, (ii) 7 and 7A. Express your answer in m/s². (Hint: 1 hour = 3600 s.)

(c) Now work out the force acting on *Voyager* at points 1 and 7. *Voyager's* mass is about 2000 kg. Explain why the force changed.

(d) Work out *Voyager's* increase in kinetic energy as it moved from point 2 to point 6. Where did this increase in kinetic energy come from?

13 The Eiffel Tower in Paris is 300 m high and can be climbed using its 1792 steps. Jacques decided to climb the tower; he took 15 minutes to do it and he has a mass of 60 kg.

(a) How much work did he do climbing the steps?

(b) What was his average power output during the climb?

(c) A croissant provides Jacques with 400 kJ of energy when digested. How many croissants should Jacques eat for breakfast, if his body is 20% efficient at transferring this energy into useful work?

(d) Explain where most of the energy from Jacques' food goes.

14 (a) The diagram shows a windmill with a rotor 100 m across. This could be used to generate electricity.

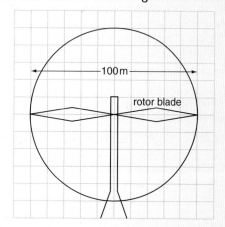

(i) Estimate the total area of the rotor blades.

(ii) The wind has a velocity of 10 m/s. The force it can cause on a surface of 1 m² is 90 N. How much work can this wind do on 1 m² in 1 s? (Work = force × distance.)

(iii) Wind is used to turn the rotor blade. The effective work done on 1 m² of the blade is 50% of that calculated in (ii). Find how much energy is transferred to the rotor in 1 s.

(iv) Calculate the maximum electrical power, in watts, which would be generated by this windmill.

(v) A conventional power station generates about 900 MW of electrical power (1 MW = 1 000 000 W). How many of these windmills would be needed to replace a power station?

(b) In unit 8 you saw where a barrier could be built across the estuary of the River Severn. This would make a lake with a surface area of about 200 km² (200 million m²).

The diagram below shows that the sea level could change by 9 m between low and high tide; but the level in the lake would only change by 5 m.

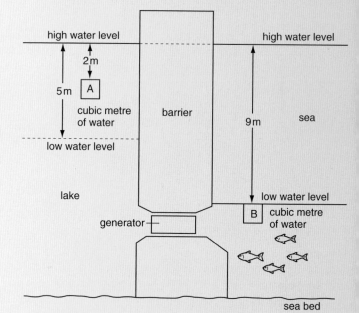

(i) What kind of energy is given up when a cubic metre of water falls from position A to position B?

(ii) A cubic metre of water has a mass of 1000 kg. The acceleration due to gravity is 10 m/s². Calculate the force of gravity on a cubic metre of water. Calculate the work that this can do as it falls from A to B. (Force = mass × acceleration.) (Work = force × distance.)

(iii) How many cubic metres of water could flow out of the lake between high and low tide?

(iv) Use your answers to parts (ii) and (iii) to find how much energy could be obtained from the tide. Assume that position A is the average position of a cubic metre of water between high and low levels in the lake.

(v) The time between high and low tide is approximately 20 000 seconds (about six hours). Use this figure to estimate the power available from the dam. Give your answers in megawatts.

(c) Explain the advantages and disadvantages of the windmill and the Severn Barrier as sources of power.

Edexcel (ULEAC)

15 The diagram shows a motor that is used to lift up a pile driver. The driver is dropped from a height of 10 m on top of the pile. The driver and pile each have a mass of 500 kg.

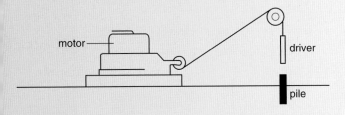

(a) How much potential energy does the driver have when it is 10 m above the pile?
(b) Calculate the speed of the driver just before it hits the pile.
(c) The driver and pile stick together on impact. Now calculate the speed immediately after impact. (Hint: use the principle of conservation of momentum.)
(d) Calculate how much kinetic energy is transferred on impact. What has happened to this energy?
(e) The driver and pile come to rest after a time of 0.1 s. Calculate the average force that the ground exerts on the pile during this time.
(f) Calculate how far the pile goes into the ground.

16 Boris has caught Mikhail the mouse and has set him to work in the tread-wheel. When Mikhail runs he can just lift Boris at a speed of 0.03 m/s.

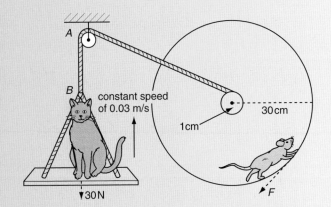

(a) How fast is Mikhail running relative to the treadwheel?
(b) What force (F) does Mikhail exert on the treadwheel? Assume the machine is 100% efficient.

17 A steel spring and a rubber band have force/extension graphs as shown. When the band is stretched to the maximum extension shown on the graph, the energy stored in the rubber is 20 J.

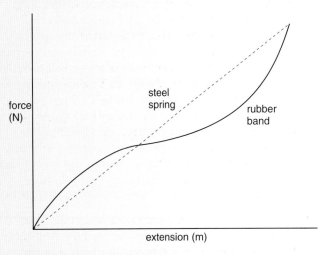

(a) When both the spring and band are stretched to the maximum extensions shown, which stores more energy? Explain your answer.
(b) The rubber band is now used in a catapult. 75% of the maximum stored energy is given to a stone as kinetic energy. The stone, which has a mass of 0.1 kg, took 0.02 s to leave the catapult. What is the maximum speed of the stone?
(c) How high could the stone be fired?

18 The Highway Code states how the braking distance, for a car with good brakes on a dry road, changes as the speed increases. The braking distance is the distance travelled by the car from the instant the brakes are applied until it comes to rest. The table shows the braking distance for different speeds.

speed (m/s)	0	9	13.5	18	22.5	27	31
braking distance (m)	0	6	14	24	38	54	75

(a) Plot a graph of braking distance (y-axis) against speed (x-axis).
(b) From the graph determine the braking distance for a car travelling at (i) 15 m/s, (ii) 30 m/s.
(c) Predict, giving your reasons, the braking distance for a car travelling at 36 m/s.
The time taken for a driver to react to a situation before actually putting on the brakes is called the thinking time, and the distance travelled during the thinking time is called the thinking distance. The thinking time is usually taken to be ⅔ second.
(d) (i) What is the thinking distance for a car travelling at 30 m/s?
(ii) What is the total stopping distance for a car travelling at 30 m/s? (Use part b)
(iii) What is the minimum distance a driver should allow from another car, also travelling at 30 m/s?

On a foggy day on a motorway the limit of visibility may be only 50 m.
(e) (i) Select and justify a suitable speed limit for these conditions.
(ii) What difference would it make to your chosen speed limit if the road were wet? Explain your answer.
(f) In any collision the wearing of a seat belt is likely to reduce the injuries suffered by a passenger. Explain in terms of momentum how the belt achieves this.
(g) A pupil put forward the theory that the braking distance is proportional to the (speed)^2. Describe an experiment which you could carry out in a school laboratory to test the theory. (Hint – use a level sand tray to brake the model car.)

OCR (MEG)

19 Diagram I shows a ski-jump on a mountain. Two ramps are covered with smooth, hard ice. The ramp WX curves near its lower end so that it is horizontal at X. An empty sledge of mass 15 kg slips from rest at W, slides down the ski-jump and eventually hits the mountainside at Y.

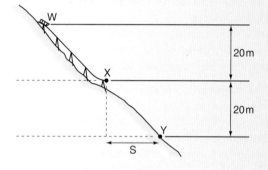

Diagram I

In answering parts (a) and (b) you may ignore the effects of friction and air resistance.
(a) (i) What is the change of the potential energy of the sledge as it moves from W to X?
(ii) With what speed does the sledge leave the ramp at X?
(iii) How long does the sledge take to travel from X to Y?
(iv) How big is the distance marked S on Diagram I?
(b) The ramp in Diagram I is replaced by a steeper one between the same levels (Diagram 2). Say what effects this will have, if any, on:
(i) the time taken for the sledge to travel from W to X
(ii) the speed with which the sledge leaves the ramp
(iii) the position of the point of impact.

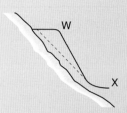

Diagram 2
(c) The sledge will probably be damaged by its impact, yet a skier can land safely. Explain how the skier manages to do this.

OCR (MEG)

20 Joy does a bungee jump. A bungee is a long elastic rope.

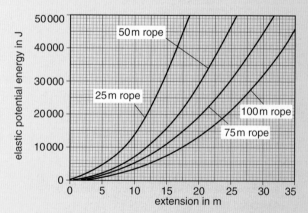

Before she jumps, she does a calculation to check her safety. Her mass is 60 kg. The rope has an **unstretched** length of 50 m.
(a) (i) Calculate the gravitational energy she has lost when the cord just begins to stretch. Use $g = 10$ N/kg.
(ii) State how much kinetic energy she has gained at this point.
(iii) Show, by calculation, that her speed at this point is approximately 32 m/s.
(b) The graph shows how the elastic potential energy of different lengths of bungee rope depends on their extension.

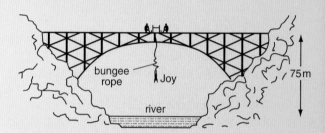

(i) Use the graph to show that Joy will **not** hit the river.
(ii) Neil decided to jump using the 50 m of rope. His mass is 80 kg. Explain why he will be less safe than Joy. There are no marks for calculations.

OCR

118

Matter

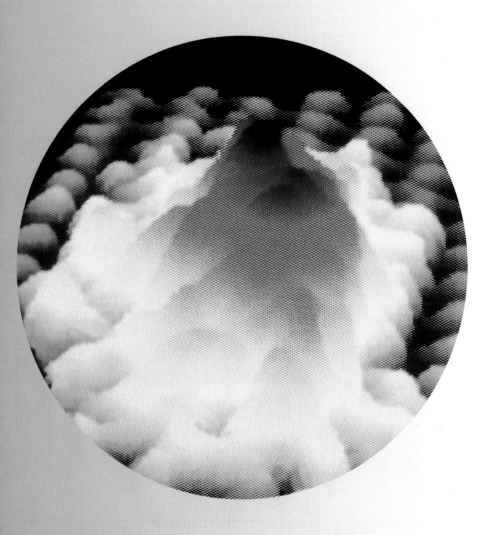

Scanning tunnelling micrograph of gold atoms on a graphite substrate. The gold atoms are shown in red, yellow and brown, while the graphite atoms are in green. The scanning tunnelling microscope uses a fine point electrode which is brought to within about 40 nanometres of the sample's surface. An interaction between the probe and sample produces a current which allows a map like this one to be constructed.

By the end of this section you should:

- understand that all matter is made from atoms
- be familiar with Brownian motion
- know that the particle structures in gases, liquids and solids are different, and know how this accounts for their different properties
- know what happens when a substance is melted or evaporated
- know and understand the three gas laws
- understand how internal combustion engines work

E

Small Particles

http://www.chem4kids.com/
matter/index.html

Everything we touch, swallow and breathe is made out of tiny particles. The smallest particles are **atoms**. There are only about 100 different types of atom. Materials which are made from only one type of atom are called **elements**. For example, aluminium contains only aluminium atoms. Some other common elements are oxygen, hydrogen, nitrogen and carbon.

The small particles in lots of materials are **molecules**. Atoms combine chemically to make molecules. For example, a water molecule is made up of two hydrogen atoms and one oxygen atom, while a carbon dioxide molecule contains one carbon and two oxygen atoms.

Atoms and molecules are far too small for us to see directly. But the photograph shows you some molecules seen through a powerful electron microscope. Electron microscopes show us that oil molecules are about 0.000 000 1 cm (10^{-7} cm) long. That means that 10 000 000 molecules put end to end would be about 1 cm long.

Discovering molecules

The idea that things were made from atoms and molecules was thought of over a hundred years ago, long before electron microscopes were invented. Below are some examples which suggest that matter is made up of small particles. **Matter** is the name which we use to describe all solids, liquids and gases.

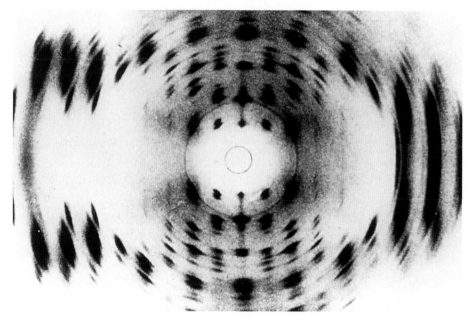

This is an X-ray diffraction photo of DNA. The dark spots are caused by X-rays being diffracted by DNA molecules. A photograph like this one played a vital part in the unravelling of the complex structure of the DNA molecule.

- A male Emperor moth uses his very large antennae to detect the scent of a female. A male Emperor moth can be attracted by the scent of a female at a distance as far as 10 km. The female produces only a small quantity of scent. This suggests that tiny particles of her scent must spread out through the air.
- There is a simple experiment which you can do for yourself, which shows that liquids are also made up of very small particles. You can take a small drop of blue

ink and put it into a glass of water. If you stir the water it will turn a very pale blue. The small particles in the ink have now been spread further apart.

● Growing crystals. Figure 1 shows how you can grow a crystal. You dissolve some copper sulphate in water to make a strong solution. Then a small crystal of copper sulphate is placed in the solution. During a week or so, this crystal grows very slowly into a larger one. This can be explained by saying that the solution contains very small particles of copper sulphate. These particles stick to the crystal so that it grows larger.

Growing a crystal is a bit like making a neat pile of wooden blocks. As another block is added the pile grows. You can see that the shape of a pyramid of blocks is the same as the shape of an alum crystal.

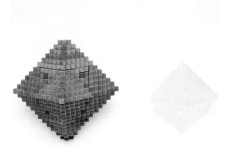

When these wooden blocks are piled together in neat rows, they form a pyramid shape. The shape of the alum crystal on the right suggests that the molecules in it are also stacked neatly in rows.

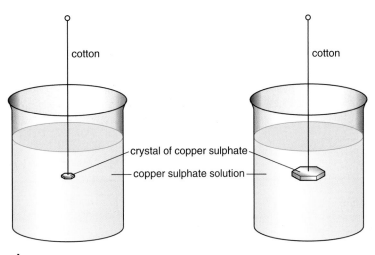

cotton

cotton

crystal of copper sulphate

copper sulphate solution

Figure 1
(a) A small crystal of copper sulphate is placed in a copper sulphate solution

(b) a week later a large crystal has grown

Homework Questions

1 When you cook a curry the smell spreads right through the house. Why does this suggest that the curry powder is made up of small particles?

2 Explain carefully why growing crystals supports the theory that solids are made up of tiny particles.

3 The South American golden dart-poison frog produces the world's most lethal poison, batrachotoxin. Only 0.002 g of this substance is enough to kill an average adult (mass 70 kg).
(a) Work out the lethal dose of this poison per gram of human flesh.

(b) Why do you think that this poison is made up of small particles?

4 In a laboratory experiment a drop of oil, volume 0.5 mm³ is dropped onto the surface of some water covered with a thin powder. The oil spreads, pushing the powder out of the way as shown.
(a) Use the diagram to estimate the area covered by oil in mm².
(b) Now calculate the thickness of the oil in mm.
(c) Explain how this experiment helps to show that oil particles are very small.
(d) Some people claim that the oil

film is only one molecule thick. Do you think this is likely?

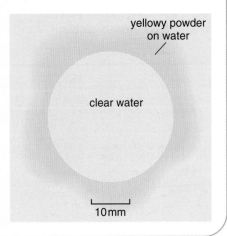

yellowy powder on water

clear water

10 mm

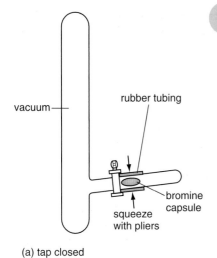

vacuum

rubber tubing

bromine capsule

squeeze with pliers

(a) tap closed

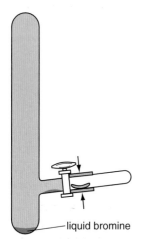

(b) tap open-the tube fills immediately

liquid bromine

Figure 1 *Bromine vapour filling a vacuum*

http://www.phy.ntnu.edu.tw/java/idealGas/idealGas.html

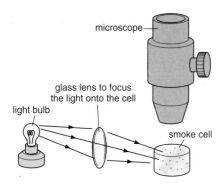

microscope

glass lens to focus the light onto the cell

light bulb

smoke cell

Figure 4

Diffusion

In the last unit you read how a male Emperor moth can detect a female moth's scent at a great distance. This supports the idea that the scent is made up of molecules and also the idea that the molecules in a gas are moving. Here are some simple experiments to show you more about the movement of molecules. In Figure 1 you can see a long tube with all the air pumped out of it. It is closed with a tap. On the other side of the tap is attached a small capsule of bromine inside some rubber tubing. The capsule is broken and then the tap is opened. As soon as the tap is opened the bromine vapour fills the long tube. This tells us that the bromine molecules are moving quickly. They are actually moving at a speed of about 200 m/s.

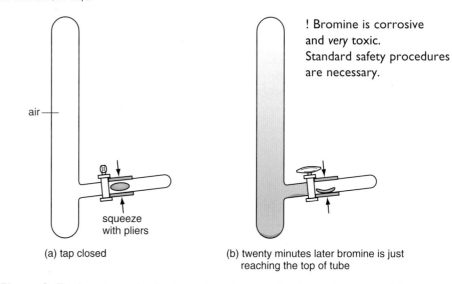

air

squeeze with pliers

(a) tap closed

! Bromine is corrosive and *very* toxic. Standard safety procedures are necessary.

(b) twenty minutes later bromine is just reaching the top of tube

Figure 2 *The bromine molecules bump into the air molecules, and are slowed down*

Figure 2 shows what happens when the experiment is repeated with air inside. This time when the tap is opened the bromine does not fill the tube quickly. After about 20 minutes the bottom half of the tube is coloured dark brown, but the top is only light brown. So although the bromine molecules travel very quickly it takes a long time for them to reach the top.

The reason for this is that the air molecules are also moving quickly. The air molecules get in the way of the bromine molecules. When two molecules bump into each other they change direction. The bromine molecules keep changing direction and so take a long time to reach the top.

This process of one substance spreading through another is called **diffusion.**

Diffusion also occurs in liquids, but only very slowly in solids. Diffusion is very important for all living things. When animals have eaten a meal, food is digested

Figure 3 *Place some ink in a glass of water. After an hour or so the water is a light blue colour. Diffusion works more slowly in liquids, which suggests that molecules move more slowly in liquids than in gases.*

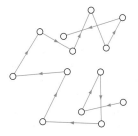

Figure 5 *The path of a smoke particle as seen through the microscope*

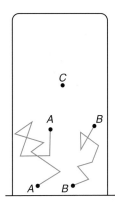

Figure 6

and diffuses into the blood. Blood then carries the food all round the body. Plants need nitrogen, potassium, phosphorus and other elements. These diffuse through the soil to the plants' roots.

Brownian motion

Robert Brown, a botanist, looked through his microscope at some grains of pollen which were in water. He noticed that the grains of pollen were moving around randomly. They jiggled from side to side.

You can see the same sort of **Brownian motion** if you look through a microscope at smoke particles. Figure 4 shows a typical experimental arrangement. A small puff of smoke is put into a smoke cell under the microscope. Light from a small bulb shines onto the cell. The smoke particles show up as tiny specks of light through the microscope. Figure 5 shows the sort of path a smoke particle follows.

The smoke particles move randomly because they are always being knocked by air molecules. These air molecules are too small to see through the microscope, but they are moving so quickly that they can deflect a much larger smoke particle.

Homework Questions

1 Figure 6 shows two bromine molecules moving in a jar full of air. Both molecules reach the top after a while.
(a) Copy the diagram and complete the paths of *A* and *B*, to show how they reached the top.
(b) Explain why bromine molecules move in this way.
(c) Further up the jar is molecule *C*. Will it reach the top before *A* and *B*?
2 (a) Describe how you would set up an experiment to observe Brownian motion.
(b) What do you see in this experiment?
(c) What evidence does Brownian motion provide for the existence of molecules?
(d) Sometimes when you are looking at a smoke particle through a microscope it suddenly disappears. Why is this?

3 When molecules are warmed up they travel faster. Explain what effect a high temperature would have on
(a) the motion of smoke particles in a smoke cell,
(b) the rate at which gases diffuse.
4 (a) Explain what diffusion is.
(b) Why does diffusion take so long, even though molecules travel at high speeds such as 200 m/s?
5 Below, you can see some data collected in a series of experiments on diffusion. An approximate time for different gases to diffuse through a distance of 10 cm is recorded.

The temperature of the gases in all experiments was 20°C. The purpose of the experiments was to study how the rate of diffusion of a molecule depends on its mass.
(a) Plot a graph of the time of diffusion (*y*-axis) against the relative mass of the molecule (*x*-axis).
(b) Ammonia has a relative molecular mass of 17. Use your graph to predict how long, on average, ammonia molecules will take to diffuse 10 cm through air.
(c) What conclusion can you draw about the relationship between speed and mass of a gas molecule at 20°C?

Substance	Relative molecular mass	Time to diffuse 10 cm through air (s)
Hydrogen	2	30
Carbon dioxide	44	160
Chlorine	71	200
Bromine	160	300
Iodine vapour	254	380

Water appears in different forms ... ice

... water ...

**http://comp.uark.edu/
~jgeabana/mol_dyn/**

When something is moving it has **kinetic energy**. In the last unit you met the idea that molecules are always on the move.

This idea is called the **kinetic theory**. The most important points in the theory are:

● Every kind of material is made of small particles (molecules or atoms).
● The sizes of particles are different for different materials.
● The particles themselves are very hard. They cannot be squashed or stretched, but the distance beween particles can change.
● The particles are always moving. The higher the temperature of a substance, the faster its particles move.
● At the same temperature all particles have the same energy. So heavy particles will move slowly and light particles will move quickly.

The last point helps to explain why hydrogen can diffuse through air much more quickly than bromine.

Solids, liquids and gases

Ice, water and steam are three different states of the same material. We call these three states solid, liquid and gas. You will now see how kinetic theory helps us to understand them.

● **Solid**. In a solid the particles are packed into rows just like apples or oranges stacked in shops (Figure 1(a)). The particles can never move out of their rows, but they vibrate around their fixed positions. As the temperature of a solid is raised the particles vibrate more and the material expands. This means that the distance between particles has increased a little.

In a solid the particles are very close to each other and held in position by very strong forces. This makes it very difficult to change the shape of a solid by squashing it or pulling it.
● **Liquid**. In a liquid the particles are still very close to each other, which means that liquids are also very difficult to compress (Figure 1(b)). The particles can now move around from place to place. A liquid can change shape to fit into any container, but its volume will remain constant at a given temperature. As a liquid warms it also expands a little, due to its particles vibrating more.

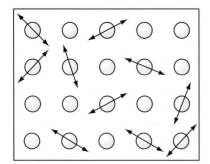

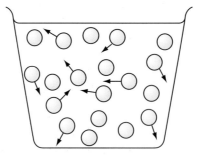

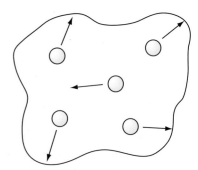

Figure 1
(a) Particles in a solid are arranged in neat rows. The particles can vibrate but do not leave their positions in the rows

(b) Particles in a liquid are close together, but free to move around

(c) Gas molecules are free to move into any available space. They move quickly and there are large distances between them

http://www.phy.ntnu.edu.tw/java/idealGas/idealGas.html

... vapour and steam. Geysers are formed when water deep in the Earth is heated under pressure. The water finds a route to the surface and boils to form a jet sometimes as much as 70 metres high.

● **Gas**. In a gas the particles are separated by big distances (Figure 1(c)). The forces between gas particles are very small. It is easy to compress a gas because there is so much space between the particles. The gas particles are in a constant state of rapid random motion. This makes a gas expand to fill any available space.

Gas pressure

A gas in a container exerts a pressure on the container walls. This is because the gas particles are always hitting the walls. The pressure caused by the gas depends on:

● The number of collisions that the particles have with the container walls per second.
● How hard the particles hit the walls.

The pressure inside a container of gas can be increased in three ways:

● Putting more molecules in the container. The number of collisions that the molecules make with the walls each second is now larger.
● Making the volume of the container smaller. The same number of molecules make more collisions with the walls, because they travel less distance between collisions.
● Heating the container. The molecules travel faster and they now hit the container walls harder and more often.

Homework Questions

1 Use the kinetic theory to help you explain the following:
(a) Some solids, like metals, are very stiff and difficult to bend.
(b) A liquid can be poured.
(c) If a gas pipe has a small hole in it, gas will escape from the pipe and you will be able to smell it a few metres away from the leak.

2 A bottle of air is sealed at room temperature and atmospheric pressure. The bottle is now placed in a refrigerator. Which of the following statements about the air in the bottle is correct?
(i) The average kinetic energy of the molecules has reduced.
(ii) The molecules are moving more slowly than at room temperature.
(iii) The molecules hit the wall of the container less often than before.
(iv) The molecules hit the walls with less force.
(v) There are fewer molecules in

the bottle than at room temperature.

3 (a) Explain, in terms of molecules, how a gas exerts a pressure on the walls of its container.
(b) The air inside an old syrup tin is heated with a Bunsen burner. The lid is pressed firmly on. Explain why the pressure inside the tin increases.
(c) If the tin is heated enough the lid flies off. Explain why.
(d) The experiment is now repeated, but with a small amount of water placed in the tin. Explain why the lid flies off at lower temperature.

4 The data in the table shows how the pressure in a gas cylinder varies with the mass of the cylinder.
(a) Plot a graph of pressure (*y*-axis) against mass (*x*-axis).
(b) Use the graph to determine the mass of the empty gas cylinder.
(c) The greatest pressure the cylinder can take safely is 20×10^5 Pa.

What will the mass of the cylinder be then?

Mass of cylinder (kg)	Pressure in the cylinder (Pa $\times$ 10⁵)
8.7	1.5
9.0	2.7
9.6	5.0
10.2	7.3

5 Describe carefully the differences between solids, liquids and gases in terms of:
(a) how the molecules are arranged in the material,
(b) how the molecules move,
(c) the separation of the molecules.

6 Explain in terms of molecular motion, why the pressure in a gas decreases if the gas is allowed to expand into a larger volume (without changing its temperature).

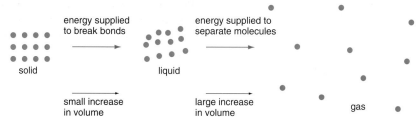

Figure 1

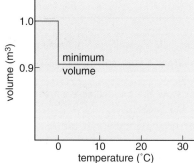

Changing solid to liquid

When a solid is heated the molecules inside it vibrate more and more quickly. If enough heat is supplied the molecules will break away from their fixed positions and start to move around. The solid has melted. The temperature at which this change happens is called the **melting point** of the material (Figure 1).

Most materials expand when they melt, because molecules are a little further apart in the liquid state. Figure 2 shows how we can use this in a greenhouse. A cylinder is filled with wax which melts at about 25°C. When air in the greenhouse reaches this temperature the wax melts and expands. This pushes the window open. This automatic window opener prevents damage to crops due to overheating.

Water is an unusual substance because it expands when it freezes (see Figure 3). Water is at its most dense at 4°C, so when a pond freezes over there is a layer of dense water at 4°C at the bottom. Ice is less dense than water which is why we see ice on the surface of ponds.

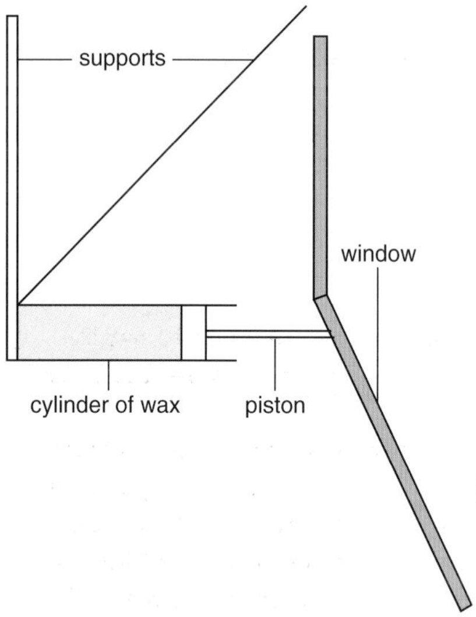

Figure 2 *Automatic window opener*

Changing the melting point

The expansion of water on freezing can be a nuisance. It causes pipes to burst in houses or in cars. To prevent freezing in car cooling systems, drivers add antifreeze. This lowers the melting point of water. When salt is added to water the melting point is lowered. This is why salt is put onto our roads in winter.

The melting point of ice can also be lowered a little by applying very large pressure to it. An extra pressure equal to that of the atmosphere will lower the melting point of ice by about 0.01°C.

Evaporation

As a liquid warms up, the average speed of the molecules in it gets larger. However, not all of the molecules in the liquid will be travelling at the same speed. Figure 4 shows that some will be travelling slowly and some more quickly. Some molecules near to the surface of the liquid have enough energy to escape. They evaporate from the liquid to form a vapour (water in the gaseous state). Evaporation from the surface of a liquid can happen at any temperature. But as the temperature gets higher more molecules have enough energy to escape. So evaporation happens at a faster rate.

Eventually the temperature rises to the **boiling point** of the liquid. At this point, evaporation also happens inside the liquid. Bubbles of vapour form inside the liquid and rise to the surface. Heat applied to a boiling liquid gives the molecules enough energy to evaporate.

Figure 3 *Volume changes on freezing for water*

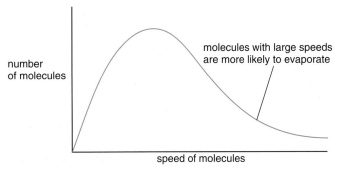

Evaporation causes cooling. This is because it is the faster (hotter) molecules which escape, leaving behind the slower (colder) molecules. The evaporation of sweat from your skin keeps you cool on a hot day. But the evaporation of water from us can also be very dangerous. You can lose heat from your body very rapidly in wet and windy conditions.

This wine cooler has been soaked in water before the wine bottle was placed in it. Evaporation of the water through the porous pot takes heat away from the wine and keeps it cool

number of molecules

molecules with large speeds are more likely to evaporate

speed of molecules

Figure 4 *The molecules in a liquid do not all travel at the same speed*

Homework Questions

1 (a) Why do you hang out washing, rather than leaving it in a pile to dry?
(b) Why does washing dry faster on warm, windy days?
(c) Why does the amount of water in the atmosphere (humidity) affect the drying rate?

2 Use Figure 3 to help you sketch a graph of the way in which the density of water changes as it freezes.

3 Explain why a saucepan will come to the boil more quickly if it is covered by a lid.

4 This question is about the water cycle – how water is carried from the sea, to fall as rain, before returning to the sea again.
(a) At A in the diagram sunlight causes water to *evaporate*; explain carefully what the italicised word means.

(b) At B water vapour has *condensed* to form clouds or water droplets. Explain the difference between water *vapour* and water *droplets*. What is meant by condensation?
(c) What is meant by a *prevailing wind*?
(d) At C the clouds rise as they approach a mountain: explain what happens to the temperature of the

air, and then why rain falls at D.
(e) How does rainwater return to the sea?
(f) When air approaches us from the South Atlantic, we experience Tropical Maritime weather; when air approaches us from Africa, we experience Tropical Continental weather. Explain what conditions to expect from these two types of weather.

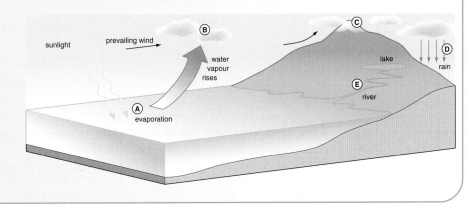

Changing boiling points

When water boils, bubbles of water vapour form inside the liquid. The pressure inside these bubbles is equal to the pressure of the air above the water. So when the air pressure changes the water boils at a different temperature. If the air pressure is greater than 1 atmosphere, water boils above 100°C; if the pressure is lower than 1 atmosphere, water boils below 100°C.

Figure 1 shows a graph of how the boiling point of water changes with pressure. You would notice this effect if you lived somewhere like Mexico City, which is 3000 m above sea level. The air pressure there is only about 0.7 atmospheres, and water boils at 90°C. At the top of Mount Everest, 9000 m above sea level, a kettle would boil at only 70°C.

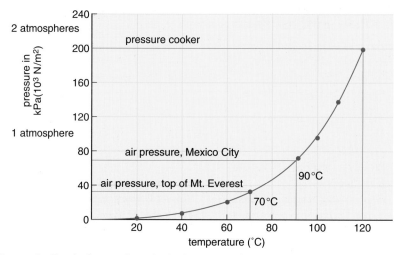

Figure 1 *Graph showing how the boiling point of water changes with pressure*

In a pressure cooker the air pressure is increased to about 2 atmospheres. The cooker has an airtight lid except for a small hole at the top. Weights are put on top of this hole so that the air pressure inside must be greater than atmospheric pressure before steam will escape. The advantage of cooking at high pressure is that the boiling point of water is raised and cooking times are considerably reduced (Figure 2, Figure 3).

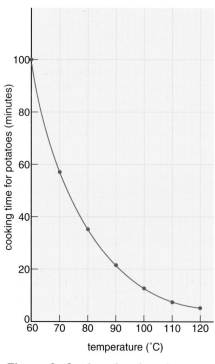

Figure 2 *Graph to show how the cooking time for potatoes decreases as the temperature is raised*

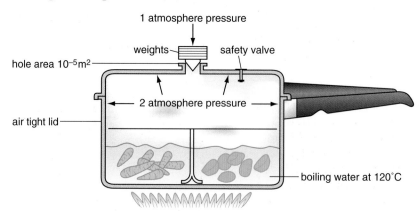

Figure 3 *A pressure cooker*

Homework Questions

1 When salt is added to water, its boiling point is increased. You often add salt to water when you cook vegetables. Does this make the vegetables cook more slowly or more quickly?

2 (a) The area of the hole in the top of the pressure cooker in Figure 4 is 10^{-5} m. What weight must be put on top of the hole to keep the pressure inside the cooker at 2 atmospheres (2×10^5 N/m²)? Remember the pressure outside is 1 atmosphere.
(b) What is the pressure inside the cooker when a weight of 0.5 N is used?

3 This question is about the time taken to cook your potatoes as you climb Mount Everest. The higher you get the longer it takes.
(a) Table 1 shows you how the air pressure drops as you climb up the mountain. Copy the table and then use Figure 1 to fill in the column of boiling points.
(b) Use Figure 2 to fill in the column for cooking times.
(c) Now plot a graph to show how your cooking times (y-axis) change with your height above sea level (x-axis).
(d) Use your graph to predict cooking times at (i) 5000 m (ii) 8500 m.
(e) Would your cooking times have changed so much if you used a pressure cooker to cook your potatoes? Explain your answer carefully.
(f) Calculate the cooking time for your potatoes at a height of 8000 m, when you use the pressure cooker (Figure 3) with a weight of 1 N.

Refrigeration

When you go to the doctor for an injection, your arm gets cleaned with some alcohol. This evaporates quickly making your arm cold. A refrigerator in your kitchen cools your food in a similar way.

Figure 4 shows a refrigerator. The cooling in a refrigerator is done by chemicals called freons, which boil at low temperatures (about −30°C). The cooling in the refrigerator occurs in the ice box where boiling freons evaporate. The freons evaporate because they absorb heat energy from the contents of the refrigerator. The freon gas then reaches the compressor which squashes the gas to a high pressure. The compression also warms the gas. From here the freon gas passes through a condensor, which cools the gas down. The gas turns back into liquid freons as it cools.

On the back of your refrigerator you will see cooling fins which cool the liquid back to room temperature. Then the freon is allowed to expand, further reducing its temperature and pressure. The freon now passes through the ice box to start the cooling cycle again.

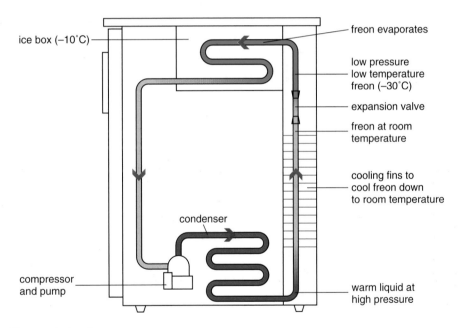

Figure 4 *A refrigerator*

Height above sea level (m)	Air pressure kPa (10^3 N/m²)	Boiling point of water (°C)	Cooking time for potatoes (minutes)
0	100	100	14
2000	79		
4000	62		
6000	47		
8000	36		

Table 1

Boyle's Law

Figure 1 shows a cylinder and piston. The pressure of the air in the cylinder can be changed by moving the piston up and down. Provided the piston is moved slowly the temperature of the gas stays the same. This apparatus can be used to see how the pressure, P, changes as the volume, V, of the air is increased or decreased (Figure 2).

Table 1 shows the sort of results you can get if you do the experiment. When the gas is compressed to half its volume the pressure is doubled. We say that the pressure of the gas is *inversely proportional* to its volume:

$$P \propto \frac{1}{V}$$

The table of results also shows that when you multiply together the pressure and volume, you always get the same number. (What is it in this example?)
When the mass of a gas stays the same, and its temperature does not change:

$$P \times V = \text{constant} \quad \text{This is } \textbf{Boyle's law}$$

Pressure (atmospheres)	Volume of air (l)	$\frac{1}{V}(l^{-1})$
0.5	2.0	0.5
1.0	1.0	1.0
2.0	0.5	2.0
4.0	0.25	4.0
10.0	0.1	10.0

Table 1

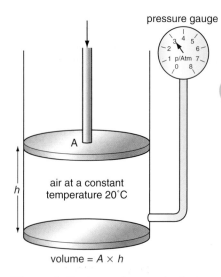

Figure 1 *Testing a piston and cylinder*

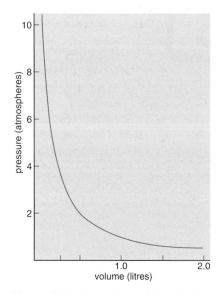

Figure 2 *As the volume of the gas is halved, the pressure doubles*

Law of pressures

Figure 3 shows you the same apparatus, placed in a large tank of water. This time the volume of the gas is kept constant. The pressure is measured at a lot of different temperatures.

The results of such an experiment are shown in Figure 4. As the temperature, T, is raised from 0°C to 100°C the pressure rises steadily from 1 to about 1.4 atmospheres. We can draw a straight line through these results. If this line is extended below 0°C you can predict what will happen to the pressure at lower temperatures. You can see that the pressure will be about 0.5 atmospheres at −136°C. At a temperature of −273°C the pressure due to the gas is nothing.

A gas exerts a pressure on the walls of its container because of its moving molecules. If a gas no longer exerts a pressure it is because the molecules have stopped moving. This means that −273°C is the lowest possible temperature. At that temperature molecules have stopped moving so we cannot cool them any further. We call −273°C **absolute zero**.

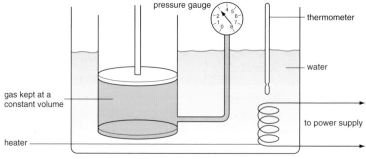

Figure 3

Absolute temperatures are measured in *degrees Kelvin*, or K. Absolute zero is 0 K and 0°C is 273 K. The size of 1 degree Kelvin is the same size as 1°C. Notice that no degree sign is used with degrees Kelvin. We write 77 K, *not* 77°K.

Figure 4 shows that the pressure of a gas is proportional to its absolute temperature, provided its volume stays the same:

$$P \propto T \quad \text{This is the } \textbf{law of pressures}$$

Charles' Law

The apparatus shown in Figure 3 can be used for a third experiment. The pressure of the gas is now kept constant. The gas is allowed to expand when it is heated.

Experimental results show that the volume of the gas is proportional to its absolute temperature, provided its pressure remains the same:

$$V \propto T \quad \text{This is } \textbf{Charles' law.}$$

http://library.thinkquest.org/12596/

Gas equation

The three gas laws may be combined into one equation, which holds true for a fixed mass of gas:

$$\frac{PV}{T} = \text{constant}$$

Example. A cylinder of gas of volume 1 m³ is initially at a temperature of 300 K and a pressure of 2 atmospheres. It is compressed to a volume of 0.5 m³ and warmed to a temperature of 450 K. What is the pressure of the gas now?

$$\frac{P_1 V_1}{T_1} = \frac{P_2 V_2}{T_2}$$

$$\text{So} \quad \frac{2 \times 1}{300} = \frac{P \times 0.5}{450}$$

$$P = 6 \text{ atmospheres}$$

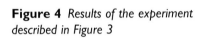

Figure 4 *Results of the experiment described in Figure 3*

Homework Questions

1 This question refers to the experiment shown in Figure 1.
(a) Use Table 1 or Figure 2 to work out the volume of the air when the pressure was:
(i) 3 atmospheres,
(ii) 8 atmospheres
(b) Use the data to plot a graph of the pressure, P, against the reciprocal of the volume, $1/V$.
(c) A student took a measure of the volume and pressure and recorded 0.16 litres and 7.0 atmospheres. Plot this point on your graph. The student made an error in measuring the pressure. Suggest what the value should have been.

2 (a) Explain what is meant by absolute zero.
(b) Why is it not possible to have a temperature of −300°C?

3 (a) Convert these temperatures to

degrees Kelvin: 100°C, 327°C, −173°C, −50°C.
(b) Convert these absolute temperatures to °C; 10 K, 150 K, 350 K, 400 K.

4 This question refers to the experiment described in Figure 3.
(a) Use the graph in Figure 4 to predict the pressure in the cylinder at:
(i) a temperature of 150 K,
(ii) a temperature of 100°C.
(b) What will the pressure in the cylinder be at 600 K?

5 The diagram (right) shows a gas storage vessel of volume 160 000 m³. The pressure in the main gas grid pipelines is about 800 kPa. In the storage vessel the pressure is just greater than 100 kPa (atmospheric pressure). Calculate the volume of gas from the grid

pipelines required to fill the gas storage vessel.

6 An airtight cylinder of gas has a volume of 0.4 m³ and pressure of 2 atmospheres at a temperature of 20°C.
(a) The cylinder expands to a volume of 1 m³ without changing its temperature. What is the pressure in the cylinder now?
(b) The cylinder is then warmed to a temperature of 100°C, without changing the volume. What is the pressure after heating the cylinder?

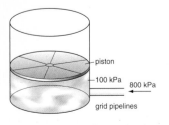

Petrol engines

If you put your finger over the end of a bicycle pump, and pump the piston up and down a few times, you find that the air inside the cylinder gets hot. As the piston moves it collides with moving molecules. The molecules rebound off the moving piston at a greater speed. This means the gas gets hotter. The pressure inside the bicycle pump cylinder increases because the air has been compressed, and then this compression warms the air up. If you compress the air slowly the temperature will stay the same because heat will escape through the sides of the cylinder (Figure 1).

Figure 2 shows how the idea is used in a **four-stroke petrol engine**.

1 On the **intake** stroke a petrol vapour and air mixture is fed into the cylinder.

2 On the **compression** stroke both the inlet and exhaust valves are closed. The piston moves up rapidly to compress the air/petrol mixture to about 1⁄10 of its original volume; the *compression ratio* is 10:1. The pressure inside the cylinder will now be about 20 atmospheres (2 MPa) and the temperature about 350°C.

3 The **working** stroke. Once the gas has been compressed the sparking plug produces a spark which starts the fuel burning. The temperature in the cylinder now rises to about 1000°C and the pressure rises to about 50 atmospheres (5 MPa). The higher pressure now forces the piston back. Although energy is used to squash the gas during the compression stroke, the working stroke gives far more energy.

4 In the **exhaust** stroke, the exhaust valve opens to allow the high pressure gases to escape.

Most cars have four **cylinders** using a four-stroke cycle. The cylinders are arranged so that they take turns in performing one of the four strokes (Figure 3). At any instant, one of the cylinders will be producing power. A car with only one cylinder would produce a very jerky ride.

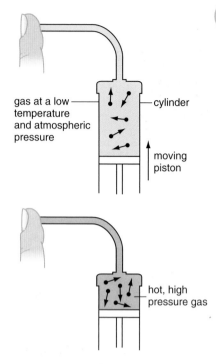

Figure 1 *Heating air up in a bicycle pump*

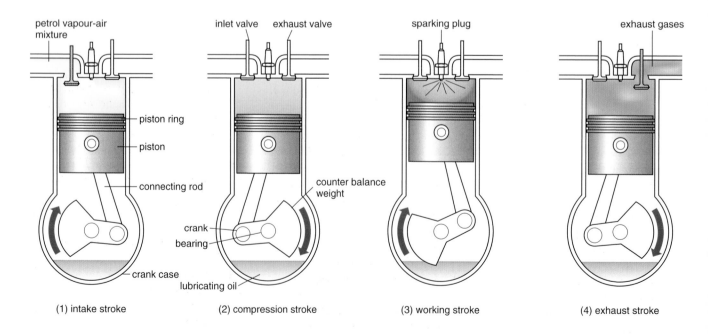

(1) intake stroke   (2) compression stroke   (3) working stroke   (4) exhaust stroke

Figure 2 *The four-stroke petrol engine*

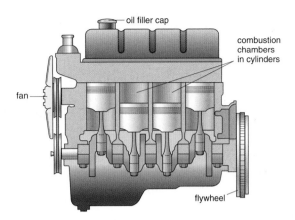

Figure 3 *A car engine cut away to show its four cylinders*

oil filler cap

combustion chambers in cylinders

fan

flywheel

Diesel engines

A four-stroke diesel engine works in a similar way to the petrol engine you have just read about. The differences are these:

http://www.howstuffworks. com/engine1.htm

- During the intake stroke only air is taken into the cylinder.
- The compression ratio of diesel engines is higher than that of petrol engines. At the end of the compression stroke the air has been squashed to about ⅟₂₀ of its original volume. At this point the temperature of the air is about 700°C, and its pressure is about 35 atmospheres (3.5 MPa).
- The diesel engine has no sparking plug. At the end of the compression stroke fuel is forced into the cylinder under high pressure. The temperature of the air is so hot that the fuel burns as soon as it has mixed into the air. When the fuel burns, the temperature inside the cylinder reaches about 2500°C and the pressure is about 100 atmospheres (10 MPa)
- Such an engine using diesel oil has a higher **efficiency** than a petrol engine.

Homework Questions

1. What is meant by the term 'compression ratio'?
2. At the beginning of the working stroke in a petrol engine the pressure in a cylinder is 5 MPa (5×10^6 N/m²). The area of the piston is 0.008 m².
   (a) Calculate the force acting on the piston.
   (b) Explain why cylinders and pistons in a petrol engine have to be well built. Why do they have to be even stronger in a diesel engine?
3. Why does a diesel engine not have a sparking plug?
4. Why do most cars have four cylinders?
5. (a) You were told in the text that

diesel engines have higher efficiencies than petrol engines. What does that mean?
(b) Use the data opposite to work out the cost of fuel to drive:
(i) a petrol-driven car 10 000 km,
(ii) a diesel-driven car 10 000 km.
(c) How far do you have to drive a diesel-fuelled car before you have recovered the extra cost of its engine?
(d) If you were buying a car which sort of engine would you choose?

6. A cylinder of air, initially at a temperature of 27°C and at atmospheric pressure 0.1 MPa, is squashed so that it occupies ⅟₁₅ of

its original volume. After being squashed, its temperature reaches 207°C. Calculate the new pressure in the cylinder.

- cost of diesel engine: £2000
- cost of petrol engine: £1300
- 1 litre of petrol will take the car 10 km
- 1 litre of diesel oil will take the car 14 km
- unleaded petrol costs 84p per litre
- diesel costs 85p per litre
- cars with diesel engines are noisier and more sluggish than petrol driven cars

SECTION E: Questions

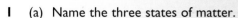

1 (a) Name the three states of matter.
(b) Suppose a substance changes from one state to another without decomposing. In which state of matter would you expect the substance to be (i) most dense, (ii) least dense, (iii) most compressible? Give reasons for your answers.
(c) There are exceptions to these generalisations, e.g. water. Water behaves differently because of 'hydrogen bonding'. In what way does the behaviour of water differ?
(d) In which of the three states of matter would you expect the particles of a substance to be:
(i) most ordered?
(ii) least ordered?
(iii) moving around freely in all directions?
(iv) vibrating to and fro about fixed positions?
(e) The ability of atoms and molecules to attract each other does not vanish when a solid substance becomes a gas. Explain why the molecules of the substance in the gaseous state are no longer held together, as they are in the solid state.

2 (a) How does increasing the temperature of a solid substance affect the way its atoms or molecules vibrate?
(b) The diagram represents some translating atoms, or molecules, of a substance in the gaseous state, at two different temperatures. In which diagram is the gas (i) hottest, (ii) coldest? How can you tell?

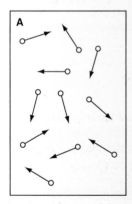 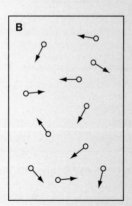

(c) Explain the terms *vibrating* and *translating*. Explain why we should use the word *average* when describing molecular motion.

3 The next diagram demonstrates an experiment which provides evidence of molecular motion. A small trace of smoke is drawn into a transparent container of air. The container is lit from the side and its contents are viewed using a low powered microscope. The smoke particles can be seen to move in a haphazard manner. This effect is called **Brownian motion**.
(a) Why don't the smoke particles fall to the bottom of the container?

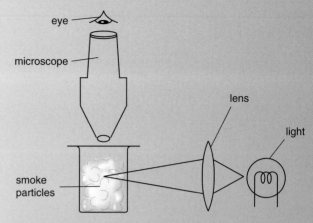

(b) Using arrows, sketch the magnified motion of a single smoke particle.
(c) Air molecules are much smaller than smoke particles and cannot be seen through the microscope. Explain how this demonstration provides evidence of their existence, and of their motion.

4 Explain the following in terms of 'molecules in motion'.
(a) When bromine is introduced into a vessel containing air, the bromine spreads out very slowly. However, if the vessel has been evacuated first, it fills with bromine very quickly.
(b) At room temperature air molecules and vapour molecules move about at very high speeds. Why do smells (vapour molecules) travel across a room very slowly?
(c) An iron bar expands when it is heated.
(d) Air trapped in a corked bottle left in strong sunlight, results in the cork blowing out.
(e) The effect described in part (d) is far more dramatic if a little wine is left in the bottle.
(f) Clothes hung on a line to dry, dry more quickly in a breeze, than in still air.
(g) If some ether is placed in a beaker and allowed to evaporate, the ether remaining in the beaker *cools*.

5 The piston for a bicycle pump is pushed in slowly until the air pressure inside the pump *trebles*. The air in the pump remains at a constant temperature of 20 °C.
(a) Describe the motion of the air molecules in the pump.

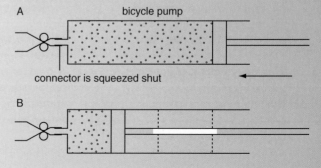

(b) Explain in terms of molecular motion why the pressure in B should be three times greater than in A.

(c) Moving the piston in very slowly ensures that the enclosed air remains at the same temperature. Why? What does this tell you about he average speed of the molecules before and after compression?

(d) What would have happened if the piston had been pushed in quickly?

(e) Explain in terms of molecular motion, why heating the enclosed air increases the pressure it exerts.

6 Smoke particles in air are seen through a microscope. The smoke particles move and make frequent changes in direction because they
A repel each other.
B attract each other.
C are able to move themselves.
D are colliding with each other.
E are colliding with invisible air particles.

OCR (MEG)

7 (a) In this diagram the bottom circle represents the molecules in the liquid. Copy and complete the top circle to represent the molecules in the gas.

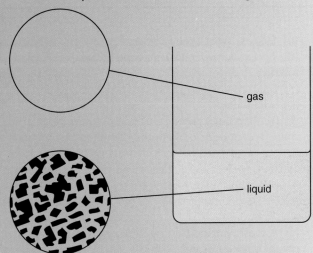

gas

liquid

(b) With reference to the diagram explain why gases can be compressed easily but liquids cannot.

(c) Brownian motion is usually shown in a school laboratory by looking at smoke specks under a microscope.

(i) Describe the motion of the smoke specks.

(ii) What causes this motion?

Edexcel (ULEAC)

8 A drop of oil, of volume 0.4 mm³, was placed on a water surface and spread out to a maximum area of 1200 mm². Assuming the oil patch was one molecule thick, what is the best estimate of the diameter of an oil molecule, in mm?

A 0.000 04   B 0.000 08   C 0.000 012
D 0.000 33   E 0.000 48

AQA (NEAB)

9 Which one of the following will cause the boiling point of water to rise?
A Reducing the pressure over the surface of the water.
B Dissolving some salt in the water.
C Boiling the water faster by increasing the supply of heat.
D Using an immersion heater instead of an external supply of heat.
E Boiling the water at a greater height above sea level.

AQA (NEAB)

10 The Kinetic Theory assumes that gases are made of rapidly moving molecules. Which of the following facts does **not** support the idea that gas molecules are moving?
A A tiny smoke particle undergoes 'Brownian Motion' when in a gas.
B Gases exert a pressure on the walls of their containers.
C Gases have lower densities than solids and liquids.
D When placed together, two gases will diffuse into each other.
E When released into an empty container, a gas will rapidly fill it.

OCR (MEG)

11 The two strokes of a four-stroke engine cycle during which only **one** valve is open are
A induction and compression.
B compression and exhaust.
C induction and exhaust.
D compression and power.

AQA (SEG)

12 When a drop of ether is put onto the skin, the skin feels cold. This is because
A liquids like ether are poor conductors of heat.
B ether is a good conductor of heat.
C the ether is an anaesthetic.
D the ether evaporates by taking heat from the skin.
E heat cannot reach the skin through the ether.

AQA (NEAB)

13 A sealed can contains air. If the can is heated the pressure of the air inside the can increases. Which of the following statements best describes why the pressure increases?
A When heated, air molecules expand and press harder on the can.
B More air molecules are created and so more molecules press on the can.
C When heated, air molecules slow down and

collide less frequently with the can.

D Air molecules are attracted to the heated sides of the can.

E When heated, air molecules move faster and collide with the can more often.

Edexcel (ULEAC)

14 At the beginning of the compression stroke in the cylinder of a diesel engine, the air is at a temperature of 127°C, at a pressure of 0.1 MPa. During the compression stroke, the volume of the air is squashed to $\frac{1}{20}$th of its original volume, and its temperature rises to 727°C. What is the pressure in the cylinder at the end of the stroke?

AQA (NEAB)

15 The diagram shows Boris in a diving bell. He is just about to explore the depths of the black lagoon. As the bell is lowered into the sea, water rises to fill the bell.

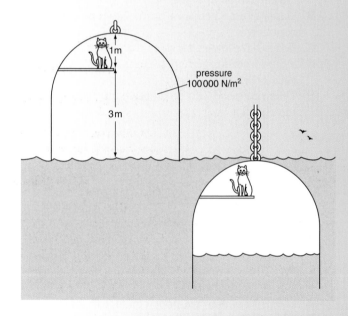

(a) Explain why water starts to fill the bell as it is lowered.

(b) the pressure below the surface of the sea is given by the formula: $P = (100\,000 + 10\,000\,d)$ N/m²; d is the depth below the surface in metres. What is the pressure of air in the diving bell at a depth of 10 m?

(d) How deep can the bell go, before Boris gets his feet wet?

16 A petrol engine repeats the same sequence of four strokes continuously. Each stroke involves the following parts of the engine: *inlet valve, outlet valve,* and *piston.* The *spark plug* produces the spark needed

to ignite (set fire to) the fuel. The diagrams on page 132 show the sequence of the four strokes. Use them to help you to answer the questions which follow.

(a) Copy and complete the table below to show the sequence of events during the four strokes.

Stroke number	1	2	3	4
Direction piston is moving (*up* or *down*)	down			up
Inlet valve position (*open* or *closed*)			closed	closed
Outlet valve position (*open* or *closed*)			closed	closed

(b) (i) In which stroke does air and petrol *enter* the cylinder?

(ii) In which stroke do the exhaust gases *leave* the cylinder?

(c) (i) Copy this flow chart. Complete the boxes to show the main types of energy transferred in the engine.

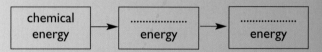

chemical energy → .... energy → .... energy

(ii) Suggest what type of energy provides the spark.

(d) (i) Explain why air is needed as part of the fuel mixture.

(ii) Explain why it is important that the fuel and air are well mixed.

(e) (i) Petrol is a mixture of compounds. Most of these compounds contain the elements carbon and hydrogen and are called hydrocarbons. Suggest two substances which are likely to be produced when a hydrocarbon burns in oxygen.

(ii) What process in living organisms is similar to this reaction?

(f) A diesel engine has the same moving parts as a petrol engine but differs in the way it works. Some of these differences are given in the table.

	Type of engine	
	Petrol	Diesel
fuel	petrol	diesel
greatest pressure just before fuel ignites	about 900 KPa	about 2200 KPa
spark needed	yes	no
efficiency	24%	40%

(i) In both types of engine the temperature of the gas mixture in the cylinder increases as the piston moves

upwards with both valves closed. Use your understanding of particles to explain why this increase in temperature happens.
(ii) In which type of engine will this increase in temperature be greater?
(iii) Suggest and explain one important difference between the general structure of the two engines.
(iv) Explain what is meant by saying that the petrol engine is *24% efficient*.
(v) Explain what happens to the remaining 76% of the energy.

AQA (SEG)

17 Which substance is a liquid at room temperature?

Substance	melting point (°C)	boiling point (°C)
A	−218	−183
B	−39	357
C	44	280
D	119	444
E	1038	2336

OCR (MEG)

18 The diagram shows some bubbles rising in a glass of a fizzy drink. Can you explain why the bubbles get larger as they rise to the surface?

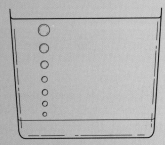

19 The next picture shows part of a chemical works in which a tanker is being filled with a chemical. The chemical is normally a gas. It is invisible, has no smell and is heavier than air. It is a non-ionic compound which is non-flammable and non-toxic.
(a) What is the *name* of the chemical?
(b) If there is a leak of the chemical, which worker will be *most* affected? Give **two** reasons for your answer.
(c) The same chemical can be used in fire extinguishers designed to put out fires involving live electrical equipment.
(i) Suggest and explain **one** reason for this.
(ii) Explain why water is unsuitable for this type of fire.
(d) Although the chemical in the tank is normally a gas, it is stored and transported as a liquid. This is because each kilogram of the chemical takes up far less space as a liquid.

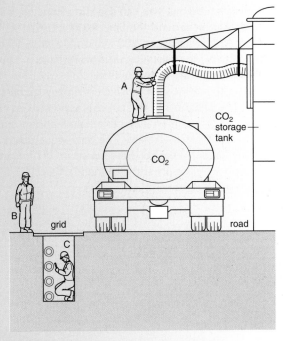

(i) Explain why the liquid chemical takes up less space.
(ii) Explain why it may be an advantage to store and transport the chemical as a liquid.
(iii) Suggest and explain one method by which the gas might be turned into a liquid.
(e) Suggest **two** safety features that you would make part of the tanker's design. Give reasons for your choice.

AQA (SEG)

20 A sealed test tube contains air at atmospheric pressure and room temperature. When it is surrounded by ice, which of the following statements about the air in the test tube is **not** correct?
A The pressure becomes lower.
B The average kinetic energy of the molecules becomes lower.
C The average momentum of the molecules becomes less.
D The molecules collide less often with the test tube.
E The average number of molecules in each cm^3 becomes less.

MEG

21 In the diagram below, you can see the planet Mars in an elliptical orbit around the Sun. At its closest (position A) Mars is about 200 million km away from the Sun. At its most distant (position B) Mars is about 250 million km away from the Sun.

Mars has a thin atmosphere which is mostly carbon dioxide. The pressure of the atmosphere changes from winter to summer. The table below shows some details of the Martian climate. The data were taken by the Viking Lander, near to the equator in 1977. Can you explain why the pressure of the Martian atmosphere changes so much?

	Average daily temperature (°C)	Average pressure (N/m²)
Position B (winter)	−73	50
Position A (summer)	−13	65

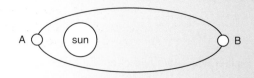

22 The diagram shows a piece of apparatus used to investigate how gas pressure varies with temperature, at constant volume. The table shows a set of results.

Temperature (in °C)	26	50	65	80	100
Pressure reading (in kN/m²)	102	110	115	120	127

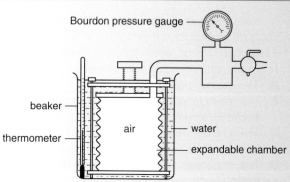

(a) Plot a graph of pressure, P (y-axis), against temperature, T, in °C (x-axis). Use it to find the pressure of the enclosed gas at 70 °C.

(b) The graph enables you to make predictions about the pressure outside the range of values plotted. How?

(c) If the gas pressure continued to vary in the way suggested by the graph, what pressure would you expect at (i) 200 °C, (ii) 0 °C, (iii) −200 °C?

(d) Is it correct to say that the pressure is proportional to temperature? Why?

(e) Where does the line cross the temperature axis (it should be between −270 and −280 °C). What will the gas pressure be at this temperature?

23 A balloon seller has a cylinder of helium gas which he uses to blow up his balloons.

The volume of the cylinder is 0.10 m³. It contains helium gas at a pressure of 1.0×10^7 N/m². The balloon seller fills each balloon to a volume of 1.0×10^{-2} m³ and a pressure of 1.2×10^5 N/m².

(a) Explain, in terms of particles, how the helium in the cylinder produces a pressure.

(b) Calculate the total volume that the helium gas will occupy at a pressure of 1.2×10^5 N/m². You can assume that there is no change in the temperature of the helium gas.

(c) Calculate the number of balloons of volume 1.0×10^{-2} m³ that the balloon seller can fill using the gas.

24 The diagram below shows a method of observing the diffusion of bromine in air.

When the bromine is released it forms a brown gas which is seen to diffuse slowly up the diffusion tube.

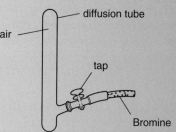

(a) Although the average speed of a bromine molecule is 350 m/s, the bromine gas only travels about 10 cm through the air in 500 s. Draw a diagram to show the path a bromine molecule takes as it travels through the air and use it to explain why diffusion is a slow process.

(b) When the experiment is repeated for air diffusing through bromine, it is noticed that the process occurs more rapidly. Suggest the reason for this.

(c) When food is being cooked at home the smells from the cooking soon travel through the house. If diffusion is such a slow process, how can you explain this?

Edexcel

25 The particle model of matter says that the molecules in a liquid are closely packed in a random way, are able to move around each other and are held together by strong forces.

(a) Explain how the particle model of matter describes the molecules in a solid.

(b) Explain why a gas will spread out quickly to fill a space.

WJEC

Heat

This solar furnace at Odeillo-Font-Romeau in France tracks the Sun as it moves throughout the day. The huge parabolic mirror (comprised of 9500 individual mirrors) reflects and focuses the heat from the Sun onto a furnace. The system is capable of producing 1000 kilowatts of thermal power, and a temperature of 3800 degrees C within the furnace itself.

By the end of this section you should:

- know the difference between heat and temperature
- understand why solids expand
- know what specific heat capacity means
- understand what is meant by latent heat
- be familiar with thermal conduction, convection and radiation

F

1

Hot and Cold

The Namib desert: daytime temperatures of 58°C have been recorded here in midsummer. However, at night, temperatures can reach freezing point. This range of temperatures makes the desert a very hostile environment for living things

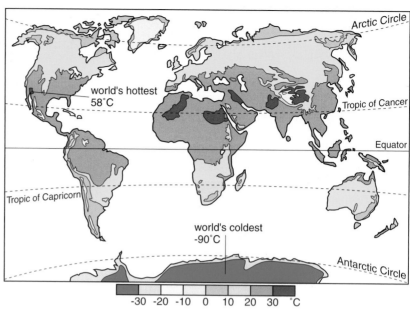

Figure 1(a) Mean temperature in July

http://www.lanly.com/heating.htm

Everybody knows the meaning of the words hot and cold. If you pick up a hot plate you burn your fingers. On a cold winter's day when you go outside without gloves, your fingers freeze. When you get too hot or too cold life becomes very unpleasant. Your body works normally at a temperature of about 37°C. You will become very ill if your body temperature rises as high as 40°C or falls as low as 34°C.

We are only comfortable wearing light clothing when the air temperature is around 10°C to 20°C. The maps in Figure 1(a) and (b) show the world's average temperatures in January and July. As you can see there are many places where it is too hot or too cold. In winter the average temperature in Verkhoyansk (Siberia) is below −40°C; the lowest temperature recorded there is about −70°C. People only survive the winter by staying indoors for months at a time. If you lived in Ethiopia you would face a different problem. The average yearly temperature in some parts of Ethiopia is about 35°C. In July the midday temperature can reach 50°C. Under such scorching conditions there is little water and food is hard to grow. Millions of Ethiopians have suffered from malnutrition or died over the years through shortages of food and water.

Life can also be uncomfortable in other places. In Bombay, you might prefer to live in an air-conditioned flat, because it gets so hot there. In Madrid, where midday temperatures reach 45°C in the summer, banks open from 9.00 am–12 noon and then again from 4.30 pm–6.00 pm. Most Spaniards have a siesta in the middle of the day, simply because it is too hot to be working outside.

Heat and temperature

It is a very common mistake to confuse the two words heat and temperature. When we talk about **heat** we mean the heat energy that we have had to put into a material to warm it up. Heat energy is measured in **joules**. The word **temperature** is used to describe how hot something is. Temperatures are usually measured in **degrees celsius** (°C).

Peter is a plumber and he uses a soldering iron which has a mass of 0.6 kg. Elsie is an electrician and she uses a soldering iron which has a mass of 0.1 kg.

The Antarctic: during the continuous darkness of mid-winter, the temperature here can be as low as −87°C

Figure 1(b) *Mean temperature in January*

They each plug their irons in and wait for them to warm up. After one minute Peter's iron has been given 20 000 J of heat and it has reached a temperature of 50°C. In that time Elsie's iron has been given 10 000 J of heat and it has reached a temperature of 100°C. Peter's iron has more heat energy than Elsie's but Elsie's iron is at a higher temperature.

Figure 2 shows the molecules in the two irons after they have been warmed up. The length of the arrows in the diagrams shows how fast the molecules are moving. The temperature is a measure of the energy of *each* molecule. The heat energy that you have to supply to warm an iron up is a measure of the total energy of *all* of the molecules.

Homework Questions

1 Use the maps of the world to help you answer the following questions.
   (a) Why do very few people live in: (i) Greenland, (ii) the centre of Australia?
   (b) Which part of the world has the greatest difference in average temperatures, between January and July?
   (c) What other factors, besides temperature, affect how many people live in a country?

2 Which will cause the worse burn:
   (i) a pan of hot water at 70°C falling on your foot, (ii) a spark from a bonfire at about 500°C landing on your hand? Explain your answer.

3 Criticise this statement: 'The heat of the inside of the Sun is about 15 million degrees celsius'.

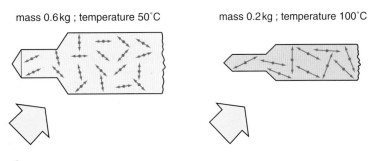

mass 0.6 kg ; temperature 50°C   mass 0.2 kg ; temperature 100°C

Figure 2
(a) 20 000 J of heat energy warmed up Peter's soldering iron to 50°C

(b) 10 000 J of heat energy warmed up Elsie's soldering iron to 100°C

2

Expansion of Solids

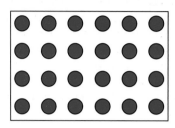

Figure 1
(a) Cold solid: atoms vibrate slowly

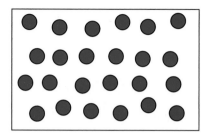

(b) Hot solid: atoms vibrate quickly and push each other apart. Expansion results

The molecules in solids and liquids are always vibrating. If the temperature falls, molecules vibrate less and they move closer together (Figure 1(a)). Then a substance will **contract**. When the temperature rises, molecules vibrate more and push each other apart. This causes substances to **expand** (Figure 1(b)). If you try to stop something expanding then very large forces may result. Sometimes these forces cause us serious problems but at other times they may be useful.

Expansion causing problems

In Saudi Arabia the temperature at midday in July can rise to as high as 50°C. But on a winter's night in January, the temperature can drop below 0°C. These large temperature changes cause problems with oil pipelines. A long straight length of pipe would soon buckle under the forces caused by expansion. The problem is solved by putting a series of expansion loops into the line. These loops make the line more flexible, so that it is free to expand or contract as the temperature changes. Figure 2 shows how the expansion of overhead power lines is tackled.

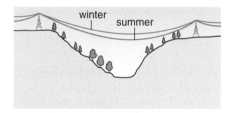

Figure 2 Engineers must allow for the expansion of overhead power lines. In summer, the lines will be longer and they will sag more

Putting expansion to use

Not all materials expand by the same amount when heated. Table 1 shows you the increase in length of various materials when they are heated through 1°C. You can see that brass expands nearly twice as much as iron for the same temperature rise. Some materials such as invar and Pyrex glass hardly expand at all. This difference in expansion between materials allows us to make a very useful device called a **bimetallic strip** (Figure 3). A strip is made out of two different metals such as iron and brass. The two metals are fixed together so that they cannot move separately. When the strip is cooled the brass contracts more than the iron so the strip bends upwards. When the strip is heated it bends the other way because the brass is now longer than the iron. This principle was used in some fire alarms and thermostats.

Material	Increase in length (mm) for 1 m heated through 1°C
aluminium	0.025
brass	0.019
iron	0.012
steel	0.011
glass (common)	0.009
glass (Pyrex)	0.003
invar (an alloy of nickel and steel	0.001

Table 1

- **Fire alarm.** Figure 4 shows the principle behind a simple fire alarm. Inside the fire detector itself there is a bimetallic switch. When the bimetallic strip gets hot it bends upwards and completes an electrical circuit. A current now flows and makes a fire alarm sound. Modern fire alarms rely on detecting smoke; this gives people an early warning.

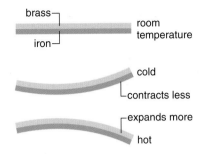

brass
room temperature
iron

cold
contracts less

expands more
hot

Figure 3 *A bimetallic strip*

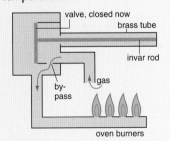

bimetallic switch

fire detector

Figure 4 *A switch for a fire alarm*

● **Thermostat**. A bimetallic switch can also be used to keep the temperature of your clothes iron constant (Figure 5). When the iron is cold the switch is up and current flows to the heating element. However, when the iron is hot the bimetallic strip bends downwards and breaks the circuit. A control knob allows you to choose your iron's temperature; hot for cotton, cooler for nylon. The hotter you want the iron to be, the more you turn the control knob downwards. This means that the bimetallic strip has to bend more before the circuit is broken, so it must be hotter.

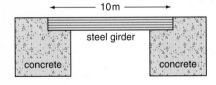

control knob
iron surface
iron
brass
bimetallic switch
iron
to heating circuit

Figure 5 *A thermostat in an iron*

Homework Questions

1 Below is a diagram of a gas oven thermostat. When the oven is hot enough the valve controlling the gas supply closes. When the oven cools down the valve opens again.
(a) Explain how it works
(b) How would you add a control knob to adjust the oven temperature?

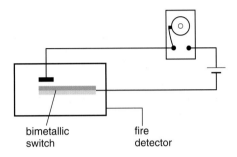

valve, closed now
brass tube
invar rod
by-pass
gas
oven burners

2 The graph shows how the current flowing in the heating element of a clothes iron changes with time.
(a) Explain why it behaves as it does.
(b) Sketch a graph to show how the temperature of the iron changes with time.

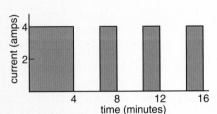

3 Look at the diagram of a bridge, and read the data below it. The bridge was built in the middle of a cold Russian winter when the temperature was −20°C. The ends of the main steel girders were fixed in cement and no room was left for expansion.
(a) By how much does a steel rod of length 10 m expand when it warms up by (i) 1°C, (ii) 40°C.
(b) Explain why the girders in the bridge are under compression in a hot summer when the temperature is 20°C.
(c) Calculate the force required to compress the bridge girder by 1 mm.
(d) Now calculate the force

compressing the girder in the summer when the temperature is 20°C.
(e) Explain what might happen to the girder or the concrete in the summer.

10m
steel girder
concrete
concrete

● A rod of steel 1 m long expands by 0.01 mm when it warms up by 1°C.
● A steel rod 10 m long with a cross-sectional area of 1 cm² needs a force of 2000 N to compress it by 1 mm.
● The cross-sectional area of the girder in the bridge is 100 cm².

3

Supplying Heat

When you want a cup of coffee you put some water in the kettle and switch it on. The water gets hotter because heat energy is being supplied which makes the molecules vibrate more rapidly. The hotter the water is, the faster the molecules move.

The amount of heat energy that must be supplied to warm up the kettle depends on two things:

- More energy is needed for a large temperature rise.
- More energy is needed if there is a lot of water in the kettle.

Warming 200 g of water from 20°C to 80°C needs 50 000 J of heat. Warming 200 g of oil from 20°C to 80°C (for making fondue) needs 40 000 J of heat. The amount of energy needed depends on the substance.

Specific heat capacities

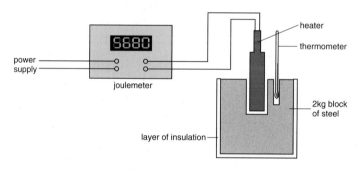

Figure 1 *An experiment to measure the heat energy required to warm up a block of steel*

You can see in Figure 1 an experiment to measure the heat energy required to warm up a block of steel. A thermometer records the temperature rise, while a Joulemeter measures the number of joules that the heater has supplied. The block of steel is wrapped in thick insulating material to make sure that no heat can escape to the surrounding air. Figure 2 shows how the temperature of the block rises as heat energy is supplied.

The amount of heat required to warm 1 kg of substance by 1°C is called its **specific heat capacity**. It is measured in units of **J/kg°C**. We can work out the specific heat capacity of steel like this. Figure 2 shows us that 18 kJ warmed the block from 20°C to 40°C.

$$18\ 000\ \text{J warmed 2 kg by 20°C}$$
$$so\ 9000\ \text{J would warm 1 kg by 20°C}$$
$$and\ \frac{9000\ \text{J}}{20} = 450\ \text{J would warm 1 kg by 1°C}$$

The specific heat capacity of steel is 450 J/kg°C. As you can see from Table 1, different substances have very different specific heat capacities. In general you can work out the heat required to warm up a substance using the equation below.

$$\text{Heat supplied} = \text{mass} \times \text{specific heat capacity} \times \text{temperature change}$$
$$\text{joules} = \text{kg} \times \frac{\text{joules}}{\text{kg°C}} \times \text{°C}$$

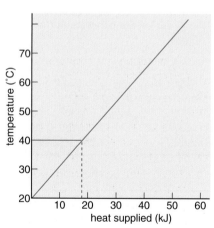

Figure 2 *A graph to show how the temperature of the steel block rises as heat energy is supplied*

Substance	Specific heat capacity (J/kg°C)
water	4200
alcohol	2400
ice	2100
concrete	800
glass	630
steel	450
copper	380
lead	130

Table 1

Example. How much heat is required to heat up the tip of Elsie's soldering iron by 400°C? The tip of the soldering iron is made of copper and has a mass of 30 g. Ignore any heat losses.

$$\text{Heat supplied} = m \times s \times (T_2 - T_1)$$
$$= 0.03 \text{ kg} \times 380 \frac{J}{kg°C} \times 400°C$$
$$= 4560 \text{ J}$$

Water has a very high specific heat capacity. This means that it absorbs a lot of heat energy when it warms up. Conversely, water gives out a lot of heat when it cools down. Several ways in which the high specific heat capacity of water is useful to us are described below:

- We are made mostly of water. This means that if we suddenly exercise, and our muscles produce a lot of heat energy, then we do not warm up too quickly.
- Water is very important for keeping our houses warm. A house central-heating system pumps hot water around the house. The hot water can release a lot of energy as it flows through radiators. If water had a low specific heat capacity, then radiators a long way from the boiler would never be warm.
- Water is capable of absorbing a lot of heat energy, so it is useful for cooling car engines (Figure 3).
- In Britain we live on an island. The fact that we are surrounded by water has a great effect on our climate. Water is so difficult to warm up and cool down that our weather is neither extremely hot nor extremely cold. Land can be warmed up or cooled down much more quickly than sea, so the temperature in the middle of a continent can change rapidly. You can see from the map on page 141 that Canada and Russia have worse winters than we do, although they are no further north.

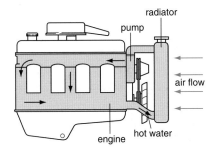

Figure 3 *A car cooling system*

Homework Questions

1 This question refers to Figure 2 which shows how the temperature of a 2 kg steel block changes as heat is supplied to it.
(a) Make a copy of the graph.
(b) Mark on the graph how the temperature would have changed if: (i) the mass was 4 kg, (ii) the mass was 1 kg, (iii) the insulating material was removed from the metal. Label these graphs (i), (ii), (iii).

2 A night storage heater contains 60 kg of concrete. How much heat is required to warm the concrete from 10°C to 40°C (see Table 1)?

3 Chen and Sally are sitting beside a lake. Chen is throwing stones into the lake. Here is an extract from their conversation.

Chen: Just think of all that kinetic energy the stone has. It is all converted into heat energy when it makes a splash in the lake. If I keep this up the lake will get warmer.

Sally: Don't be stupid, it would take all day!

Comment on their conversation.

4 Julie has an outdoor swimming pool which is 20 m long, 10 m wide and 2 m deep.
(a) When the pool is full, what is the volume of water in it?
(b) The density of water is 1000kg/m³: what mass of water is there in the pool?
(c) It is necessary to warm the water from 17°C to 22°C. How much heat energy does that require?
(d) During a hot summer spell the sun shines on the pool for an average of 8 hours a day. While the sun shines, the pool absorbs energy at a rate of 60 kW. How much energy is absorbed each day?
(e) Roughly how many days does it take the pool to warm up to 22°C? (Ignore any heat losses at night.)
(f) Julie decided to warm the pool with electrical heaters. How much would it cost her to warm up her pool by 5°C? The electricity company charges 2p for 1 MJ of energy.

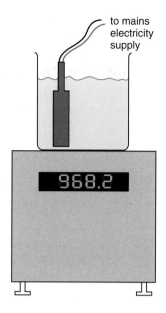

Figure I *An experiment to measure how much heat energy is used to boil water*

In the last unit you learnt that when heat energy is supplied to a substance it warms up. However, this is not always the case. Heat energy must be supplied to melt ice or to boil water. You have seen pans of water boiling on a cooker. The cooker gives heat to the water but the boiling water never gets any hotter than 100°C. The energy that is supplied is used to evaporate molecules. The energy required to turn 1 kg of a liquid at its boiling point into 1 kg of vapour is known as the **specific latent heat of vaporisation**. It is measured in joules per kilogram (J/kg).

Figure 1 shows a simple experiment that allows you to measure how much heat energy is used to boil water. A beaker of water is boiling on top of an electric balance. The heater is supplying heat energy at a rate of 1000 W. In a time of 250 s the reading on the balance dropped from 1000 g to 900 g. From this we can see that 100 g (or 0.1 kg) boiled away in that time.

How much energy is needed to turn 1 kg of boiling water at 100°C into vapour at 100°C (Figure 2)?

$$\text{Heat supplied} = 1000\,\frac{\text{J}}{\text{s}} \times 250\ \text{s}$$
$$= 250\ 000\ \text{J}$$

This boiled away 0.1 kg. So ten times as much energy, 2 500 000 J, will boil away 1 kg of water (Figure 2).

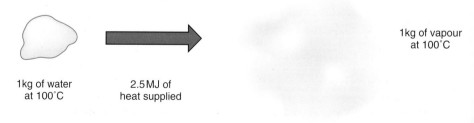

1kg of water
at 100°C

2.5MJ of
heat supplied

1kg of vapour
at 100°C

Figure 2 *The specific heat of vaporisation of water is 2.5 MJ/kg*

Melting and casting

Casting is a very important process which is used in many different industries. For example, pipes, valves, guns and pistons are all manufactured by casting metal. Figure 3 shows you how this process works. Molten metal is poured into a mould which has been made exactly to the shape of a pipe. When the metal has solidified and cooled again the mould can be removed. Usually the moulds are made from sand which has been made rigid with a resin.

If you were in business making metal castings you would find you had a large electricity bill. You would be using a very large amount of energy to heat up and melt your metal. Figure 4 shows a graph of how the temperature of a piece of aluminium changes as heat is supplied to it in a furnace. Over the region AB the heat energy is used to warm up the aluminium. At B the aluminium begins to melt. By C aluminium has melted completely and the temperature begins to rise again. You can see that it takes almost as long to melt the aluminium as it does to warm it up. So the energy required to melt the aluminium is large. This energy is called the **latent** (or hidden) **heat of fusion**. The *specific latent heat of fusion* of aluminium is the heat energy required to melt 1 kg of aluminium.

Ice also needs a lot of energy to melt it, which is why if you want a cold drink you will put a couple of ice cubes into your glass. Also an ice pack is a very effective way of removing heat from body tissues. If you have a bad bruise, try an ice pack to help reduce the swelling.

Figure 4

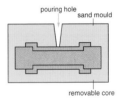

Figure 3 *Metal casting*
(a) The finished pipe

(b) How it is cast

Homework Questions

1 When is it possible to supply heat to a substance without a temperature change?

2 This question refers to the aluminium which was heated in the furnace. How its temperature changed is shown in Figure 4. Some additional data are shown in the table below.

- Mass of aluminium heated = 80 kg
- Time of heating = 1000 s
- Power of heaters in the furnace = 80 kW

(a) At what temperature did the aluminium melt?
(b) How long did it take to warm the aluminium up to its melting point?
(c) How much heat was supplied to the aluminium in that time?
(d) Use the equation:
Heat supplied = $m \times s \times (T_2 - T_1)$
to calculate the specific heat capacity of aluminium.
(e) How much heat was supplied to melt the aluminium?
(f) How much heat energy is required to melt 1 kg of aluminium?
(g) Figure 4 shows how the temperature changes in an imaginary ideal furnace, which loses no heat to its surroundings. Real furnaces do lose heat. Make a copy of Figure 4 and add to it a second graph to show how the temperature would change in a real furnace.

3 Icebergs come from the Arctic or Antarctic ice caps; they are made from fresh water. It has been suggested that icebergs could be towed from the Arctic to North Africa to supply water to countries that suffer from drought. Comment on this proposal.

4 A sample of molten wax is put in a boiling tube and allowed to cool. A graph of the temperature of the wax against time is shown below.
(a) What is the melting point of the wax?
(b) Explain why the temperature remains constant for about 15 minutes.

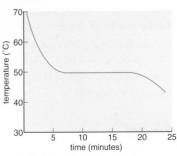

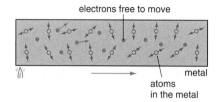

electrons free to move

metal

atoms
in the metal

Figure 1
(a) Heat is conducted quickly by fast-moving electrons

insulator

hot   cold

(b) Heat is conducted slowly by atoms bumping into each other

When you walk around your house in bare feet you will notice that your feet feel warm as long as you stay on a carpet. But if you go into a kitchen which has tiles on a concrete floor your feet will soon feel cold. You notice this effect because the tiles are good **conductors** of heat. A good conductor of heat will carry heat away from your body quickly; this makes you feel cold.

Table 1 shows you materials which conduct heat well and those which are poor conductors or **insulators**. All metals are good thermal conductors and materials such as plastic, wood and air are insulators. When heat is transferred by conduction, hot atoms pass some of their kinetic energy to colder neighbouring atoms. Metals contain electrons that are free to move. When one end of a metal rod is heated, energy can be carried away from the hot end of the rod by fast moving electrons (Figure 1(a)). In a thermal insulator there are few electrons which are free to move, and heat is transferred more slowly by hot atoms bumping into colder atoms (Figure 1(b)).

Material	Conductivity (W/mK)	
copper	385	good conductors
iron	72	
concrete	5	
glass	1	
brick	0.6	
water	0.6	
fat	0.046	
wool	0.04	
air	0.025	poor conductors

Table 1 *This table showing **conductivities** allows you to compare how well two different materials will conduct heat. A concrete floor will take heat away from your feet far faster than a woollen carpet*

Keeping warm

If you look at Table 1 you can see that fat, wool and air are all poor conductors of heat. It is no surprise then, that these three substances are important for keeping warm-blooded animals (including us) at the right temperature. If you have ever been swimming in the North Sea you will know how rapidly you get cold. Your skin is in contact with cold water and you are losing heat by conduction. In really cold Arctic waters you could not survive more than a few minutes. Seals, however, spend all of their lives in cold water. They are protected from losing heat by conduction by a very thick layer of fat (blubber) which surrounds all of their body.

Birds have feathers and other animals have fur or hair. Fur and feathers are poor conductors of heat, but the way they reduce heat loss is by trapping a thick insulating layer of air.

We have few hairs to keep us warm. If we stand naked, moving air currents soon take heat away from us. However, wearing clothes traps air, so keeping us warm.

This robin has fluffed out her feathers to trap a layer of air. Air is a poor conductor of heat and so she manages to keep warm even in cold weather

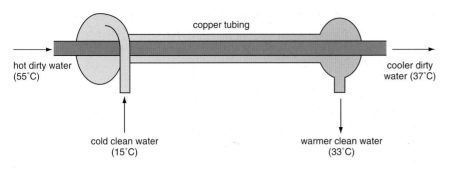

Figure 2 *A heat exchanger for a laundry*

Figure 3 *Heat exchanger wall made of metal*

Heat exchange

Figure 2 shows a double pipe heat exchanger that is being used in a laundry. Hot dirty water from the washing goes through the central pipe. Clean cold water flows round the outside of the pipe. The idea is to warm up the clean water using heat from the dirty water. This helps to reduce the laundry's heating bill.

Figure 3 shows part of the wall of another heat exchanger. The following points make sure that as much heat is removed from the hot liquid as possible:

- The wall of the container should be made from a good conductor (usually metal).
- The wall should be thin, so that heat is conducted rapidly.
- The surface area should be large to conduct more heat.
- The temperature difference between the cooling water and the hot liquid should be large.
- More heat is extracted from the hot liquid if it flows slowly through the heat exchanger.

Homework Questions

1 Here is part of a conversation between Peter, Ramesh and Lorraine, who are talking about keeping warm in winter.

Peter: I think string vests are ridiculous, they are just full of holes. How can they possibly keep you warm?

Ramesh: I heard on the radio that it was better to wear two vests than one. How can they do any good?

Lorraine: It's not the vest that keeps you warm, it's the air underneath them.

Comment on this conversation.

2 This question refers to the laundry's heat exchanger shown in Figure 2. What effect will the following changes have on the final temperature of the clean water that is being warmed up?
(a) Iron tubing is used instead of copper.
(b) Thinner copper tubing is used for the wall of the heat exchanger.
(c) The length of the heat exchanger is increased.
(d) The hot dirty water is made to run faster.

3 Why do power stations need heat exchangers?

4 (a) Explain in terms of the motion of particles how
(i) a metal conducts heat,
(ii) wood conducts heat.
(b) The diagram below shows a piece of wood with a ring of brass round part of it. A piece of paper has been stuck partly across the wood and partly across the brass. A flame is now applied gently underneath the paper as the wood is turned slowly. Explain what you expect to happen and why.

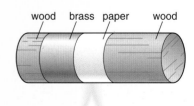

5 If you had a fur coat, explain why it would be even warmer if you wore it inside out.

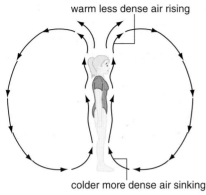

Figure 1 *Convection currents near a person in a room*

To make a hot air balloon fly you need a burner which heats up the air inside the balloon. When air is heated it expands and its density becomes less. When hot air is surrounded by colder, more dense air, it rises. This is the same principle as a cork submerged in water floating to the surface.

Figure 1 shows how air circulates if you stand, with most of your clothes off, in the middle of a room. Your body heats up air next to it, which then rises. Colder air flows down near the walls to replace the warmer air. The currents of air which flow are called **convection currents**.

Heat can be transferred by convection in *liquids* and *gases*, but not in solids. Although most liquids and gases do not transfer heat very well by conduction, they do transfer heat quickly by convection. Convection currents allow large quantities of hot liquid or gas to move and give heat to a colder part. If we wore no clothes our bodies would lose lots of heat by convection. By wearing clothes we trap a layer of air which acts as an insulator.

Exactly the same idea is used to reduce heat losses from your house. Your loft is full of air and convection currents there can cause a large amount of heat loss. Lofts can be insulated with felt or glass fibre. To stop convection in the cavity between inner and outer walls, it is possible to pump in polystyrene foam. The foam has lots of air trapped in it and so is a poor conductor of heat. Double glazing also traps air, in a layer between two pieces of glass (Figure 2).

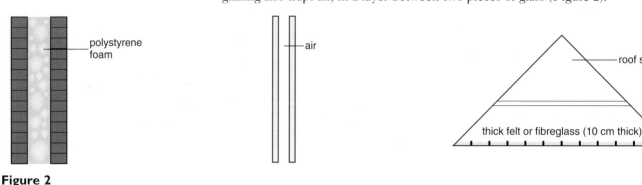

Figure 2

(a) Cavity wall insulation | (b) Double glazing | (c) Loft insulation

Convection currents also play an important part in our weather systems. Winds are convection currents on a large scale. You have probably noticed when you have been sunning yourself on the beach that there is usually a sea breeze (Figure 3). In the daytime the land warms up quickly. This causes a rising air current and a breeze blowing in from the sea. Seabirds are quick to take advantage of these rising currents of air, and can soar upwards without flapping their wings.

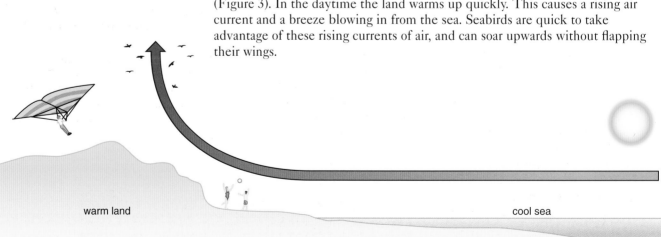

Figure 3 *The large specific heat capacity of the sea means that it stays cool. The land warms quickly, and warm air rises above the land*

Convection in water

When water is heated it too will transfer heat energy by convection. Figure 4 shows a simple way that you can show this in a laboratory. Place some potassium permanganate crystals at the bottom of a flask of water. When heat is supplied from underneath the dissolved potassium permanganate rises showing the path of the currents.

It is possible to circulate water around the heating system of a house using convection currents. Figure 5 shows such a heating system. The boiler must be put at the lowest point in the house. The hot water rises upwards to the roof. The water then feeds the radiators and finally the cool water is returned to the boiler.

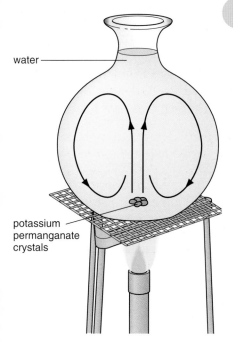

Figure 4 *A laboratory experiment to show convection currents in water*

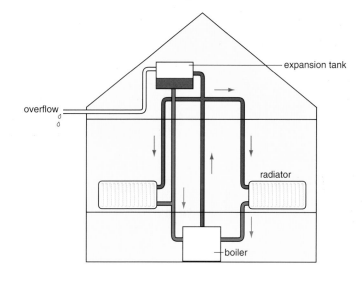

Figure 5 *This system of circulating water is suitable for a small house only. In a large house a pump is used to help push the water round*

Homework Questions

1 Heat cannot be transferred by convection in a solid. Explain why.
2 Figure 3 shows the direction of a sea breeze in daytime. At night, land cools down more quickly than the sea. Draw a diagram to show the direction of the sea breeze at night.
3 Explain how glider pilots can manoeuvre their gliders to great heights without using an engine.
4 About a hundred years ago in Cornish tin mines, fresh air used to be provided for the miners through two ventilation shafts shown below.
(a) To improve the flow of air, a fire was lit at the bottom of one of the shafts. Explain why.
(b) One day, Mr Trevethan, the owner of the mine, had an idea. To make the ventilation even better he lit another fire at the bottom of the second shaft.
Comment on this idea.

5 This question is about the cost of insulating a house. At the moment the house has no loft insulation, cavity wall insulation or double glazing.
(a) Use the data provided to decide which method of insulation provides the best value for money.
(b) How many years do you have to wait before the double glazing has paid for itself?
6 Explain why a candle will not light in a weightless spacecraft in outerspace, even if it has a plentiful supply of oxygen.

- Yearly heating bill for house: £700
- Cost of double glazing: £5000 This would reduce the fuel bill by 20% a year
- Cost of loft insulation: £450 This would reduce the fuel bill by 30% a year
- Cost of cavity wall insulation: £1800 This would reduce the fuel bill by 25%

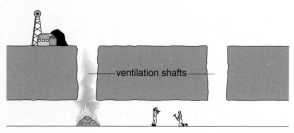

Radiation

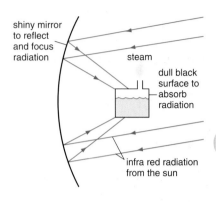

shiny mirror to reflect and focus radiation

steam

dull black surface to absorb radiation

infra red radiation from the sun

Figure 1 *A solar furnace*

Radiation is the third way by which heat energy can be transferred from one place to another. Heat energy from the Sun reaches us by radiation. The Sun emits electromagnetic waves which travel through space at high speed. Light is such a wave, but the Sun also emits a lot of **infra-red** waves (or infra-red radiation). Infra-red waves have longer wavelengths than light waves. It is the infra-red radiation that makes you feel warm when you lie down in the sun. Infra-red radiation travels at the same speed as light; as soon as you see the Sun go behind a cloud you feel cooler.

Good and bad absorbers

Infra-red radiation behaves in the same way as light. It can be reflected and focussed using a mirror. Figure 1 shows the idea behind a solar furnace. The shiny surface of the mirror is a poor absorber of radiation, but a good reflector. Radiation is absorbed well by dull black surfaces. So the boiler at the focus of the solar furnace is of a dull black colour.

Good and bad emitters

Figure 2 shows an experiment to investigate which type of teapot will keep your tea warm for a longer time. One pot has a dull black surface, the other is made out of shiny stainless steel. Radiation which is emitted from the hot teapots can be detected using a thermopile and a sensitive ammeter. When you do the experiment you will find that the black teapot emits more radiation than the shiny surface. So a shiny teapot will keep your tea warmer than a black teapot.

● Black surfaces are good absorbers and good emitters of radiation
● Shiny surfaces are bad absorbers and bad emitters of radiation

thermopile

Figure 2 *A sensitive instrument called a thermopile can detect radiation*

The greenhouse effect

In Italy, where the average temperature in the summer is about 5°C higher than in Britain, tomatoes grow very well. It is a great help to a tomato grower in Britain if he uses a greenhouse. On a warm day the temperature inside a greenhouse can be 10°C or 15°C higher than outside (Figure 3). Infra-red radiation from the sun passes through the glass of the greenhouse, and is absorbed by the plants and soil inside. The plants radiate energy, but the wavelength of the emitted radiation is much longer. The longer wavelengths of radiation do not pass through the glass and so heat is trapped inside the greenhouse. The temperature rises until the loss of heat through the glass by conduction balances the energy absorbed from the Sun.

Some people worry that a similar greenhouse effect could be happening in our atmosphere. As we continue to burn fossil fuels we are filling our atmosphere with carbon dioxide and other chemicals. As these chemicals absorb long wavelength radiation emitted from the Earth's surface, the average temperature of the Earth increases. The planet Venus has a greenhouse effect on a large scale. Its atmosphere is mostly carbon dioxide, and its average surface temperature is about 460°C, hot enough to melt some metals.

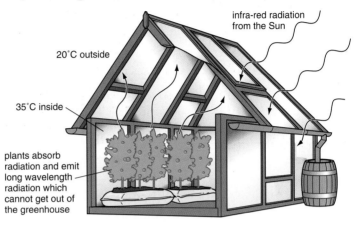

Figure 3

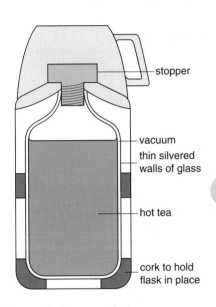

Figure 4 *A vacuum flask*

Vacuum flask

A vacuum flask (thermos flask) keeps things warm by reducing heat losses in all possible ways. The flask is made with a double wall of glass and there is a vacuum between the two walls. Conduction and convection cannot take place through a vacuum. The glass walls are thin, so that little heat is conducted through the glass to the top. Heat can be radiated through a vacuum, but the glass walls are silvered like a mirror so that they are poor emitters of radiation. The stopper at the top prevents heat loss by evaporation or convection currents (Figure 4).

Homework Questions

1 Explain why the following is true in terms of heat transfer.
   (a) A concrete floor feels much colder than a wooden floor when walked on with bare feet, although the temperature of each floor is the same.
   (b) Clean snow does not melt quickly in bright sunshine, though dirty snow does.
   (c) Some casserole dishes which are used in ovens are black, but the outside of an electric kettle is shiny.
   (d) After finishing the London marathon, athletes are wrapped in aluminium-coated plastic sheets.

2 Explain three ways in which a vacuum flask helps to keep drinks warm.

3 The diagram below shows how the Earth receives radiation from the Sun in daytime and re-radiates energy at night.
   (a) Explain why, although the Earth has been receiving radiation from the Sun for millions of years, its temperature remains roughly the same.
   (b) Why is the density of radiation falling at A higher than at B or C?. Use this fact to explain why the Earth has a hot equator and cold poles.
   (c) Where is the greatest radiation loss from the Earth at night?
   (d) Make a sketch of the Earth to show how two convective processes transfer energy from the equator to the poles.
   (e) What names do we give to these convective processes?

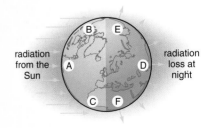

Keeping warm in the house

Suppose you are a heating engineer who wants to know what size of central heating system to install in a house. You can calculate the heat losses from a house using **U-values**. If a material transfers heat well it has a *high* U-value; if the material is a good insulator is has a *low* U-value. You can see some values for U-values in Table 1. An engineer can calculate the rate of loss of heat using this equation:

$$\text{Rate of heat loss (watts)} = U\text{-value} \times \text{area} \times \text{temperature difference}$$
$$= \frac{W}{m^2{}^\circ C} \times m^2 \times {}^\circ C$$

We can use the data provided to calculate the rate at which heat is lost from a poorly insulated house. The outside temperature is 0°C and the house is to be kept at 15°C. The data are given in Table 2

Heat loss per second, $H = U \times A \times T$

- Ceiling area: $H = 2 \times 100 \times 15 = 3000$ W
- Walls: $H = 1 \times 200 \times 15 = 3000$ W
- Floor: $H = 1 \times 100 \times 15 = 1500$ W
- Windows $H = 5 \times 30 \times 15 = 2250$ W
- Doors $H = 5 \times 10 \times 15 = 750$ W
  Total = 10 500 W

So you would need to install a heating system capable of producing at 10 kW. If the house owner used a gas central heating system continuously at this rate it would cost about £30 per week.

	U-values W/m²°C
Uninsulated house	
● Uninsulated roof	2.0
● Cavity wall	1.0
● Floor without carpets	1.0
● Windows, single glazed	5.0
● Doors	5.0
Insulated house	
● Insulated roof	0.3
● Cavity filled wall	0.5
● Floor with carpets	0.3
● Windows, double glazed	2.5
● Doors with draught excluders	3.0

Table 1

- Ground floor area = 100 m²
- Ceiling area = 100 m²
- Area of brick wall = 200 m²
- Area of windows = 30 m²
- Area of doors = 10 m²

Table 2

Keeping cool

If you have ever done any long-distance running, you will know that you get very hot indeed and that your efforts cause you to sweat a lot. You will see from the data provided on the next page that marathon runners can suffer severe problems due to temperature changes of the body or loss of water (dehydration).

The bar graphs help to explain the problems which marathon runners face. Figure 1(a) shows that Sarah generates heat in her muscles at a rate of 1000 W; for her body to remain at a safe temperature she must lose this excess energy at the same rate. Sarah loses energy mostly through the evaporation of water through her lungs, and also by sweat evaporation. She also loses energy by convection and conduction (and a little by radiation) as she runs through the air.

At relatively cool temperatures (18°C) Sarah loses excess heat quite easily. At 23°C, she loses less by conduction, convection and radiation (200 W), but she loses more energy by sweat evaporation (800 W). However her body temperature remains stable because she is still producing heat at a rate of 1000 W. At a temperature of 28°C, the temperature difference between her and the air is small, and the rate of heat loss due to conduction, convection and radiation is small (100 W). The bar graphs show that her total rate of heat loss (900 W) is smaller than her total rate of heat production (1000 W). Sarah's body temperature will start to rise; heat exhaustion might be the result unless she takes on lots of water to drink and to splash on her body to cool her down.

- First we will use the data (Figure 1(b)) to calculate how much water one runner, Sarah, loses in a three hour marathon when the temperature is 18°C. At this temperature she loses heat due to evaporation at the rate of 600 W.

Marathon running data

- Mass of runner = 60 kg
- Specific heat capacity of water = 4200 J/kg°C
- Specific latent heat of vaporisation of water = 2.5 MJ/kg
- At rest an athlete produces heat energy at a rate of 100 W
- Average body temperature = 37°C
- The body can only work normally between 33°C and 41°C

Over 3 hours the heat lost is:

$$\text{Heat lost} = 600\,\frac{\text{J}}{\text{s}} \times (3 \times 3600)\text{s}$$

$$= 6\,500\,000\text{ J}$$

$$= 6.5\text{ MJ}$$

But 2.5 MJ of heat evaporates 1 kg of water, so she loses $\frac{6.5}{2.5} = 2.6$ kg of water in the race.

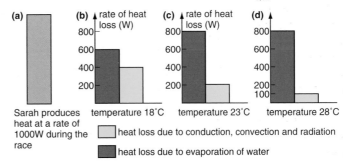

(a) Sarah produces heat at a rate of 1000W during the race

(b) rate of heat loss (W) — temperature 18°C

(c) rate of heat loss (W) — temperature 23°C

(d) temperature 28°C

☐ heat loss due to conduction, convection and radiation

■ heat loss due to evaporation of water

Figure I

Keeping warm at the end of a marathon. The shiny blanket is a poor radiator of heat

- When marathon runners finish a race they are wrapped up in bags to stop them cooling too quickly. When Sarah finishes her race and rests, her body will only be *producing* heat at a rate of 100 W, but she is still *losing* it at a rate of 1000 W (600 W due to evaporation, 400 W due to other processes). So she loses heat from her body at a rate of 900 W. If this is allowed to happen even for 10 minutes, she will become very cold. In 10 minutes:

$$\text{heat lost} = 900\text{ J/s} \times (10 \times 60)\text{s} = 540\,000\text{ J}$$

We can calculate her loss in temperature using:

$$\text{Heat lost} = \text{mass} \times \text{specific heat capacity} \times \text{temperature drop}$$

$$\textit{so}\ \text{temperature drop} = \frac{H}{ms} = \frac{540\,000\text{ J}}{60\text{ kg} \times 4200\text{ J/kg°C}}$$

$$= 2.1°\text{C}$$

Homework Questions

House heating

1 Use the data provided to work out the rate of heat loss from the same house, if it is insulated well.

2 Some people think that it is more important to insulate the walls than to put in double glazing. This seems sensible because the windows are small. Comment on this idea.

3 Use your answer to question 1 to calculate the cost of heating an insulated house per week. The following steps will help.
(a) What is the rate of energy loss from the insulated house? (Answer to question 1.)
(b) How much energy does the house lose in 24 hours? Explain your answer in MJ.

(c) To keep the house at a stable temperature, how much energy must be supplied in 24 hours?
(d) The cost of gas heating is 0.4p per MJ. Now calculate the cost of heating per week.

Marathon running

4 Explain why as the air temperature rises, a marathon runner loses more heat by evaporation of sweat, and less by conduction, convection and radiation.

5 If Sarah loses as much as 3 kg of water, she will suffer severe effects from dehydration.
(a) Explain why she could be in danger if the air temperature is more than 23°C.
(b) What action can a runner take

to avoid dehydration?

6 Use the marathon running data box for this question.
(a) What will happen to Sarah's body temperature if she runs when the air temperature is 28°C? Assume that she has no means of cooling other than those suggested in the graphs.
(b) How much extra heat energy is she producing: (i) per second, (ii) per hour?
(c) Calculate by how much her body temperature will have increased after one hour.
(d) Explain why Sarah is unlikely to finish a marathon if the temperature is as high as 28°C, unless she consumes water.

SECTION F: Questions

1 Diagram (i) illustrates an instrument used to measure the time that the Sun shines during the day. The blackened glass bulb contains mercury and is supported inside an evacuated glass case. Diagram (ii) shows how the connecting wires are arranged inside tube A.

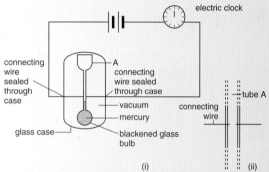

(i)

(ii)

(a) How does energy from the Sun reach the mercury? Give a reason for your answer.
(b) Explain why the clock starts when the Sun shines.
(c) Why is tube A of small cross-sectional area?
(d) Explain why blackening the bulb ensures that the mercury level falls rapidly when the Sun ceases to shine.

OCR (MEG)

2 The diagram shows a circuit in which an immersion heater is used to heat a metal block. The heater supplies energy at the rate of 50 W.

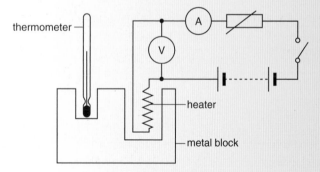

(a) How many joules of energy are supplied each second?
(b) The heater is switched on for 300 seconds. During this time the temperature rises from 20°C to 50°C.
(i) Calculate the energy supplied.
(ii) If the mass of the block is 2 kg, calculate the energy required to raise the temperature of 1 kg of the material by 1°C.
(iii) What name is given to the quantity you have calculated in (b)(ii)?
(c) When the experiment is performed as shown above, the measured rise in temperature is smaller than expected.

(i) Why is the measured rise smaller?
(ii) How would you change the apparatus to make the measured rise in temperature closer to the expected value?

AQA (NEAB)

3 In an experiment in which equal masses of lead and a lead-tin alloy called solder were allowed to cool, the following cooling curves were obtained.

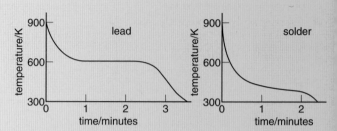

(a) For the lead:
(i) what was the physical state of the lead after 30 seconds,
(ii) what was happening to the lead at 600 K,
(iii) what is 600 K in Celsius units,
(iv) why did the temperature of the lead remain constant at 600 K for some time?
(b) State **two** important differences between the lead and the solder which can be deduced from these cooling curves.
(c) Solder is often used by plumbers to repair burst pipes by filling the fracture with solder. Why is solder better than lead for this purpose?

AQA (NEAB)

4 25% of the heat lost to the surroundings from a house passes through the roof of the house.

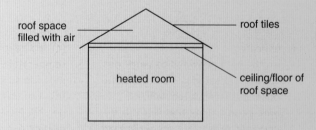

(a) Name **two** other areas of a house from which heat is lost to the surroundings.
(b) (i) State the main method by which heat is transferred through the ceiling.
(ii) Explain how the heat passing through the ceiling is transferred through the roof space to the roof tiles.
(c) Explain carefully why a covering of fibre glass on the floor of the roof space reduces the heat loss through the roof.

WJEC

5 A hot liquid loses heat by conduction, convection, radiation and evaporation. The vacuum flask shown below is designed to prevent hot liquids becoming cold.

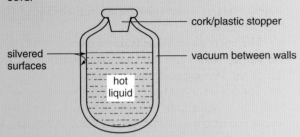

(a) Explain how the vacuum between the walls reduces the heat loss from the hot liquid.
(b) Explain how and why the cork/plastic stopper reduces the heat loss from the hot liquid.

WJEC

6 A heating engineer designs a storage heater, which must contain either concrete or oil. Electric elements are used to heat up the heater at night when electricity costs less.

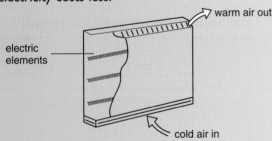

(a) The storage heater contains a box measuring 1.0 m long, 0.5 m high and 0.2 m deep.

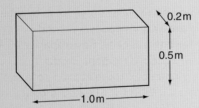

Calculate the volume of this box.
Use the equation below.
You **must** show how you work out your answer.

volume = length × depth × height

(b) The engineer works out the mass of concrete which would fill the box. He writes this in the table.

material	energy to raise the temperature of 1 kg by 1 deg C	density	mass of material to fill box
concrete	3400 J	2200 kg/m³	220 kg
oil	2000 J	760 kg/m³	kg

Calculate the mass of the oil.
(c) The engineer decides to use concrete blocks to store energy.
Look at all the information in the table.
Write down **two** reasons which support this decision.
(d) The box is filled with concrete blocks.
Each of the concrete blocks has a mass of 5 kg.
One of the blocks is heated from 15 °C to 65 °C.
Calculate the energy gained by this block.
Use the equation below. You **must** show how you work out your answer.

$$\text{energy gained} = \text{mass} \times \text{specific heat capacity} \times \text{temperature rise}$$

(e) The hot concrete block is put in contact with a cold concrete block. Both blocks are covered with a good insulator so that no heat is lost. The graph shows how the temperature of each block changes with time.

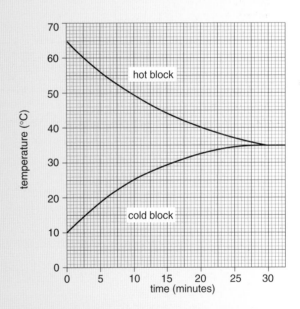

(i) Use the graph to calculate the average rate of cooling of the hot block between 5 and 10 minutes.
You **must** explain how you work out your answer.
(ii) How can you tell from the graph that the cold concrete block has a larger mass than the hot concrete block?

(f) The graph shows that
◆ initially the hot block cools down and the cold block warms up.
◆ after 30 minutes the temperatures of both blocks become steady.
A model for explaining how energy transfers

between the blocks involves the random transfer of tiny packets of energy.
Use your ideas about these energy packets and the rate at which they transfer energy to explain these observations.

OCR

7 (a) The diagram below shows radiation from the Sun arriving at the Earth's surface at two places and the possible movement of an air mass between the North pole and the equator.

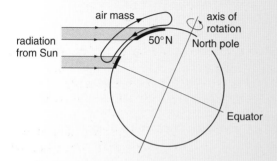

(i) How does the intensity of radiation arriving at the equator compare with that arriving at latitude 50° North?
(ii) State how this affects the average surface temperatures at the equator and at latitude 50° North.
(iii) The diagram shows the possible movement of air between the North pole and the equator. Explain how the circulation of the air shown is produced.

Edexcel

8 The next diagram shows how energy from the Sun can be used to heat a house.
Water from the storage tank is pumped through the solar panel.
In the solar panel, the water passes through copper pipes that are painted black.
The water is then returned to the storage tank.
(a) (i) Explain why the pipes in the solar panel are painted black.

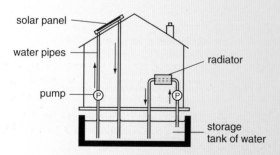

(ii) Plastic pipes are cheaper than copper pipes. Explain why copper pipes are used in the panel rather than plastic ones.
(b) Write down ONE advantage and ONE disadvantage of using solar panels rather than gas to heat a house.
(c) The solar panel takes water from the bottom of the storage tank. The radiator takes water from the top of the storage tank. Explain why.
(d) The house is heated by pumping warm water from the storage tank through radiators. The diagram below shows the position of a radiator in a room. Describe how the radiator heats the room. Copy the diagram and add to it to illustrate your answer.

Edexcel

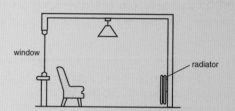

9 The diagram below shows an electric kettle.

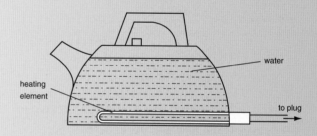

(a) Name and explain the process by which all the water in the kettle becomes heated.
(b) Water has a specific heat capacity of 4200 J/kg°C. Explain what this statement means.
(c) The element of the electric kettle supplies energy at the rate of 2800 J/s. The kettle contains 2 kg of water at 16 °C.
(i) Use the formula

$$\text{Energy transferred (J)} = \text{mass (kg)} \times \text{specific heat capacity (J/kg °C)} \times \text{change in temperature (°C)}$$

to find the energy required to raise the temperature of the water to 100 °C.
(ii) Calculate the time taken to raise the temperature of the water to 100 °C.
(d) Explain why, in practice, the time taken would be longer than that calculated in (c).

WJEC

10 Mr Adams is a neurosurgeon. Recently he had to operate on Polly. She had a giant aneurysm. An aneurysm is like a balloon that has blown out from the side of an artery in the brain. Aneurysms occur when the wall of the artery is weak. They are very dangerous since they could burst and bleed into the brain.

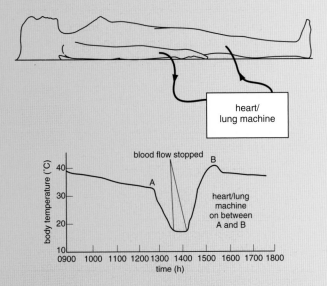

Polly's aneurysm was so large that it was necessary to stop the blood flowing into the brain. At normal body temperatures the brain dies in a few minutes without a blood supply. But at 15°C the brain can last for nearly an hour without a blood supply. To cool her down Polly's blood was passed through a heart/lung machine. The graph shows how her body temperature changed during the day. The operation was successful and Polly has now recovered completely.
(a) Use the graph to work out how long it took Mr Adams to remove the aneurysm
(b) Between 1420 h and 1520 h Polly was warmed up again. By how much did her temperature rise in that time?
(c) Polly's mass is 60 kg. How much heat was needed to warm her up again? Assume that 4000 J of heat energy warms up 1 kg of Polly by 1°C.
(d) What was the power of the heater in the heart/lung machine?

11 Meteors are small pieces of matter made mostly of iron. Like the Earth, meteors are in orbit around the Sun. Meteors travel very quickly and can cause a lot of damage when they hit something. The craters on the Moon were made by meteors. Fortunately few meteors hit the surface of the Earth. This is because our atmosphere slows them down in a very short time. Some data about a meteor are shown.

- Mass of meteor = 0.01 kg
- Speed of meteor entering atmosphere = 30 000 m/s
- Specific heat capacity of iron = 500 J/kg°C

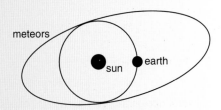

(a) Calculate the kinetic energy of the meteor as it enters the atmosphere. Use the formula:
Kinetic energy = ½ × mass × (speed)²
(b) Explain why the meteor slows down in the atmosphere.
Andrew and Kate are having a discussion about meteors. Andrew says: 'the kinetic energy of the meteor is turned into heat energy. I worked out that the final temperature of the meteor is about 900 000°C, using the equation:
energy transformed = mass × specific heat capacity × temperature change.'
(c) Use the data to show how Andrew got this answer. What assumption did he make?
Kate says: 'I read in a book that a meteor only reaches a temperature of about 20 000°C in the atmosphere. Your answer must be wrong. This is because you have forgotten that the meteor is losing heat.'
(d) Discuss what Kate says. Can you think of ways that the meteor will lose heat? What else will happen to the surface of the meteor at that temperature?
(e) Explain why very few meteors reach the surface of the Earth.

12 The time taken to cook an egg is:
- proportional to the mass of the yolk,
- proportional to the distance between the yolk and the shell,
- inversely proportional to the surface area of the shell.
Elaine decides to cook an ostrich egg for breakfast. Ostrich eggs are 3 times as long as hens' eggs. Elaine likes her hens' eggs boiled for 5 minutes. How long should she boil the ostrich egg for?

13 An electric heater, which has a power rating of 6 kW, is used to produce hot water for a bathroom shower. Cold water from the main water supply flows directly to the shower heater at a temperature of 10°C. Water flows through the shower at a rate of 2.4 litres per minute.

(a) Calculate the temperature of the hot shower water. (I litre of water requires 4200 J to warm it through 1°C.)

(b) Calculate the cost of the shower, if electricity costs 7p per kWh. Assume a shower lasts 5 minutes.

(c) Another shower has a heater rated at 5 kW, but the water flowing has a temperature of 50°C. Why can this happen?

(d) What happens to the water temperature if the water pressure drops?

(e) Explain any safety features that should be built into the shower.

14 This question is about the comparative costs of heating a bath by using gas and electricity. Below you can see an old gas bill charging the householders £128.47 for 290 therms of gas. The 'therm' is a unit of energy. The calorific value of the gas gives the amount of energy released when 1 m³ of gas is burnt; this is 38.5 MJ/m³ or 1032 Btus per cubic foot. A 'Btu' is a 'British thermal unit'.

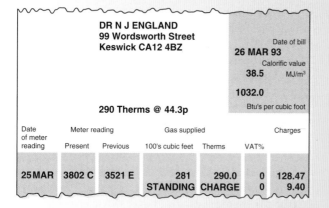

		DR N J ENGLAND				
		99 Wordsworth Street			Date of bill	
		Keswick CA12 4BZ			26 MAR 93	
					Calorific value	
					38.5 MJ/m³	
					1032.0	
		290 Therms @ 44.3p			Btu's per cubic foot	

Date of meter reading	Meter reading		Gas supplied			Charges
	Present	Previous	100's cubic feet	Therms	VAT%	
25 MAR	3802 C	3521 E	281	290.0	0	128.47
			STANDING	CHARGE	0	9.40

(a) How many different units of energy appear on the gas bill?

(b) Use the information on the bill to show that 10^5 Btu equal 1 therm.

(c) For this part of the question you need to know that 1 m³ = 35.3 ft³.
Work out the calorific value of the gas in:
(i) MJ/ft³,   (ii) Therms/ft³.
(iii) Now show that 1 therm equals 106 MJ.
(iv) Calculate the cost of providing 1 MJ of energy by burning gas.

(d) (i) A bath requires about 100 kg of water. We will assume that the water needs to be warmed from 10°C to 50°C. Calculate the energy required to warm the water. (1 kg of water needs 4.2 kJ to warm it through 1°C. Give your answer in MJ.)

(ii) Calculate the cost of heating the water using gas. Assume the gas boiler is 60% efficient.

(iii) Calculate the cost of heating the water using

electricity. Assume the immersion heater warms the water with 100% efficiency. The cost of electricity is 6.6p per kWh. [1 kWh = 3.6 MJ]

(iv) Why is electrical heating more efficient than gas heating?

(e) The gas board now charges 1.477p per kWh. How does this compare with the old price?

15 The diagrams show a simple solar panel. Water is pumped slowly through thin copper tubing which has been painted a dull black colour. The tubing has been embedded in an insulating material.

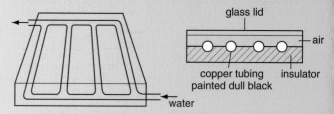

(a) Why is thin copper tubing used and why has it been painted black?

(b) Why does a glass lid improve the efficiency of the solar panel?

(c) Which material would you choose to insulate the bottom of the panel?

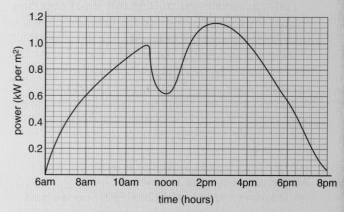

(d) The graph shows how the power of sunlight falling on 1 m² of solar panel varies throughout a bright summer's day.

(i) Explain the variation through the day. What do you think happened round about noon?

(ii) Use the graph to estimate the total energy absorbed by the panel during the day. Assume the panel absorbs 20% of the incident radiation; express your answer in kWh.

(iii) A typical house needs about 10 kWh of energy per day. Estimate the size of panel needed to supply energy to a house through the summer months.

(e) Comment on the limitations of solar power in Britain.

Waves and Sound

Waves carry energy and information. Different types of wave enable us to see, hear, watch television and communicate by phone

By the end of this section you should:

- know the difference between transverse and longitudinal waves
- understand that waves can reflect, refract, interfere and diffract
- know how loudness, pitch and quality of a sound wave relate to its shape
- know that there are three types of seismic waves
- know that light is an electromagnetic wave, and only a small part of the electromagnetic spectrum
- be able to explain how radio waves are used for communication purposes
- know some ways in which objects vibrate

1 Introducing Waves

Waves do two important things; they carry energy and information. You have seen ocean waves crashing into a sea wall at high tide. Those waves certainly carry energy.

When you watch television you are taking advantage of radiowaves. These waves carry energy and information from the transmitting station to your house. Light and sound waves carry energy and information from the television set to your eyes and ears.

Waves on slinkies

One of the best ways for you to learn about waves is to see them moving along on a stretched 'slinky' or spring. Figure 1 shows a slinky lying on the floor. When you move your hand up and down some humps move away from you along the slinky. Although the wave energy moves along the slinky, the movement of the slinky itself is up and down. If you tie a piece of string to the slinky, you will see that it moves in exactly the same way as your hand did to produce the waves. This sort of wave is called a **transverse wave**. The particles carrying the wave in the slinky move at right angles to the direction of wave motion. Water ripples on the surface of a pond and light waves are examples of transverse waves.

Aerials transmit radiowaves. These convey energy and information.

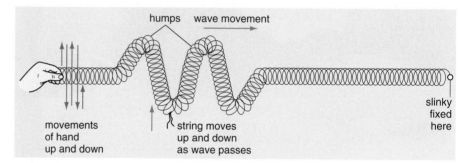

Figure 1 A transverse wave moving along a slinky

You produce a different kind of wave when you move your hand backwards and forwards along the slinky (Figure 2). Your hand compresses and then expands the slinky. The wave is made up of compressions and expansions which move along the slinky. This time a piece of string tied to the slinky moves backwards and forwards along it. Again, this is how your hand moved to produce the waves. This sort of wave is called a **longitudinal wave**. The particles carrying the wave in the slinky move backwards and forwards along the direction of wave motion. Sound waves are longitudinal.

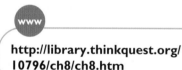

http://library.thinkquest.org/10796/ch8/ch8.htm

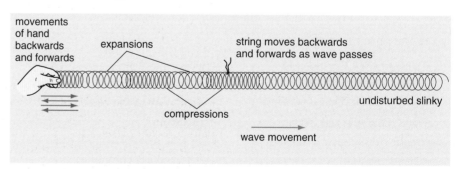

Figure 2 A longitudinal wave moving down a slinky

162

Sea waves carry a lot of kinetic energy. Sea waves also carry some information – about the weather conditions at sea.

Describing waves

Figure 3 is a graph showing the displacement of a slinky along its length at one moment. The arrows on the graph show the direction of the motion of the slinky; a larger arrow represents a larger speed.

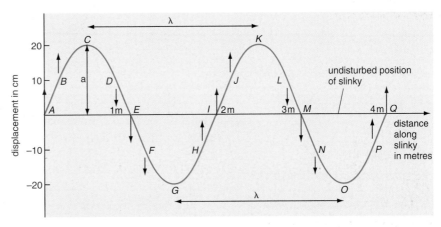

Figure 3 *The displacement of a slinky along its length. The arrows on the graph show the direction of motion of the slinky*

http://member.aol.com/
nicholashl/waves/waves.htm

- **Phase**. Points *B* and *J* are moving in phase. They are moving in the same direction, with the same speed. They also have the same displacement away from the undisturbed position of the slinky. *F* has been displaced in the opposite direction to *B* and *J*, and is moving in the opposite direction. *F* is out of phase with *B* and *J*. However, *F* moves in phase with *N*.
- The **wavelength** of a wave motion is the shortest distance between two points which are moving in phase. You can think of a wavelength as the distance between two 'humps'. We use the Greek letter λ (*lambda*) for the wavelength.
- The **amplitude** of a wave is the greatest displacement of the wave away from its undisturbed position. You can think of the amplitude as the height of a 'hump'.
- The **frequency**, *f*, of the wave is the number of complete waves produced per second. There are two complete waves in Figure 3. The unit of frequency is waves per second or *hertz* (Hz); 1 kHz means 1000 Hz; 1 Mhz means 1 000 000 Hz.
- The **time period** of a wave, *T*, is the time taken to produce one complete wave.

Wave velocities

The **velocity** of a wave, v, is the distance travelled by a wave in one second. The velocity of waves down a particular slinky is the same for all wavelengths. Figure 4(a) shows waves moving on a slinky with frequency 3 Hz and wavelength 0.4 m. In one second three waves have been produced, so the distance travelled by the first wave is $3 \times 0.4 = 1.2$ m. The wave velocity is 1.2 m/s. For any wave (see Figure 4(b)) we can calculate the wave velocity using the formula:

$$\text{Velocity} = \text{frequency} \times \text{wavelength}$$
$$v = f \times \lambda$$

http://www.physics.nwu.edu/ugrad/vpl/waves/wavetypes.html

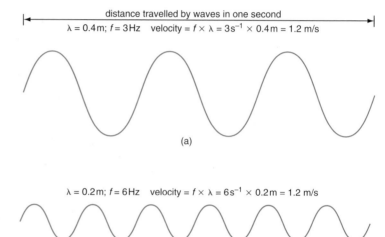

distance travelled by waves in one second
$\lambda = 0.4\,\text{m}; f = 3\,\text{Hz}$ velocity $= f \times \lambda = 3\text{s}^{-1} \times 0.4\,\text{m} = 1.2$ m/s

(a)

$\lambda = 0.2\,\text{m}; f = 6\,\text{Hz}$ velocity $= f \times \lambda = 6\text{s}^{-1} \times 0.2\,\text{m} = 1.2$ m/s

(b)

Figure 4 *The speed of waves along a slinky is the same for all wavelengths; high frequency waves have short wavelengths.*

Homework Questions

1 Use diagrams to explain what is meant by (i) a longitudinal wave, (ii) a transverse wave. Give two examples of each.

2 How would you use a slinky to demonstrate that waves can transmit both energy and information?

3 Make a sketch of a wave to illustrate what is meant by the terms (i) amplitude, (ii) wavelength.

4 The time periods of two waves are (i) 0.1 s (ii) 0.25 s. What are their frequencies?

5 (a) The length of a railway carriage is 28 m. A passenger at a station counts ten carriages passing him in 14 seconds. How fast is the train travelling?
(b) Waves pass an anchored yacht at a rate of five crests every 20 seconds. The crests are separated by a distance of 7 m. Calculate
(i) the frequency of the waves,
(ii) the speed of the waves.

6 Copy Figure 4(a). Underneath it draw a wave travelling on the same slinky with a frequency of 5 Hz. What is the wavelength of this wave?

7 This question refers to the graph in Figure 3.
(a) What is the wavelength of the wave?
(b) What is the amplitude of the wave motion?
(c) The frequency of the wave motion is 2 Hz. What is the time period of the wave?

(d) Calculate the speed of the wave.
(e) Give a point moving in phase with: (i) I, (ii) B, (iii) M.
(f) Make a sketch of the wave motion in Figure 3. Use the arrows showing the direction of movement of the particles in the slinky to draw in the position of the slinky a short time later.
(g) In which direction is the wave moving?

8 A radio station produces waves of frequency 200 kHz and wavelength 1500 m.
(a) What is the speed of radio waves?
(b) Another station produces waves with a frequency 600 kHz. What is their wavelength?

2 Water Waves

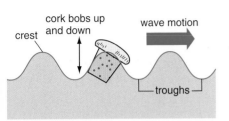

crest
cork bobs up and down
wave motion
troughs

Figure 1 *Ripples on water are transverse waves*

You can learn more about the nature of waves by studying ripples which move over the surface of water. It is easy to show that these ripples are transverse waves. If you look at a floating cork you will see it bob up and down as ripples travel along the surface of the water (Figure 1).

You can produce water waves in a ripple tank, by lowering a dipper into the water (Figure 2). A motor vibrates the dipper up an down to produce waves continuously. A beam of wood produces straight waves, and a small sphere produces circular waves. If you shine a light from above the tank you will see bright and dark patches on the screen below. These patches show the positions of the crests and troughs of the waves.

Ripples caused by a drop of water

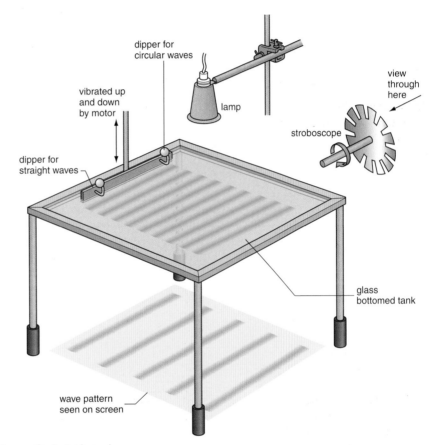

dipper for circular waves

vibrated up and down by motor

lamp

view through here

stroboscope

dipper for straight waves

glass bottomed tank

wave pattern seen on screen

Figure 2 *A ripple tank*

Using a stroboscope

Water waves move quite quickly and it can be difficult to see them. However, if you look through a rotating stroboscope you can make the waves appear stationary. The stroboscope is a disc with 12 slits in it. If you rotate the disc twice a second you will see the ripple tank 24 times a second. The waves will appear stationary when the dipper produces waves with a frequency of 24 Hz. Each time there is a slit in front of your eye one wave has moved forwards to the position of the next wave.

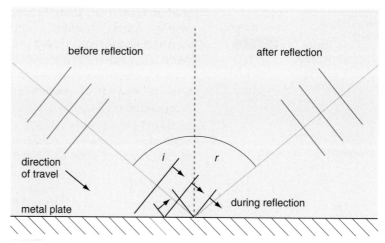

Figure 3 *Reflection of waves off a plane surface; angle of incidence, i = angle of reflection, r*

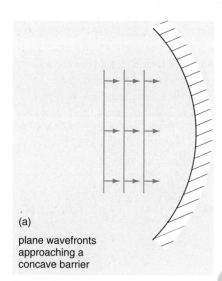

(a)

plane wavefronts
approaching a
concave barrier

Figure 4*(a)*

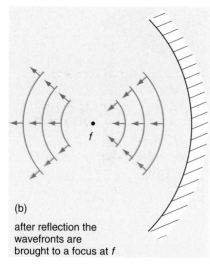

(b)

after reflection the
wavefronts are
brought to a focus at *f*

Figure 4*(b)*

Reflection

In Figure 3 you can see a computer simulation of waves approaching a straight metal barrier in a ripple tank. In the diagram, a line is drawn at right angles to the surface of the barrier. This line is called the **normal**. The angle between the normal and the direction of travel before reflection is called the **angle of incidence**, *i*. The angle between the normal and the direction of travel after reflection is called the **angle of reflection**, *r*. When waves are reflected, *i* always equals *r*. Figures 4 and 5 show some further examples of water waves being reflected.

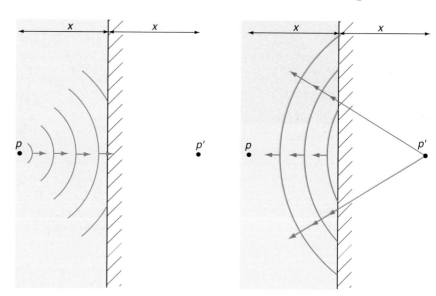

Figure 5

(a) *Circular wavefronts spread out from a point*

(b) *After reflection, the waves appear to have come from the point behind the barrier*

Refraction

In Figure 6 you can see some waves going from a region of deep water to shallow water. A region of shallow water in a tank can be made with a glass plate. In shallow water, waves travel more slowly than they do in deep water. There must be the same number of waves passing through both the deep and shallow regions. This means the frequency of the waves is the same. The speed of the waves is given by the equation $v = f \times \lambda$. So when the wave slows down in shallow water the wavelength must be less. In Figure 7 you can see some waves approaching a region of shallow water at an angle. They slow down and change direction. This is called **refraction**.

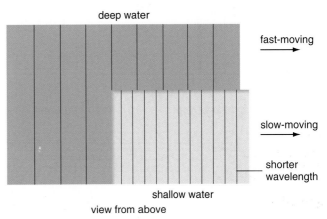

deep water

fast-moving

slow-moving

shorter wavelength

shallow water

view from above

(b) Waves going from deep water to shallow water

glass plate

side view

(a)

Figure 6

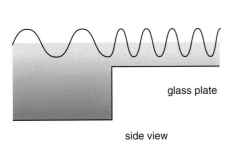

fast (deep water)

slow (shallow water)

Figure 7 *Water waves are refracted when they enter shallow water*

Homework Questions

1 Draw careful diagrams to show how waves are reflected in the following cases.

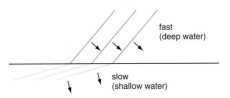

(a)

(b)

30°

(c)

2 The diagram shows a view looking down on to a ripple tank. One end of the tank has been tipped so that the water is deeper at one end than the other.

(a) Which end is deeper?
(b) Explain why the waves do not spread out as circular ripples.

3 What is meant by the term refraction? What causes waves to refract?

4 Draw careful diagrams to show how the waves are refracted in the following cases.

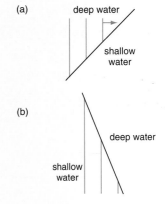

(a) deep water

shallow water

(b) deep water

shallow water

5 A propeller with two blades rotates twenty times a second. You look at it through a hand stroboscope with 10 slits.
(a) Why does the propeller look stationary if you rotate the stroboscope twice per second?
(b) What do you see if the stroboscope rotates 4 times per second?

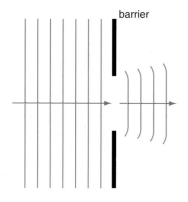

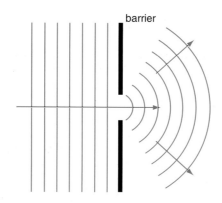

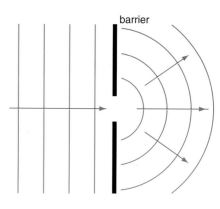

Figure 1

(a) Small wavelength, large gap

(b) Small wavelength, smaller gap

(c) Large wavelength, small gap

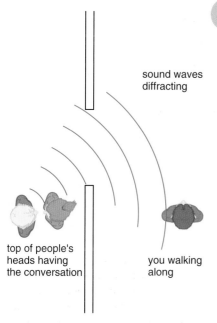

Figure 2 *A 'bird's eye view' of a conversation overheard through a doorway*

sound waves diffracting

top of people's heads having the conversation

you walking along

http://www.physics.nwu.edu/ugrad/vpl/waves/superposition1.html

Diffraction

When waves pass through a small hole, they spread out. This is called **diffraction**. You can see the diffraction of water waves in a ripple tank. Figure 1 shows you what happens when waves go through a series of gaps in barriers.

In Figure 1(a) the gap is large in comparison with the wavelength of the waves. The waves only spread out a little. In Figure 1(b) the gap is smaller. The waves spread out more. In Figure 1(c) the wavelength is larger than the gap and the waves now spread out completely.

Sound also diffracts. This tells us that sound is carried by waves. Figure 2 shows the sort of position you might find yourself in. You are walking down a corridor and you can hear two people talking through an open door, but you cannot see them. The sound waves do not travel in a straight line. They spread out and change direction as they pass through the doorway. That is why you can hear them talking even though you cannot see them.

We also think that light is carried by waves. So why can't we see round corners? You cannot see the people talking in Figure 2, because light waves have very small wavelengths. This means that when light waves go through a doorway they hardly diffract at all. Sound waves have much longer wavelengths, so they diffract through the doorway.

In this photograph you can see water waves diffracting as they pass through a harbour entrance. Water waves have a large wavelength, and so they spread out a lot when they diffract

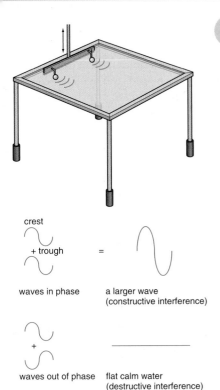

crest
+ trough   =

waves in phase   a larger wave
(constructive interference)

+

waves out of phase   flat calm water
(destructive interference)

Figure 4 *A ripple tank set up to show the interference of waves*

Interference

Some interesting patterns can be produced in a ripple tank when two small dippers make waves together. The two dippers produce a series of crests and troughs. These spread out and overlap as shown in Figure 3.

There are some places where the waves from the two dippers arrive *in phase*. This means that the two crests or two troughs arrive at the same time. The two crests move the water upwards to make a larger wave. So in some places, the water moves up and down *more* than it does with only one dipper working. We call this **constructive interference**.

At other places in the ripple tank, waves from the two dippers are arriving *out of phase*. This means that when a crest arrives from one dipper a trough arrives from the other. This time the effect of the two waves is to cancel each other out. The water does not move at all; it is as if the dippers have been switched off. We call this **destructive interference** (Figure 4).

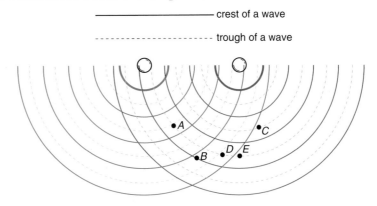

———————————— crest of a wave

- - - - - - - - - - - - - - - - - trough of a wave

Figure 3

Homework Questions

1 Astronomers use radio telescopes to detect radio waves from distant galaxies. A lot of radio waves have wavelengths a few metres long. Radio telescope dishes are about 100 m across. This means that the radio waves are only diffracted by a small amount. Explain why.

2 In an experiment in a ripple tank, straight water waves are produced with a frequency of 20 Hz. The waves travel at a speed of 40 cm/s through a gap in a barrier of width 1 cm.
(a) Calculate the wavelength of the waves.
(b) Draw a diagram to show how the waves would spread through the gap. Explain how you decided what to draw.
(c) Draw another diagram to show

what happens when the gap is made 4 cm wide.

3 In Figure 3 which of the points A, B, C, D, E will show (i) constructive interference (ii) destructive interference? Explain your answer.

4 The two diagrams below show slinkies with moving humps on them. Draw diagrams to show the shape of the slinkies (i) when the humps meet, (ii) after the humps have passed through each other.

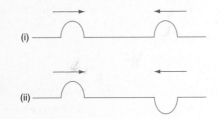

5 Use the information below to sketch a graph of the displacement of the point A against time. Your time axis should cover the next four seconds after the instant shown in the diagram.

- The wavelength of both sets of waves is 0.5 m.
- The amplitude of the waves is 0.2 m.

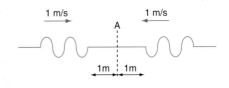

Sound Waves

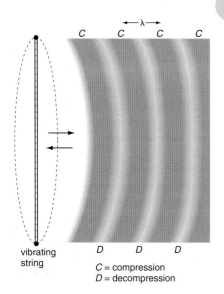

Making and hearing sounds

When you pluck a guitar string the instrument makes a noise. If you put your finger on the string you can feel the string vibrating. Sounds are made when something vibrates. The vibrations of a guitar string pass on energy to the air. This makes the air vibrate.

Sound is a longitudinal wave. Molecules in air move backwards and forwards along the direction in which the sound travels. In Figure 1 you can see that when the guitar string moves to the right it compresses the air on the right hand side of it. When the string moves to the left the air on the right expands. The string produces a series of **compressions** and **decompressions**. In a compression the air pressure is greater than normal atmospheric pressure. In a decompression the air pressure is less than normal atmospheric pressure.

Compressions and decompressions travel through air in the same way that compressions will move along a slinky. Your ear detects the changes in pressure caused by sound waves. When a compression reaches the ear it pushes the ear drum inwards. When a decompression arrives, the ear drum moves out again. The movements of the ear drum are transmitted through the ear by bones. Then nerves transmit electrical pulses to the brain.

vibrating string

D D D

C = compression
D = decompression

Figure 1 *A vibrating guitar string*

Speeds of sound (m/s)	Material
330	air
1500	water
5000	steel

Table 1

Speed of sound

The speed of sound depends on which material it travels through. Sound waves are transmitted by molecules knocking into each other. In air, sound travels at about 330 m/s. In solids and liquids, where molecules are packed more tightly together, sound travels faster (Table 1). In a vacuum there are no molecules at all. Sound cannot travel through a vacuum, although light can.

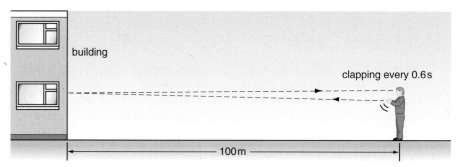

Figure 2 *Measuring the speed of sound through air*

Figure 2 shows a simple way for you to measure the speed of sound through air. Stand about 100 m away from a building and clap your hands. Sound waves will be reflected back to you from the building. When you hear the echo, clap again so that you clap in time with the echo. A friend, watching you clapping your hands, times 10 claps in 6 seconds. Now, you know that the sound took 0.6 s to travel 200m (to the wall and back again).
So the speed of sound is given by:

$$V = \frac{d}{t}$$

$$= \frac{200 \text{ m}}{0.6 \text{ s}} = 330 \text{ m/s}$$

http://www.umanitoba.ca/linguistics/russell/138/sec4/acoustl.htm

http://library.thinkquest.org/2662/

http://library.thinkquest.org/19537/

http://www.physics.nwu.edu/ugrad/vpl/waves/sound1.html

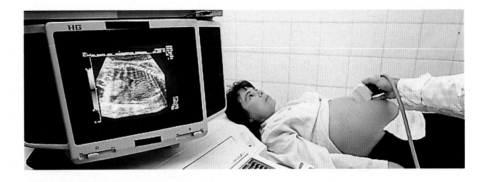

In this picture ultrasound emitted by the probe placed on the mother's stomach is reflected by the foetus. A computer builds up a picture from those reflected waves, which, unlike X-rays, are perfectly safe. In this photograph we can see a healthy baby boy.

Ultrasonic depth finding

We use the name **ultrasound** to describe very high frequency sound waves. These waves have such a high frequency that we cannot hear them. Because ultrasound has a high frequency, the waves have a short wavelength. This means that it is possible to produce a narrow beam of ultrasound without it spreading out due to diffraction effects.

Ships use beams of ultrasound for a variety of purposes. Fishing boats look for fish, destroyers hunt for submarines or explorers chart the depth of the oceans. Figure 3 demonstrates the idea. A beam of ultrasonic waves is sent out from the bottom of a ship. The waves are reflected from the sea bed back to the ship. The longer the delay between the transmitted and reflected pulses, the deeper the sea is (Figure 4).

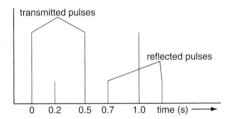

Figure 4 *Ultrasound pulses for a depth of 150 m*

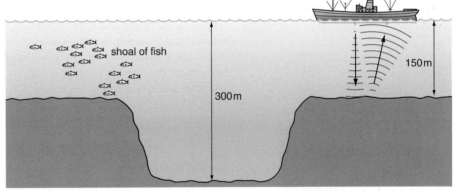

Figure 3 *Ultrasonic depth finding*

Homework Questions

1 The frequency of a sound from your mouth is 250 Hz.
(a) Calculate the wavelength of this sound (use Table 1 to find the speed).
(b) Explain why sound is diffracted when it leaves your mouth.

2 (a) Ultrasound can be used to examine a baby inside a mother's womb.
(i) How do waves help to build up an image?
(ii) Why is ultrasound preferable to X-rays?
(b) Explain how you could use ultrasound waves to check for cracks in railway lines.
(c) A bat can find its supper by using ultrasonic waves for echo-location. Explain how this process works. Could we find our supper through echo-location?

3 The ship in Figure 3 sends out short pulses of ultrasound every 0.5 s; the frequency of the waves is 50 kHz (50 000 Hz).
(a) The duration of each pulse is 0.01 s. How many complete oscillations of the ultrasound waves are emitted during that time?
(b) Use the information in Figures 3 and 4 to show that the ultrasound travels at a speed of 1500 m/s through water.
(c) Sketch a graph, similar to Figure 4, to show both the transmitted and reflected pulses when the ship reaches point A.
(d) What difficulties does the ship face when trying to measure depths of around 500 m?
(e) Calculate the wavelength of the ultrasonic waves.
(f) Why is it important to use a *narrow* beam of ultrasound waves? Why is it not possible to produce such a narrow beam of ordinary sound waves?

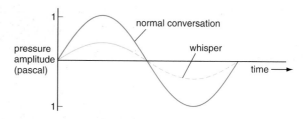

Figure 1   *Sound waves caused by the human voice*

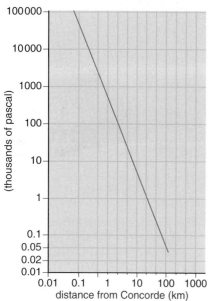

Figure 2

Loudness

Your ears are very good detectors of energy. A disco produces sound energy at a rate of about 40 W. You find this very noisy. If you were to light a disco with one 40 W light bulb, everyone would complain that it was too dark.

Your ears detect sounds over a wide range of frequencies. You can hear frequencies as low as 20 Hz, and as high as 20 000 Hz. Your ears are most sensitive to frequencies of about 2000 Hz. So a note at a frequency of 2000 Hz sounds louder than a note of frequency 10 000 Hz which carries the same energy. A loud noise makes your ear drums move a long way, while a very quiet noise has only a small effect on your eardrums. The loudness of a noise depends on the pressure caused by the sound wave. During normal conversation your voice will cause the air pressure to change by about 1 pascal (1 N/m²). Your voice produces a pressure wave of amplitude 1 pascal (Figure 1). This is a small change in comparison with atmospheric pressure (100 000 pascals).

Loud noises can be very unpleasant and can damage your hearing. There are laws in force which limit the noise that industrial machinery, cars and aeroplanes are allowed to make. A sonic boom from Concorde can be heard over very great distances. Figure 2 shows roughly how the pressure caused by Concorde changes with distance. Exactly how far sound travels depends on many factors such as the strength and direction of the wind.

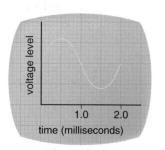

(a) waveform of tuning fork of low pitch

Pitch

We use the term **pitch** to describe how a noise or a musical note sounds to us. Bass notes are of low pitch, treble notes are of high pitch. Men have low-pitched voices, women have voices of higher pitch. The pitch of a note is related directly to its frequency. The higher-pitched notes are the notes with higher frequency.

Figure 3 shows a data logger being used to analyse the waveform of the sound from a tuning fork. Once the data has been collected it can be down-loaded and displayed on a computer's VDU; Figures 3(a) and (b) confirm that higher pitched sounds have higher frequencies.

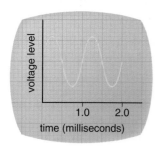

(b) waveform of tuning fork of higher pitch

Figure 3

Quality

On a piano the note that is called middle C has a frequency of 256 Hz. This note could be played on a piano or a violin, or you could sing the note. Somebody listening to the three different sounds would recognise straight away whether you had sung the note or played it on the piano or violin. The **quality** of the three notes is different. The quality of a note depends on the shape of its waveform. Although two notes may have the same frequency and amplitude, if their waveforms are of a different shape you will detect a different sound (Figure 4).

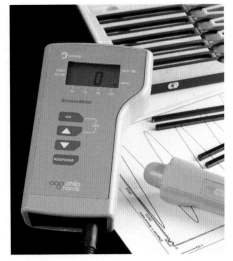

Every musical instrument can play notes of the same pitch; the quality of each note however, varies widely between instruments

This data logger can be used to record the waveforms produced by different instruments

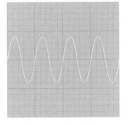

(a) flute

(b) trumpet

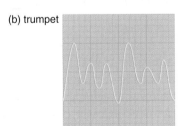

(c) piano

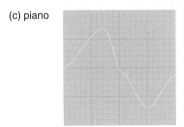

(d) violin

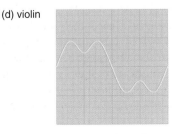

Figure 4 *Data-logger readings from various instruments*

Homework Questions

1 Use the data below, and Figure 2, to answer these questions.
(a) At approximately what distance from Concorde will the sound level be enough to interrupt a conversation?
(b) Work out roughly how far you need to be from Concorde so that you cannot hear it.

Noise level	Pressure amplitude in thousandths of a pascal
Painfully loud	100 000
Normal conversation	1000
Quiet countryside	1
Too quiet to be heard	0.02

(c) Explain why it is necessary to have laws controlling the noise levels near airports.

2 (a) Use the data in Figure 3 to calculate the frequencies of the sounds emitted from the two tuning forks.
(b) Using the same scales as Figure 3, sketch the forms of notes from tuning forks of frequencies (i) 2000 Hz; (ii) 750 Hz.

3 Look at Figure 4. The data logger collected information about the four musical instruments for the same length of time in each case.

(a) Which note has the highest frequency?
(b) Which instrument is played most loudly?
(c) Which instrument is played most softly?
(d) Which two instruments are playing notes of the same pitch?

4 An electronic synthesizer produces the two pure notes A and B as shown (right). It produces a third note C by adding the two waveforms together.
(a) Copy the two waveforms carefully onto some graph paper.
(b) Add the two waveforms together to produce the waveform of C.
(c) Does C sound louder than A or B?
(d) How does the frequency of C compare with: (i) A, (ii) B?
(e) Does C have the same quality as A or B?

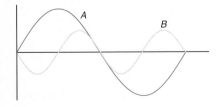

Internal structure of the Earth

The Earth is nearly spherical, but is slightly flattened at the poles. Its structure and surface resemble that of a cracked egg. The 'cracked shell' is the thin crust, the 'white' is the mantle, and the 'yolk' the core (Figure 1). The concentric layers increase in thickness, density and temperature towards the centre.

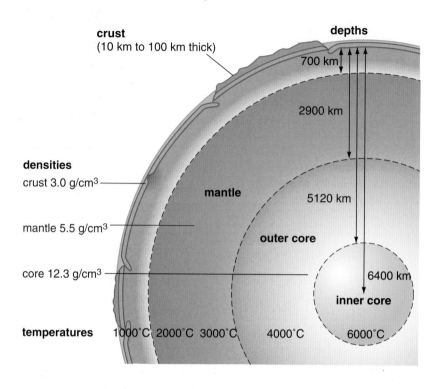

Figure I *Cross-section of the Earth to show its internal structure*

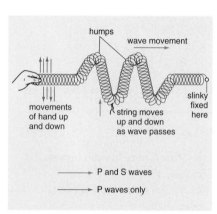

Figure 2(a) A tranverse wave moving down a slinky. S-waves travel through the Earth like this, causing rock to oscillate at right angles to the direction of wave movement.

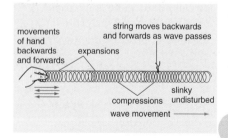

Figure 2(b) A longitudinal wave moving down a slinky. P-waves travel through the Earth like this, causing a series of compressions and expansions in rock along the direction of wave movement.

The Earth's crust is very thin and is broken into many parts of various sizes, called plates. These float on the denser mantle, parts of which are molten. Over periods of millions of years, slow moving convection currents in the mantle cause movements in the plates above them. Such movements shape the surface of the Earth, forming mountain ranges and rift valleys; they provide the energy for volcanoes and cause earthquakes as giant pieces of rock slip abruptly past each other.

Evidence for the Earth's Structure

Much detail of the Earth's structure comes from the study of earthquakes. During an earthquake, the crust ruptures. Energy generated at the focus of the earthquake creates a train of shock (**seismic**) waves. These extend outwards through the Earth and their pathways are shown in Figure 3. Earthquake energy creates three main types of waves: **P or primary waves; S, secondary or shear waves; L, longitudinal or surface waves**. L waves are slow moving and travel through the crust. P and S waves move faster and travel through the deeper layers of the Earth (Figure 3). P waves travel through liquids and solids. S waves travel through solids; they cannot pass through the Earth's liquid outer core. From the movement of these waves we can obtain evidence for the Earth's internal

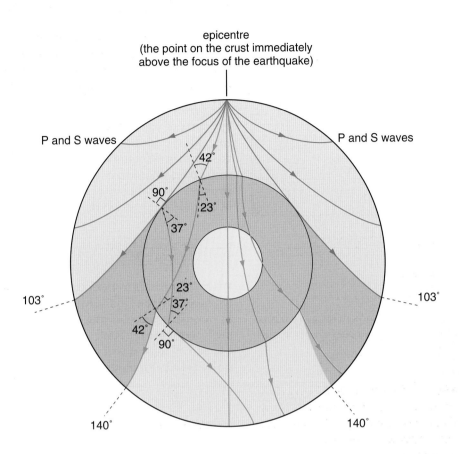

Figure 3 *Cross-section of the Earth showing the paths of seismic waves from an earthquake. Both P and S waves (in blue) spread out to angles of up to 103° from the epicentre, but S waves cannot travel through the liquid core. P waves (in green) entering the liquid core slow down and are focused (like light waves through a lens) into the region at the bottom of the diagram (angles > 140°). No P wave travelling through the liquid outer core reaches the 'P wave shadow zone'. However, weak P waves are detected in that zone, which have been speeded up, and therefore refracted, by the solid inner core*

structure. Surface waves roll invisibly through the Earth's crust. Around the **epicentre** of an earthquake (right above the focus) these waves cause the most damage to buildings.

Seismic waves

The velocities of seismic waves depend on the density and elasticity of the rock they are passing through. Rigid rock transmits waves faster than loose sediments or molten rocks, because it springs back more readily when compressed or distorted. The more dense a rock is the more slowly it transmits a wave. Both the density and elasticity of rocks increase with depth, but the elasticity rises faster than the density. Consequently, both P wave and S wave velocities increase as they go deeper into the Earth's mantle. However, when P waves enter the molten outer core they slow down considerably. P waves speed up again slightly on entering the solid inner core. Figure 4 shows the variation of wave velocities with depth.

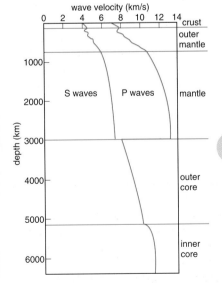

Figure 4 *This graph shows the variation of P and S wave velocities with depth in the Earth*

S waves are transverse waves. The rock oscillates at right angles to the direction of the wave motion. S waves can only travel through solids, because only a rigid body can provide the sideways forces to restore the rock to its original position. Liquids flow so they cannot provide the sideways or shear forces. P waves are longitudinal waves. They are like sound or shock waves, which are well illustrated by a series of compressions and expansions passing along a slinky. See Figure 3.

S waves do not register on seismometers at an angle greater than 103° from the epicentre of the earthquake, because they cannot travel through the liquid outer core. Most P waves also cut out at angles greater than 103° but reappear at angles greater than 140°. Between 103° and 140° a **shadow zone** exists in which little earthquake information is received. Some weak P waves, however, do enter the shadow zone, either by being refracted outwards by the solid inner core, or by being reflected back off the Earth's surface.

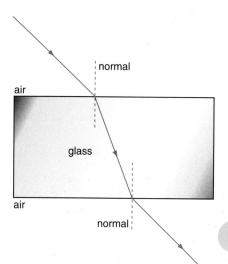

Figure 5 *Light rays refracted by a glass block; seismic waves obey the same rules of refraction*

Refraction

When light passes from air to glass it is slowed down and it is refracted towards the normal; when light leaves glass and enters air it refracts the other way (Figure 5). Seismic waves obey the same rules of refraction. In Figure 3 you can see how the P waves are refracted towards the normal as they enter the outer core. At such a boundary some waves will also be reflected; similarly when light strikes a surface some is transmitted and some is reflected.

Homework Questions

1 In California, you can see orange groves with trees growing in perfect, straight lines. However, there are some orange groves in which the lines of trees are for some reason kinked. They were not planted like that.
(a) What is the cause?
(b) In what interesting geological area are these orange groves?

2 Although some very deep holes have been drilled into the Earth, none has ever reached the mantle. We have no direct evidence of the nature of the interior of the Earth. Our knowledge is based on indirect evidence. What is this evidence and what has it told us about the Earth's interior?

3 This question is about seismic waves; you will find it useful to refer to Figures 3 and 4.
(a) When P waves enter the core at Point A they are refracted. Explain carefully using the data in Figure 4 the direction of this refraction.
(b) Explain fully why seismic waves travelling through the Earth follow curved paths.
(c) S waves can travel only to depths of about 3000 km. Why is this the case?
(d) How can you tell from Figure 4 that the outer mantle of the Earth has many separate layers or discontinuities in it?
(e) A seismic station is about 1000 km from the epicentre of an earthquake. P and S waves reach it travelling close to the Earth's surface. Approximately how long is the interval between the two types of waves reaching the station?

4 (a) S and P seismic waves pass through the Earth. Explain the nature of these waves.
(b) Which type of wave can pass through the core? Explain why the other type of wave is confined to the mantle.

5 The diagram shows light from a point source spreading out on to a converging lens below it.
(a) Why is there a 'shadow zone' on the screen below the lens? Copy the diagram and mark where this zone is.
(b) How does this experiment help to explain why there is a P-wave shadow zone for seismic waves emitted from an earthquake?
(c) It is suggested that the lens behaves rather like the outer core of the Earth. What sort of lens would you use to represent the solid inner core of the Earth? Add this lens to your diagram to illustrate its effect on the light.

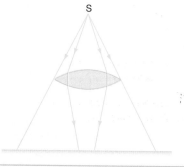

Electromagnetic Waves

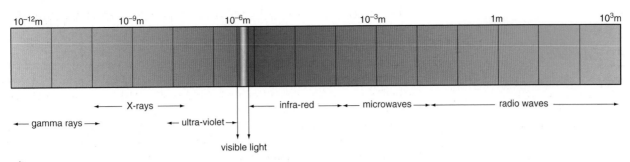

X-rays

gamma rays

ultra-violet

visible light

infra-red — microwaves — radio waves

Figure 1 *The electromagnetic spectrum*

You will already have heard of radio waves and light waves. These are two examples of **electromagnetic waves**. There are many sorts of electromagnetic wave, which produce very different kinds of effect. Figure 1 shows you the full *electromagnetic spectrum*. The range of wavelengths in the spectrum stretches from 10^{-12} m for gamma rays to about 2 km for radio waves.

All the waves you have met so far travel through some material. Sound waves travel through air, seismic waves travel through the Earth, water ripples travel along the surface of water. Electromagnetic waves can travel through a vacuum; this is how energy reaches us from the Sun. The energy is carried by changing electric and magnetic forces. These changing forces are at right angles to the direction in which the wave is travelling. So electromagnetic waves are transverse waves (Figure 2).

Figure 2 *In an electromagnetic wave, energy is carried by oscillating electric and magnetic forces. These forces are at right angles to the direction in which the wave travels*

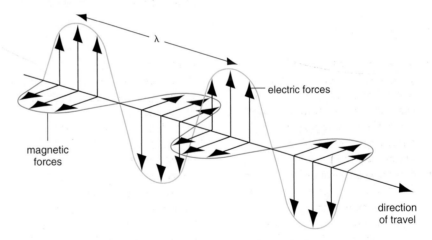

electric forces

magnetic forces

direction of travel

Electromagnetic waves show the usual wave properties. They can be reflected and refracted. They show diffraction and interference effects. In a vacuum all electromagnetic waves travel at the same speed of 3×10^8 m/s. However, electromagnetic waves travel at slower speeds when they travel in a material. For example, light travels at a slower speed in glass.

- **Radio waves.** Radio 4 broadcasts on longwave use a wavelength of 1500 m; Capital Radio uses a wavelength of 194 m. These radio waves are produced by high frequency oscillations of electrons in aerials. Radio waves with wavelengths of a few hundred metres are used in local and national radio (see Figure 3).

  Radio waves with wavelengths of a few centimetres are used to transmit television signals and international phone calls. If you make a phone call to America your radio signals are sent out into space by large aerial dishes, like the one you can see in the photograph on the next page. These signals are received by a satellite in orbit around the Earth. Then the signals are relayed to another aerial dish in America. It is important to use short wavelengths for international communications, so that a narrow beam of waves can be directed towards the satellite. Long wavelengths would be diffracted, so not much energy would reach the satellite.

www

http://www.purchon.com/
physics/electromagnetic.htm

http://www.smgaels.org/
physics/home.htm

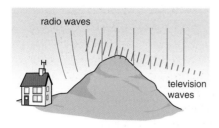

Figure 3 *Long and medium wavelength radio waves will diffract around hills and houses. However, waves used for TV signals are of short wavelengths. These will not bend around hills so well; this house will have poor TV reception*

- **Microwaves** have wavelengths between radiowaves and infra-red waves; it should be remembered that the distinction between various types of electromagnetic wave is fairly arbitrary.

  The short wavelength radiowaves described above could also have been described as microwaves. The other well known use of microwaves is to heat food in ovens. Microwaves of a particular wavelength are chosen which are absorbed by water molecules. Microwave cooking provides the advantage that the waves can penetrate to the middle of the food, thereby cooking the inside as well as the outside. This is much faster than the conventional method of cooking, where heat is conducted to the inside. Microwave ovens must be made of metal in order to trap the waves inside them; this is important to make sure we do not cook ourselves!

- **Infra-red waves** have wavelengths between about 10^{-4} m and 10^{-6} m. Anything that is warm will lose energy by giving out infra-red radiation. You lose some heat energy by radiation. You can certainly feel the infra-red radiation given out, or *emitted*, by an electric fire. Prolonged exposure of the skin to sunlight can cause sunburn, due to infra-red rays.

  Infra-red photography can be used to measure the temperature of objects. The hotter something is, the more infra-red radiation it gives out.

- **Light waves** form the part of the electromagnetic spectrum to which our eyes

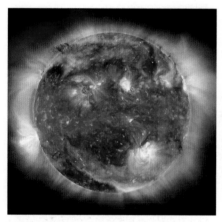

This is an ultra-violet image of the Sun. Very hot objects like the sun produce these waves. Astronomers often 'see' what space looks like in wavelengths other than visible light. Imagine if our eyes detected infra-red light as opposed to visible light – how different would the world look?

A large satellite communications dish which is designed to receive radio messages. The main dish collects the radio waves and directs them towards the secondary reflector, held above the main dish on four supports. This, in turn, reflects them down onto the receiver, the mast at the centre of the main dish.

are sensitive. Red light has a wavelength of 7×10^{-7} m and violet light a wavelength of 4×10^{-7} .

- **Ultra-violet waves** have wavelengths shorter than light – approximately 10^{-8} m or 10^{-9} m. While infra-red waves are emitted from hot objects (1000°C or so), ultra-violet waves are emitted from even hotter objects 4000°C and above). The Sun and other stars are sources of ultra-violet 'light'. Exposure to ultra-violet waves can damage your eyes, and prolonged exposure to ultra-violet light from the sun can damage your skin and cause skin cancer.

- **X-rays** have wavelengths of about 10^{-10} m. These rays can cause damage to body tissues, so your exposure to them should be limited. X-rays are now widely used in medicine. X-rays of short wavelengths will pass through body tissues but will be absorbed by bone. Such rays can be used to take a photograph to see if a patient has broken a bone.

  Slightly longer wavelength X-rays are used in body scanning. These X-rays are absorbed by body tissues and doctors can build up a picture of the inside of a patient's body. This allows doctors to investigate whether a patient has cancer.

- **Gamma rays** are very short wavelength electromagnetic waves which are emitted from the nucleus of atoms. Gamma rays are very penetrating and large doses of gamma radiation are harmful. These rays have many industrial, agricultural and medical uses (see Section L).

Homework Questions

1 (a) How does an electromagnetic wave carry energy? Draw a diagram to help explain your answer.
(b) Electromagnetic waves are emitted from objects when electrons oscillate rapidly backwards and forwards. How do you think electromagnetic waves are detected?

2 (a) Why are short wavelength radio waves needed for mobile phone communications?
(b) Give two reasons why microwave ovens are made from steel.
(c) Which electromagnetic waves cause (i) sunburn, (ii) skin cancer?
(d) Give three examples of how electromagnetic waves are used in your life every day.

3 In the table below you can see some data showing typical values of wavelengths and frequencies for different types of radio wave.

(a) Copy the table. Then use the equation $v = f \times \lambda$ to fill in the missing values.
(b) Which wave would you use for (i) a local radio station (ii) television broadcasts to the USA. Explain your choice.

4 The diagram (below) shows a side view of a radio dish. Explain why the receiver is placed some distance away from the dish. (A diagram may make your answer clearer.)

Type of radio wave	Wavelength (m)	Frequency (MHz)
Long	1500	
Medium	300	
Short	10	
VHF		100
UHF		3000

(VHF = very high frequencies, UHF = ultra high frequencies).

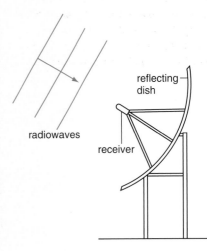

reflecting dish

radiowaves

receiver

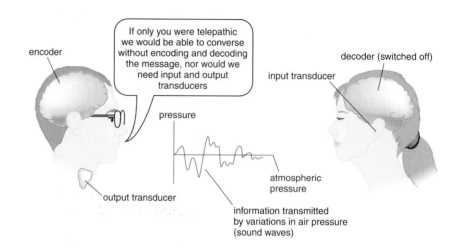

Figure 1 *Information can be carried in these pulses on the slinky. The amplitude and shape of the pulses are important*

Waves carry energy and information, which allow us to communicate with each other. You could communicate in code by sending pulses along a stretched spring or slinky (Figure 1). The length and shape of the pulses carry the information or message. Most of us are lucky enough to be able to communicate by talking and listening to each other.

A communications system can only work if it contains a number of **fundamental building blocks**. Figure 2 illustrates this idea, by examining what is required for two people to talk to each other.

Figure 2 *Speech communication system*

- **Encoding.** The message is sent in code (or language). The speaker's brain encodes the message and transmits it by electrical pulses to the voice box.
- **Output transducer.** A transducer is a device that changes the way our information signal is carried. Here the voice box changes electrical pulses into sound waves.
- **Transmission.** Once the sound waves leave the voice box the signal has been sent or transmitted. The information is now carried in the pressure variations of the sound wave.
- **Input transducer.** The sound waves reach the ear of the listener. These waves make the ear drum vibrate, which then transmits electrical messages to the brain.
- **Decoding** The brain now can decode the message; however, if you do not understand the language or you are not concentrating, the message does not get through.
- **Storage and retrieval.** Once the message has been understood the brain *stores* it in the memory. Later the message can be *retrieved* or remembered. To help the brain, you take notes in class, which are stored in a file and retrieved when it is time to revise.
- **Amplification.** Sometimes a person's hearing is not so good. Then a hearing aid amplifies the sound. A hearing aid contains a tiny microphone to receive the signal, which is amplified and retransmitted by a speaker to the ear.

When you ring up a friend and speak to her on the phone, the communication system is a little more complicated. There are two more transducers; your mouthpiece turns sound waves into electrical pulses which travel along the phone line, and her earpiece turns the electrical pulses back into sound waves. When she is out, you might leave a message on the answerphone. The message is stored on magnetic tape, ready for retrieval when she comes home.

Mobile phones rely on microwaves and digital codes

Radio systems

This section concentrates on the broad outline of a radio system. To understand radiocommunication more fully, you need to read Unit G9 too; Unit K5 tells you more about amplifiers.

Transmitting the signal

A microphone detects sound waves and turns them into audio frequency (AF) electrical pulses; this is the input transducer. The **modulator** encodes the message, by mixing in the audio frequency information, with the radio frequency carrier signal. This is amplified and transmitted from the aerial; in Figure 3 you can see the radio wave represented by oscillating electric and magnetic fields.

Receiving the signal

The process is now put into reverse. A receiving aerial picks up the radio transmission. The signal is amplified before being passed to the **demodulator** which separates out the radio and audio frequencies. The demodulator decodes the signal (see Figure 4). Finally, the audio signal is amplified, before the electrical pulses drive the loudspeaker which produces the sound. The loudspeaker is the output transducer.

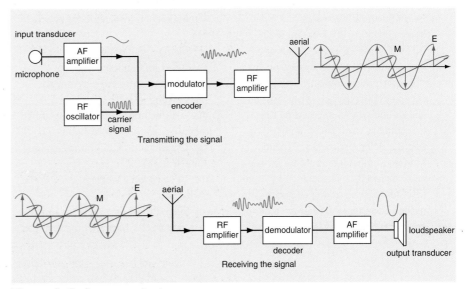

Figure 3 *Radio communication system*

Decoding the signal

Figure 4 shows the circuit to decode or demodulate the signal. The amplitude modulated RF signal, V_{aa}, is passed into a diode. Without a capacitor or resistor in the circuit, the signal would come out like the voltage V_{bb}: the diode only conducts one way. These rectified pulses, V_{bb}, charge up the capacitor (see Unit K2), while the diode is conducting. When the diode is not conducting the capacitor partly discharges through the resistor. The value of the resistance must be carefully chosen. If R is too small, the capacitor discharges too quickly and too much of the RF signal gets through to the output. If R is too big the capacitor does not discharge fast enough to follow the AF signal properly. The final smoothed output signal is shown.

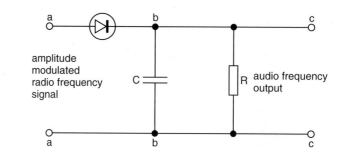

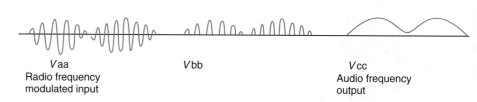

Vaa
Radio frequency
modulated input

Vbb

Vcc
Audio frequency
output

Figure 4 *Decoding a signal*

Homework Questions

1 Below, several means of communicating information are listed. Choose three of them and draw block diagrams to explain how the information is transmitted and received in each case. Your answers should include an account of the transducers used and the encoding and decoding processes. Explain how each message could be stored and retrieved.
(a) One ship signalling to another in morse code using flashes on a lamp.
(b) Watching television.

(c) Making an international phone call.
(d) Using a bar code reader at the checkout in a supermarket.
(e) Sending a message by e-mail.
(f) Writing a letter.

2 Make an estimate of how long these messages took to be transmitted:
(a) Christopher Columbus reaching America, 1492.
(b) Wellington's victory at Waterloo, 1815.
(c) Sixty thousand casualties in the first day of the Battle of the Somme,

1916.
(d) Neil Armstrong landing on the Moon, 1969.

3 What is meant by the terms (i) audio frequency, (ii) radio frequency. Explain your answer with reference to sound waves and carrier waves.

4 (a) Think of an animal you know something about, and discuss how it sends and receives messages.
(b) How do the colours on plants send messages to animals?

Aerials and polarisation

Aerials transmit or receive radio waves. Any conductor can act as an aerial, but for efficient transmission and reception it is necessary to design aerials carefully. In Figure 1 radio waves are being transmitted by a **dipole** aerial. This aerial consists of two vertical wires, each of which is one quarter of a wavelength long. The waves are emitted equally in all horizontal directions.

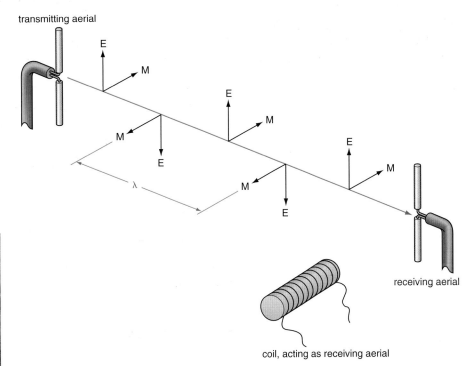

Figure 1

In the top photograph a fisherman can't see any fish because of glare from the Sun reflecting off the water. The bottom photograph is what he sees when he puts his polaroid sunglasses on. The glare is much reduced and now he can see the fish. This is because the sunglasses only transmit light with oscillations in one direction.

The waves in Figure 1 are shown travelling towards a receiving aerial, which is identical to the transmitter. The receiving aerial detects radio waves when it is placed vertically. When it is turned so that its wires lie in a horizontal plane it detects nothing. The waves transmitted from the dipole aerial are **polarised**. In this case they are vertically polarised, so that the electric field of the wave lies in a vertical plane; the magnetic field is at right angles to the electric field and lies in a horizontal plane. When the receiving aerial lies in a vertical plane, electrons in it are made to oscillate up and down by the changing magnetic and electric fields. Now there is a current in the aerial which can be detected by a meter. Radio waves can also be detected by a coil. Note how the coil in Figure 1 is placed so that its axis lies parallel to the magnetic field of the waves. This changing field induces a current in the coil, as you would do by pushing a bar magnet in and out.

Figure 2 shows what happens to an electromagnetic wave when it passes through a polarising filter. To help to see the effect of polarisation, only the electric field of the wave is shown. At A the electric field of the wave can oscillate in any plane (at right angles to the direction in which the wave travels). After

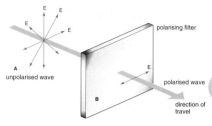

Figure 2

passing through the filter at B, the wave's electric field only oscillates in a horizontal plane. The wave is polarised. By rotating the polariser, the plane of polarisation may be rotated too.

Ground, sky and space waves

Radio waves can travel to us by three different routes.

* Some waves are conducted along the ground or across an ocean. These are called **ground** or **surface waves**. Low frequency waves (long waves) can travel up to 1500 km along the ground. Higher frequency waves lose energy rapidly over the ground, so their range is much less.
* Some radio waves travel towards the sky, but are reflected back towards the Earth's surface by the **ionosphere**. These are called **sky waves**. Waves with frequencies below about 30 MHz are reflected by the ionosphere, but higher frequency waves can pass through it. The ionosphere is a region of the atmosphere stretching from about 100 km to 500 km above the Earth's surface. In this region molecules have been ionised by radiation from the sun.

    Sky waves of long, medium and short wavelengths can travel several thousand kilometres round the Earth due to multiple reflections.
* VHF and UHF waves and microwaves are not reflected by the ionosphere. These waves can only be transmitted round the world with the help of communications satellites. These are called **space waves**. It is also possible to transmit space waves directly over a distance of about 100 km provided that the transmitter is on a mountain and there is nothing to get in the way.

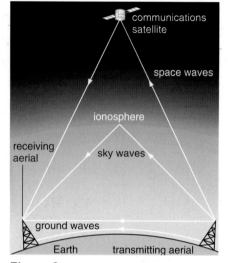

Figure 3

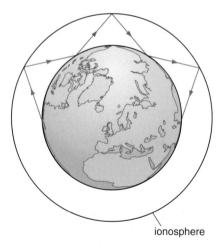

Figure 4 *How sky waves can travel around the Earth*

Frequency band	Wavelength	Use of waves
Low frequency 30 kHz–300 kHz	Long wave 10 km–1 km	National radio (Radio 4)
Medium frequency 300 kHz–3 MHz	Medium wave 1 km–100 m	National and local radio (Radio 1)
High frequency 3 MHz–30 MHz	Short wave 100 m–10 m	International radio Amateur and CB radio
Very high frequency (VHF) 30 MHz–300 MHz	10 m–1 m	Shipping, military and police communication
Ultra high frequency (UHF) 300 MHz–3 GHz	1 m–10 cm	TV, radiophones, aircraft guidance systems
Microwaves frequencies > 3 GHz	Less than 10 cm	Telephone calls, communications satellites, radar

This table shows the variety of radio waves and some of their uses

Modulation

A radio station might broadcast on a frequency of 3 MHz and yet the sounds we hear, voices or music, are in the audio range of frequencies 20 Hz to 20 kHz. The information about the sound is carried by modulating the radio waves. This can be done in two ways.

- **Amplitude modulation (AM).** Sound waves are first turned into electrical oscillations. These signals are then mixed in with the radio **carrier** waves. The information from the sound is then carried by varying the amplitude of the radio carrier wave (Figure 5).

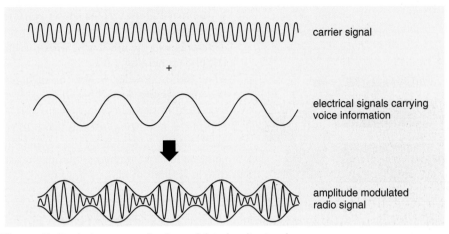

Figure 5 *Producing an amplitude modulated radio signal*

- **Frequency modulation (FM).** Here the information about the sound waves is carried by varying the frequency of the carrier waves (Figure 6). The frequency of the carrier waves increases for a positive information signal, and decreases for a negative information signal.

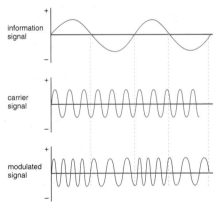

Figure 6 *Frequency modulation*

Homework Questions

1 (a) Explain what is meant by polarisation.
(b) Why does the direction of your TV aerial matter?
(c) How do polaroid sunglasses help skiers?
(d) Find out how polaroid sunglasses work and write a brief explanation.

2 In 1901 Marconi succeeded in transmitting the letter 's' in Morse code across the Atlantic. However, the first television signals were not transmitted across the Atlantic until 1960. Explain how the radio waves travelled round the world in each case.

3 (a) Explain the difference between AM and FM radio.
(b) Find one station which transmits on AM and one on FM. Give the carrier frequency for each station.

4 There are three routes which radiowaves can take between transmitters and receivers around the Earth.

(a) What are the names given to those waves taking different routes?
(b) Draw a diagram to illustrate these routes.
(c) Which waves have frequencies less than 2 MHz?
(d) Which waves have frequencies in the range 3–30 MHz?
(e) Which waves have frequencies above 30 MHz?
(f) What is the ionosphere?
(g) Which waves are affected by changes in the atmosphere?

At the beginning of the century, your great great grandparents were happy to walk several miles to see friends or relations. We still visit friends of course, but often we pick up the phone for a chat instead. Now we can call anywhere in the world. The signals our voices make are carried by electrical, light or radio waves.

Look at Figure 1. This shows you the principle of the telephone in your home. When you speak your voice produces sound waves, which cause pressure differences in the air. These pressure changes act on the mouth piece of the telephone, making a cone move in and out. The movements of the cone squeeze some carbon powder. When the carbon is squashed, its electrical resistance becomes slightly less. This allows a larger current to flow from the battery. In this way, the information is carried along the wire by electrical waves. At the other end of the line, someone can listen to your voice. The electrical pulses are turned back into sound waves by the ear piece, which is like a small loudspeaker. The changes in current change the magnetising effect of the magnet. This moves a disc in and out to make sound waves.

In the past telephone systems transmitted electrical signals through copper wires, like these ones.

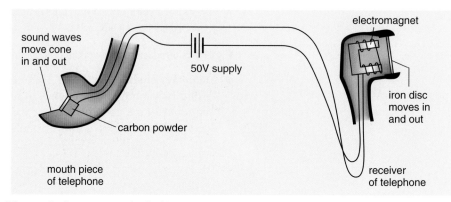

Figure 1 *A conventional telephone system*

Modern telephone systems transmit telephone messages by sending pulses of light down glass fibres. Optical cables have several advantages over the old copper wires.

Optical fibres are made from thin, flexible glass. Light which has been totally internally reflected emerges from the ends. Light travels along the entire tube with little absorption. Modern telephone systems use optical fibres in place of copper wires.

- Optical cables are less bulky than copper cables. The resistance of a copper wire is proportional to its length, and inversely proportional to its cross-sectional area. So a thick wire has less resistance than a thin wire of the same length. This is why copper cables are so bulky; less energy is lost in a thick, low resistance cable.
- More messages can be carried at the same time in an optical fibre.
- There is less 'crackle' on the line. A signal in one fibre does not affect its neighbour.
- Less energy is lost in optical cables. Signals travel 20 km without the need for amplification; signals in copper wires need amplification by **repeaters** every 2 km. As a wave travels along a cable, or fibre, its intensity (and amplitude) decrease due to energy losses; this process is called **attenuation**.

Overseas telephone calls are carried by microwaves (Figure 2). The microwaves are transmitted via a satellite. These waves are electromagnetic waves with a frequency of a few gigahertz. When you speak to someone via a satellite link, you will notice a delay before they reply.

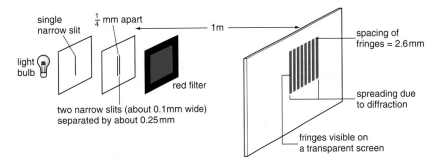

Figure 3 *An arrangement to see the interference of light*

correspond to places of constructive interference; here the red light waves arrive in phase. At the dark places the light waves arrive out of phase; this is destructive interference.

The wavelengths of light are too small for you to measure with a ruler as you did with microwaves. However, there is a formula which will help you.

$$\text{Wavelength} = \frac{\text{fringe spacing} \times \text{slit separation}}{\text{distance from slits to screen}}$$

Using the information in Figure 3, we can work out the wavelength for red light

$$= \frac{(2.6 \times 10^{-3}\ \text{m}) \times (2.5 \times 10^{-4}\ \text{m})}{1\ \text{m}}$$

$$= 6.5 \times 10^{-7}\ \text{m}$$

Fringes can be produced using other colours, for instance green and blue. From the formula above you can see that the wavelength is proportional to the fringe spacing. So red light has the longest wavelength and blue light the shortest.

When white light is used, you see a whole series of colours. This is because white light is made up of all colours. Each colour has a different wavelength. At some angles red light interferes constructively, while at other angles blue light does, and so on.

Homework Questions

1 Red, green and blue fringes were obtained using exactly the same apparatus but different filters. The wavelength of the red light is 6.5 × 10⁻⁷ m. The fringe spacing for the red, green and blue fringes are 2.6 mm, 2 mm and 1.8 mm respectively. Use this information to work out the wavelengths of green and blue light.

2 This question is about the interference fringes shown in Figure 3.
(a) The screen is moved further away from the slits. What difference does that make to: (i) the spacing of the fringes, (ii) the brightness of the fringes?
(b) The slits are moved further apart. What difference does that make to the spacing of the fringes?
(c) The slits are made slightly narrower. What difference does that make to: (i) the spacing of the fringes, (ii) the brightness of the fringes, (iii) the number of fringes that you can see?

3 Opposite, you can see a thin layer of oil floating on a puddle of water. You can see a ray of light that is partly reflected from the surface of the oil, and then partly reflected from the water surface. Explain why if you look at oil on water you can

see patches of colour.

SECTION G: Questions

1 (a) This diagram shows a ship 800 m from a cliff. A gun is fired on the ship. After 5 seconds the people at the front of the ship hear the sound of the gun again.

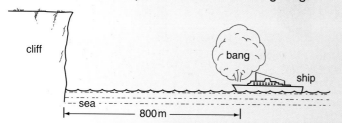

cliff

bang

ship

sea

|← 800 m →|

(i) What is the name of this effect?
(ii) What happens to the sound at the cliff?
(iii) How far does the sound travel in 5 seconds?
(iv) Use the equation below to calculate the speed of sound:

$$\text{Speed} = \frac{\text{distance travelled}}{\text{time taken}}$$

(b) The diagram below shows three people standing around a house.

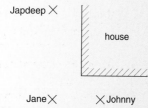

Japdeep ✕

house

Jane ✕   ✕ Johnny

(i) Who could see Johnny?
(ii) Who could hear Johnny?
(iii) To answer (i) you have assumed that light travels in straight lines. What did you assume about sound when you answered (ii)?
(c) The following diagrams show experiments which could be done in a ripple tank.

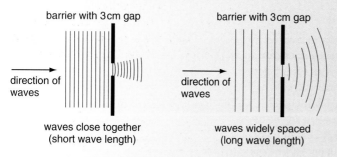

barrier with 3 cm gap

direction of waves

waves close together (short wave length)

barrier with 3 cm gap

direction of waves

waves widely spaced (long wave length)

You will see that the waves spread out after going through the gap in the barrier. This effect is called diffraction. In which experiment did waves spread out less?
(d) The next diagram shows a ship searching for a submarine. It sends out narrow beams of sound such as AB and AC. Ordinary sound is not satisfactory. Ultrasound has to be used.
(i) What is ultrasound?

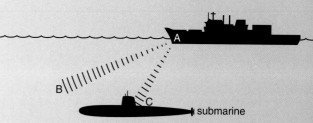

A

B

C submarine

(ii) Why is ultrasound necessary?
(e) Below is an oscilloscope on the ship.

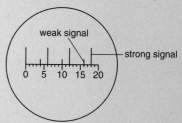

weak signal

strong signal

0 5 10 15 20

The numbers on the scale show times in tenths ($\frac{1}{10}$) of a second. Pulses of ultrasound are sent out every 6 tenths of a second. These are shown on the oscilloscope as strong signals. Weaker signals are received when ultrasound is directed on path AC (see (d) above).
(i) How much time passes between the strong signal going out and the weak signal coming in?
(ii) Ultrasound travels with a speed of 1500 m/s in water. How far is the submarine from the ship?
(f) Ultrasound is used to obtain an image of an unborn baby.

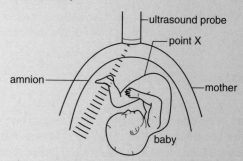

ultrasound probe

point X

amnion

mother

baby

(i) Why is ultrasound used, rather than X-rays?
(ii) When ultrasound goes from one type of material or tissue to another it may be reflected. Explain why ultrasound is reflected at X.

Edexcel (ULEAC)

2 In the next diagram S_1 and S_2 are two loudspeakers. The speakers are both supplied by the same voltage source. The speakers produce a note of frequency 165 Hz.
(a) The speed of sound is 330 m/s. Calculate the wavelength of the sound waves.
(b) Edward walks from y to x. At y, the sound seems loud; and, at x, it seems loud. But in between x and y

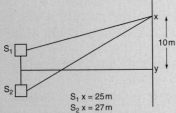
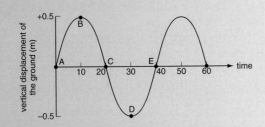

S₁ x = 25 m
S₂ x = 27 m

the loudness decreases. Explain Edward's observations clearly.
(c) The connections to one of the speakers are reversed. Explain what Edward hears now as he walks from x to y.
(d) The frequency of the note is changed to 660 Hz. Describe what Edward hears as he walks between x and y.

3 An earthquake produces seismic waves which travel around the surface of the Earth at a speed of about 6 km/s. The graph shows how the ground moves near to the centre of the earthquake as the waves pass.

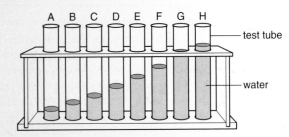

(a) What is the time period of the waves?
(b) What is the frequency of the waves?
(c) Calculate the wavelength of the seismic waves.
(d) Explain why the ground is moving most rapidly at times C and E.
(e) When is the ground accelerating at its greatest rate?
(f) Use the graph to estimate the vertical speed of the ground at the time marked C.
(g) Make a sketched copy of the graph. Add to it a second graph, to show the ground displacement caused by a second seismic wave of the same amplitude but twice the frequency.
(h) Discuss whether high frequency or low frequency seismic waves will cause more damage to buildings.
(i) The diagram shows seismic waves passing a house. The waves produce ground displacements that have a vertical component YY¹ and a horizontal component XX¹. Which component is more likely to make the house fall down?
Explain your answer.

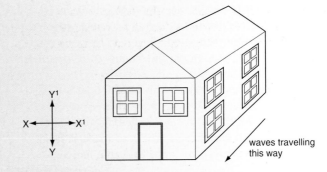

waves travelling this way

4 (a) The diagram below shows a simple musical instrument made by James in his science class. To make a note he gently blows over the top of the test-tubes which contain water.

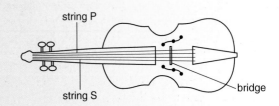

A B C D E F G H

— test tube

— water

(i) James gently blows over the tubes. What happens to the air in the test-tubes?
(ii) Which test-tube will make the note with the lowest frequency?
(iii) The depth of the water in the test-tubes changes the frequency of the note. Name ONE thing which James could do that would change the loudness of the note.
(iv) Linda, instead of blowing over the test-tubes, taps them with a pencil. Explain why she will not produce notes of the same frequency as James.
(b) The diagram shows a violin. It consists of four strings, **P, Q, R** and **S**. String **P** produces the highest frequency notes and string **S** the lowest frequency notes.

string P

string S

bridge

(i) What is it that vibrates to make the notes?

(ii) The notes produced from a particular string can be changed by sliding your finger up towards the bridge. What happens to the frequency of the note when this is done?

(iii) Each string is exactly the same length but each string produces a different note when bowed. Give THREE things that could be different for the strings which would cause them to make different notes even through they are the same length.

Edexcel (ULEAC)

5   Read this article about whales, then answer the questions that follow.

(a) Explain why the reflection and refraction of waves shown in the diagram help the whales to communicate over large distances.

(b) Explain why creatures living at the bottom of the sea cannot communicate over long distances.

(c) Wallis, an amorous bull whale, is prepared to swim for a day to find a mate. After singing for half an hour, he gets a response from Wendy 7 minutes after he stops. How far away is she, and will Wallis bother to make the journey? (Assume Wendy replies as soon as Wallis finishes his serenade.)

Whale Song

Not only are blue whales the largest animals in the world, but they are also the noisiest. They give out low frequency sounds which allow them to communicate over distances of thousands of kilometres.

The whales are helped in their long distance communications because the sounds they give out are trapped in the upper surface layers of the ocean. Sounds which hit the surface of the sea at a shallow angle are reflected back. Sounds which travel downwards are turned back upwards. At greater depths sound travels faster, because the water is more compressed. This causes sound waves to be refracted as shown in the diagram. This is similar to the refraction of light waves on a hot day, which allows us to see a mirage. Only in the top layers of the ocean does sound travel a long way. The sounds are trapped, rather like light waves in an optical fibre.

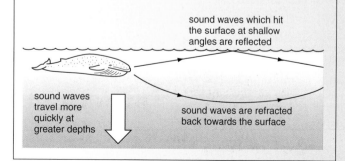

sound waves which hit the surface at shallow angles are reflected

sound waves travel more quickly at greater depths

sound waves are refracted back towards the surface

• Wallis can swim at 15 km/h.
• Sound travels at about 1500 m/s in water.

(d) Why are there long pauses in whale conversations?

(e) Explain carefully how the refraction of sound waves shown in the diagram tells us that sound travels faster at greater depths. Draw a diagram to show what would happen to whale sounds if sound travelled more *slowly* at greater depths.

(f) On a hot day, it is common to see a mirage on a road as you drive along. The mirage is an image of the sky. Draw a diagram to explain how mirages occur. (Hint: light travels slightly faster in the hot air just above the road surface.)

6   (a) Two marine biologists, Dr Fritz Muller and his research student Floella are discussing whale sounds.

Floella: We are 50 km away from a whale now. If we were 100 km away the intensity of his sound would be halved. This is because the sound has spread out into twice the area.

Fritz: That is a good idea, but I think it will be less due to energy losses.

(i) Comment on this conversation.

(ii) Analyse the data in the table to see who is right.

Intensity of sound (arbitrary units)	Distance from whales (km)
80	50
47	80
29	125
17	200
14	240

(b) Dolphins also use sound waves to communicate under water. They use high frequencies, which do not travel very far.

(i) High frequency sound has the advantage of being able to transmit more information. Explain why. What sort of information might dolphins want to exchange?

(ii) Suggest why dolphins do not need to communicate over long distances.

7   (a) Use the information from the diagram of a wave to write down a value for the

(i) amplitude,

(ii) wavelength of the wave.

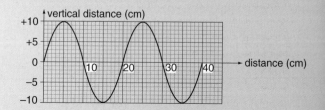

(b) If the wave was produced in 0.2s,
   (i) calculate the period of the wave.
   (ii) Use the equation $frequency = \dfrac{l}{period}$
       to calculate the frequency of the wave.
(c) (i) Copy the original diagram and add to it a new wave with a wavelength of 40 cm and an amplitude of 5 cm.
   (ii) If this new wave was produced in the same time, what is its frequency?

WJEC

8 The diagram below shows the crests of water waves in a ripple tank moving from deep to shallow water.

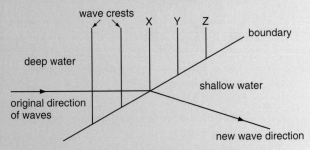

(a) Copy and complete the diagram to show the crests of waves **X, Y** and **Z** in the shallow water.
(b) (i) Measure and write down the wavelength of the water waves in the deep water.
   (ii) Write down, **in words**, the equation connecting wave speed, frequency and wavelength.
   (iii) If the deep water waves travel at a speed of 13.5 cm/s, calculate the frequency at which they were produced.
(c) When the waves travel from deep to shallow water they change direction. State **two** other differences which occur.
(d) Water waves are *transverse* waves. Explain what this means.
(e) Explain how earthquake (seismic) waves provide information about the internal structure of the earth.

WJEC

9 The electromagnetic spectrum is the name given to a family of waves that includes light, infra red and ultra violet radiations. All members of the family can travel through a vacuum with the same high velocity.

Electromagnetic waves are produced when the energy of electrically charged particles is changed in some way. The greater the change in energy, the shorter the wavelength of the electromagnetic wave produced. Radio waves, with a wavelength of up to 10 km and gamma (γ) rays with wavelengths of a thousand millionths of a millimetre are found at opposite ends of the electromagnetic spectrum.
(a) Name **one** part of the electromagnetic spectrum

   (i) that is **not** mentioned in the above passage,
   (ii) that has a wavelength shorter than that of visible light.
(b) Give **one** reason why radio waves have a longer wavelength than gamma (γ) rays.
(c) State **one** practical use of
   (i) infra red radiation,
   (ii) ultra violet radiation.

WJEC

10 (a) The graph below shows how the output voltage from a microphone depends on the frequency of the sound being detected.

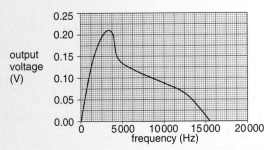

   (i) In testing a microphone, why is it important to keep the amplitude of the sound the same?
   (ii) What is the frequency of the highest pitched sound that the microphone can detect?
   (iii) Estimate the frequency at which the microphone is most sensitive.
   (iv) The range of human hearing is 20 Hz to 20 000 Hz.
       Explain whether this microphone would be suitable for use in a music recording studio.
(b) Studio records used to be made on magnetic tape. The information can be transferred onto other tapes, vinyl discs (records) or compact discs (CDs).

Describe the differences in the ways that information is stored on records and CDs.

Edexcel

11 The diagrams below show three ways in which radio waves can travel.

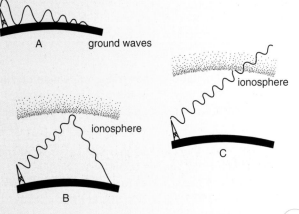

The ground waves in diagram A follow the Earth's curvature. The radio waves shown in diagram B are reflected by the ionosphere. The radio waves shown in diagram C are able to travel through the ionosphere.

(a) Write down the names of the waves shown in diagrams **B** and **C**.

(b) Explain how the diagrams show that each wave is attenuated as it travels.

(c) Radio 4 is broadcast from England. A motorist driving away from England through France can receive the Radio 4 long wave signal on her car radio.

  (i) Which of the diagrams shows the way in which long wave signals travel?

  (ii) How does attenuation affect the signal she receives as she continues to drive south?

  (iii) Explain why she is unable to receive the Radio 4 VHF signal.

Edexcel

12 The next diagram shows a simple AM (amplitude modulation) radio system for generating a radio signal.

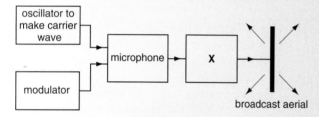

(a) What does the microphone do?

(b) What is required in box **X** to make the signal strong enough to be received over a wide area?

(c) The wave trace for the carrier wave is shown. Copy **Box 1** and sketch a possible wave trace for the audio wave. Copy and show in **Box 2** how the carrier wave is reshaped by the modulator.

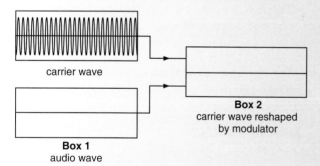

Box 2
carrier wave reshaped by modulator

Box 1
audio wave

(d) Each radio station sends out a modulated carrier wave in this way. How is it possible to listen to the signal from just one radio station at a time?

OCR

13 In recent years there has been a rapid growth in the number and use of mobile telephones. Mobile telephones use radio waves for transmitting speech. They have to use frequencies that are not already used by radio stations.

(a) Radio waves used for mobile telephones have a typical wavelength of 0.30 m. Calculate the frequency of these radio waves, given that their speed is 3.0×10^8 m/s.

(b) Mobile telephones can be used to communicate throughout Europe using satellite links. A set of three satellites, each in an elliptical orbit, is used to give 24 hour coverage. The diagram below shows the orbit of one of these satellites.

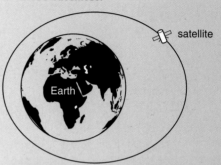

  (i) Draw an arrow on the diagram to show the gravitational force acting on the satellite.

  (ii) Describe how the size of this force changes as the satellite makes one orbit of the Earth.

  (iii) Copy the diagram and place an M where the acceleration of the satellite is greatest.

(c) The diagram below shows how a dish aerial is used to focus waves and transmit them to the satellite. Focusing the radio waves minimises the effects of diffraction.

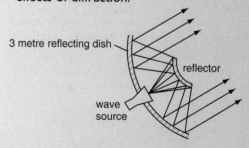

  (i) Explain why it is important to minimise the effects of diffraction.

  (ii) What TWO factors affect the amount of diffraction that takes place when a wave passes through an opening?

  (iii) The waves used for satellite transmission have a much shorter wavelength than the 0.30 m used by the mobile telephones. Suggest why a wavelength of 0.30 m is unsuitable for satellite transmission.

(d) Transatlantic telephone calls can be carried either using satellite links or by optical fibres on the seabed.

Describe how optical fibres can be used to carry telephone calls. Suggest ONE advantage and ONE disadvantage of using optical fibres rather than satellite links.

Edexcel

Light and Optics

The Sun emits more energy as light than it does at any other wavelength. Animals' eyes are specially adapted to take advantage of this.

By the end of this section you should:

- understand how shadows are formed
- understand why we see images in mirrors
- know that light can be refracted
- be able to define total internal reflection, and know the conditions when it will occur
- understand how lenses work
- know how the eye allows us to see, and how glasses compensate people with poor eyesight
- know that white light is made from the primary colours

Rays and Shadows

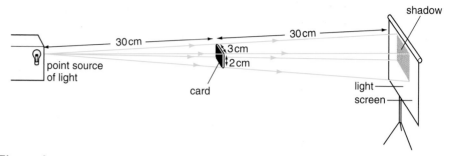

Figure 1

Shadows and eclipses

Shadows are formed when something blocks the path of light. In Figure 1 you can see a piece of card held in front of a small source of light. Some light misses the card and travels on, in a straight line, to the screen. A sharp shadow is formed on the screen behind the card.

Not all shadows are so sharp. If the source of light is large then the shadows have two parts. In the middle of the shadow there is a dark part called the **umbra**. Around the edges of the shadow there is a lighter region called the **penumbra**. A good example of the shadow formation is provided by eclipses of the Sun and Moon.

An eclipse of the Sun occurs when the Moon passes between the Earth and the Sun. The Moon is a lot smaller than the Sun but it is closer to us. It is just possible for the Moon to cover the Sun completely. When this happens there is a **total eclipse** of the Sun. During a total eclipse of the Sun the sky goes black and it is possible to see stars. It is only possible to see a total eclipse of the Sun if you are in the umbra of the shadow (Figure 2). If you are inside the penumbra of the shadow you will only see a **partial eclipse** of the Sun. Only part of the Sun is covered during a partial eclipse. An eclipse of the Moon happens when the Moon passes behind the Earth and into the Earth's shadow (Figure 3).

www

http://library.thinkquest.org/
10796/ch8/ch8.htm

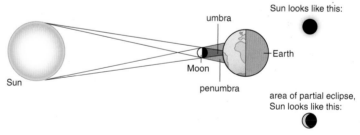

Figure 2 *An eclipse of the Sun*

A partial lunar eclipse. The upper left-side of the Moon has entered the darkest part of the Earth's shadow (the umbra) and the red tint is due to the filtering effect of the Earth's shadow – the same effect can be seen as the Sun sets.

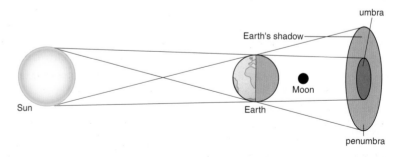

Figure 3 *An eclipse of the Moon*

⚠️Never look at the Sun through a magnifying glass, binoculars or telescope. You would damage your eyes badly or even cause blindness.

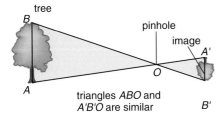

triangles *ABO* and *A'B'O* are similar

So $\dfrac{AB}{AO} = \dfrac{A'B'}{A'O}$

$AB = \dfrac{A'B'}{A'O} \times AO$

$= \dfrac{10 \text{ cm}}{30 \text{ cm}} \times 30 \text{ m}$

$= 10 \text{ m}$

The pinhole camera

You can make a simple pinhole camera out of a cardboard shoe box. A small hole is put in one end. The other end of the box should be removed and a piece of tissue paper put in its place. If you now take the box outside and point it at some trees, you will see an image of them on the tissue paper. If you want to take a photograph of the trees, you must use a light-proof box. The photograph is made by allowing the light to fall onto a piece of photographic paper instead of the tissue paper (Figure 4).

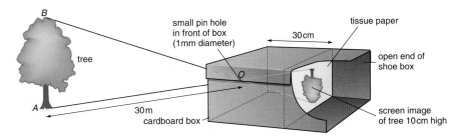

Figure 4 *The principle of the pinhole camera*

The light from the trees travels through the pinhole in a straight line. This causes the image to be upside down. Provided the hole is small the image of the tree will be sharply defined. If the hole is too big the tree will look blurred.

The size of the image lets you work out the height of the tree, which is 30 m from the pinhole.

Homework Questions

1 Work out the area of the shadow in Figure 1.

2 (a) Draw diagrams to illustrate (i) an eclipse of the Moon, (ii) an eclipse of the Sun.
   (b) The diagram below shows how an annular eclipse of the Sun can happen. During an annular eclipse the Moon is further away from the Earth than in a total eclipse. Sketch how the Sun would appear when viewed from: (i) X and (ii) Y.

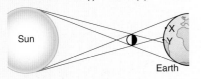

3 Venus moves in an orbit closer to the Sun than the Earth's orbit. In the diagram you can see Venus in three positions marked V_1, V_2, V_3. On the right, X, Y and Z show how Venus looked when seen on three occasions through a telescope. Match X, Y and Z to the positions of Venus.

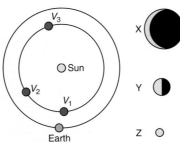

4 (a) Explain why making the hole larger in a pinhole camera makes the image more blurred. Illustrate your answer with a diagram.
   A student used a pinhole camera to form an image of the Sun. She investigated how the size of the Sun's image depended on the size of the pinhole. The table shows her results.
   (b) Plot a graph of image size (y-axis) against hole diameter (x-axis).
   (c) The student has made an incorrect measurement of the diameter of the hole. Which measurement is wrong and what should it have been?
   (d) Use the graph to predict what the diameter of the Sun's image would be for a very small hole.
   (e) Use your answer to part (d) and the extra data provided to calculate the Sun's diameter.

- Distance of Earth to Sun: 150 million km
- Length of pinhole camera: 500mm

Diameter of Sun's image (mm)	6.5	8.0	9.5	11.0	12.5
Diameter of hole (mm)	2.0	3.5	4.0	6.5	8.0

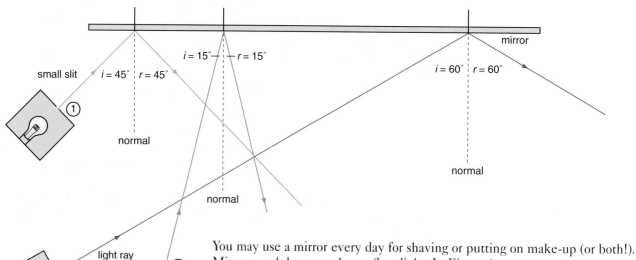

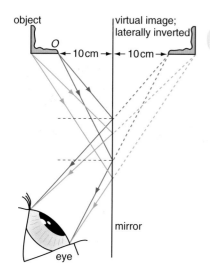

Figure 1 *Reflection of light rays from a mirror*

Figure 2 *Light is reflected from a rough surface in all directions*

You may use a mirror every day for shaving or putting on make-up (or both!). Mirrors work because they reflect light. In Figure 1 you can see an arrangement for investigating how light is reflected from a mirror. A ray box is used to produce a thin beam of light. Inside the ray box is a light bulb; light is allowed to escape from the box through a thin slit.

Before the light ray strikes the mirror it is called the **incident ray**. The *angle of incidence*, i, is defined as the angle between the incident ray and the normal. The **normal** is a line which passes at right angles through the mirror surface. After the ray has been reflected it is called the **reflected ray**. The angle between the normal and this ray is called the *angle of reflection*, r.

There are two important points about reflection of light rays which can be summarised as follows:

- The angle of incidence always equals the angle of reflection; $i = r$.
- The incident ray, the reflected ray and the normal always lie in the same plane.

All surfaces can reflect light. Shiny smooth surfaces produce clear images. Figure 2 shows that light is reflected in all directions from a rough surface so that there is no clear image.

An image in a plane mirror

We can use the rules about reflection to find the **image** of an **object** in a plane (flat) mirror. In Figure 3 the object is an L shape. Rays from the L travel in straight lines to the mirror where they are reflected ($i = r$). When the rays enter your eye they appear to have come from behind the mirror. This sort of image is called a **virtual image**. Your brain thinks that there is an image behind the mirror, but the L is not really there. You cannot put a virtual image onto a screen. An image which can be put onto a screen (like the one in a pinhole camera) is called a **real image**.

Figure 3 *Seeing an image in a mirror*

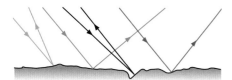

An example of some mirror writing

You can also see that the image appears to be the same distance behind the mirror as the object is in front of it. The image also appears to be back-to-front. You will have seen this effect when you look into a mirror. When you lift your right hand, your image lifts its left hand. The image is said to be **laterally inverted**.

● An image in a plane mirror is virtual, laterally inverted and the same size as the object.

Figure 4 shows how it is possible to produce the illusion of a ghost in a play. The technique is known as 'Pepper's Ghost'. A large sheet of glass is placed diagonally across the stage. The audience can see a wall through the glass on the darkened stage. An actor is hidden from the audience in the wings. He is brightly illuminated so that his image is reflected by the glass for the audience to see. When the actor walks off the stage, his image (the ghost) appears to leave by walking through the wall.

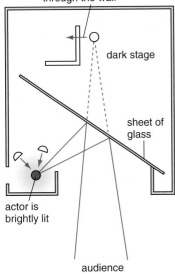

Figure 4 *Pepper's Ghost*

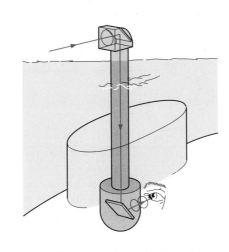

Figure 5 *You can make a simple periscope using two mirrors*

Homework Questions

1 (a) Describe the image that you will see when you look through the periscope as shown in Figure 5.
(b) At what angle must the mirrors be fitted into the periscope?
2 John runs towards a mirror at 5 m/s. At what speed does his image approach him?
3 (a) How many 10p coins will the eye see reflected in these mirrors?
(b) Draw diagrams to show how each image is formed.
4 Show how the word CALCULATOR would look when reflected in a mirror.
5 The diagram on the far right shows a split image range finder that fits into a camera.

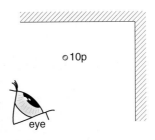

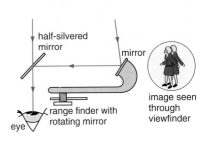

(a) Explain why you see two images.
(b) How do you adjust the range finder to focus the camera?
6 Copy these diagrams on the right and complete the paths of the rays after reflections in the mirrors. Use a protractor to draw your diagrams accurately.

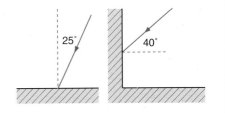

3 Refraction of Light

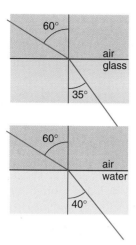

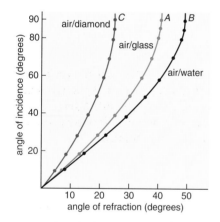

Figure 1 *Light travels more slowly in glass than it does in water. So a light ray bends more when it goes into glass*

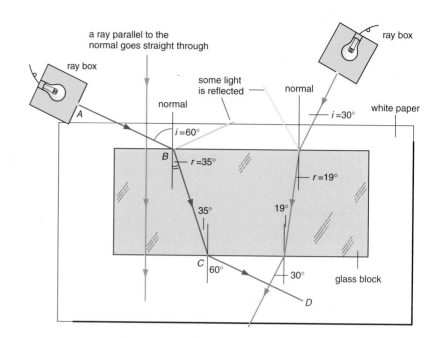

Figure 2 *Refraction of light rays by a glass prism*

Figure 3 *These graphs show how r depends on i when light travels from air into (a) glass (b) water and (c) diamond*

www

http://member.aol.com/
nicholashl/waves/waves.htm

When a light ray travels from air into a clear material such as glass or water, you can see the ray change direction. This is called **refraction**. Refraction happens because light travels faster in air than in other substances (Figure 1).

The amount by which a light ray bends when it goes from air into another material depends on two things:

- What the material is.
- The angle of incidence.

Figure 2 shows you an experiment to study how light rays bend when they go into a block of glass. The angle i between the normal and the incident ray, AB, is the angle of incidence. The angle r between the normal and refracted ray, BC, is the angle of refraction. The experiment shows these points:

- The light ray is bent towards the normal when it goes into the glass. The angle of incidence is greater than the angle of refraction.
- When the light ray leaves the block of glass it is bent away from the normal.
- If the block has parallel sides, light comes out at the same angle as it goes in.

Real and apparent depth

When a light ray leaves water and goes into air it is refracted. This effect makes a pond look more shallow than it really is. In Figure 4 someone is leaning over a pond to look at a fish. Light rays from the fish travel up to the surface of the water. At the water surface these rays are bent away from the normal. When these rays enter the eye, the person imagines that these rays come from I not O. What is seen is a **virtual image** of the fish. This image is closer to the surface than the fish itself.

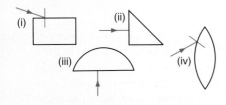

James demonstrates refraction in the pool

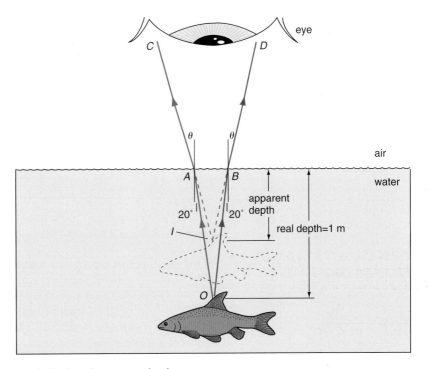

Figure 4 *Real and apparent depth*

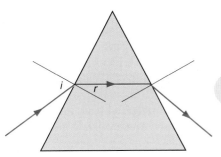

Figure 5 *Light is refracted by a triangular prism*

Refraction by prisms

You learnt some simple rules about refraction from the experiment shown in Figure 2. You can apply these rules to predict what will happen to light rays going into any shape of block. In Figure 5 you can see a light ray passing through a triangular glass **prism**. Notice that as the ray goes into the prism it is bent towards the normal; as it leaves the prism it is bent away from the normal.

Homework Questions

1 When a light ray goes into glass it bends towards the normal; when it comes out it bends away from the normal. Use this rule to sketch the path of the rays through the blocks in these cases.

2 (a) Make a copy of Figure 4. Mark in only the rays *OB* and *OA*. Use a protractor to measure the angle 20° as shown.
(b) Use the information in Figure 3 to work out what the angle θ should be.

(c) Now draw in the rays *BD* and *AC*.
(d) Use your scale diagram to calculate the apparent depth of the fish.

3 Draw diagrams to explain why a swimming pool of constant depth looks shallower at the far end.

4 When a light ray goes from air into a clear material you see the ray bend. How much the ray bends is determined by the **refractive index** of the material.

(a) Look at the table of data. How is the refractive index of a material related to the speed of light in it?
(b) A light ray strikes three materials with angle of incidence of 60°. These materials are: (i) glass, (ii) water, (iii) diamond. Use Figure 3 to calculate the angle of refraction in each case.
(c) Which bends light more, glass or perspex? Perspex refractive index = 1.4.

Material	Speed of Light (10^8 m/s)	Refractive Index
Air	3.0	1
Glass	2.0	3/2
Water	2.25	4/3
Diamond	1.25	2.4

Total Internal Reflection

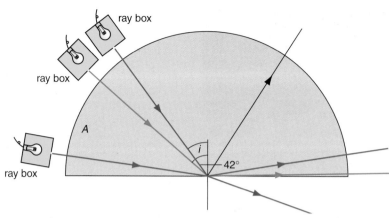

Figure 1 *Refraction and reflection in a glass block*

In the last unit you learnt that when a light ray crosses from glass into air, it bends away from the normal. However, this only happens if the angle of incidence is small. If the angle of incidence is too large all of the light is reflected back into the glass. This is called **total internal reflection**. Figure 1 shows how you can see this effect for yourself in the lab. Three rays of light are directed towards the centre of a semicircular glass block. Each ray crosses the circular part of the block along the normal, so it does not change direction. However, when a ray meets the plane surface there is a direction change. For small angles of incidence, the ray is refracted (red ray). Some light is also reflected back into the block (shown as a black line on the diagram). At an angle of 42° the ray is refracted along the surface of the block. This is called the **critical angle** (blue ray). If the angle of incidence is greater than this critical angle then all of the light is reflected back into the glass (green ray). The critical angle varies from material to material. While it is 42° for glass, for water it is about 49°.

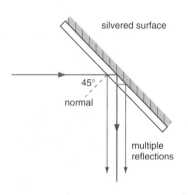

Total internal reflection in prisms

An ordinary mirror has one main disadvantage: the silver reflecting surface is at the back of the mirror. So light has to pass through glass before it is reflected by the mirror surface. This can cause several weaker reflections to be seen in the mirror, because some light is reflected off the glass/air surface.

These multiple reflections can be a nuisance, for example in a periscope. We can avoid the extra reflections by using prisms. In Figure 2(b) the light ray *AB* meets the back of the glass prism at an angle of incidence of 45°. This angle is *greater* than the critical angle for glass, so the light is totally reflected. There is only one reflection because there is one surface. Total internal reflection by prisms is also put to use inside binoculars and cameras.

Refraction and cars

Refraction and reflection are put to use in your car. It is important that your rear lights are clearly visible to the car behind you. At the same time they must not dazzle the driver of a following car. Figure 3 shows how this is achieved. The cover of the rear light is made with a series of points. Any light that is travelling directly backwards is refracted to the side. A similar shape of plastic is used in the reflectors on the back of cars and bicycles. This time the light from the headlights of a car passes straight through a plane plastic surface (Figure 4). Then the total internal reflection occurs at the inside surfaces of the pointed plastic.

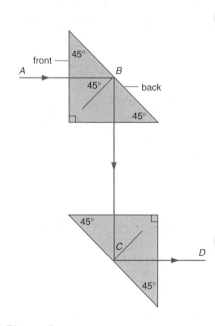

Figure 2
(a) Reflection from a mirror
(b) Reflection from two prisms to make a periscope

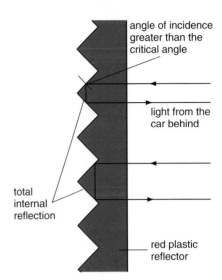

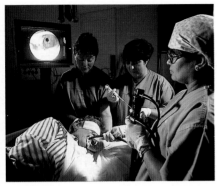

This photo shows an endoscope being used to investigate the abdomen. The fibre optic bundle allows the doctor to view inside the patient

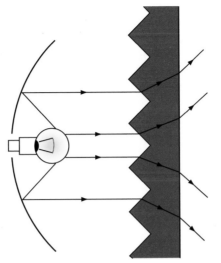

Figure 3 *A car rear-light cover*

angle of incidence greater than the critical angle

light from the car behind

total internal reflection

red plastic reflector

Figure 4 *A reflector for a car or a bicycle*

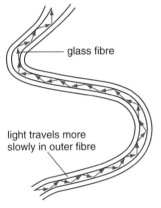

glass fibre

light travels more slowly in outer fibre

Figure 5 *Internal reflection traps light inside the glass fibres of an endoscope*

Optical fibres

Glass fibres are now used for carrying beams of light (Figure 5). The fibres usually consist of two parts. The inner part (core) carries the light beam. The outer part provides protection for the inner fibre. It is important that light travels more quickly in the outer part. Then the light inside the core is trapped due to total internal reflection.

Surgeons use a device called an *endoscope* to examine the inside of patients' bodies. This is made of two bundles of fibre optics. One bundle carries light down inside the patient, and the other tube allows the surgeon to see what is there. Optical fibres are also in use by British Telecom. A small glass fibre, only about 0.01 mm in diameter, is capable of carrying hundreds of telephone calls at the same time. These fibres have replaced the old copper cables in telephone systems.

Homework Questions

1 Turn back to the last unit. Explain how the graphs in Figure 3 can help you work out critical angles. What are the critical angles of glass, water and diamond?

2 Explain, with the help of a diagram, what the fish in the diagram below will see as he looks upwards.

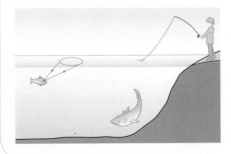

3 Below, you can see a ray of light entering a five-sided prism (pentaprism) in a camera. The ray undergoes three internal reflections before emerging. Copy the diagram and mark in the ray's path.

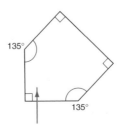

135°

135°

4 Describe in detail three uses for internal reflection. Illustrate your answer with diagrams.

5 The diagram below shows sunlight passing through a prismatic window that is used to light an underground room.

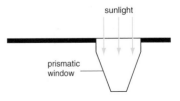

sunlight

prismatic window

(a) Copy the diagram and show the path of the rays through the window.
(b) Explain why the window is shaped this way.

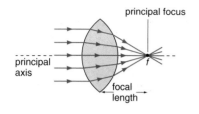
principal focus
principal axis
focal length
f

Every day of your life you use a converging lens; there is one in each of your eyes. There are also converging lenses in many optical instruments such as telescopes, cameras and slide projectors.

Converging lenses are usually made from glass and they have two nearly spherical surfaces. When a light ray enters the glass it is refracted towards the normal, and then away from the normal when it leaves (Figure 1).

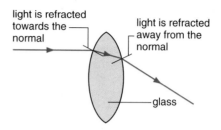
light is refracted towards the normal
light is refracted away from the normal
glass

Figure 1 *Refraction by curved lens surfaces*

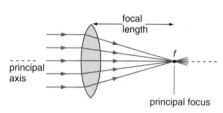
focal length
f
principal axis
principal focus

Figure 2
(a) A fat lens is a strong lens; it has a short focal length. Its curved surface refracts the light through a large angle (b) A thin lens is a weak lens; it has a longer focal length than the fat lens

In Figure 2 you can see what happens to a lot of rays which are parallel to the **principal axis**. Each ray is refracted by a different amount, depending on where it meets the lens. After these rays have passed through the lens they converge and meet at a point. This point is called the **principal focus** of the lens. The **focal length**, *f*, of the lens is the distance between the lens and the principal focus. Each lens has two principal focuses. If the rays were to come from the right in Figure 2, they would come to a focus on the left of the lens.

Figure 3 shows how a lens can focus rays that are not parallel.

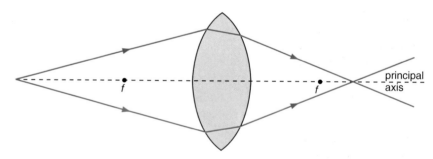
f
f
principal axis

Figure 3 *A lens can also focus rays that are not parallel; this time the rays meet behind the principal focus*

Finding the image

If you know the focal length of a lens and the position of an object, you can work out where the lens will form an image of that object. You can construct a scale drawing using any two of the three rays shown in Figure 4(a).

- A ray parallel to the principal axis is refracted through the principal focus.
- A ray through the centre of the lens, C, does not change its direction.
- A ray through the principal focus on the first side of the lens is refracted parallel to the principal axis.

This is the method for making a scale drawing like Figure 4(a).
(1) Draw the principal axis and thin line (AB) to show the lens.
(2) Mark the position of the principal focuses. In this example the focal length is 10 cm.
(3) Mark the position of the object. In this case, it is 20 cm away from the lens.

(4) Draw the three construction rays from the top of the object. The top of the image is where these rays meet. The image can now be drawn in; the bottom of the image lies on the principal axis.

In Figures 4(b) and (c) you can see two other examples of ray diagrams. In all cases the images are real and inverted, but the sizes of the images vary. When the object is a long distance from the lens the image is small and close to the lens. When the object is just outside the focal length of the lens, the image is magnified and a large distance from the lens. A real image can be projected onto a screen.

Homework Questions

1 The diagram below shows light rays from a small object O, passing through a lens and forming an image at I.

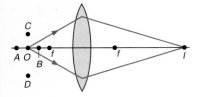

(a) Copy the diagram. Add to the diagram the position of the image, for each of the object positions, A, B, C, D. Mark your images A', B', C', D' to correspond to each object position.
(b) What would happen to the image if a piece of card covered the bottom half of the lens?

2 In Figure 4 you can see that the image is magnified if the object is close to the lens. We define the magnification as:

$$M = \frac{\text{height of image}}{\text{height of object}}$$

(a) Work out the magnification for each of the images in Figure 4.
(b) Take careful measurements to prove that this formula is also true:

$$\frac{\text{image height}}{\text{object height}} = \frac{v}{u}$$

where v is the distance between the image and the lens, and u is the distance between the object and the lens.

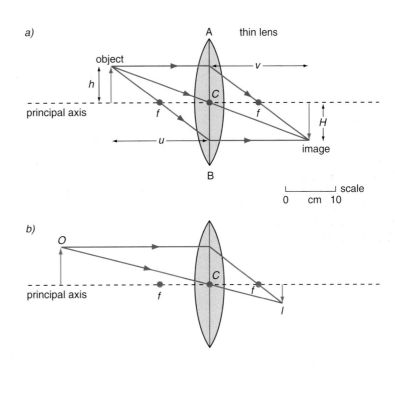

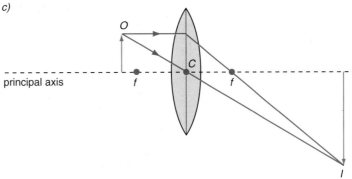

Figure 4 *In drawing these scale diagrams we show all of the refraction occurring at the centre of the lens along line AB in Figure 4(a), which is a good approximation for a thin lens*

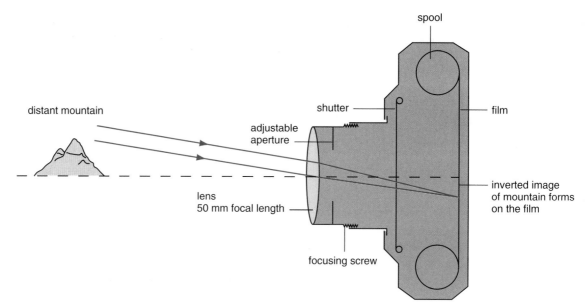

Figure 1 *A camera*

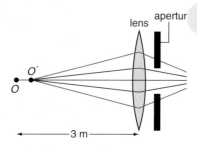

Figure 2 *The depth of focus is larger if a small aperture is used. In this diagram the camera is correctly focused on an object 3 m away. Rays from O' will be out-of-focus if they pass through all of the lens*

The camera

A diagram of a simple camera is shown in Figure 1. The purpose of the lens is to project an image of a distant object (a mountain, for example) onto a film. When you want to take the photograph, pressing a button opens up the shutter to allow light to fall on to the film.

However, before you take a photograph you need to consider these points.

- **Choice of film.** A 'fast' film is more sensitive to light than a 'slow' film. The fast film needs less time to take a photograph than a slow film. The advantage of faster film is that you can take a photograph when the light is poor, or when something is moving quickly. The disadvantage of a fast film is that it produces poorer quality pictures than a slow film.
- **Focusing.** Your picture must be in focus. To focus, move the lens backwards and forwards with the focusing screw. For distant objects the lens is moved back towards the film. For closer objects you move the lens forwards.
- The **shutter speed** controls the amount of light coming into the camera. On a dark day you might choose a shutter speed of 1/30 s, while on a bright day you can use a faster speed of 1/60 s.
- **f-number.** This refers to the diameter of the aperture (gap). If you set your aperture at f/8, it means that its diameter is 1/8 of the focal length of the lens. The f-number, like the shutter speed, controls the amount of light coming into the camera. A wide gap allows more light in. The f-number also determines the depth of focus of your photograph (Figure 2). A small gap (a small f-number, such as f/22) will give a large depth of focus. This means that things both near to and far from the camera will be in focus.

The slide projector

Figure 3 shows how a slide projector works. A brightly illuminated slide (A) is used as an object for the projector lens (B). This lens projects an image of your slide on to a screen a few metres away. A 500 W light bulb (C) is used to make the slide bright. A concave mirror (D) behind the bulb reflects light forwards. The two condenser lenses (E) then converge the light towards the slide. A heat filter (F) is used to prevent the slide being damaged.

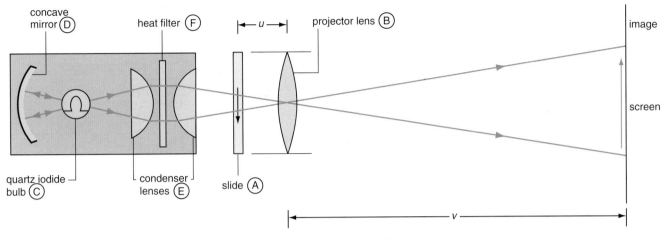

Figure 3 *The principle of the slide projector*

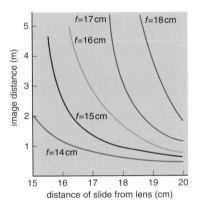

Figure 4 *Graphs to show how the distance of the slide from the lens affects the image distance. Graphs for five different lenses are shown*

Light bulbs produce infra-red waves as well as light. The heat filter absorbs the infra-red waves, which would heat up the slide. The filter does however let light through. The slide projector is cooled by a fan which blows air through it. Vents on top of the projector allow the warm air to escape.

In this slide projector, the distance, u, between the lens and slide can be adjusted between 15 cm and 20 cm. What lens should you choose for the projector? It is important that the slide is just outside the focal length of the projector lens. This makes sure that you see a large image on the screen. So a lens with a focal length of about 15 cm will be the best. Figure 4 gives a series of graphs for different lenses, to show how the distance, u, affects the distance between the image and lens, v.

Homework Questions

1 A photographer takes three photographs. The first is of an old painting in a darkened room (f/2, 1/15 second, fast film); the second is of the Taj Mahal at midday (f/16, 1/30 second, slow film); the third is of a car cornering (f/4, 1/1500 second, fast film). Explain in each case what factors affected the photographer's choice of: (i) speed of film, (ii) shutter speed, (iii) f-number.

2 A lens of focal length 15 cm is used in the slide projector in Figure 3.

(a) Use Figure 4 to work out how far the slide is from the lens to project an image: (i) 3 m from the lens, (ii) 5 m from the lens.
(b) A slide measures 35 mm × 23 mm. What is the size of the picture on the screen, when the distance between the projector and the screen is 3 m? This formula may help:

$$\frac{\text{image height}}{\text{object height}} = \frac{\text{image distance } (v)}{\text{object distance } (u)}$$

(c) The lens in the projector breaks. The shop only has lenses of focal length 14 cm, 16 cm and 19 cm. Which one would you choose? Why?

3 (a) Copy Figure 1 showing only the lens, the film and rays from the mountain,
(b) Next to your sketch, add a second diagram to show rays entering the camera from an object only 3 m away from the lens. Show how the lens has been moved to ensure the picture is in focus.

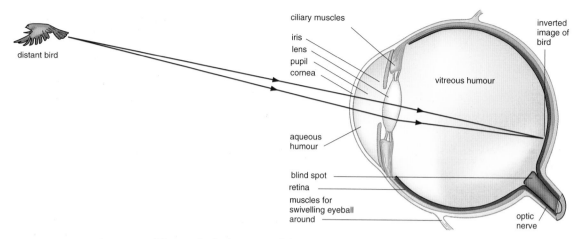

Figure 1 *A plan view of the human eyeball*

ciliary muscles
iris
lens
pupil
cornea
vitreous humour
inverted image of bird
distant bird
aqueous humour
blind spot
retina
muscles for swivelling eyeball around
optic nerve

Figure 1 shows you what an eyeball would look like if you could see it from the top. Below are listed the important points about the working of the eye:

- The eyeball is roughly spherical and keeps its shape due to the liquids inside it, the **vitreous humour** and the **aqueous humour**.
- The eye **lens** makes an image of a distant object on the **retina**.
- The retina contains cells which are sensitive to light. Some cells (**cones**) detect different colours, and other cells (**rods**) respond to the brightness of light.
- The **optic nerve** carries signals from the retina to the brain. Although the image on the retina is upside down, the brain sorts this out for us so we can see things the right way up.
- The amount of light that enters the eye is determined by the size of the **pupil**. The **iris** acts like the aperture of a camera. In bright light it closes down to protect the eye. In the dark the iris opens up to allow the eye to gather more light.

Focusing the eye

Your eye is most relaxed when you are looking at distant objects. The eye then focuses parallel rays onto the retina (Figure 2(a)). When you are looking at distant objects, your eyes cannot focus on something that is close to you at the same time. The lens is not strong enough to converge rays coming from nearby on to the retina. To look at something close to you, the eye lens has to change shape. The **ciliary muscles** make the lens fatter (Figure 2(b)). The light is now bent more when it goes through the lens and can be focused on the retina. This focusing process is called **accommodation**.

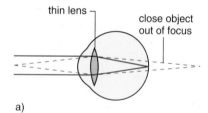

thin lens
close object out of focus

a)

Wearing spectacles

A normal eye is able to see both near and distant objects clearly. However, it is quite common for people to suffer from either short or long sight:

- Someone who is short-sighted (myopic) can see things nearby, but cannot focus on distant objects. The problem is that the eye lens is too powerful, or their eyeball is slightly mishaped. Parallel rays from distant objects are focused in front of the retina. This can be corrected by using a **diverging lens**. A diverging lens will spread the rays out, so the eye can now bring them to focus on the retina (Figure 3).
- People who are long-sighted cannot focus on objects that are close to the eye. However, they may be able to see clearly things far away. This time the

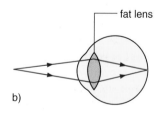

fat lens

b)

Figure 2
(a) A thin lens focuses parallel rays onto the retina
(b) A fat lens is needed to look at objects close to the eye

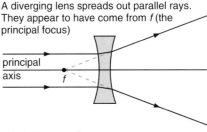

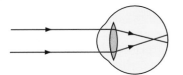

(a) A short-sighted eye cannot see distant objects

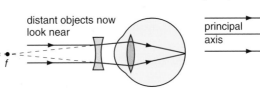

(b) A diverging lens corrects short sight

(c) A diverging lens

Figure 3

problem is that the eye lens is too weak. So rays from objects close to the eye converge at a point behind the retina. This sight defect can be corrected by using spectacles with a **converging lens** (Figure 4).

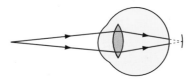

(a) A long-sighted eye cannot see close objects

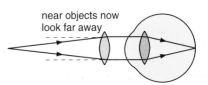

(b) A converging lens corrects long sight

Figure 4

Binocular vision

Fast food, Kenyan style!

An animal which has both eyes at the front of the head is usually a hunter. Those animals which have eyes at the sides of the head make good meals for the hunters. Having eyes at the sides of the head gives an animal a wide range of vision. That is important if you do not want to get eaten. With two eyes at the front of your head, your brain gets two slightly different views of everything. This is very helpful when it comes to judging distances. If you are hunting your supper like the lioness in the photograph, you need to know how far away it is. Try putting a pencil in each hand and touching the points together; you will find it easy with both eyes open but difficult if you close one eye.

Homework Questions

1 (a) Suggest three ways in which the eye and the camera are similar.
(b) What is different about the way a camera and an eye focus light?

2 (a) Draw a diagram to show a normal eye focusing parallel rays from a distant object onto its retina.
(b) Draw a second diagram to illustrate how this eye accommodates to focus on an object closer to it.

3 (a) What is meant by a long-sighted eye?
(b) Explain how this eye defect can be corrected.

4 Instead of wearing spectacles some people prefer to wear contact

lenses to improve their eyesight. Contact lenses are curved pieces of plastic which fit directly onto the cornea. Below are three shapes of lens, A, B and C. Lens C is used to correct for longsightedness; the right hand side of the lens causes light to diverge, but the left hand side converges light more strongly.
(a) Which side of each lens sticks on the eye, (the left or the right side)?

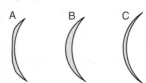

(b) Which eye defect is corrected by using (i) lens B, (ii) lens A?
(c) Which eye has the more severe defect, the one wearing lens B or the one wearing lens C? Explain your answer.

5 Some ophthalmic surgeons use lasers to change the shape of the cornea to correct short-sighted eyes. Explain the principle behind this operation.

6 Close your right eye and look at the blue dot. Move your eye closer to the page until the red dot disappears. What causes this blind spot?

If you look into the sky when it has been raining (and if it is sunny or reasonably bright), you are quite likely to see a rainbow. White light from the sun is a mixture of many different colours. When sunlight passes through raindrops in the sky it is split up into its separate colours (Figure 1).

You can produce your own 'rainbow' or **spectrum** of colours by using a *prism*. In Figure 2 a ray of white light is split into its separate colours. Blue light is bent more by the prism than the red light. This tells us that blue light is slowed down more by the glass than the red light. The splitting of white light into colours is called **dispersion**.

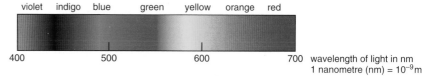

Figure 1 *The colours of the rainbow. Different colours have different wavelengths*

Making and mixing coloured lights

In your eyes there are cells called cones which are sensitive to colours. There are three types of cone cell; one which detects red light, one which detects green light and one which detects blue light. Red, green and blue are called the **three primary colours**. They cannot be made by mixing together other colours. Most other colours *can* be made by mixing together various amounts of the primary colours.

You can make red, green or blue light with a filter (Figure 3). A red filter, for example, allows red light to pass through it but absorbs all the other colours of light. The red light would be absorbed by a green filter. So if you looked at white light through a green and a red filter, placed together, you would see nothing. Figure 4 shows you the sort of effect that you will see if you mix together light of the three primary colours.

You can do this by using three slide projectors, one with a red filter, one with a green filter and one with a blue filter. Where the three colours overlap in the middle, white light is produced. At other places the **secondary colours** are produced. Cyan is a mixture of green and blue; magenta is a mixture of red and blue; yellow is a mixture of red and green.

Figure 2 *A prism can produce a spectrum from white light*

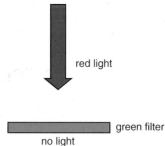

Figure 3

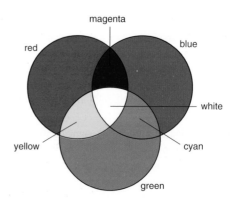

Figure 4 *Red, blue and green are the primary colours*

Rainbows are produced when raindrops split sunlight into separate colours in much the same way as a prism

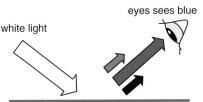

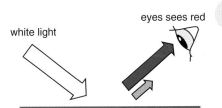

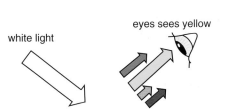

Figure 5

Making colours by reflection

Things appear coloured because they absorb some colours of light and reflect others. For example a shirt may look blue because it reflects blue light and absorbs the other colours. In fact, it is not quite as simple as that. The blue shirt will probably reflect a little green and violet light as well, but the shirt looks blue to the eye. Other colours behave in the same way (Figure 5). The blue shirt will look blue as long as you look at it in white or blue light. However, if you shine red light on the shirt it will look black, because there is no blue light for it to reflect.

What colour shirt would you get if you dyed it in a mixture of yellow and blue dyes? The answer is green. The yellow dye absorbs blue and violet, but reflects green, yellow and red. The blue dye absorbs yellow, orange and red, but reflects violet and green. The only colour that is *not* absorbed is green. Mixing paints and dyes gives a different effect from mixing light. If you mix green and red light you get yellow. If you mix green and red paint you get a nasty dark mess!

Homework Questions

1 Inspector Grappler of the vice-squad is on patrol in New York. He is in disguise wearing a red cap, blue shirt and green trousers. Copy and fill in the table below to show what colour he looks in red, yellow or blue light.

Colour of light	cap	shirt	trousers
Red			
Yellow			
Blue			

2 What colour of paint will you get if you mix yellow and cyan paints?

3 (a) You look at a blue car through (i) a blue filter, (ii) a red filter. What colour do you see in each case? (b) You look at a yellow book through (i) a red filter, (ii) a blue filter. What colour do you see in each case?

4 (a) The diagram below shows a beam of white light entering a prism. Copy and complete the diagram to show how the light passes through the prism.

(b) Explain with reference to your diagram what is meant by dispersion. What causes dispersion?

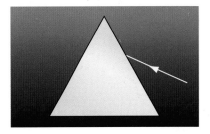

SECTION H: Questions

1 Red, green and blue lamps are arranged as shown; each lamp emits light in all directions. A metal plate is placed between the lamps and a white screen.
(a) What colours will be seen at A, B, C, D and E?
(b) Where will the screen appear white?

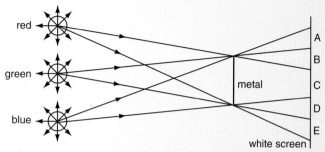

2 Copy the diagram and complete it to show how the incoming light ray is reflected from mirrors X and Y.

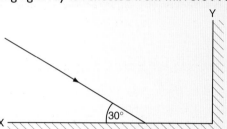

3 The diagram shows five different shapes of lens.
(a) Which is the strongest converging lens?
(b) Which is the weakest converging lens?
(c) Which lens could correct for myopia?

A   B   C   D   E

4 Copy the diagrams below, and complete them to show how the light rays pass through each block of glass.

(1) 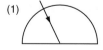   (2)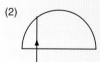

(3)   (4)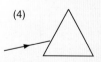

(5)   (6)

5 The diagram shows a simple plan view of the eye.

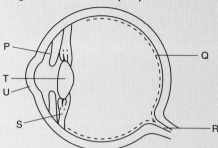

(a) Name the parts of the eye that each label points to.
(b) Stefan leaves a dark room and goes outside into bright sunlight. What effect does this have on the pupil of the eye?
In the retina there are millions of light-sensitive cells. There are two kinds, called rods and cones. The cones enable us to distinguish colours. In a normal eye there are three types of cone. One responds to red light, one to green and one to blue.
(a) How can an eye detect: (i) yellow light, (ii) magenta light, (iii) white light?
(d) A person who suffers from red-green colour blindness cannot distinguish between red and green. Explain what might be wrong with his cone cells.

6 The diagram shows light from the Sun falling onto a lens.

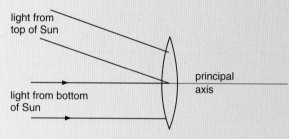

(a) Explain why light rays coming from the Sun are parallel.
(b) Copy the diagram and complete it to show the position of the Sun's image. The focal length of the lens is 10 cm.
(c) Using the same scale make a second sketch to show the size and position of the Sun's image produced by a lens of focal length 20 cm.

Lens	Diameter (cm)	Focal length
A	5	5
B	5	20
C	5	10
D	10	50

(d) Use the data in the table to select the best lens for each of these jobs: (i) burning a piece of paper with the Sun's rays, (ii) projecting an image of the Sun to look for sun spots.
⚠Never view the Sun directly through a telescope or lens.

7 (a) Copy and complete diagram (1) to show refraction and dispersion by a prism. Explain why dispersion occurs.
(b) Light is also dispersed by droplets of water. Copy and complete diagram (2) and use it to explain why we can see rainbows.

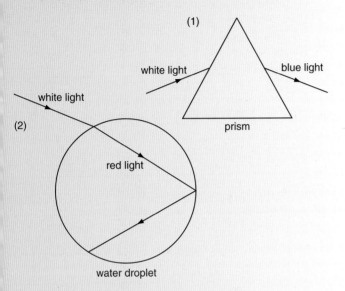

(1)

white light   blue light

prism

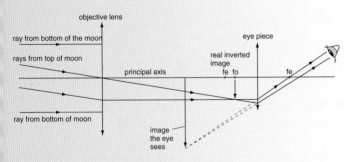

white light

(2)

red light

water droplet

8 The diagram below shows the path of two rays from the top of the Moon passing through an astronomical telescope. You may want to look at www.howstuffworks.com/telescopes.htm to help you.

objective lens

eye piece

ray from bottom of the moon

rays from top of moon

real inverted image

principal axis   fe fo   fe

ray from bottom of moon

image the eye sees

(a) Copy the diagram and show the passage of the two rays from the bottom of the Moon. It will make the diagram clearer to use different coloured pencils or pens.
(b) Describe the image that the eye sees.
(c) Explain why the telescope magnifies more if:
(i) the objective lens has a long focal length
(ii) the eye lens has a short focal length.

9 (a) Some binoculars use prisms to turn light through 180°.

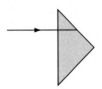

(i) Copy and complete the diagram below to show the path of the light as it passes through and out of the prism.
(b) Name ONE other instrument which uses a prism to reflect light.

10 The diagram shows a ray of light incident at point **A** inside a glass fibre optic cable. The ray of light is totally internally reflected at **A** and eventually passes out into the air from point **B**.

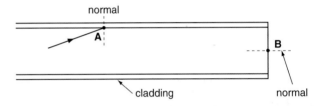

normal

A

B

cladding   normal

(a) Copy then draw on the diagram the path taken by the ray of light
(i) between **A** and **B**,
(ii) as it passes into the air from **B**.
(b) Explain carefully
(i) why the light is totally internally reflected inside a fibre optic cable,
(ii) why the light is able to emerge at **B**.

WJEC

11 The diagram shows a simple camera. The lens has to be screwed in or out to get the image in focus on the film. This movement depends on the position of the object being photographed. The graph shows how the

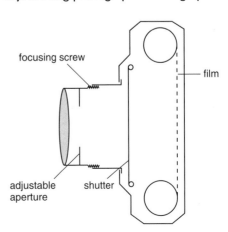

focusing screw

film

adjustable aperture   shutter

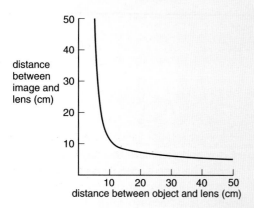

separation of the lens and film depends on the distance of the object from the lens. The focal length of the lens is 50 mm. The distance between the lens and the film can be varied between 50 mm and 60 mm.

(a) Draw ray diagrams to show how the lens forms an image of an object (i) a long way away, and (ii) 30 cm from the lens. In each case state the distance between the lens and the film.

(b) Explain why the camera cannot focus on something 20 cm from its lens. How would you adapt the camera so that it could take a photograph this close up?

12 This question is about how a magnifying glass works. Look at diagram 1 below; here an eye is looking at a ladybird at a distance of about 25 cm. This distance is about as close as an adult eye can focus on an object (young eyes can often focus closer than this). This is called the **near point of vision**. Now look at diagram 2. The same eye is viewing the ladybird through a converging lens, placed so that the ladybird lies inside the focal length of the lens. You can see how the rays from the ladybird's head are diverging when they reach the eye. So the rays appear to come from behind the lens.

(a) Copy diagram 2 and extend the rays 1 and 2 to show where the image appears to be.

(b) The image should be close to the near point of vision; now explain why the image appears magnified. (It might be helpful to compare the angles α and β

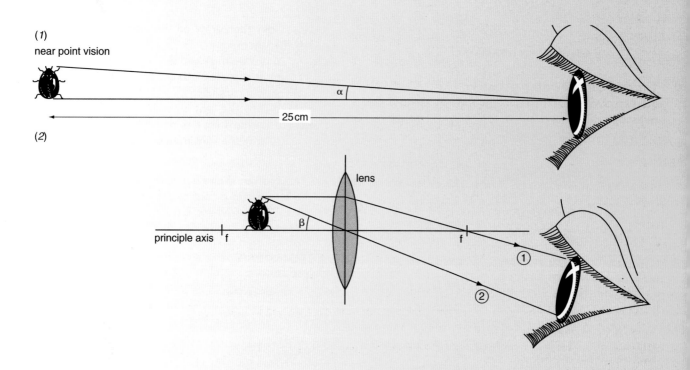

Electricity

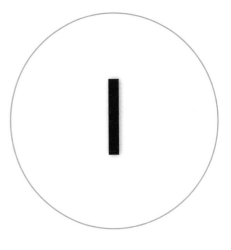

A large city such as New York uses a phenomenal amount of energy to function. Without electricity, life as we know it would be very different.

By the end of this section you should:

- understand what static electricity is and how it is created
- know what electric current is
- know the difference between series and parallel circuits
- be able to define the volt
- know Ohm's Law
- understand resistance
- know how to calculate electrical power
- be able to understand electrical circuits
- know how electricity is supplied to the home and how electrical appliances are kept safe
- understand how electron beams are produced
- know what the cathode ray tube is used for
- know what is meant by the photoelectric effect

We all take electricity for granted. At home you can turn on a light or a fire at the flick of a switch. You may very well take a snack out of the fridge or deep freeze and cook it in your microwave oven, before sitting down in front of your favourite television programme. Without electricity, our lives would be completely different and less comfortable.

Electrical charge

Electricity was discovered a long time ago when the effects of rubbing materials together were noticed. You will have seen these effects for yourself. If you take a shirt off in a dark room you can hear the shirt crackle and you may also see some sparks. A well-known trick at children's parties is to rub a balloon and stick it on to the ceiling. You have probably felt an electrical shock after walking across a nylon carpet. In these examples, you, or the balloon, have become charged as a result of **friction** (rubbing).

There are two types of electrical charge, positive and negative. A **positive** charge is produced on a perspex ruler when it is rubbed with a woollen duster. You can put **negative** charge onto a plastic comb by combing it through your hair.

Some simple experiments show us that like charges repel each other, and unlike charges attract each other. These experiments are shown in Figure 1.

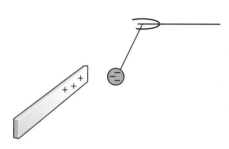

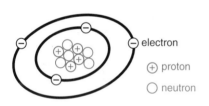

Figure 1 *Attraction or repulsion?*
(a) Like charges repel

(b) Unlike charges attract

Where do charges come from?

There are three types of small particle inside atoms. There is a very small centre of the atom called the **nucleus**. Inside the nucleus there are **protons** and **neutrons**. Protons have a positive charge but neutrons have no charge. The **electrons** carry a negative charge and they move around the nucleus. The size of the charge on an electron and on a proton is the same. Inside the atom there are as many electrons as protons. This means that the positive charge of the protons is balanced by the negative charge of the electrons. So the atom is neutral or uncharged (Figure 2).

When you rub a perspex ruler with a duster some electrons are removed from the atoms in the ruler and are put onto the atoms in the duster. As a result the ruler has fewer electrons than protons and so it is positively charged. But the duster has more electrons than protons and is negatively charged (Figure 3).

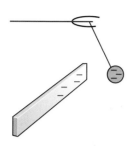

- electron
- ⊕ proton
- ○ neutron

Figure 2 *This beryllium atom is neutral. Four negatively-charged electrons balance four positively-charged protons*

http://www.eskimo.com/~billb/ele-edu.html

http://sln.fi.edu/franklin/scientst/electric.html

http://library.thinkquest.org/2763/

Picking up litter

You may know that you can use your comb to pick up small pieces of paper, but it is quite difficult to explain it. Figure 4 shows the idea. The comb is negatively charged after combing your hair, so when it is placed close to the paper, **electrons** in the paper are pushed to the bottom or **repelled**. The top of the paper becomes positively charged and the bottom negatively charged. The negative charges on the comb attract the top of the paper upwards. The same charges repel the bottom, but the positive charges at the top of the paper are closer to the comb. As a result the upwards force is bigger than the repulsive downwards force and the piece of paper is picked up.

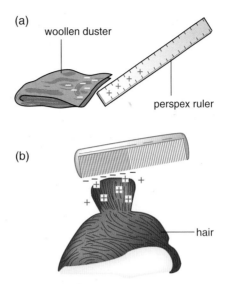

(a)

woollen duster

perspex ruler

(b)

hair

Figure 3 *Charging by friction*

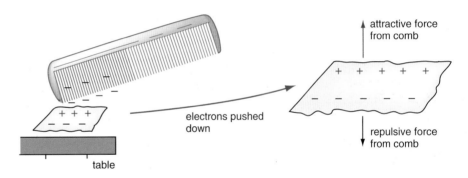

attractive force
from comb

repulsive force
from comb

electrons pushed
down

table

Figure 4 *Your comb can pick up small pieces of paper*

Homework Questions

1 (a) List 4 machines, at home, that work on electricity.
(b) How would you manage without these machines in a power cut that lasts for 3 days?

2 (a) The diagram below shows 2 small plastic balls. The balls are charged. What can you say about the charges on the balls?

(b) Draw the forces acting on each ball.

3 In the text at the top of the page, you read that electrons are removed from atoms by rubbing. An electron needs energy to remove it from an atom. Explain, using scientific terms, how rubbing provides this energy.

4 You charge up a plastic rod by rubbing it with a duster; explain how you would determine whether the rod carries positive or negative charge.

5 (a) You rub a balloon on your shirt and it (the balloon) becomes positively charged. Explain in terms of electron movement how the 'charging' occurs.
(b) You now hold the balloon close to the wall. The balloon sticks to the wall. Use the electron theory to explain this.

Spark hazards

A sailor who works on board an oil tanker has to wear shoes which conduct electricity. We say a material conducts electricity if a charge can flow through it. Metals are conductors of electricity. Materials like plastic and rubber do not conduct electricity; they are called insulators. Wearing shoes with rubber soles on board a tanker could be extremely dangerous. When the sailor moves around the ship in rubber shoes, charges can build up on him as he works. Then when he touches the ship, there will be a small spark as charge flows away from his body. Such a spark could ignite oil fumes and cause an explosion. Some very large explosions have destroyed tankers in the past. So sailors wear shoes with soles which conduct. Now any charge on him flows away and he cannot make a spark.

Sparks are most likely to ignite the oil when it is being unloaded. To avoid this, the surface of the oil is covered with a 'blanket' of nitrogen. This gas does not burn, so a spark will not cause an explosion.

Lightning

Large thunderclouds have strong convection currents inside them. Ice crystals are carried up and down by these currents and they can become charged as a result of a frictional process. The bottom of a thundercloud gains a large negative charge.

When a thundercloud passes over a tall building or tree, it can discharge itself with devastating effect. A flash of lightning releases about 1000 million joules of energy. The photographs show the sort of damage which lightning can cause.

A tall building is protected by a lightning conductor consisting of a thick metal strip on the outside of the building, which is connected to spikes at the top of the building and a metal plate in the ground (Figure 1). When a thundercloud passes overhead, the points of the lightning conductor become positively charged. The size of the electric forces are such that positive and negative ions are produced. These ions can help to discharge the thundercloud gradually, so if a lightning strike does occur it is likely to be less energetic and therefore less damaging.

A lightning strike on the Eiffel Tower, photographed in 1919. A large electrical charge builds up on the base of a cloud until it creates a conducting path through the air; the lightning flash occurs when the charge on the cloud flows to the ground.

Troy Trice at home with the clothes he was wearing when he was struck by lightning. Eyewitnesses say that the bolt burnt through his helmet and blew his shoes off. His breathing stopped, but he was resuscitated and has made a full recovery.

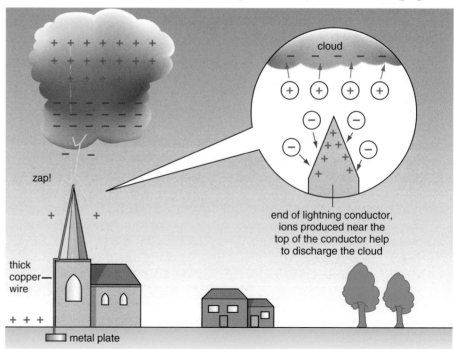

Figure 1

Electrostatic precipitation

Many of our power stations still burn coal to produce electrical energy. When coal is burnt a lot of soot is produced. It is important to remove this soot before it gets into the atmosphere. One way of doing this is to use an **electrostatic precipitator**. Inside the precipitator there are some wires which carry a large negative charge. As the soot passes close to these wires the soot particles become negatively charged. These particles are repelled away from the negative wires and are attracted to some positively charged plates. The soot sticks to the plates, and can be removed later. Some large precipitators, in power stations, remove 30 or 40 tonnes of soot per hour.

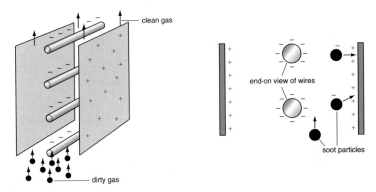

Figure 2 *Soot particles in dirty fumes are removed in an electrostatic precipitator*

Photocopying

Nowadays, most offices have a photocopying machine. The key to photocopying is a plate which is affected by light. When the plate is in the dark its surface is positively charged. When the plate is in the light it is uncharged.

An image of the document to be copied is projected on to the plate (Figure 3(a)). The dark parts of the plate become charged. Now the plate is covered with a dark powder, called **toner**. The particles in the toner have been negatively charged (Figure 3(b)), so the toner sticks to the dark parts of the plate, leaving a dark image. Next, a piece of paper is pressed on to the plate. This paper is positively charged, so the toner is attracted to it (Figure 3(c)).

Finally, the paper is heated. The toner melts and sticks to the paper, making the photocopy of the document (Figure 3(d)). In modern photocopiers the whole process takes less than a second.

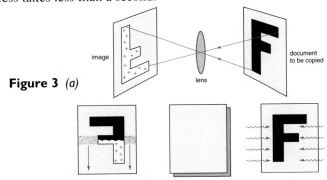

Figure 3 *(a)*

(b) Negatively charged toner powder sticks to the image

(c) The image is transferred to the paper

(d) The final image is fixed by heating

http://www.school-for-champions.com/science/staticexpl.htm

Homework Questions

1   The tyres on aircraft are made from special rubber that conducts electricity. Explain why.

2   (a) Explain why a photocopier needs toner powder. Why does the powder need to be charged?
    (b) When you get your photocopy out of the copier it is usually warm. Why?
    (c) The lens in Figure 3(a) produces an image of the document, which is upside-down and back-to-front. Explain why the final image is the right way round.

3   (a) Explain this: When you polish a window using a dry cloth on a dry day the window soon becomes dusty. Why does this not happen on wet days?
    (b) Cling film is a thin plastic material that is used for wrapping up food. When you peel the film off the roll it sticks to itself. Can you suggest why this happens?

4   Why should lightning conductors be:
    (i) fixed to the ground,
    (ii) made of metal,
    (iii) pointed,
    (iv) at the highest point on a building?

Electric Current

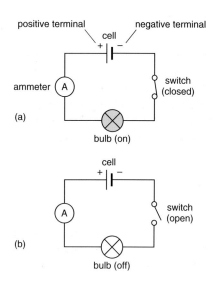

(a)

(b)

Figure 2 *An electrical circuit*

Conductors	Insulators
Good	Rubber
Metals e.g. Copper	Plastics e.g.
Silver	Polythene
Aluminium	PVC
Moderate	Perspex
Carbon	China
Silicon	Air
Germanium	
Poor	
Water	
Humans	

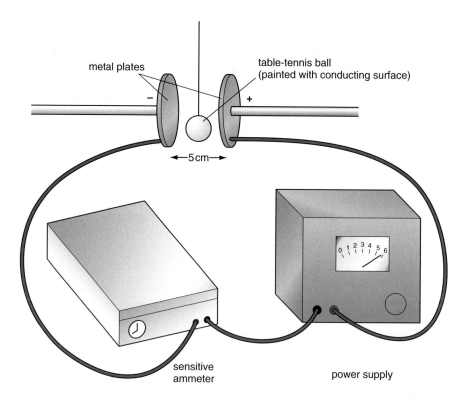

Figure 1

Electric currents consist of moving electric charges. A demonstration of the nature of an electric current is shown in Figure 1. An electrical supply has been used to put static charge onto two electrical plates. A conducting metal sphere, which has been suspended between the two plates, bounces backwards and forwards. When the ball touches the negative plate it becomes negatively charged; it is repelled from the negative plate and attracted towards the positive plate. A sensitive ammeter which is connected between the electrical supply and plates registers a current, just as an ammeter does when a battery lights a bulb, Figure 2(a).

A complete conducting path is required for a current to flow; if a switch is opened the current stops, Figure 2(b). The same idea applies when water flows round your central heating system. You must have a complete pathway (or circuit), so that the water goes from the boiler to the radiators, and back to the boiler to be warmed up again.

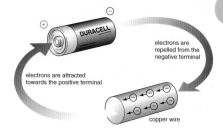

Figure 3 *A current is a flow of charge*

Which materials conduct?

Metals are good conductors of electricity. Each metal atom has at least one loosely held electron which is free to move. When a current passes through a wire, it is because negatively charged electrons are repelled from the negative terminal of a cell and are attracted towards the positive one. Currents are also carried by positively or negatively charged ions. The word ion is used to describe an atom which has gained or lost an electron; a positive ion has lost an electron and a negative ion has gained an electron. Your body is full of ions, so you conduct electricity. Electrical signals from your brain travel along nerves to instruct muscles. Because you are a conductor, you can get a shock from the mains supply. Materials which do not conduct electricity are called insulators.

Which way does current flow?

Before it was appreciated that currents are often carried by the flow of electrons, scientists decided to think of a current as the flow of positive charges. Therefore arrows on circuit diagrams show what we call the **conventional current** flowing from the positive terminal of a battery to the negative terminal. Figure 4 shows three examples of a conventional current flowing from left to right. The current can be carried either by positive particles moving to the right, or by negative particles moving to the left, or both.

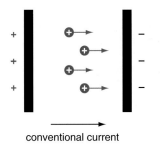

conventional current

(a) Positive particles in a semiconductor

Circuit diagrams and symbols

Figure 2 gives two simple examples of circuit diagrams. Such diagrams are useful to represent the path of a current. The table below shows commonly used symbols to represent the various parts of an electrical circuit.

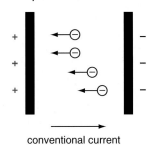

conventional current

(b) Electrons in a metal

Effects of an electric current

Electric currents produce three effects on their surroundings.

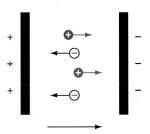

conventional current

(c) Positive and negative ions in a solution

Figure 4

- Heating and Lighting.
  This effect has already been mentioned in Figure 2(a). The current causes the filament of a light bulb to glow white hot. Electric currents are used in our homes for heating, cooking and lighting.
- Chemical Change.
  The passing of an electric current through a solution can produce a chemical change. For example, a current passing through a solution of copper sulphate causes copper to be deposited at the cathode (negative terminal).
- Magnetic Effect.
  When a current flows it produces a magnetic field, which can be detected by a plotting compass placed near the wire. These magnetic effects are discussed in Section J.

Circuit symbols			
cell	─┤├─	ammeter	─(A)─
battery	─┤├··┤├─	voltmeter	─(V)─
lamps	─⊗─	microphone	I⊏
open switch	─o⌿o─	bell	⌂
resistor	─⊏⊐─	buzzer	⊅
variable resistor	⟋	loud speaker	⊅⊨
diode	─▷├─	motor	─(M)─

Homework Questions

1. (a) Explain what an electric current is.
   (b) What is meant by an electrical conductor?
   (c) Why are metals good electrical conductors?
2. (a) What are the three effects which an electrical current can produce?
   (b) Give examples of how we put each effect of an electrical current to practical use.
3. Copy the diagram of the plates and ball from Figure 1 (do not include the wires, meter and supply).
   (a) The ball is moving to the left. Mark your diagram to show the sign of the charge carried by the ball, and draw an arrow to show the direction of the conventional current.
   (b) Later the ball travels to the right. What charge does the ball carry, and in which direction does the conventional current now flow? Explain your answer.
4. (a) Draw a circuit to show current passing from a battery, through an ammeter, resistor, light bulb, switch, then back to the battery.
   (b) Design a circuit with two switches so that you can turn a light on or off either at the top or bottom of a staircase.

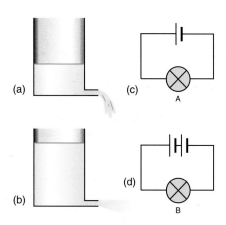

Figure 1

http://library.thinkquest.org/
28032/

Below there are two statements written about a torch battery which is connected to a torch bulb. Which one is correct?

Statement A: *The battery can be thought of as a provider of energy, which is transferred to the electrons as they pass through the battery, and transferred by the electrons as they pass through the bulb, to heat and light energy.*

Statement B: *The battery in an electrical circuit can be compared with a pump in a water circuit. Electrons in the wire are forced to move through the wires by the battery, just as water is forced to move through the pipes by the pump.*

The answer is that both ideas are correct. Electrons are provided with energy by the battery. But it is also a useful idea to compare electrical and water circuits, because understanding how water flows helps us to understand electrical circuits too.

Batteries and brightness

Figure 1(a) shows a tank of water with an outlet pipe at the bottom; water flows out at a slow rate. When the depth of water in the tank is increased in Figure 1(b), the pressure of water at the bottom of the tank is increased and water flows out at a faster rate.

The cell in an electrical circuit provides an 'electrical pressure' which pushes electrons through the bulb. In Figure 1(c) one cell pushes electrons through the bulb at a slow rate and the bulb is dull; electrical energy is being transferred into heat and light energy at a slow rate. In Figure 1(d), two cells push the electrons round the circuit more quickly and the bulb is brighter; electrical energy is now being transferred into heat so light energy more quickly.

The idea of the water tank can be used in other circuits too.

Series circuits

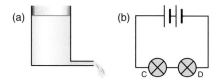

Figure 2

In Figure 2(a) the depth of the water is the same as in Figure 1(b), but a longer outlet pipe has been put on the tank. The water flows out more slowly than before, because a longer pipe offers more resistance to the flow of water.

In Figure 2(b), two cells push electrons through two bulbs one after the other; these bulbs are said to be **in series**. Two bulbs offer more resistance to the flow of the electrons than one, so the current is less and the bulbs C and D are dimmer than bulb B.

Parallel circuits

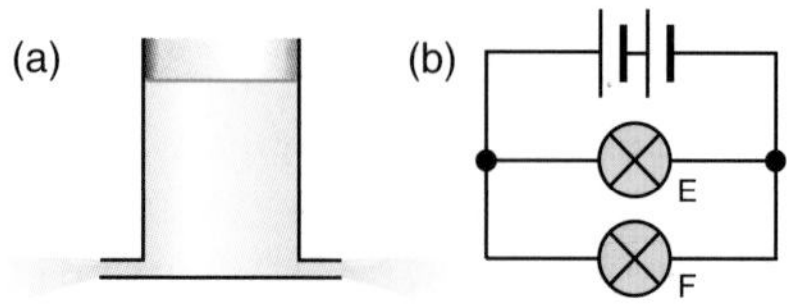

Figure 3(a) shows another tank, but with two outlet pipes similar to the one in Figure 1(b). The depth of the water in Figure 3(a) is the same as before; water runs out of each outlet pipe at the same rate as the water in Figure 1(b), because the water pressure is the same on each pipe. This means that the tank will empty twice as quickly when it has two outlet pipes.

Figure 3(b) shows two cells pushing electrons through two bulbs, which are side by side. These bulbs are said to be **in parallel**. Each bulb is attached to two cells, which provide the same 'electrical pressure' as the cells in Figure 1(d). The bulbs B, E and F are all of the same brightness. However, the cells in Figure 3(b) will run down more quickly than the cells in Figure 1(d), because the two bulbs use energy more quickly than one.

Figure 3

Homework Questions

1 (a) Write down the rate of flow of water along pipes A and B.
(b) Write down the electric current flowing along wires A and B.

In questions 2, 3 and 4 the cells and bulbs are identical. A **single bulb** connected to a **single cell** glows with **normal brightness.**

2 (a) State whether bulbs A–F are brighter than normal, of normal brightness, duller than normal or off. (b) Later the switches are closed in all the circuits. Describe the brightness of bulbs A–F now.

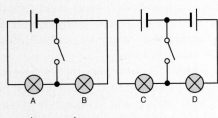

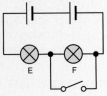

3 Which bulb will be brighter, or will they be the same?
(a) G or H? (b) J or K? (c) G or L?
(d) N or P? (e) I or J? (f) M or P?

4 Look at the circuits 1–5. In which circuit do the cells (i) last longest, (ii) last for the least time?

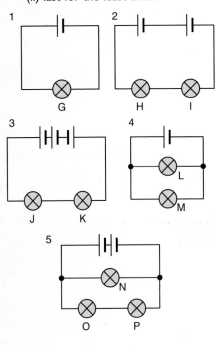

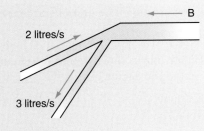

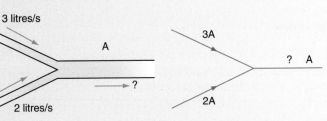

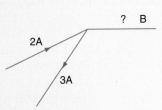

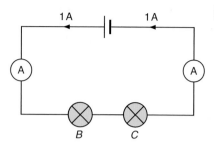

Figure 1 *An electrical circuit*

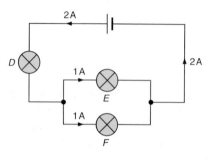

Figure 2 *A current is a flow of charge*

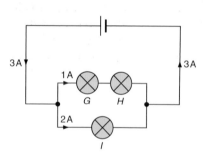

Figure 3

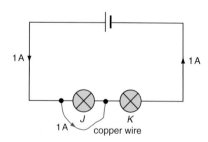

Figure 4

Splitting the current

We cannot lose current as it goes round a circuit (see Figure 1). The same current flows through bulbs B and C (and through the cell). The bulbs are in **series**. You can measure the current going into the bulbs and out of the bulbs with two ammeters. Both ammeters read 1 A. If they did not read the same, we would have lost some electrons.

Exactly the same idea applies if we have a circuit with branches in it. In Figure 2 a current of 2 A goes through bulb D. Then the current splits to go through bulbs E and F; each bulb gets a current of 1 A. But then 2 A flows back to the negative terminal of the cell.

The currents do not always split equally. More current goes through the easier path. In Figure 3 it is easier for the current to go through bulb I, than it is to go through bulbs G and H; so 2 A goes through bulb I, and 1 A through the other two bulbs.

Figure 4 shows a **short circuit**. Bulb J has been shorted out by some copper wire. The current takes the easy path through the wire. No current goes through the bulb J so it is off.

Current rules

- All parts of a series circuit receive the same current
- The same current goes into a juntion as comes out
- More current goes through the easier path

Measuring Charge and Current

We measure the current in a circuit using an ammeter. The unit of current is the **ampere** (A), though most of us call it an amp.

When the current is big (10 A), the charge moves quickly round the circuit. When the current is small (0.001 A) the charge moves slowly round the circuit. Current is the rate at which charge flows round the circuit.

$$\text{current } (I) = \frac{\text{charge } (Q)}{\text{time}(t)}$$

$$I = \frac{Q}{t}$$

We could measure charge by counting the number of electrons flowing. However, electrons have only a very small charge. Our unit of charge is the **coulomb** (C). 1 coulomb is equivalent to the charge carried by six million million million (6×10^{18}) electrons.

$$1 \text{ amp} = 1 \text{ coulomb/sec}$$

Voltage

Look at the circuit in Figure 5. Will the bulb work if you take the cell away? Of course it will not. The cell provides the energy for the bulb to light. The cell turns chemical energy (from the substances inside it) into electrical energy. The cell gives energy to the electrons to move around the circuit. When the electrons reach the bulb their energy is transferred into heat and light energy.

There is an electrical energy difference between the positive and negative

Many cells down the backbone on this electric eel act to produce a large voltage between its nose and tail. This voltage can be used to kill prey

terminals in the cell. This energy difference is measured by the cell's **voltage**. (Voltage is also known as **potential difference** or **p.d.**) We use a voltmeter to measure voltages. Notice that the voltmeter is connected across the cell (in **parallel**), not in series with it.

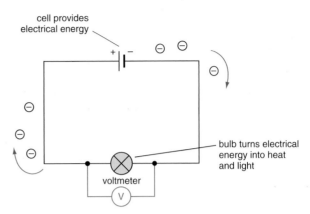

Figure 5

A transistor radio uses a 9 volt (9 V) battery. If you put your tongue across the terminals of a 9 V battery you can feel a little tingle. (DON'T use a battery of more than 9 V). Mains electricity is supplied at 230 V, although it used to be supplied at 240 V. A shock from the mains gives your body a lot of energy. A mains shock is very painful and could kill you.

Figure 6 shows a circuit to supply two headlamps from a car battery. The bulbs are in parallel and each gets the 12 V from the battery.

If you put the two bulbs in series, they are dimmer. Each one only gets half the battery voltage (Figure 7). The battery voltage does not always split equally. A brighter bulb uses more energy. So it gets more of the voltage (Figure 8). Notice that the sum of the voltages across the bulbs is always equal to the battery voltage. This is because the energy provided by the battery equals the energy used by the bulbs.

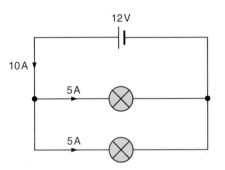

Figure 6 *A circuit to supply two headlamps from a car battery*

Voltage Rules

- Bulbs in parallel receive the same voltage
- Adding the voltage across the bulbs in series gives the battery voltage
- A larger voltage across a bulb in a series circuit means that bulb is using more energy than the bulb with a smaller voltage across it.

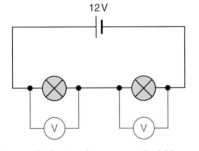

Figure 7 *Each voltmeter reads 6 V*

Defining the Volt

The greater the voltage of a supply, the greater the amount of energy transferred to the circuit.

A potential difference of 1 volt exists between two points in a circuit, when 1 joule of electrical energy is transferred to other forms of energy as 1 coulomb passes between those points.

Figure 8 may be used as an example. A coulomb of positive charge at A would have 12 J of electrical potential energy. By the time the coulomb has moved to B, 10 J of energy has been transferred to heat and light in bulb (1), leaving 2 J of electrical potential energy. Those 2 J of electrical potential energy are then transferred to heat and light in bulb (2). The coulomb of charge reaches C having used up its electrical potential energy. Bulb (1) uses five times as much energy as bulb (2).

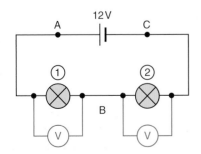

Figure 8 *The brighter bulb gets the larger voltage*

High voltages can kill!

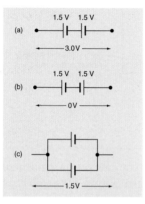

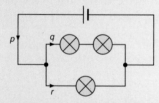

Figure 9

It is important to realise that it is not the coulombs which get used up, but the energy which they carry; the same number of coulombs pass point A as pass point C each second. The battery gives each coulomb 12 J of energy, which is transferred to the circuit before the coulomb returns to the battery.

1 volt = 1 joule/coulomb

Cells and Batteries

A battery consists of two or more electrical cells. Figure 9 shows three ways in which two cells may be connected. In series: (a) the voltages add up to produce a larger voltage, provided the cells 'face' the same way; (b) if the cells face in opposite directions the resultant voltage is zero. In parallel: (c) the voltage produced by the two cells is still 1.5 V, but the battery behaves likes a larger cell, so energy can be provided for longer.

Homework Questions

1 Which current in the diagram below is the largest, *p*, *q* or *r*? Which is the smallest?

2 Copy the diagrams below and mark in the missing values of current.

3 Some industrial machines use a 415 V supply. Explain why no machines use a 415 V supply in your home.

4 Explain carefully the energy changes that occur when a cell is connected to light a bulb.

5 (a) The bulbs below are identical. A₃ reads 0.2 A. What do ammeters A₁ and A₂ read?

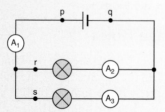

(b) How many coulombs pass each of points *p*, *q*, r and s, in 1 minute?
(c) In 1 minute how much energy has been transferred to each bulb?

6 A lightning flash delivers a charge of 5 C; the potential difference between the cloud and Earth is 100 million volts.
(a) The flash lasts for 0.002 s. What is the average value of the current?
(b) (i) How much energy is transferred by the flash of lightning?
(ii) To what forms of energy is the electrical energy transferred?

7 In the circuit below, a voltmeter connected across *AB* measures 6 V. What does the voltmeter measure across:

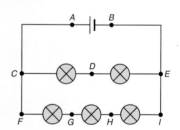

(i) *CD*, (ii) *GH*, (iii) *FI*, (iv) *EI*, (v) *DI*, (vi) *DH* (quite hard)?

8 What is the potential difference between points *A* and *B* in this diagram?

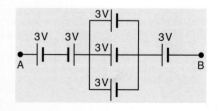

A view of several electrical insulators at an electricity distribution facility near a power station

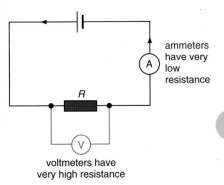

ammeters have very low resistance

R

voltmeters have very high resistance

Figure 2

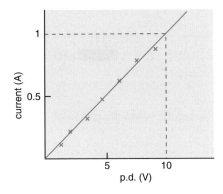

Figure 3

Figure 1 *Moving through a resistor, electrons (red circles) keep bumping into atoms (yellow circles). This makes the resistor hotter*

Figure 1 shows a resistor in a circuit. If we want to calculate the current flowing through it we need to know how much **resistance** it has. A resistor which has a large resistance only allows a small current through it. A small resistance allows a large current through.

$$Resistance~(R) = \frac{\text{p.d. across resistor, in volts } (V)}{\text{current flowing through it, in amperes } (I)}$$

or

$$R = \frac{V}{I}$$

The unit of resistance is the ohm, symbol Ω. Large resistances are measured in thousands or millions of ohms. So, $1000~\Omega = 1~k\Omega$ (1 kilohm); and $1~000~000~\Omega = 1~M\Omega$ (1 megaohm).

In an electrical circuit it is the resistors, not the wires connecting them to the battery, which get hot. The enlarged picture of a resistor in Figure 1 helps to show you why. Electrons are being pushed around the circuit by the battery and they collide with the atoms in the resistor. Energy is given to the atoms so that they vibrate faster – this means the resistor is getting hotter.

Measuring resistance

The simplest way for you to measure resistance is shown in Figure 2. The voltage across the resistor is measured using the voltmeter. The current flowing through the resistor can be read from the ammeter. Then the resistance can be calculated using the formula: $R = V/I$. A voltmeter has a large resistance so hardly any current flows through it. If current does flow through the voltmeter, the ammeter measures the extra current, and this will give you the wrong answer.

You can increase the current flowing through your resistor by increasing the number of cells. You can then plot a graph of the current against the voltage. If your resistor is made from a metal or from carbon, your graph will look like Figure 3. The graph shows us that the resistance of the resistor does not change as the current increases. Such a resistor is said to be **ohmic** – one that obeys **Ohm's Law**.

Ohm's Law states that for some conductors, the current flowing is proportional to the voltage, provided the temperature does not change.

You can use the circuit in Figure 4 to see that the resistance of a wire is proportional to its length. A resistance wire is stretched between AB and a steady current of 1 A flows through it. A voltmeter is attached to one end of the wire at A, and the other end of the voltmeter can be connected to any point on the wire. Table 1 shows some typical results. You can see that double the length of wire gives double the resistance.

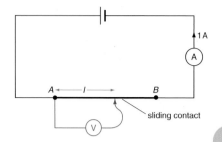

Voltage (V)	Current (A)	Resistance (Ω)	Wire length (cm)
2.0	1.0	2.0	15
4.0	1.0	4.0	30
8.0	1.0	8.0	60
12.0	1.0	12.0	90

Table 1

Figure 4 *The resistance of a wire becomes bigger, the longer it is*

Combination of resistors

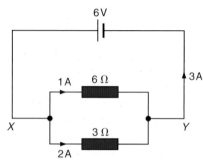

(a) Resistors in parallel

* **Series.** The last experiment with a wire makes it easy to make a rule to work out the total resistance of two or more resistors in series. If the length of the wire is doubled the resistance is doubled. So when resistors are in series we simply **add** them to work out the total resistance. You can see in Figure 5 that the resistance between X and Y is 20 Ω.

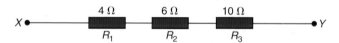

Figure 5 *Resistors in series: $R = R_1 + R_2 + R_3$*

* **Parallel.** Working out how to combine resistors in parallel is harder. Figure 6 shows you an example. The most important point you should realise is that the resistance between X and Y must be *less* than either of the 3 Ω or 6 Ω resistors. When you put a resistor in parallel with another, you increase the *total* current, therefore you have made the resistance *smaller*.

  Using the equation $I = V/R$ you can see that a 6 V battery will drive 1 A through the 6 Ω resistor, and 2 A through the 3 Ω. So the *total* current flowing out of the battery is 3 A. You can now calculate the combined resistance of the two resistors.

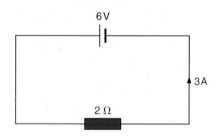

(b) The total resistance is smaller; in this example the two resistors in (a) are the same as one 2 Ω resistor

Figure 6

$$R = \frac{V}{I} = \frac{6\,\text{V}}{3\,\text{A}} = 2\,\Omega$$

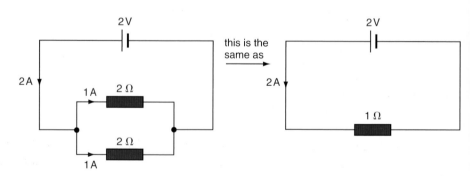

Figure 7 *Putting two resistors of the same value in parallel halves the resistance*

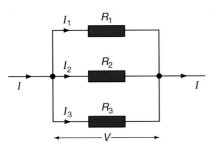

Figure 8

Sometimes it can be useful to apply a formula to work out the resistance of resistors in parallel. In Figure 8 there are three resistors R_1, R_2, R_3 in parallel; they have currents of I_1, I_2 and I_3 passing through them respectively. Because the resistors are in parallel, they have the same voltage across them, V. The total current $I = I_1 + I_2 + I_3$, but $I = V/R$

So $\dfrac{V}{R} = \dfrac{V}{R_1} + \dfrac{V}{R_2} + \dfrac{V}{R_3}$ dividing both sides by V gives

$$\frac{1}{R} = \frac{1}{R_1} + \frac{1}{R_2} + \frac{1}{R_3}$$

Homework Questions

1 Use the data in Table 1 to calculate the resistance of 1 m of the wire.

2 Figure 3 shows an I/V graph for a resistor. Calculate its resistance.

3 (a) Calculate the resistance of the following combinations of resistors.

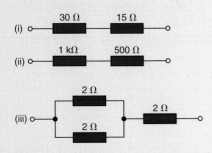

(b) Calculate the current which a 4.5 V battery supplies to each combination (when connected across the red terminals).
(c) Calculate the potential difference across each *separate* resistor when the 4.5 V battery is connected across each combination.

4 (a) For the following diagram work out the current flowing through: (i) the 12 Ω resistor, (ii) the 4 Ω resistor, (iii) the battery.

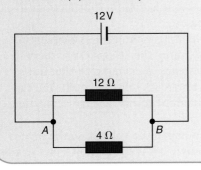

(b) What single resistor has the same value as these two resistors which are connected in parallel?
(c) What is the combined resistance of a 2 Ω, a 3 Ω and a 6 Ω resistor connected in parallel?

5 (a) Use the information in the diagram to calculate the voltage across the 12 Ω resistor.
(b) Now calculate the voltage across the bulb. Use this answer to calculate the bulb's resistance.
(c) Work out the new current in the circuit when the following separate changes are made (assume the bulb's resistance stays the

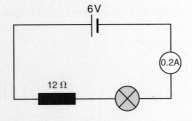

same): (i) an extra 12 Ω resistor is added in series with the bulb, (ii) an extra 12 Ω resistor is added in parallel with the first 12 Ω resistor.

6 How does the resistance of a wire depend on its thickness? Bob chose five different thicknesses of resistance wire, each of length 1 m. The measurements he made are shown in the table below.
(a) Why did he cut each wire to the same length?
(b) What conclusions can you draw from his experiment?
(c) Bob cuts a length of 3 m of this type of wire which has a cross-sectional area of 0.22 mm². What is its resistance?

Diameter (mm)	Cross-sectional area (mm²)	Resistance (Ω)
0.374	0.110	10
0.315	0.078	14
0.264	0.055	20
0.189	0.028	40
0.156	0.019	56

7

Changing Resistance

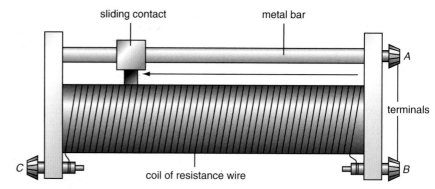

sliding contact   metal bar

A

terminals

C   coil of resistance wire   B

Figure 1 *A variable resistor*

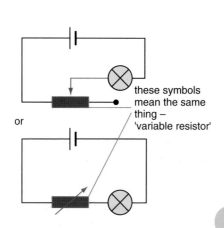

these symbols mean the same thing – 'variable resistor'

or

Figure 2 *These circuits show the symbols for a variable resistor*

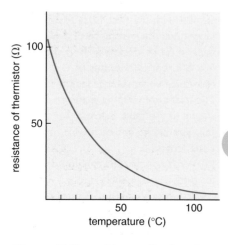

Figure 3 *The resistance of a thermistor changes with temperature*

Variable resistors

In Figure 1 you can see one type of **variable resistor**. It can be used as a fixed resistor by using terminals B and C, when the current goes through the full length of resistance wire, or it can be used as a variable resistor, when you use terminals C and A. The current now flows along the thick metal bar, then down through the sliding contact and along the coil of resistance wire to C. The metal bar has a very small resistance, so the further the contact slides towards C, the less the resistance becomes. When the sliding contact is half way down the bar, the resistance between A and C is about half of the total resistance of the coil between B and C. Figure 2 shows the circuit symbols for a variable resistor.

The thermistor

A **thermistor** is a resistor whose resistance changes considerably with temperature (Figure 3). At low temperatures a thermistor's resistance is high, but as the temperature rises the resistance becomes less. At low temperatures, electrons are fixed onto atoms and so cannot move. As the electrons get hotter they receive enough energy to escape from their atoms, so the thermistor becomes a better conductor. Materials whose resistances change in this way are known as semiconductors. Carbon and silicon are two materials whose resistances decrease as they get hotter.

Resistance of a light filament

The filament of a light bulb also changes with temperature, but its resistance gets bigger as the temperature rises. In this case the number of electrons carrying the current remains constant as the temperature rises. However, the increased vibrations of the atoms as they get hotter makes it harder for the electrons to pass through the filament, so the resistance increases.

You can investigate the resistance of the light filament using the circuit in Figure 4. The variable resistor allows you to control the brightness of the bulb. Moving the slider towards Y reduces the resistance, R, so more current flows, making the bulb brighter. Moving the slide towards X dims the bulb. You can show your results by plotting a graph of the current against voltage across the bulb (see Figure 5).

You can see that the current is *not* proportional to the voltage, so the light filament does not obey Ohm's Law. Some simple calculations shown on the graph

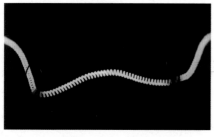

A close-up of the tightly coiled tungsten filament in a light bulb

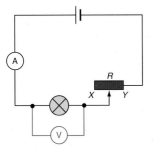

Figure 4

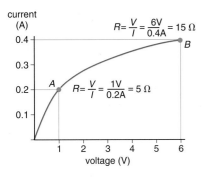

$$R= \frac{V}{I} = \frac{6V}{0.4A} = 15 \ \Omega$$

$$R= \frac{V}{I} = \frac{1V}{0.2A} = 5 \ \Omega$$

Figure 5

show you how the resistance changes. At point A, where the current is only 0.2 A and the bulb is quite cool, the resistance is 5 Ω. At B the bulb is hot, having a current of 0.4 A going through it, and the resistance is now 15 Ω.

Manufacturing light bulbs

The wire used to make the filament of a light bulb is *tungsten*, which has a melting point of 3400 °C. When the filament is working, its temperature is about 2500 °C. At that temperature most other metals have melted. For the light bulb to work on the mains voltage of 230 V, the filament needs a high resistance. This is usually about 1000 Ω. Metals are good conductors, so metal wires have low resistances. 1 m of tungsten wire with a diameter of 1 mm has a resistance of 90 Ω (at 2500 °C). To make a filament have a larger resistance it must be made of very fine wire (thinner than your hair). The 1 m length of filament is coiled tightly, and then coiled again to fit into the bulb, as shown in the photograph.

The next difficulty is that tungsten at high temperatures would oxidise in air, so the filament is placed in a mixture of argon and nitrogen gases. Even so, the filament's life is limited because at such high working temperatures it tends to evaporate. Next time a light bulb blows at home, look at it. You will see that the glass bulb has blackened due to the evaporated tungsten. Nevertheless the average light bulb has a lifetime of about 1000 hours. That is excellent value for money, at a cost of about 50p!

Homework Questions

1   Figure 1 shows a variable resistor. The resistance of the coil between B and C is 100 Ω. With the slider in its present position estimate the resistance between the terminals (i) A and B (ii) A and C.

2   Draw a circuit diagram to show how you would use a battery and variable resistor to control the speed of a motor.

3   The circuit below shows a 24 Ω variable resistor connected in series with a 16 Ω resistor.
(a) What are the maximum and

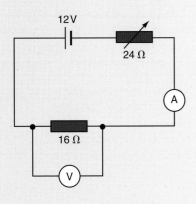

minimum values of the total resistance in the circuit?
(b) Calculate the maximum and minimum values of the current which the ammeter can record.
(c) Calculate the maximum and minimum values of the voltmeter reading.

4   A thermistor, whose resistance changes with temperature as shown in Figure 3, is put in series with a 48 Ω resistor as shown below.

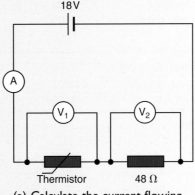

(a) Calculate the current flowing through the circuit when the thermistor is at a temperature of

(i) 20°C, (ii) 80°C.
(b) Sketch graphs to show how V_1 and V_2 vary as the thermistor's temperature changes between 20°C and 80°C. Put as much detail as possible on the graphs.

5   Three light bulbs are put in a circuit as shown below; they are identical to the bulb whose I/V graph is shown in Figure 5.
(a) Use that graph to calculate the battery voltage.
(b) Calculate the current flowing through the battery when switch S is opened.

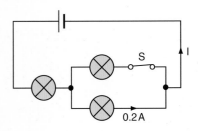

8

Electrical Power

Electric cars recharging their batteries using solar power. The black photovoltaic panels convert sunlight into electrical energy, which feeds into the cars through the orange connecting wires. Such cars produce no gaseous emissions, and therefore no pollution.

Measuring the power

When you switch on a fire to warm up a room, electrical energy is transferred to heat energy. If you want to know how quickly the room is going to warm up you need to know the rate at which electrical energy is used, or the power used by the fire. **Power used = Energy used/second** (see Section D4).

You can work out the electrical power, P, used in a circuit, if you know the voltage of the supply, V, and the current, I, by using the formula:

$$P = V \times I$$

Power is measured in **joules per second** (J/s) or **watts** (W).

Often power used comes in rather large units. For example 1 bar of an electric fire uses about 1000 W; this is called a **kilowatt** (**1 kW**). If you want to talk about power stations you will need to use **megawatts**. 1 megawatt is 1 000 000 W. A large power station can produce 2000 MW of electrical power. In the cold spell of January 1987, Britain's peak power usage was 48 300 MW. Table 1 shows you the power used, and the operating currents and voltages of several electrical devices.

Device	Power (W)	Operating voltage (V)	Current (A)
Torch bulb	0.9	3	0.3
Hair drier	480	240	2.0
Mains bulb	100	240	0.4
Electric kettle	3000	240	12.5
Iron	1000	240	4
TV set	60	240	0.25
Car starter motor	1200	12	100
Pocket calculator	0.0003	3	0.0001
Milk float	3600	72	50

Table 1

Electricity bills

What is it that you pay the electricity board for? You pay for the energy which you use and it costs you about 7p for 1 unit. The unit that the electricity board uses is the kilowatt hour (kWh). If you leave a 1 kW fire on for 1 hour you have used 1 kWh of energy.

The kilowatt hour does not look like a unit of energy; but it is. We can turn a kilowatt hour into joules like this:

$$\text{Energy used} = \text{Power} \times \text{time}$$
$$= 1000 \text{ W} \times 3600 \text{ s}$$
$$= 3\,600\,000 \text{ J}$$

Example. What does it cost to cook a turkey for 6 hours using a 2 kW electric oven?

$$\text{Energy used} = 2 \text{ kW} \times 6 \text{ h}$$
$$= 12 \text{ kWh}$$

Each kWh costs 7p, so total cost $12 \times 7\text{p} = 84\text{p}$

Homework Questions

1 Use the formulae $P = VI$ and $V = IR$, to show that $P = I^2R$ and $P = V^2/R$ may also be used to calculate the power delivered to an electrical circuit.

2 (a) Calculate the current flowing in this circuit.

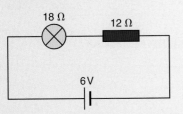

(b) What power does the battery deliver to the circuit?
(c) How much power is the light bulb using?

3 An electric kettle has an element of resistance 24 Ω. Calculate how much power it uses when it is connected to the mains (supply voltage 240).

4 (a) A houseowner goes away for two weeks' holiday. To deter burglars she leaves on two 100 W light bulbs in the house while she is away. If 1 kWh of electricity costs 7p, how much do these bulbs cost her over the two weeks?
(b) What does it cost to use a 1 kW iron for 30 minutes?

5 (a) (i) A mains bulb is marked 240 V, 60 W. What do these markings mean?
(ii) Calculate the working current of the bulb.
(iii) What is the bulb's resistance when working normally.
(iv) Light bulbs are connected to the mains in parallel. Explain the advantages this provides.
(b) A string of Christmas tree lights consists of 20 bulbs connected in series; a bulb works normally when a current of 0.025 A passes through it.
(i) When the lights are connected to a mains supply of 240 V, how much voltage is there across each bulb?
(ii) How much power is delivered to each bulb?
(iii) What is the resistance of each bulb?
(iv) What advantage is there of connecting these bulbs in series, and what disadvantage?
(v) You decide to design a 0.3 W, 240 V Christmas tree light. What will the bulb's resistance be? Explain why such a bulb would be impractical.

Circuit Calculations

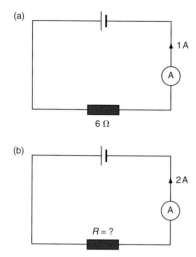

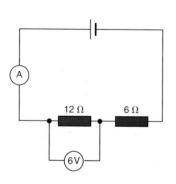

Figure I

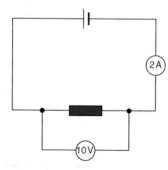

Figure 2

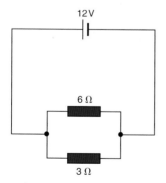

Figure 3

Figure 4

In the previous sections you have learnt the basic rules about electrical circuits. The best way to make sure that you have understood them is to practise by solving problems. In this section, some examples are given, but most of the work is to be done by you.

Resistance

You can compare the value of two resistors using an ammeter and a cell; the larger resistor lets less current through. In Figure 1(a) the cell drives a current of 1 A through a 6 Ω resistor; in Figure 1(b) the same cell drives a current of 2 A through a second resistor whose value is not known. Because the current is more than 1 A, the second resistor must have a resistance less than 6 Ω. In fact its value is 3 Ω; the current is twice as big as before, so the resistance is half the previous value.

Resistance, Voltage and Current Calculations

The value of a resistor may be calculated using an ammeter and a voltmeter; for example, in Figure 2,

$$R = \frac{V}{I}$$

$$= \frac{10\ V}{2\ A}$$

$$= 5\ \Omega$$

More complicated problems may be solved with the help of the Current and Voltage rules on pages 228 and 229. For example, you might be asked to calculate the battery voltage in Figure 3.

The current flowing through the 12 Ω resistor is:

$$I = \frac{V}{R}$$

$$= \frac{6\ V}{12\ \Omega}$$

$$= 0.5\ A$$

The voltage across the 6 Ω resistor is:

$$V = I \times R$$

$$= 0.5\ A \times 6\ \Omega$$

$$= 3\ V$$

The battery voltage is the sum of the voltages across the two resistors, which is 9 V.

Power calculations

Similar care needs to be taken to calculate the power developed in a resistor. For example how much power is produced by the 3 Ω in Figure 4?
Each resistor has 12 V across it. So the current through the 3 Ω resistor is:

$$I = \frac{12\ V}{3\ \Omega}$$

$$= 4\ A$$

So the power developed is:

$$P = 12 \text{ V} \times 4 \text{ A}$$
$$= 48 \text{ W}$$

Homework Questions

1 The cells in Figures 1–4 are identical; the ammeter in circuit 1 reads 1 A.

(a) Calculate the missing values, A_1, A_2 and R_1.

(b) You decide to replace the two resistors in circuit 4 with a single resistor. What value are you going to choose? Explain your answer.

(c) Explain how you would use an ammeter and a cell to compare the value of two resistors.

1

2
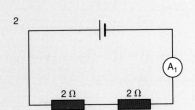

3
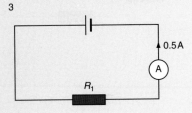

4
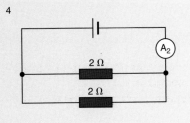

2 In each of the circuits 5–9, state which is the larger of R_1 and R_2.

5   6
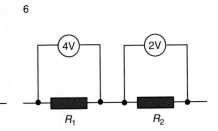

7
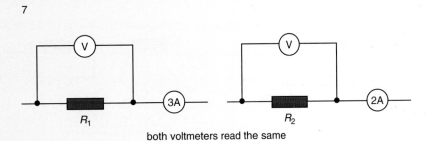

both voltmeters read the same

8
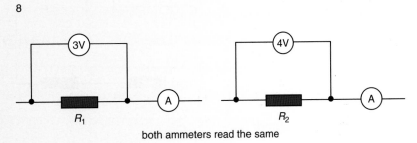

both ammeters read the same

9
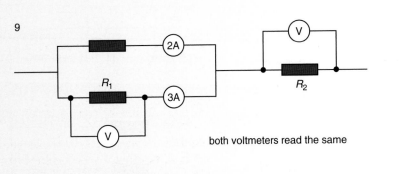

both voltmeters read the same

Homework Questions

3 For each of the circuits 10–19 calculate the missing ammeter or voltmeter readings or missing resistances.
   (a) Find V_1, V_2 and A in circuit 10.
   (b) Find V_1, V_2 and A in circuit 11.
   (c) Find V_1, V_2 and A in circuit 12.
   (d) Find V in circuit 13.
   (e) Find R and A in circuit 14.
   (f) Find R in circuit 15.
   (g) Find V_1, V_2, A_1 and A_2 in circuit 16.
   (h) Find A_1, A_2 and V in circuit 17.
   (i) Find R_1, R_2 and A in circuit 18.
   (j) Find V in circuit 19.

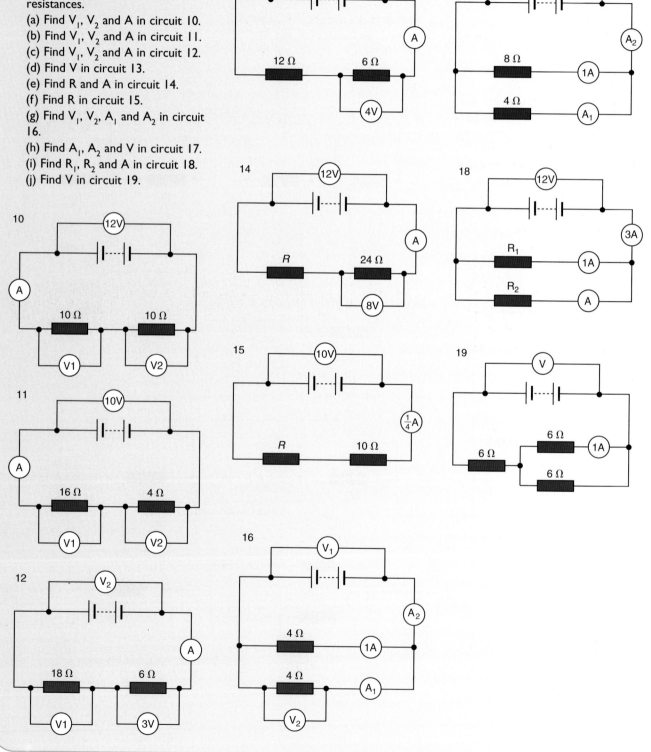

Homework Questions

4 (a) Calculate the current that each of the following 240 V appliances takes under normal operating conditions:
   (i) a 60 W bulb
   (ii) a 300 W TV
   (iii) a 960 W toaster
   (iv) a 1.2 kW heater
   (v) a 3 kW shower.
   (b) Calculate the resistance of each of the appliances above when they are working under normal operating conditions.

5 The table below shows the electrical appliances used by a family during the course of one week. Calculate the week's electricity bill. Assume the cost of electricity is 8p per kWh. To help you calculate the cost, copy the table and fill in the missing values.

6 Circuits A and B show two possible arrangements of two 60 Ω resistors for a mains electric fire.
   (a) Which of the two settings do you think will correspond to the 'high' setting on the fire and which to the 'low' setting?
   (b) Calculate the current drawn from the mains in each case.
   (c) Calculate the power used in each case.

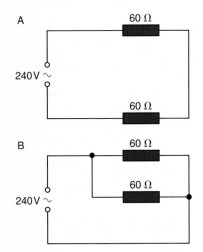

Appliance	Power rating (W)	Hours per week in use	kWh per week	Cost per week (p)
microwave	1000	0.5	0.5	8
12 light bulbs	60 each	40		
TV	250	20		
computer	400	10		
fridge	500	12 (when the compressor is on)		
shower	2500	2		
cooker	4500	4		
lawn mower	720	2		

Alternating current

The electricity supply to your home is an **alternating current** supply (**a.c.**). The voltage of the supply is 230 V. Figures 1(a) and (b) show two light bulbs, one on a 230 V mains a.c. supply and the other on a 230 V d.c. supply. They both have the same brightness, so each supply delivers the same power to the light. Figure 1(c) shows how the voltage across each lamp varies with time. For the d.c. supply the voltage is constant at 230 V. However, for the light powered by the a.c. supply, the voltage across it changes from +325 V to −325 V. When the voltage becomes negative the lamp still works. It simply means that the current is flowing the other way round – just like turning the battery around in a circuit. 325 V is the peak voltage of the mains supply. The reason that the peak voltage is bigger than 230 V is because for part of the time the mains voltage is near to zero, and at those times little power is given to the lamp. So the peak voltage has to be more than 230 V to make up for those times when little power is given to the light bulb.

We call 230 V the **root mean square** (*r.m.s.*) **value** of the mains supply. In general

$$\text{r.m.s. voltage} = \frac{\text{peak voltage}}{\sqrt{2}}$$

The frequency of the mains supply is 50 Hz, which means that there are 50 complete voltage cycles per second.

Mains supply to your house

The mains electricity supply comes into your house on two cables called the **live** and **neutral**. In any circuit, you must have two wires. The current comes into the house on one wire and returns to your local substation on the other. The live wire is the dangerous wire – the voltage on this wire changes between +325 V and −325 V. The voltage on the neutral wire is close to zero. Figure 2 illustrates how your cooker is wired to the mains. Notice how the direction of current flow reverses during one voltage cycle.

Figure 3 shows a plan of your house wiring. The supply comes through a main fuse and the electricity meter, and then to the fuse box. The fuse box is the distribution point for your house's electricity supply. In the box there are about six fuses which lead to different circuits in the house. The size of the fuse depends on the current which flows in the circuit (see page 244). Cookers, immersion heaters or electric shower heaters use large currents and so have their own circuit.

● Your house will have two or three **ring main circuits**, which supply all the wall sockets. On each ring main there are usually about 10 sockets. Notice that all the sockets are in parallel, so the full mains voltage is supplied to everything that is plugged into a socket. The advantage of using a ring main circuit is that current can flow two ways into a particular socket. So the connecting wires can be thinner, because they carry a smaller current than they would do otherwise. In addition to the live and neutral wires, the ring main circuit carries an **earth wire**. The earth wire is there for reasons of safety (see page 245).

● The lights for your house have their own circuit. Again each light fitting is in parallel, so that each light bulb receives the mains voltage of 230 V. Light bulbs draw a small current (about 0.4 A for a 100 W bulb) so about 10 lights can be safely run through a 5 A fuse.

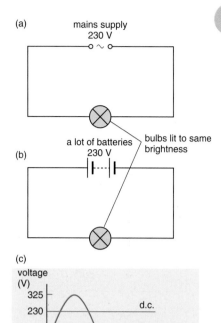

Figure 1

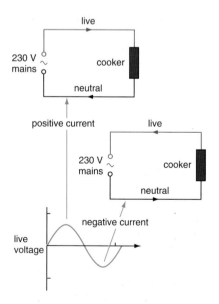

Figure 2

Circuits in buildings are usually protected by fuses, which 'blow' if too much current flows through them. This fuse box in a flat has fuses for a number of circuits. Circuit breakers are now often used instead of fuses.

⚠ **It is important that the supply is turned off before fuses are changed.**

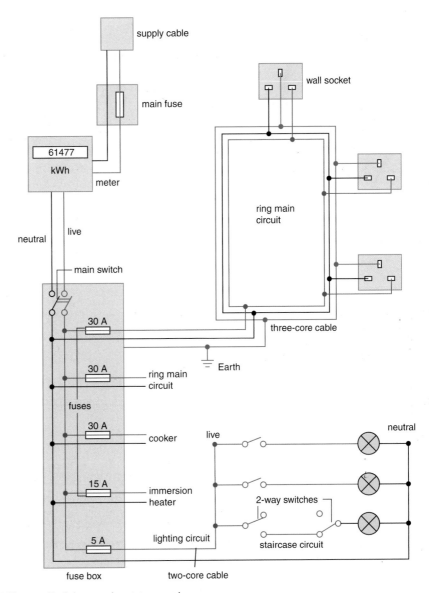

Figure 3 *A house electricity supply*

Homework Questions

1 Explain what is meant by an alternating current.

2 Why do we say that the mains voltage is 230 V, when its maximum value is 325 V?

3 What is the advantage of using a ring main circuit?

4 What is the greatest number of 60 W bulbs that can be run off the mains, if you are not going to overload a 5 A fuse?

5 A hot water tank containing 0.2 m³ of water (200 kg) is to be heated from 15°C to 40°C by an immersion heater drawing a 15 A current from the mains supply (230 V). (i) What is the power of the heater? (ii) What is the resistance of the heater? (iii) How much energy is used to warm up the tank? (1 kg of water needs 4200 J to warm it up by 1°C),

(iv) How long will it take to warm up the tank, (v) How much does it cost to warm up the tank, if 1 kWh costs 7p?

6 An electric shower uses a 230 V, 15 A power supply.
(a) Calculate the electrical power supply used by the shower heater.
(b) Calculate the cost of a 10 minute shower if 1 kWh costs 7p.

11 Electrical Safety

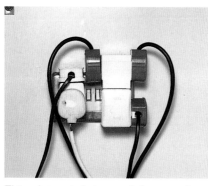

This adaptor is being used dangerously; far too many devices are plugged into it. Question 5 opposite shows the problems that can occur

Although electricity is very useful to us it can also be very dangerous. Electrical faults can cause fires which damage property and sometimes result in injury or death. You can also give yourself a very painful electric shock from the mains, and electric shocks do occasionally kill people. The purpose of this unit is to teach you how to keep your home safe.

Fuses

The main purpose of a fuse is to prevent a fire, although a fuse can also prevent damage to expensive electrical equipment. In electrical cables which are bent and twisted it is quite common for the electrical insulation to crack and break. For example this could easily happen with your electric lawn mower or an iron. As a result of the broken insulation, the live wire could come directly into contact with the neutral wire. This would short-circuit the electrical device (Figure 1).

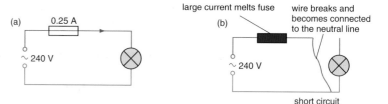

Figure I

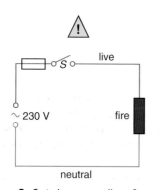

Figure 2 *Switches, as well as fuses, are put into the live wire*

Normally, the current flowing through the connecting wires is quite small: 0.25 A in our example. By contrast, if there is a short circuit, the resistance in the circuit is so small that the current becomes very large: 100 A or more. Such a large current would cause enormous heating and a fire is the likely result. However, a fuse protects against fire. A fuse contains a thin piece of resistance wire which melts easily if the current becomes too large. So when a fault happens, the fuse melts and the circuit is broken (Figure 1(b)).

The fuse is put into the *live* wire. Then if a fault occurs and the fuse melts, the live (dangerous) wire is disconnected. Switches are also put into the live wire for the same reason. If a switch is put into the neutral wire, you could get a shock from an electric fire element even though it is switched off (Figure 2).

All devices are protected by a fuse in the plug, and if that fails, the main fuse box in the house also has a fuse for each circuit. Nowadays, it is quite common to find **circuit breakers** in houses. If the current becomes too big the circuit breaker throws open a switch which can be reset when the fault has been corrected.

Choosing a fuse

When wiring up a plug you should always choose the right fuse for the device you are going to use. For example, what fuse should you use for a 1000 W iron?

Appliance	Power (W)	Normal Current (A)	Recommended Fuse (A)
Lamp	100	0.4	3
TV set	70	0.3	3
Hair drier	500	2.2	5
Toaster	1200	5.2	13
Kettle	2750	12.0	13

Table I

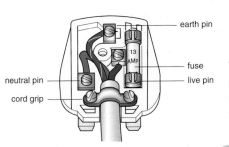

Figure 3 *A correctly wired plug*

$$P = V \times I$$

$$I = \frac{P}{V} = \frac{1000 \text{ W}}{230 \text{ V}} = 4.3 \text{ A}$$

The most commonly used fuses in the home are 3 A, 5 A, and 13 A. So you should choose the 5 A for your iron, then the fuse will blow if any small extra current flows due to a fault. Table 1 shows some appliances and their recommended fuses.

Wiring a plug

You will often want to wire up a new plug to some electrical device. Don't rush at it; it will take you at least 15 minutes to do it well. Figure 3 shows you what it should look like when finished. These are the points to watch for:

- Make sure the wires are in the right place; earth is green/yellow, live is brown and neutral is blue.
- Do not strip the insulation back too far.
- Make sure the main thick cable is held in the cord grip.
- Do the screws up well.
- Choose the right fuse.

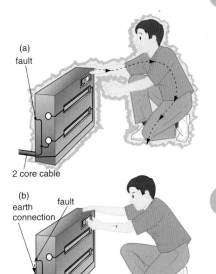

Figure 4

Earthing appliances

The pictures in Figure 4 tell a story. In (a) a fault has developed in an electric fire and the live wire has come into contact with the metal casing. The man gets a shock. In (b) the casing was attached to earth, so as soon as the live wire touched the case, a large current flowed and the fuse blew. In the second case the man does not get a shock.

A lot of modern appliances are made out of plastic, such as the bases of electric lamps. In these cases there is no need for an earth wire since plastic does not conduct electricity. This method of protection is called **double insulation** and it is shown by the sign. ▣

Homework Questions

1 (a) Explain why we need fuses and how they work.
(b) Why is it dangerous to put a fuse in the neutral wire?
(c) Why do we earth the outer metal casings of electrical devices?

2 The diagram shows a thermal circuit breaker. Explain how it works, and how it can be reset.

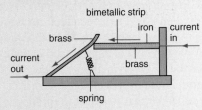

3 (a) Why is it dangerous to touch an electrical device with wet hands?
(b) Explain three special precautions

taken over the use of mains electricity in the bathroom.

4 An earth leakage trip works by detecting the strength of magnetic fields in both neutral and live wires.
(a) Why should the strength of magnetic field be the same from the live and neutral wires?
(b) If the live and neutral wires produce different magnetic field strengths, what has happened?
(c) Explain how an earth leakage trip can save lives.

5 The devices shown in the table below are all drawing current through an adapter plugged (foolishly) into a single socket.
(a) Copy the table and fill in the column to show how much current each device takes.
(b) What fuse should be fitted for each device?
(c) What is the total current which goes through the adapter from the mains? Comment on its size.
(d) How should these devices be connected to the mains?

Device	Power	Voltage	Current
Kettle	2.8 kW	230 V	
Fan Heater	1.7 kW	230 V	
Iron	1.0 kW	230 V	

12 Electron Beam Tubes

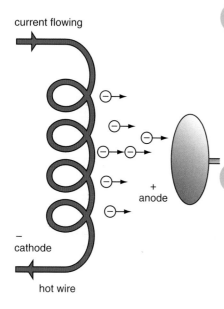

current flowing

anode

+

−

cathode

hot wire

Figure 1 *Thermionic emission*

Thermionic emission

When a current goes through a wire, the wire gets hot. At very high temperatures some electrons have enough energy to escape from the wire. If the wire is charged negatively the electrons are repelled and can be collected by a positive plate (Figure 1). The positive plate is called an **anode** and the negative wire the **cathode**. When this effect (thermionic emission) was first discovered, the emitted electrons were called **cathode rays**, because they were emitted from the cathode.

The Maltese Cross tube

Figure 2 shows how a '**Maltese Cross**' tube works. A 6 V battery is connected to the filament so that it is hot enough to give out electrons. A 4000 V power supply is then connected across the cathode and anode. The negative electrons are attracted towards the positive anode. Some of the electrons hit the Maltese Cross and go back to the power supply. Others carry on, and hit the fluorescent screen. When an electron hits the screen, its kinetic energy is used to make the fluorescent screen give out some light.

You can control the brightness of the fluorescent screen in two ways. First the voltage of the supply to the anode can be increased. This makes the electrons travel faster, so they will have more kinetic energy when they hit the screen. Second, the filament can be made hotter by making a bigger current flow through it. Then more electrons are given out, so more electrons hit the screen.

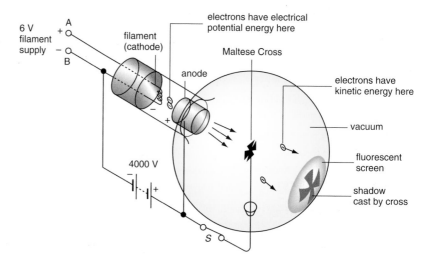

Figure 2 *A Maltese Cross tube. A metal cross lies in the path of the electrons, so a shadow is cast on the fluorescent screen*

The cathode ray oscilloscope

Figure 3 shows a **cathode ray oscilloscope** (CRO). Electrons are accelerated away from a heated filament by the pull of a positive anode. Then the electrons travel through a vacuum until they hit a fluorescent screen. Unlike the Maltese Cross tube the CRO produces a very fine beam of electrons, which produces a small spot of light on the screen. The beam is focused by the two anodes. The brightness of the spot is controlled by the grid. If the grid is charged slightly negative, electrons from the filament are repelled so that fewer of them hit the screen. This makes a smaller, duller spot.

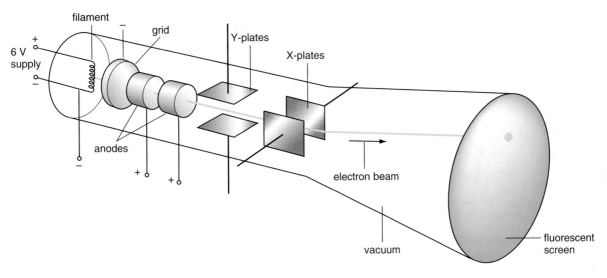

Figure 3 *A cathode ray oscilloscope (CRO)*

The electron beam can be deflected vertically or horizontally by charging the Y-plates or the X-plates. Figure 4 illustrates how the X and Y plates may be charged to deflect the beam. In this diagram you are looking down the length of the oscilloscope, through the screen towards the deflection plates. Notice that when alternating current is applied to the Y-plates a vertical line is produced. As a result of the alternating current, the charge on the Y-plates is switching around very rapidly. Sometimes the top plate is positive, but a fraction of a second later it is negative. This makes the electron beam switch quickly from being deflected upwards to being deflected downwards. The switching occurs so rapidly that the spot on the screen has no time to fade, and we therefore see a continuous straight line.

Homework Questions

1 Look carefully at Figure 2.
(a) (i) Does it matter which way round the 6 V battery is connected to the filament? (ii) Does it matter which way round the 4000 V supply is connected? Explain your answers.
(b) What change would you see if you reduced the voltage between the cathode and the anode to 2000 V?
(c) Why do we have to keep a vacuum in the tube?
(d) The diagrams below show the shadow at the end of the Maltese Cross tube. In one of them the switch S is open, in the other it is closed. Can you explain their shapes?

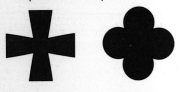

(i) *S closed*   (ii) *S open*

2 Draw diagrams similar to those in Figure 4 to show the deflection of the spot in an oscilloscope in the following cases:
(a) top Y-plate negatively charged, bottom Y-plate positively charged;
(b) alternating current supplied to both Y and X plates together.

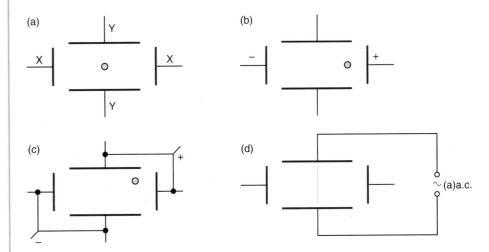

Figure 4

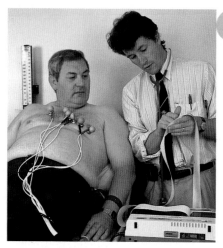

A doctor conducts an electrocardiography (ECG) examination on a man to monitor the state of his heart

The time base

In the last unit you read how the X and Y plates in an oscilloscope can be used to deflect the electron beam. What really makes the oscilloscope useful to us is its time base. The **time base circuit** works like this. A changing voltage is applied to the X-plates of the CRO, so that the spot moves across the screen from left to right. The moment the spot reaches the right-hand side of the screen it returns immediately to the other side to start its journey across the screen again. Figure 1 shows how the voltage applied to the X plates varies with time.

The time base allows us to look at changing voltages (*signals*). The CRO plots a graph of voltage (*y*-axis) against time (*x*-axis). We can apply a signal to the Y-plates so that the spot is moving up and down. At the same time, the time base makes the spot move sideways. A typical signal is shown in Figure 2. In this diagram the right-hand dial shows you that each centimetre in a vertical direction means a voltage of 2 V. So the peak voltage is 4 V. The left-hand dial shows you that the beam crosses the screen horizontally, taking 2 ms (0.002 s) for each centimetre. One complete cycle of the voltage waveform takes 4 squares of the grid, or 8 ms. The time period of the cycle is 8/1000 s. Therefore the frequency is 1000/8 = 125 cycles per second or 125 Hz (f = 1/T).

Oscilloscopes are widely used in industry to monitor and display changing signals. They are also useful in hospitals where they are used to show the strength and frequency of a patient's heart beat, or to build up a picture after an X-ray or ultrasound scan.

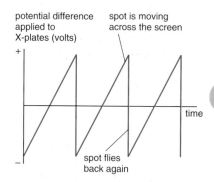

Figure I How the voltage applied to the X-plates varies with time

Televisions

Getting our television pictures is a complicated process, but the television set itself is rather like a CRO. A TV screen is made up of lots of small dots which are blue, green or red. These are the three primary colours, and if they are mixed together they make white. Various combinations of the colours can make the other colours. Table 1 gives some examples.

To make a colour picture the TV set needs three electron beams, as shown in Figure 3. A beam of electrons leaves the 'green' gun and passes through a hole in the shadow mask. Then the beam hits a small fluorescent spot that gives out green light. Similarly electron beams leave the other two guns and hit fluorescent spots that give out blue and red light. The purpose of the shadow mask is to make sure the beams hit the right part of the screen. The small holes in it only allow the beam to hit a small part of the screen.

Like an oscilloscope, the television has a time base. The whole television picture is built up by the beams sweeping backwards and forwards across the screen very rapidly indeed. The beams go from top to bottom of the screen in about 0.025 seconds. During this time they have crossed the screen about 625 times.

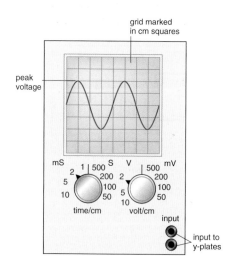

Figure 2 A typical CRO signal

Blue	Green	Red	Mixture
●	●	●	○ white
●	●		● cyan
	●	●	● yellow
●		●	● magenta

Table I

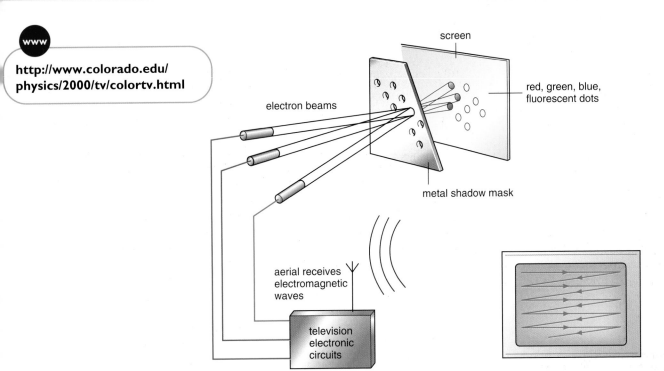

screen

red, green, blue,
fluorescent dots

electron beams

metal shadow mask

aerial receives
electromagnetic
waves

television
electronic
circuits

Figure 3 *The principle of the colour television*

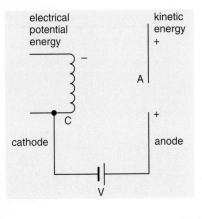

Figure 4 *The time taken for the beam to travel from top to bottom of a screen is 0.025 seconds*

Homework Questions

1 Look at the signal in Figure 2. Draw another diagram to show how the signal looks when you make these two separate changes: (i) increase the Y-gain to 1 V/cm, (ii) increase the time base speed to 1 ms/cm.

2 The diagram shows a waveform on an oscilloscope screen; the time base is set to 1 ms/cm and the Y-gain control to 2 V/cm. Calculate the peak voltage and frequency of the a.c. supply

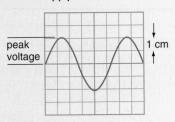

peak
voltage

1 cm

3 Explain why a colour television needs three electron beams. What colour do you see on the screen when two red spots are illuminated for every blue and green spot?

4 The purpose of this question is to enable you to work out the speed of an electron in a CRO tube.
(a) Refer to the diagram below.
(i) Explain why an electron near the cathode, C, has electrical potential energy.
(ii) Why does the electron have kinetic energy near the anode, A?
(b) By using the definition of the volt, page 229, show that the electron transfers eV joules of electrical potential energy to kinetic energy when the electron moves from C to A; e is the charge on the electron, V is the potential difference between C and A.
(c) Write down an expression for the electron's kinetic energy at A, in terms of its mass, m and velocity, v.
(d) Use your answers to (b) and (c) to calculate the velocity of an electron which has been accelerated through a potential difference of 4000 V. Assume it started from rest

near the cathode; the mass of an electron is: $m = 9.1 \times 10^{-31}$ kg; the charge of an electron is: $e = 1.6 \times 10^{-19}$ C.
(e) If the electron current is 1.2×10^{-6} A, calculate the number of electrons flowing per second. [Hint: current = number of electrons per second $\times$ charge on each electron.]

electrical
potential
energy

kinetic
energy
+

A

C

cathode

+

anode

V

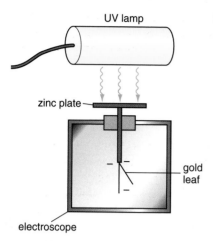

UV lamp

zinc plate

gold
leaf

electroscope

Figure 1

http://www.iop.org/Physics/
Electron/Exhibition/

Photoelectric effect

Electrons can be knocked out of the surface of some metals, when light of short wavelength falls on them. This is called the **photoelectric effect**; Figure 1 shows the apparatus which would be used to demonstrate this. Short wavelength ultra-violet (UV) light irradiates a clean, polished zinc plate, which is placed on top of an electroscope. When the electroscope is negatively charged the UV light causes it to discharge.

Figure 2 summarises three important experimental results which help us to understand this effect.

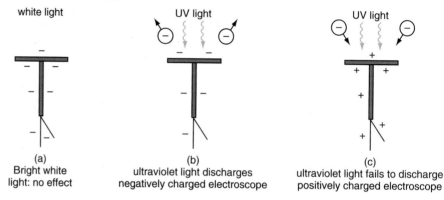

white light	UV light	UV light
(a)	(b)	(c)
Bright white light: no effect	ultraviolet light discharges negatively charged electroscope	ultraviolet light fails to discharge positively charged electroscope

Figure 2

(a) A strong source of light from an ordinary 100 W light bulb does not discharge the negatively charged electroscope.

(b) A weak source of light (2 W) from a short wavelength ultra-violet lamp, discharges a negatively charged electroscope.

(c) A weak source of ultra-violet light does not discharge a positively charged electroscope.

Photons

The photoelectric effect can be explained by the idea of photons.

- Light and electromagnetic radiation is emitted and absorbed in packets of energy called **photons**.
- The energy of the photon is directly proportional to the frequency of the radiation. Thus radiowave photons carry low energies, while gamma-ray and X-ray photons carry large energies.
- One photon interacts with one electron.

These theories can now be used to explain the experiments in Figure 2.

(a) Photons emitted from a white light are too low a frequency to knock out an electron from the zinc plate. Energy has to be given to an electron to take it away from the metal, and these photons are not energetic enough.

(b) Ultra-violet photons are energetic enough to dislodge electrons from the zinc. One photon is absorbed by one electron; the photon's energy does work to remove an electron from the metal and also provides the electron with kinetic energy.

(c) Ultra-violet photons dislodge electrons from the metal, but the positive charge on the electroscope pulls the electrons back. No discharge occurs.

Figure 3

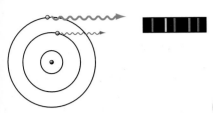

Figure 4 *Electrons fall from a high level to a lower level. The blue photon carries more energy than the red photon.*

The nature of light is hard to understand. We need to use the wave theory of light to explain phenomena such as diffraction, interference and polarisation, but we can only explain the photoelectric effect using a particle theory. Light shows both wave and particle properties; we call this **wave-particle duality**.

Spectra

The photon theory helps us to understand the nature of electrons in atoms. A hot metal filament emits a continuous spectrum of light; we see all the colours of the rainbow (Figure 3). In a metal, electrons are free to move and can have any amount of kinetic energy. When an electron loses energy in a collision it emits a photon; these photons can have any amount of energy so we see a continuous spectrum.

On the other hand, if you examine the light coming from a hot gas, you see only a few specific colours. This is called a line spectrum. This observation leads to the idea that electrons in atoms can only exist in certain specific energy levels. Energy, from a flame for example, can excite an electron to a higher energy level. A short time later, the electron falls back to its original, lower level, and the extra energy is emitted as a photon. Because each atom only has a small number of energy levels, we only see a small number of such 'lines', see Figure 4.

X-ray production

Figure 5 shows the principle behind the production of X-rays. A heated cathode produces electrons by thermionic emission. These electrons are accelerated by a large potential difference of about 10 kV. The anode in this apparatus consists of a dense metal such as tungsten. When electrons strike the metal they decelerate rapidly, transferring their kinetic energy into photons of energy. Because the electrons are travelling quickly they have a large quantity of kinetic energy, so they produce high frequency, short wavelength photons; X-rays typically have wavelengths of about 10^{-10} m.

The photon theory helps to explain why UV rays, X-rays and γ-rays present a hazard to us which other types of electromagnetic radiations do not. While excessive doses of any electromagnetic wave can burn us, the shorter wavelengths can cause cancer. The short wavelength radiations produce high energy photons, which can penetrate our skin and cause damage to a cell nucleus. Radiographers working with X-rays must take precautions to protect themselves.

Homework Questions

1. (a) What is the photoelectric effect?
   (b) How would you demonstrate this effect?
   (c) Explain how the theory of photons helps to account for the photoelectric effect.

2. A teacher tries to explain the photoelectric effect with an analogy. She says that if you sprinkle sugar out of a window on to a crowded street you will irritate a lot of people. However, if you drop a few kilogram bags of sugar you will knock a few people out.
   (a) What is an analogy?
   (b) To what, in the analogy above, are these things analogous: (i) light photons, (ii) UV light photons, (iii) electrons?
   (c) Discuss the extent to which this is a good analogy.

3. (a) Explain why X-rays and γ-rays are dangerous.
   (b) What precautions do radiographers take?

4. What evidence is there that electrons can only exist in a small number of energy levels in atoms?

5. Look at Figure 5. What changes will you notice in the X-rays if these two separate changes are made:
   (i) the anode-cathode voltage is reduced to 9 kV?
   (ii) the filament voltage is increased to 8 V?

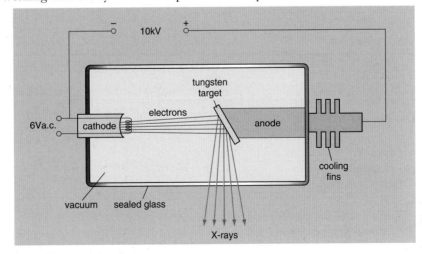

Figure 5

SECTION I: Questions

1 Burning coal in power stations produces large amounts of ash, dust and waste gases. All of these cause environmental problems. An electrostatic precipitator in the chimney removes ash and dust from the waste gases.

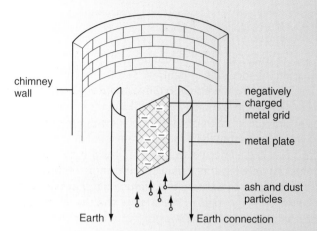

It consists of a metal wire grid surrounded by two large metal plates connected to earth. The wire grid is given a very large negative charge. The ash and dust particles become negatively charged as they pass the wire grid. They then move towards the metal plates and lose their negative charge.

(a) State **two** environmental problems caused by burning coal.

(b) Explain clearly why the ash and dust particles move towards the metal plates.

(c) State what happens to the negative charges given up by the ash and dust particles at the metal plates.

WJEC

2 The diagram shows a circuit for emergency lighting. If the mains supply fails the relay switch closes and the lamps operate from the 12 V batter.

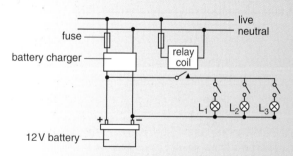

(a) Write down ONE reason for connecting the lamps in parallel.

(b) When switched on, the current in each lamp is 5 A.

(i) Calculate the current in the battery when all three lamps are switched on.

(ii) Calculate the power of each lamp.

(c) Lamps in emergency lighting circuits are connected to the battery using thick wires. Mains lamps of the same power are connected using thinner wires. Explain why.

3 This question is about electrostatic charge. The picture shows an aircraft being refuelled.

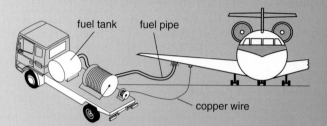

(a) Explain how electrostatic charge can build up during refuelling.

(b) During refuelling, a copper wire is connected between the aircraft and the tanker. Without the wire a charge would build up on the aircraft.

(i) Why is a build-up of charge on the aircraft dangerous?

(ii) A build-up of charge can produce a large voltage between the aircraft and the tanker. Explain, in terms of energy, what is meant by **voltage**.

(iii) With the wire attached, the charge passes safely back to the tanker. Why does the charge now pass back to the tanker?

(c) It takes 20 minutes to refuel the tanker. The wire connecting the aircraft to the tanker is thin because the current is **very** small. A charge of 0.12 mC moves round the circuit. Calculate the average current in the wire during refuelling.

You **must** show how you work out your answer.

WJEC

4 Diagram (1) below shows the inside of a mains-operated hair drier. The fan can blow either hot or cold air. Diagram (2) is a circuit diagram of the same drier showing how it is wired up.

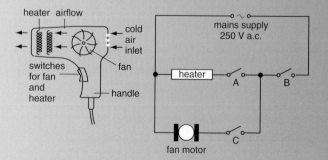

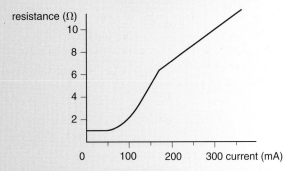

(a) Copy the table below and show, by placing ticks in the spaces, which switches need to be ON to get the result shown.

(You may use each switch more than once, once, or not at all.)

Result	Switch A	Switch B	Switch C
a blow of cold air			
a blow of hot air			

(b) The heater must not be on without the fan.
(i) Which of the switches, A, B, C, must always be on to achieve this?
(ii) Explain carefully what you would expect to happen if the fan failed to work when the heater was on.
(c) The manufacturer wishes to include a two-speed fan. This could be done by connecting a suitable resistor across one of the switches as follows:

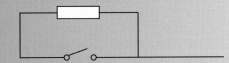

(i) Copy diagram (2) and draw a resistor across the correct switch in order to make a two-speed fan.
(ii) When the switch is open, will this give a fast or slow speed? Explain your answer.
(d) The details on the hair drier are 250 V, 500 W. Calculate the current from the mains supply when the drier is working at the stated power.
(e) Fuses for the mains of 3 A, 5 A and 13 A are available.
(i) Which fuse would you choose for use in the plug attached to the drier?
(ii) Which wire in the mains cable should be connected to the fuse?
(f) A girl needs to use the drier for 10 minutes. Calculate the energy converted during this time.
(g) The manufacturer makes a different hair drier which will work from a 12 V car battery. You are required to find the power taken by the 12 V drier. Copy and complete the circuit diagram below to show how you would connect up an ammeter and voltmeter to do this.

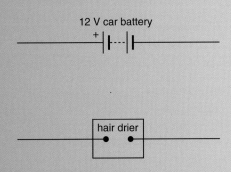

12 V car battery

hair drier

5 The graph shows how the resistance of a bulb varies with the current through it.
(a) What is the value of the resistance of the bulb when it is not switched on?
(b) The bulb can be used as a simple overload protection and warning device for use with model railway controllers. The bulb is placed in one of the wires leading to the track, as in the circuit diagram below.

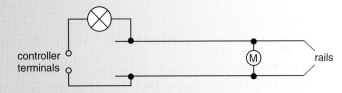

controller terminals

M

rails

When operating normally the current through a model railway locomotive is about 250 mA.
(i) What is the potential difference across the bulb when 250 mA passes through it?
(ii) If the output voltage of the controller is 12 V, what is the potential difference across the motor when 250 mA passes? (Assume the resistance of the rails is negligible.)

The train derails and short-circuits the two rails (i.e. it joins the two rails together by a good conductor).

(iii) State and explain what happens to the bulb when this occurs.

OCR (MEG)

6 Two light bulbs (A and B) light normally when connected to a 5 V battery. The graph on the next page shows how the current varies with the applied voltage (potential difference) for each bulb.
(a) When they are working normally, what is the resistance of each bulb?
(b) A 5 V battery is connected across XY.
(i) Which bulb will be brighter?
(ii) How much power is used by each bulb?
(c) The bulbs are now connected in series. Describe carefully what happens as the voltage across PQ is increased slowly from 0 to 5 V.

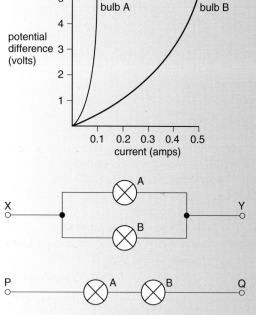

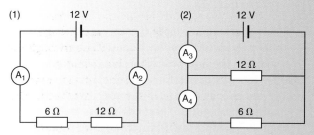

7 (a) Calculate the readings on each of the four ammeters A₁, A₂, A₃, A₄, shown in diagrams (1) and (2).

(1) 12 V

(2) 12 V

(b) Calculate the power transformed in each of the resistors shown in the diagrams.

8 An electric iron is marked 240 V, 720 W.
(a) Explain the meaning of these markings.
(b) Calculate the normal working current of the iron.
(c) What is the resistance of the iron element?
(d) Which fuse would you use for the iron: 3 A, 5 A or 13 A?
(e) Explain why it is important to have a fuse.

9 The manufacturers of a new bulb claim that its long life and high efficiency will save you about £60 during its lifetime, if you use it rather than the normal bulb. It emits the same amount of light as a normal bulb, but it uses less power.

	Cost	Lifetime	Power rating
'long life' bulb	£12	12 000 h	20 W
normal bulb	50p	1 000 h	100 W

(a) Explain what is meant by 'high efficiency'.
(b) Use the data in the table to investigate the truth of the claim. (At today's prices, electricity costs 7p per kWh).

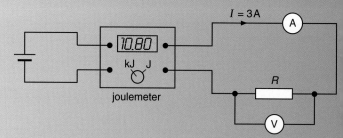

10 In the circuit shown, a battery delivers energy to a resistor. This energy is measured by a joulemeter. After 5 minutes, 10.80 kJ of energy have been supplied to the resistor.
(a) Use the information in the diagram to calculate the number of coulombs that flowed round the circuit in 5 minutes.
(b) How much power was transferred to the resistor? (Use the formula: power = energy supplied/time.)
(c) Now work out the voltage across the resistor, R. (Use the formula: $P = V \times I$.)
(d) Calculate the energy carried by each coulomb of charge, using your answer to part (a). Your answer should confirm that the voltage measures the number of joules of energy carried by each coulomb of charge.

A potential difference (voltage) of 1 volt exists across a resistor if 1 joule of energy is transferred to the resistor when 1 coulomb of charge passes through it.

(e) Use the definition of the volt to work out the speed of an electron reaching the anode of this electron gun. The mass of an electron is 9.1×10^{-31} kg and its charge is 1.6×10^{-19} C.

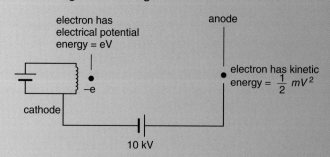

11 On the next page you can see a typical waveform on the screen of an oscilloscope. Also shown are the Y-gain and time base controls of the oscilloscope.
(a) What is the peak voltage of the signal?
(b) What is the time period of one oscillation of the signal?

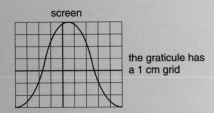

screen

the graticule has a 1 cm grid

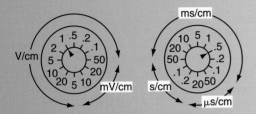

V/cm   mV/cm   s/cm   ms/cm   μs/cm

(c) Calculate the frequency of the signal.

(d) Make a sketch to show what the trace would look like if two changes are made together: the time base changes to 1 ms per cm, and the Y-gain is changed to 2 V per cm.

12 The following circuit shows an ammeter and a voltmeter connected to a power supply and a resistance wire. The connector **B** is joined to a length of resistance wire **DC**.

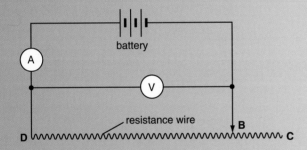

battery

A

V

resistance wire

B

D ~~~~~~~~~~~~~~~~~~~~~~~~~~~~~~ C

(a) (i) Write down, **in words**, the equation connecting resistance, current and voltage.
   (ii) With **B** in the position shown, the voltmeter reads 10 V and the ammeter 2 A. Calculate the resistance between **D** and **B** in ohms.
(b) The connector **B** is moved towards **D**. State the effect this would have on
   (i) the circuit current.
   (ii) The circuit resistance.

WJEC

13 The table shows the power rating of appliances used in the home.

Appliance	Power rating
fire	2000 W
television	250 W
kettle	2.5 kW
hairdrier	1200 W
vacuum cleaner	800 W

(a) If all the appliances were used for the same length of time, state which one would
   (i) use the least amount of electricity,
   (ii) Cost the most to run.
(b) Calculate
   (i) the power of the fire in kW,
   (ii) the cost of using the fire for 2h if one unit of energy (kWh) costs 8p.
   You may use the following equations

Energy used (kWh) = power (kW) × time (h),

Cost = number of units × cost per unit.

WJEC

14 A 2800 W washing machine is operated on a 230 V mains supply.
(a) (i) Write down, **in words**, the equation connecting power, current and voltage.
   (ii) Calculate the current that flows through the washing machine when it is working.
   (iii) Suggest a suitable value for the fuse that should be placed in the plug attached to the washing machine.
(b) Explain carefully the purpose **and** action of
   (i) a *fuse*,
   (ii) an *earth leakage circuit breaker*.

15 (a) (i) Describe how a miniature circuit breaker (m.c.b.) protects an electrical circuit.
   (ii) State the **two** main advantages a m.c.b. has over a fuse.
(b) The table below gives information about the use of some household appliances.

Copy and complete the table, showing your working.

WJEC

Appliance	Power	Time used	Energy used (kWh) Power (kW) × Time (h)	Total cost Energy used (kWh) × Cost per unit (8p)
Fire	2 kW	4h	8 kWh	64p
Fan heater		7h	8.4 kWh	

16 When the switch **S** is closed, charge is transferred, producing an electric current which flows through the circuit lighting the lamp.

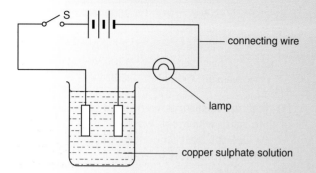

(a) Explain how the charge is transferred through the
   (i) metal connecting wires,
   (ii) copper sulphate solution (the electrolyte).
(b) (i) Write down, **in words**, an equation connecting current, time and charge.
   (ii) If a current of 0.2 A flows through the lamp in the above circuit, calculate the amount of charge transferred in 2 minutes.

WJEC

17 Sam is investigating how the resistance of a lamp changes as she alters the current through it.

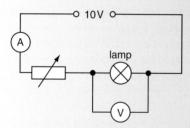

She uses this circuit.
(a) She adjusts the setting of the variable resistor. Explain how this affects the current.
(b) She records the values of the voltage across the lamp as the current changes. She plots this graph.

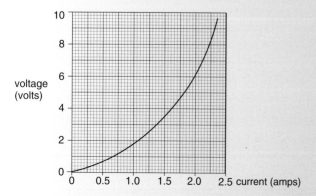

(i) Use the graph to find the value of the current when the voltage is 4.0 V.
(ii) Calculate the resistance of the lamp when the voltage is 4.0 V.
   You **must** show how you work out your answer.
(c) How can you tell from the graph that the resistance of the lamp increases between 4.0 V and 8.0 V?

OCR

18 (a) The table below shows the current in three different electrical appliances when connected to the 240 V mains a.c. supply.

Appliance	Current in A
kettle	8.5
lamp	0.4
toaster	4.8

(i) Which appliance has the greatest electrical resistance?
   How does the data show this?
(ii) The lamp is connected to the mains supply using thin, twin-cored cable, consisting of live and neutral connections.
   State TWO reasons why this cable should not be used for connecting the kettle to the mains supply.
(b) (i) Calculate the power rating of the kettle when it is operated from the 240 V a.c. mains supply.
   (ii) A holiday-maker takes the kettle abroad where the mains supply is 120 V.
   What is the current in the kettle when it is operated from the 120 V supply? You can assume that the resistance of the kettle does not change.
   (iii) The kettle is filled with water. Explain how the time it takes to boil the kettle changes when it is operated from the 120 V supply.

Edexcel

Magnetism and Electromagnets

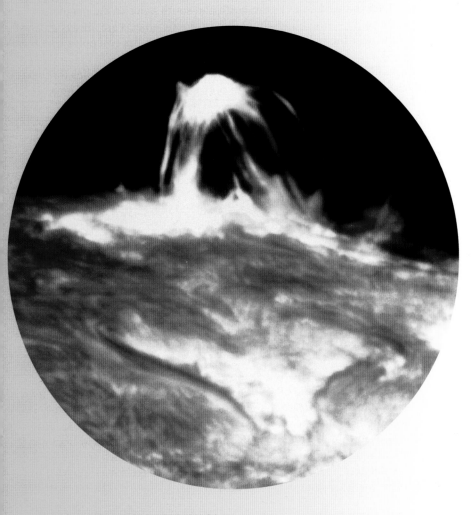

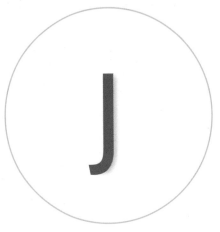

A solar flare erupting from the Sun's surface. The eruption of magnetically charged material is forced into curved paths by the Sun's strong magnetic field.

By the end of this section you should:

- know what a magnetic field is
- know that an electric current can produce a magnetic field
- know how to magnetise materials
- understand what is meant by the motor effect
- know how an electric motor works
- understand how electromagnets work and why they are useful
- know what electromagnetic induction is
- understand how generators work
- be able to explain how a transformer works, and know how they can be used to transmit electricity

J

Magnets

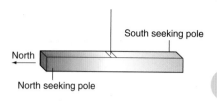

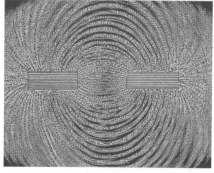

Some metals, for example iron, cobalt and nickel, are **magnetic**. A magnet will attract them. If you drop a lot of pins on to the floor the easiest way to pick them all up again is to use a magnet.

Poles

In Figure 1 you can see a bar magnet which is hanging from a fine thread. When it is left for a while, one end always points north. This end of the magnet is called the **north-seeking pole**. The other end of the magnet is the **south-seeking pole**. We usually refer to these poles as the north and south poles of the magnet.

The forces on pins, iron filings and other magnetic objects are always greatest when they are near the poles of a magnet. Every magnet has two poles which are equally strong.

When you hold two magnets together you find that two north poles (or two south poles) repel each other, but a south pole attracts a north pole (Figure 2).

South seeking pole

North

North seeking pole

Figure 1

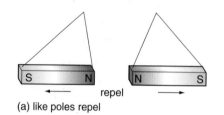

repel

(a) like poles repel

attract

(b) unlike poles attract

Figure 2

Magnetic fields

There is a magnetic field in the area around a magnet. In this area there is a force on a magnetic object. If the field is strong the force is big. In a weak field the force is small.

The direction of a magnetic field can be found by using a small plotting compass. The compass needle always lies along the direction of the field. Figure 3 shows how you can investigate the field near to a bar magnet, using a compass. We use magnetic field lines to represent a magnetic field. Magnetic field lines always start at a north pole and finish on a south pole. When the field lines are close together then the field is strong. The further apart the lines are the weaker the field is. (Magnetic field lines are not real, but they make a useful model which helps us to understand magnetic fields.)

Computer artwork of the magnetic field around two magnets, as revealed by iron filings

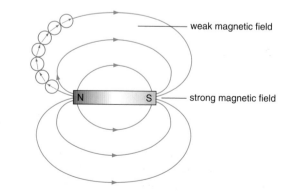

weak magnetic field

strong magnetic field

plotting compass

Figure 3

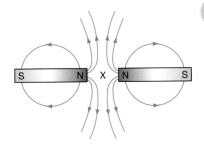

Figure 4 *X is a neutral point; a compass placed here can point in any direction*

http://www.windows.ucar.edu/
cgi-bin/tour_def?link=/
earth/Magnetosphere/
overview.html

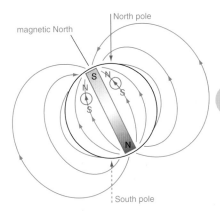

Figure 6 *The Earth's magnetic field*

Combining magnetic fields

The pattern of magnetic field lines close to two (or more) magnets becomes complicated. The magnetic fields from the two magnets combine. The field lines from the two magnets *never* cross. If field lines did cross, it would mean that a compass would have to point in two directions at once.

Figure 4 shows the sort of pattern when two north poles are near each other. The field lines repel. At the point X there are no field lines. The two magnetic fields cancel out. X is called a neutral point.

Figure 5 shows the pattern produced by a north and south pole. Notice that there is an area where the field lines are equally spaced and all point in the same direction. This is called a uniform field.

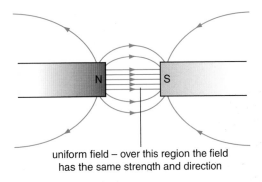

uniform field – over this region the field has the same strength and direction

Figure 5

The Earth's magnetic field

Figure 6 shows the shape of the Earth's magnetic field. Magnetic north is not in the same place as the geographic North Pole. At the moment magnetic north is in the sea north of Canada. Over a period of centuries the direction of the field alters.

The north (seeking) pole of a compass points towards magnetic north. Unlike poles attract. This means that magnetic north behaves like a south-seeking magnetic pole.

Homework Questions

1 (a) The diagram shows a bar magnet surrounded by four plotting compasses. Copy the diagram and mark in the direction of the compass needle for each of the cases B, C, D.

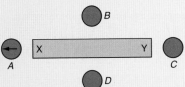

(b) Which is a north pole, X or Y?

2 Draw carefully the shape of the magnetic field surrounding these magnets. Mark in any neutral points.

3 Two bar magnets have been hidden in a box. Use the information in the diagram to the right to suggest how they have been placed inside the box.

4 Give three examples of where you might use permanent magnets in the home. Describe each situation.

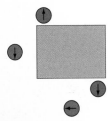

5 Refer to Figure 6 showing the Earth's magnetic field.
(a) Compare the strength of the magnetic field at the equator and at the geographic North Pole. Which is stronger?
(b) Why is a compass very difficult to use near to the North magnetic pole?

The field near a straight wire

In Figure 1, a long straight wire carrying an electrical current is placed vertically so that it passes through a horizontal piece of hardboard. Iron filings have been sprinkled onto the board to show the shape of the field. Below are summarised the important points of the experiment:

- If the current is small, the field is weak. But if a large current is used (30 A) the iron filings show a circular magnetic field pattern.
- The magnetic field gets weaker further away from the wire.
- The direction of the magnetic field can be found using a compass. If the current direction is reversed, the direction of the magnetic field is reversed.

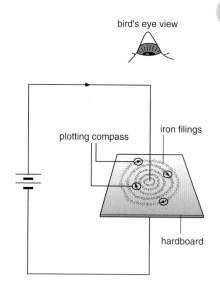

Figure 1 *This experiment shows there is a magnetic field around a current-carrying wire*

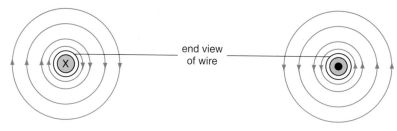

Figure 2

Figure 2 shows the pattern of magnetic field lines surrounding a wire. When the current flows into the paper (shown ⊗) the field lines point in a clockwise direction around the wire. When the current flows out of the paper (shown ⊙) the field lines point anticlockwise. The **right-hand grip rule** will help you to remember this. Put the thumb of your right hand along a wire in the direction of the current. Now your fingers point in the direction of the magnetic field.

The field near coils of wire

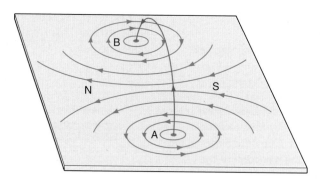

Figure 3 *The magnetic field near a single loop of wire*

Figure 3 shows the magnetic field around a single loop of wire, which carries a current. You can use the right-hand grip rule to work out the field near to each part of the loop. Near A the field lines point anticlockwise as you look at them, and near B the lines point clockwise. In the middle, the fields from each part of the loop combine to produce a magnetic field running from right to left. This loop of wire is like a very short bar magnet. Magnetic field lines come out of the left-hand side (north pole) and go back into the right-hand side (south pole). Figure 4 shows the sort of magnetic field that is produced by a current flowing through a long coil or **solenoid**. The magnet field from each loop of wire adds on to the next. The result is a magnetic field which is like a long bar magnet's field.

The iron filings show the shape of the magnetic field around a solenoid

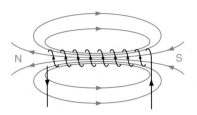

Figure 4 *The magnetic field near a long solenoid*

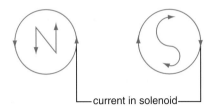

current in solenoid

Figure 5 *This is a good way to work out the polarity of the end of a solenoid*

Producing large magnetic fields

The strength of the magnetic field produced by a solenoid can be increased by:

- using a larger current,
- using more turns of wire,
- putting some iron into the middle of the solenoid.

But there is a limit to how strong you can make a magnetic field. If the current is made too large the solenoid will get very hot and start to melt. For this reason large solenoids must be cooled by water. There is a limit to the number of turns of wire you can put into a space. Eventually iron becomes magnetically 'saturated' and its magnetisation gets no stronger.

Nowadays, the world's strongest magnetic fields are produced by **superconducting magnets**. At very low temperatures (about 4 K) some materials, such as niobium and lead, become superconductors. A superconductor has no electrical resistance. This means that a current can flow without causing any heating effect. So a large magnetic field can be produced by making enormous currents (5000 A) flow through a solenoid which is kept cold in liquid helium.

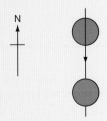

A coloured three-dimensional magnetic resonance imaging scan of a healthy human brain, seen from the front. This technique, using magnetic fields, allows doctors to examine organs non-intrusively.

Homework Questions

1 The diagram below shows two plotting compasses, one above and one below a wire. Draw diagrams to show the position of the needles when: (i) there is no current, (ii) the current is very large (30 A), (iii) the current is small (1 A).

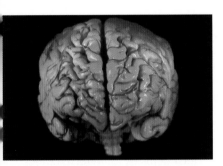

2 The diagram shows a long perspex tube with wire wrapped round it to make a solenoid.
(a) Copy the diagram and mark in the direction of the compass needles 1–6, when the current flows through the wire.

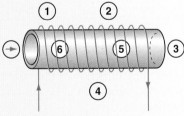

(b) Which end of the solenoid acts as the South Pole?
(c) In which direction do the needles point when the current is reversed?
(d) Copy the diagram again, leaving out the compasses. Draw magnetic field lines round the solenoid.

3 The diagram represents a wire placed vertically, with the current flowing out of the paper towards you. Draw the magnetic field lines round the wire, showing how the field decreases with distance.

4 Diagram (i) below shows an electron moving around the nucleus of an atom.

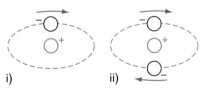

i) ii)

(a) Explain why this atom is magnetic. (Remember: a moving electron produces a current.)
(b) Sketch the shape of the magnetic field near the atom.
(c) What happens to the magnetic field if the electron moves the opposite way?
(d) What can you say about the atom in diagram (ii)? Is it more or less magnetic than the other atom?

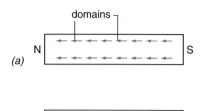

domains

N ⟶ S

(a)

(b)

Figure 2

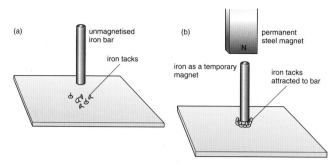

(a) unmagnetised iron bar

iron tacks

(b) permanent steel magnet

N

iron as a temporary magnet

iron tacks attracted to bar

Figure 1 *An iron bar will act as a magnet when there is a permanent magnet near it*

Magnetic domains

Steel can be a permanent magnet; once a piece of steel has been magnetised it remains a magnet. Iron can be a temporary magnet; iron is only magnetised when in a magnetic field. This field can be provided by a magnet or by a solenoid (Figure 1).

We think that the insides of magnetic materials are split up into small regions, which we call **domains**. Each domain acts like a very small magnet. In any iron or steel bar there are thousands of domains. The idea helps us to understand permanent and temporary magnets.

In a steel bar, once the domains have been lined up, they stay pointing in one direction (Figure 2(a)).

In an iron bar the domains are jumbled up when there is no magnet near (Figure 2(b)). But as soon as a magnet is put near to an iron bar the domains are made to line up. So an iron bar will be attracted to either a north or south pole of a permanent magnet.

Magnetic memories

We use magnetic tapes to store information. These tapes are used for recording music or as computer memories. The tape is coated with very small magnetic particles. The direction of magnetisation of these particles is changed by applying a strong magnetic field. The information is stored in the pattern of the magnetised particles.

Jo's film is stored on magnetic tape

Magnetising

One way to make a magnet out of an unmagnetised steel bar is to stroke it with a permanent magnet. The movement of the magnet along the steel bar is enough to make the domains line up (Figure 3(a)).

A magnet can also be made by putting a steel bar inside a solenoid. A short but very large pulse of current through the solenoid produces a strong magnetic field. This magnetises the bar.

The apparatus shown in Figure 3(b) can be used as an **electromagnet** if an iron bar is used instead of a steel bar in the solenoid. When a current is switched on the iron becomes magnetised; when the current is switched off the iron is no longer magnetised. Electromagnets are widely used in industry.

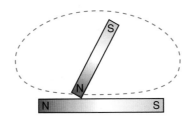

Figure 3
(a) To magnetise a steel bar stroke it 20 times like this

(b) Magnetisation using a solenoid

car battery to produce
a large current

Demagnetising

To make a steel bar lose its magnetism you need to jumble up the domains inside the bar. There are three ways to do this:

● Hit the bar with a hammer.
● Put the bar inside a solenoid which has an alternating current supply. The alternating current produces a magnetic field which switches backwards and forwards rapidly. The domains are left jumbled up after the current has been reduced gradually to zero.
● Heat the bar to about 700°C. At low temperatures the atoms inside the steel line up to magnetise each domain. At a very high temperature the atoms vibrate at random so much that each domain is no longer magnetised.

Homework Questions

1 (a) Tracey has magnetised a needle as shown below. She then cuts the needle into four smaller bits as shown. Copy the diagram and label the poles A–H.

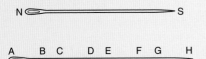

(b) Lee says 'this experiment helps to show that there are magnetic domains in the needle'. Comment on this observation.

2 The diagram below shows an electromagnet. As the current increases the magnet can lift a larger load, because the domains in the iron core line up more and more.

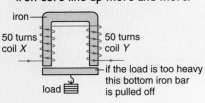

iron

50 turns
coil X

50 turns
coil Y

if the load is too heavy this bottom iron bar is pulled off

load

Load (N)	Current (A)
0	0
5	0.5
8.5	1.0
12.0	2.0
14.0	3.0
14.8	4.0
15.0	5.0

(a) Use the data provided to draw a graph of the load supported (y-axis) against current (x-axis).
(b) Use the graph to predict the load supported when the current is: (i) 1.5 A, (ii) 6.0 A.
(c) Sketch on your graph how the load varies with current when each of the coils X and Y has: (i) 25, (ii) 100 turns.
(d) What happens when you reverse the windings on coil X?
(e) Make sketches to show how the domains are lined up when the current (in the original diagram) is:

(i) 0, (ii) 0.5 A, (iii) 5 A.
(f) Use your answer to part (e) to explain why there is a maximum load which an electromagnet can lift.

3 The diagram shows the magnetic field close to a bar magnet, and an iron tack below it.
(a) Draw a diagram to show how the domains are aligned in the tack.
(b) Explain *carefully* why the tack is attracted to the magnet. Would the tack be attracted if the field were uniform?
(c) What happens if a south magnetic pole is placed close to the tack? Explain your answer.

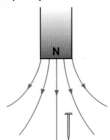

The Motor Effect

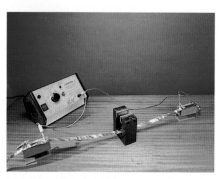

Aluminium foil carrying a current is pushed out of a magnetic field

In the photograph you can see a piece of aluminium foil which has been fixed between the poles of a strong magnet. When there is a current through the foil it is pushed upwards away from the magnet. This is called the **motor effect**. It happens because of an interaction between the two magnetic fields, one from the magnet and one from the current.

In Figure 1 below you can see the way in which the two fields combine. By itself the field between the poles of the magnet would be nearly uniform. The current through the foil produces a circular magnetic field. The magnetic field from the current squashes the field between the poles of a magnet. It is the squashing of the field that catapults the foil upwards.

The force acting on the foil is proportional to:

- the strength of the magnetic field between the poles
- the current
- the length of the foil between the poles.

Fleming's left-hand rule

To predict the direction in which a wire moves in a magnetic field you can use the **left-hand rule** (Figure 1). Spread out the first two fingers and the thumb of your left hand so that they are at right angles to each other. Let your first finger point along the direction of the magnet's field, and your second finger point in the direction of the current. Your thumb then points in the direction in which the wire moves.

This rule works when the field and the current are at right angles to each other. When the field and the current are parallel to each other, there is no force on the wire and it stays where it is.

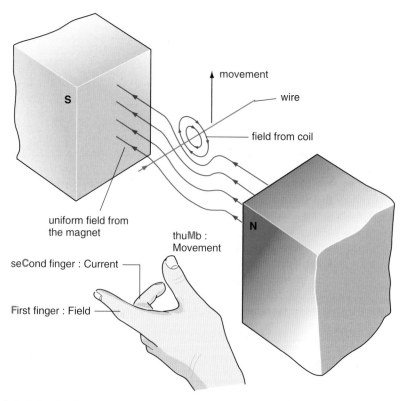

Figure 1 *Left-hand rule*

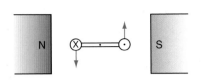

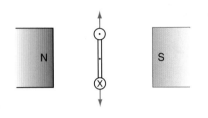

Figure 3

(a) The end-on view of the wire loop in Figure 2. The turning effect is maximum in this position

(b) In this position the forces acting on the coil produce no turning effect

Ammeters

Figures 2 and 3 show the idea behind a moving coil ammeter. A loop of wire has been pivoted on an axle between the poles of a magnet. When a current is switched on, the left-hand side of the loop moves downwards and the right-hand side moves upwards. (Use the left-hand rule to check this.) If nothing stops the loop, it turns until side *DC* is at the top and *AB* is at the bottom. However, when a spring is attached to the loop it only turns a little way. When you pass a larger current through the loop, the force is larger. This will stretch the spring more and so the loop turns further.

The photograph in the questions section shows how a model ammeter can be made using a coil of wire, a spring and some magnets.

An ammeter is sensitive if it turns a long way when a small current flows through it. The sensitivity of an ammeter will be large when:

- a large number of turns is used on the coil
- strong magnets are used
- weak springs are used.

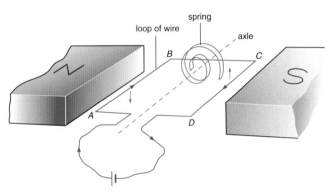

Figure 2 *The principle of the moving-coil ammeter*

Homework Questions

1 (a) The diagrams show: (i) a pair of magnets, (ii) a wire carrying a current into the paper. Sketch separate diagrams to show the magnetic fields near each of (i) and (ii), when they are well separated.
(b) The wire is now placed between the poles of the magnets. Sketch the combined magnetic field. Add an arrow to show the direction in which the wire moves.
(c) Which way does the wire move when: (i) the current is reversed, (ii)

the north and south poles are changed round?

2 This question is about the model ammeter shown in the photograph. The graph shows the angle that the coil turned through, against the current flowing through the coil.
(a) Use the graph to work out the current when the angle is: (i) 30°, (ii) 50°.

(b) Make a sketch of the graph. Add to it further graphs to show the deflection for different currents when the ammeter is made: (i) with stronger springs, (ii) with twice the number of turns on its coil.
(c) Could this ammeter be used to measure alternating currents? Explain.
(d) (Quite hard) Why is the graph not a straight line?

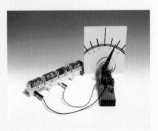

(i)

(ii)

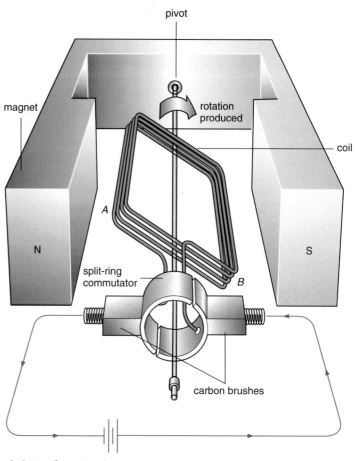

Figure 1 *A design for a simple motor*

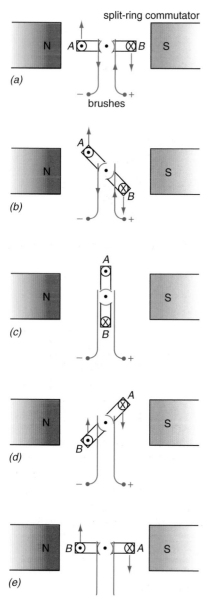

Figure 2

In the last unit you learnt that a coil carrying a current rotates when it is in a magnetic field. However, the coil can only rotate through 90° and then it gets stuck. This is not good for making a motor. We need to make a motor rotate all the time.

Figure 1 shows the design of a simple motor which you can make for yourself. A coil carrying a current rotates between the poles of a magnet. The coil is kept rotating continuously by the use of a **split-ring commutator**. This causes the direction of the current in the coil to reverse, so that forces continue to act on the coil to keep it turning. Figure 2 explains the action of the commutator.

A current flows into the coil through the commutator so that there is an upwards push on side *A*, a downwards push on *B* (Figure 2(a)). The coil rotates in a clockwise direction (Figure 2(b)).

When the coil reaches the vertical position no current flows through the coil. The coil continues to rotate past the vertical due to its own momentum (Figure 2(c)).

Now side *A* is on the right-hand side. The direction of current flowing into the coil has been reversed (Figure 2(d)).

Side *A* is pushed down and side *B* is pushed upwards. The coil continues to rotate in a clockwise direction (Figure 2(e)).

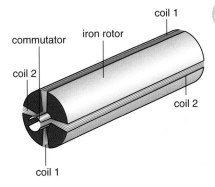

coil 1
iron rotor
commutator
coil 2
coil 2
coil 1

(a)

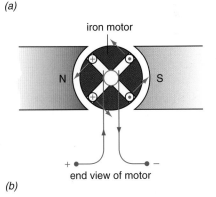

iron motor

N   S

end view of motor

(b)

Figure 3

Commercial motors

You use electric motors every day. Every time you put your washing into the washing machine or use a vacuum cleaner, you are using an electric motor. Your car also uses an electric motor to get it started. For these sorts of use, motors need to be made as powerful as possible.

Here are some of the ways which can be used to make a motor more powerful (Figure 3):

- A large current should be used.
- As many turns as possible should be put on the coil.
- More than one coil can be put on the rotor. Each coil then experiences a force, so the total force turning the motor is larger.
- The coils can be wound on an iron core to increase the magnetic field.
- Curved pole pieces make sure that the magnetic field is always at right angles to the coils. This gives the greatest turning effect.

A cut-away view of a Black and Decker drill, showing the electric motor and gears inside it

Homework Questions

1 Name three machines (other than those mentioned in the text) which use electric motors.

2 What two properties of carbon make it a good material to use for motor brushes?

3 (a) Look at Figure 2. Which position is the motor likely to stick in?
(b) Explain why the motor shown in Figure 3 is less likely to stick.

4 Copy Figure 3(b) and draw in some field lines to show the shape of the magnetic field.

5 The motor shown to the right is used to lift up a load.
(a) Use the information in the diagram to calculate the following:
(i) the work done in lifting the load,
(ii) the power output of the motor

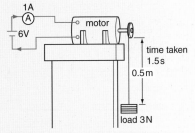

1A
6V
motor
time taken
1.5s
0.5m
load 3N

while lifting the load, (iii) the electrical power input to the motor.
(b) Calculate the efficiency of the motor.
(c) Explain carefully the energy changes which occur during the lifting process.

6 The next diagram shows how an electric motor can be made using an electromagnet. You can see the forces acting on the coil when a current flows.

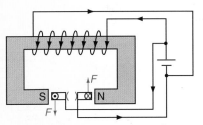

S   N
F
F

(a) The battery is now turned round. What effect does that have on: (i) the polarity of the magnet? (ii) the direction of current in the coil? (iii) the forces acting on the coil?
(b) Would this motor work with an a.c. supply? Explain.
(c) Why are the electromagnet and coil run in parallel from the battery, not in series?

Electromagnets in Action

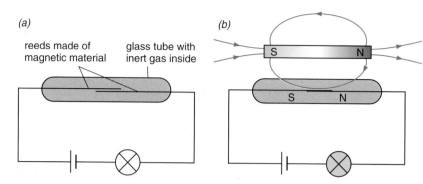

Figure 1

Reed switches

Two reeds made of magnetic materials are enclosed inside a glass tube. Normally these reeds are not in contact so the switch is open (Figure 1(a)). When a magnet is brought close to the reeds they become magnetised so that they attract each other. The switch is now closed (Figure 1(b)). These switches can be used to work circuits using a magnetic field. This field can be supplied using a permanent magnet or a solenoid (Figure 2).

Figure 2 *Reed switches can also be opened and closed using the magnetic field from a solenoid. This device is sometimes called a reed relay*

Relays

A car starter motor needs a very large current of about 100 A to make it turn round. Switching large currents on and off needs a special heavy-duty switch. If you had such a large switch inside the car it would be a nuisance since it would take up a lot of space. The switch would spark and it would be unpleasant and dangerous. A way round this problem is to use a relay.

Figures 3(a) and 3(b) show how a car starter relay works.

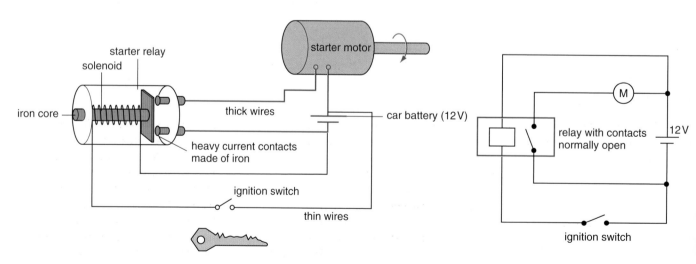

Figure 3

(a) A car starter relay

(b) The circuit diagram for the starter motor

Inside the relay a solenoid is wound round an iron core. When the car ignition is turned, a small current magnetises the solenoid and its iron core. The solenoid is

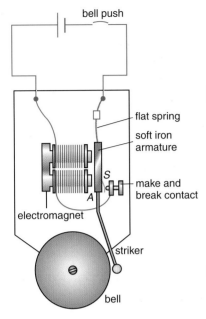

bell push

flat spring

soft iron armature

S

A

make and break contact

electromagnet

striker

bell

Figure 4 *An electric bell*

attracted towards the heavy-duty electrical contacts, which are also made of iron. Now current can flow from the battery to the starter motor. The advantage of this system is that the car engine can be started by turning a key at a safe distance!

Electric bells

Figure 4 shows the idea behind an electric bell. When the bell push is pressed the circuit is completed and a current flows. The electromagnet becomes magnetised and the soft iron is attracted to the electromagnet. The movement of the iron causes the striker to hit the bell. As the bell is hit, A moves away from S and the circuit is broken. The electromagnet is now demagnetised and a spring pulls the iron back to its original position. The circuit is remade and the process starts over again. The striker can be made to hit the bell a few times every second.

The moving-coil loudspeaker

The loudspeaker in your radio and television sets is probably made like the one shown in Figure 5. A loudspeaker is an example of a transducer. Transducers turn one form of energy into another.

Electrical signals from the radio cause the current flowing in the coil to change. A change in the current causes a change in the magnetic force acting on the coil. In this way the paper cone is made to move in and out. The vibrations of the cone produce sound waves.

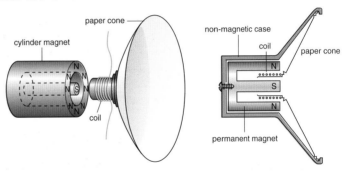

paper cone

cylinder magnet

coil

non-magnetic case

coil

paper cone

S

N

N

permanent magnet

Figure 5 *The moving-coil loudspeaker*

Homework Questions

1 The diagram below shows the detonator circuit for a magnetic mine. This sort of mine is placed on the seabed in shallow water. The detonator is activated when it is connected across the battery. Explain how a ship can trigger the mine.

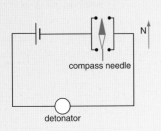

compass needle

N

detonator

2 This question is about the relay circuit in Figures 3(a) and 3(b).
(a) Why is the coil made of insulated wire?
(b) Explain why iron is used in the centre of the solenoid.
(c) When the switch is turned the motor starts, which in turn starts the petrol engine. Explain, step by step, how this process works.
(d) (i) The current through the motor is 100 A. Why is it important to use thick wires?
(ii) The resistance of the relay coil is 48 Ω. Calculate the current which

flows through it when connected to the car battery in Figure 3(a).
(iii) Why is it an advantage to use thin wire in the relay circuit?

3 (a) Use the left hand motor rule to explain why a current causes the coil to move in or out in Figure 5.
(b) Now explain how an alternating current can cause a loudspeaker cone to vibrate.
(c) How is the intensity of the emitted sound controlled?
(d) How is the pitch of the sound controlled?

Electric motors work because forces act on current-carrying wires which are placed in magnetic fields. A motor converts electrical energy into mechanical energy. The process can be put into reverse. If you turn a small motor by hand you produce a current. Then mechanical energy has been turned into electrical energy. This is called **electromagnetic induction**.

Size and direction of current

Figure 1 shows an experiment to find out what affects the making of a current.
(1) **Direction of movement.** To get a current the wire must cut across lines of magnetic field. The wire must be moved up and down along the direction XX'. There is no current if the wire moves along ZZ' or YY'. Reversing the direction of movement reverses the current. If moving the wire up makes the meter move to the right, moving the wire down will make the meter go to the left.
(2) **Size of current.** You can make a larger current flow in the following ways:

- Moving the wire more quickly. When the wire is stationary between the poles of the magnet there is no current.
- Using stronger and bigger magnets.
- Looping the wire so that several turns of wire pass through the poles.

These facts about electromagnetic induction were first discovered by Faraday.

The device shown here is used at airports to check that passengers are not carrying any guns or bombs. Metal objects cause changes in an electromagnetic field when they pass through the 'doorway'. A circuit detects the changes and sets off an alarm

http://www.vvm.com/
~radioray/html/e101-22.htm

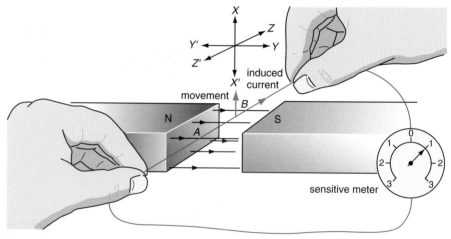

Figure 1

Energy changes

In Figure 2(a) a current is being produced by moving a magnet into a solenoid. When the current flows a compass needle is attracted towards end Y. So end Y behaves as a south pole and end X as a north pole. This means that as the magnet moves towards the solenoid there is a magnetic force which repels it. There is a force acting against the magnet, so you have to do some work to push it into the solenoid. The work done pushing the magnet produces the electrical energy.

In Figure 2(b) the magnet is being pulled out of the solenoid. The direction of the current is reversed and now there is an attractive force acting on the magnet. The hand pulling the magnet still does work to produce electrical energy. When the switch S is opened, there is no current. So the magnet can move in and out of the coil without any repulsion or attraction.

When a current is produced by electromagnetic induction, energy is always used to create the electrical energy. In the example described in Figure 2 the energy originally came from the muscles pushing the magnet.

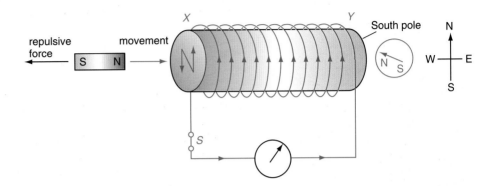

Figure 2(a)
Lenz's law of electromagnetic induction says: 'When a current is induced it always opposes the change in magnetic field that caused it.' The end X of the solenoid is a north pole. So the effect of the induced current is to push the magnet back. This opposes the motion of the magnet, and agrees with Lenz's law

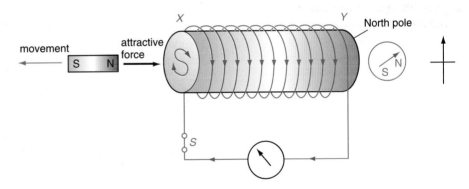

Figure 2(b)
Now the magnet moves away. X is now a south pole so the magnet is attracted to the solenoid. This opposes the motion and so agrees with Lenz's law

An electromagnetic flow meter

Figure 3 shows a way to measure the rate of flow of oil through an oil pipeline. A small turbine is placed in the pipe, so that the oil flow turns the blades round. Some magnets have been placed in the rim of the turbine, so that they move past a solenoid. These moving magnets induce a voltage in the solenoid which can be measured on an oscilloscope (Figure 3(b)). The faster the turbine rotates, the larger is the voltage induced in the solenoid. By measuring this voltage an engineer can tell at what rate the oil is flowing.

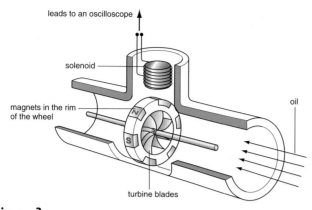

Figure 3
(a) An electromagnetic flow meter

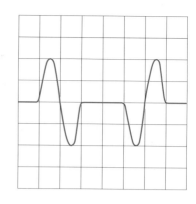

(b) The oscilloscope trace. The time base is set so that the dot crosses the screen in 0.05 seconds

Homework Questions

1 (a) In Figure 1 (page 270) the wire moves up at a speed of 2 m/s. This makes the ammeter kick one division to the right. Say what will happen to the meter in each of the following cases: (i) the wire moves up at 4 m/s, (ii) the wire moves down at 6 m/s, (iii) the wire moves along YY′ at 3 m/s, (iv) the magnets are turned round and the wire moved up at 3 m/s, (v) a larger pair of magnets is used so that the length of the wire AB in the magnetic field is doubled. The wire is now moved up at 2.5 m/s with the strength and direction of the field, as shown in Figure 1.
(b) In the diagram, explain which arrangement will produce a larger deflection on the meter.

2 This question refers to the flow meter shown in Figure 3.
(a) The poles on the wheel rim are arranged alternately with a north,

then south pole facing outwards. Use this fact to explain the shape of the oscilloscope trace.
(b) Sketch the trace on the oscilloscope for the following (separate) changes: (i) the number of turns on the solenoid is made 1.5 times larger, (ii) the flow of oil is increased, so that the turbine rotates twice as quickly.
(c) Use the information in Figures 3(a) and 3(b) to calculate how many times per second the turbine is rotating.
(d) Gita and Sarah are two apprentice engineers who are using the flowmeter for the first time. This is part of a conversation they have about the meter.

Sarah: Because a current is induced there must be a force that opposes the motion. This means that the turbine will slow down the oil flow.
Gita: The resistance of the oscilloscope is very large so only a small current can flow. So the slowing down effect can be ignored.
Comment on their conversation.

3 The diagram shows a heavy copper pendulum which swings backwards and forwards from A to C, between the poles of a strong magnet. As the wire moves, a current is made to flow through the resistor R; a data logger is used to record how the voltage changes across R.
(a) Give two reasons why you would expect the current to be greatest as

the pendulum moves past B.
(b) Sketch a graph to show what voltage the data logger records as the pendulum swings from A to C and back again. Mark your graph clearly to show the points A, B and C.
(c) On the same axes sketch the voltage you would observe when (i) the pendulum is released from a greater height, (ii) the polarity of the magnets is reversed.
(d) Explain carefully the energy changes which occur when the pendulum swings from A to B (i) with S closed, (ii) with S open.
(e) It is observed that the pendulum swings take longer to die away when the switch is open, than when the switch is closed. Explain why.
(f) The pendulum is replaced by a heavier one; it is released again from A. What effect will you notice on (i) the graph drawn in part (b), (ii) the time taken for the swings to die away? Explain your answer.

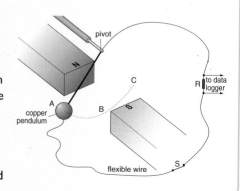

Generators

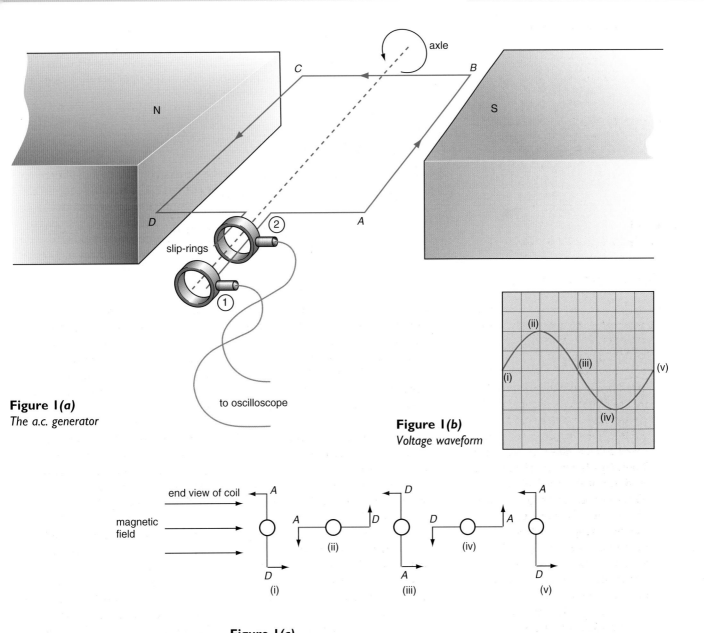

Figure 1(a)
The a.c. generator

Figure 1(b)
Voltage waveform

end view of coil

magnetic field

Figure 1(c)
Position of coil

The a.c. generator (alternator)

Figure 1 shows the design of a very simple **alternating current** (a.c.) generator. By turning the axle you can make a coil of wire move through a magnetic field. This causes a voltage to be induced between the ends of the coil.

You can see how the voltage waveform, produced by this generator, looks on an oscilloscope screen. In position (i) the coil is vertical with *AB* above *CD*. In this position the sides *CD* and *AB* are moving parallel to the magnetic field. No voltage is generated since the wires are not cutting across the magnetic field lines.

When the coil has been rotated through a ¼ turn to position (ii), the coil produces its greatest voltage. Now the sides *CD* and *AB* are cutting through the magnetic field at the greatest rate.

In position (iii), the coil is again vertical and no voltage is produced. In position (iv) a maximum voltage is produced, but in the opposite direction. Side *AB* is moving upwards and side *CD* downwards.

The d.c. generator (dynamo)

Figure 2 shows how **direct current** (d.c.) can be generated. The design of the dynamo is very similar to that of the alternator in Figure 1. The difference is that the ends of the coil are now fixed to a split-ring commutator rather than two separate slip rings. Now it does not matter which side, *AB* or *CD*, moves upwards, current will always flow out of one side of the commutator. So direct current is produced.

The d.c. generator is identical to the d.c. motor in design. However, a motor is used to turn electrical energy into kinetic energy; whereas the dynamo turns kinetic energy into electrical energy.

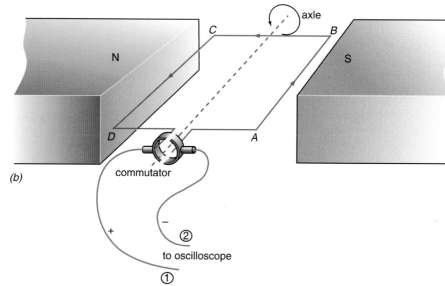

(b)

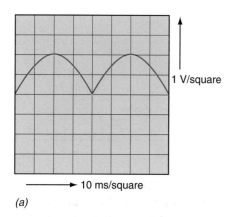

(a)

Figure 2 *The d.c. generator*

Producing power on a large scale

The electricity which you use in your home is produced by very large generators in power stations. These generators work in a slightly different way from the ones you have seen so far.

Instead of having a rotating coil and a stationary magnet, large generators have rotating magnets and stationary coils (see Figure 3). The advantage of this set-up is that no moving parts are needed to collect the large electrical current which is produced.

The important steps in the generation of electricity in a power station (Figure 4) are these:

(1) Coal is burnt to boil water.

(2) High pressure steam from the boiler is used to turn a turbine.

(3) The drive shaft from the turbine is connected to the generator magnets, which rotate near to the stationary coils. The output from the coils has a voltage of about 25 000 V.

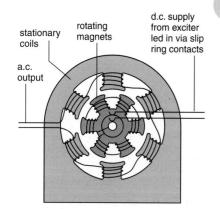

Figure 3 *A section through a large generator*

(4) The turbine's drive shaft also powers the **exciter**. The exciter is a direct current generator which produces current for the rotating magnets, which are in fact electromagnets.

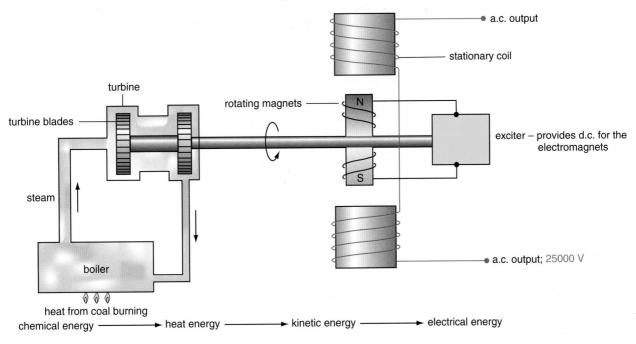

Figure 4 *The layout of a power station*

Homework Questions

1 (a) Copy Figure 2(b) and mark on the graph the places where the coil is: (i) horizontal, (ii) vertical.
(b) On the same graph show how the voltage appears when the coil is rotated in the opposite direction: (i) at the same speed, (ii) at twice the speed.

2 In the diagram the dynamo is connected to a flywheel by a drive belt. The dynamo is operated by winding the handle. When Surindra turns the handle as fast as she can, the dynamo produces a voltage of

6 V. The graph shows how long the dynamo takes to stop after Surindra stops winding the handle. The time taken to stop depends on how many bulbs are connected to the dynamo.
(a) Explain the energy changes which occur after Surindra stops winding the handle: (i) when the switches S_1, S_2 and S_3 are open (as shown), (ii) when the switches are closed.
(b) Why does the flywheel take longer to stop when no light bulb is

being lit by the dynamo?
(c) Make a copy of the graph. Use your graph to predict how long the flywheel turns when you make it light 4 bulbs.

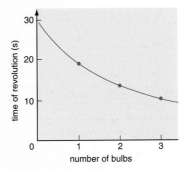

(d) The experiment is repeated using bulbs which use a smaller current. They use 0.15 A rather than 0.3 A. Using the same axes, sketch a graph to show how the running time of the dynamo depends on the number of bulbs, in this second case.

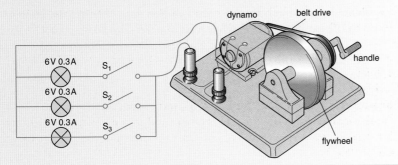

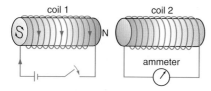

Figure 1

This transformer delivers power to the national grid

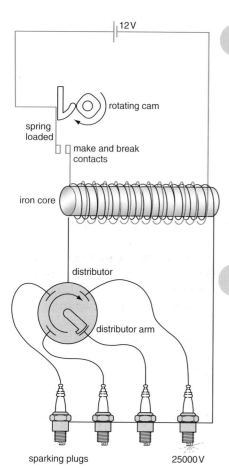

Figure 2 An induction coil in a car

Mutual inductance

In Figure 1 (above left) when the switch is closed in the first circuit, the ammeter in the second circuit kicks to the right. For a moment a current flows through coil 2. When the switch is opened again the ammeter kicks to the left.

Closing the switch makes the current through coil 1 grow quickly. This makes the coil's magnetic field grow quickly. For coil 2 this is like pushing the north pole of a magnet towards it, so a current is induced in coil 2. When the switch is opened the magnetic field near coil 1 falls rapidly. This is like pulling a north pole away from coil 2. Now the induced current flows the other way.

The ammeter reads zero when there is a constant current through coil 1. A current is only induced in the second coil by a changing magnetic field. This happens when the switch is opened and closed.

The induction coil

Inside the cylinders of a car's engine, the mixture of air and petrol explodes when it is ignited by a sparking plug. To make sparks, large voltages, about 25 000 V, are needed. Figure 2 shows how this is done.

Two solenoids have been wound round an iron core. The red solenoid is connected to the car battery through a pair of make-and-break contacts. When the circuit is complete a current flows. The iron core becomes magnetised and a strong magnetic field is produced. As the cam rotates the circuit is broken. This causes the magnetic field to fall very rapidly. A very large voltage is now induced in the second (black) solenoid, which has a large number of turns. The rotating distributor arm feeds the high voltage to each sparking plug in turn.

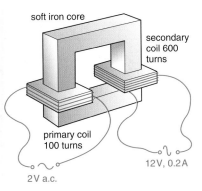

soft iron core

secondary coil 600 turns

primary coil 100 turns

12V, 0.2A

2V a.c.

(a) A step-up transformer

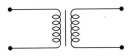

(b) The circuit symbol for a transformer
Figure 3

A small transformer for use in a laboratory

Transformers

A **transformer** is made by putting two coils of wire onto a soft iron core as shown in Figure 3. The primary coil is connected to a 2 V alternating current supply. The alternating current in the primary coil makes a magnetic field which rises and then falls again. The soft iron core carries this changing magnetic field to the secondary coil. Now a changing voltage is induced in the secondary coil. In this way, energy can be transferred continuously from the primary circuit to the secondary circuit.

Transformers are useful because they allow you to change the voltage of a supply. For example, model railways have transformers which decrease the mains supply from 230 V to a safe 12 V. These are **step-down transformers**. The transformer in Figure 3 steps *up* the voltage from 2 V to 12 V.

To make a step-up transformer the secondary coil must have more turns of wire in it than the primary coil. In a step-down transformer the secondary has fewer turns of wire than the primary coil.

The rule for calculating voltages in a transformer is:

$$\frac{V_s}{V_p} = \frac{N_s}{N_p}$$

V_p = primary voltage; V_s = secondary voltage; N_p = number of turns on the primary coil; N_s = number of turns on the secondary coil.

Homework Questions

1 (a) In Figure 1 when the switch is opened the ammeter kicks to the left. Describe what happens to the ammeter during each of the following (i) the switch is closed and left closed so that a current flows through coil 1, (ii) the coils are pushed towards each other, (iii) the coils are left close together, (iv) the coils are pulled apart.
(b) The battery is replaced by an a.c. voltage supply which has a frequency of 2 Hz. What will the ammeter show when the switch is closed?

2 (a) Explain why the black solenoid in Figure 2 must have a large number of turns.
(b) Will the car still work if the black circuit is connected to the battery, and the red solenoid to the distributor? Explain your answer.

3 Explain why a transformer does not work when you plug in the primary coil to a battery.

4 The question refers to Figure 3.
(a) What power is used in the secondary circuit?
(b) Explain why the smallest current which can be flowing in the primary circuit is 1.2 A.
(c) Why is the primary current likely to be a little larger than 1.2 A?

5 The table below gives some data about 4 transformers. Copy the table and fill the gaps.

Primary turns	Secondary turns	Primary voltage (V)	Secondary voltage (V)	Step-up or step-down
100	20		3	
400	10 000	10		
	50	240	12	
	5 000	33 000	11 000	

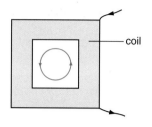

(a) Eddy currents flow in an unlaminated core

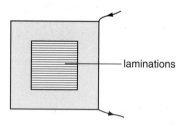

Figure 1
(b) Laminations help to stop eddy currents flowing

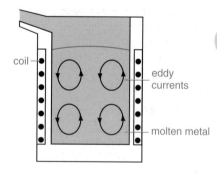

Figure 2 *An induction furnace which puts eddy currents to good use. In this furnace, scrap metal is melted down for re-use. The heating is due to eddy currents which are induced in the metal itself. These are induced by an alternating current flowing through a coil on the outside of the furnace*

Power in transformers

We use transformers to transfer electrical power from the primary circuit to the secondary circuit. Many transformers do this very efficiently and there is little loss of power in the transformer itself. For a transformer which is 100% efficient we can write:

> Power supplied by primary circuit = Power used in the secondary circuit
>
> $$V_p \times I_p = V_s \times I_s$$

In practice transformers are not 100% efficient. These are the most important reasons for transformers losing energy:

- The windings on the coils have a small resistance. So when a current flows through them they heat up a little
- The iron core conducts electricity. Therefore the changing magnetic field from the coils can induce currents in the iron. These are called **eddy currents**. To reduce energy lost in this way the core is laminated. This means the core is made out of thin slices of iron with sheets of insulating material between each slice (Figure 1).
- Energy is lost if some of the magnetic field from the primary coil does not pass through the secondary coil.
- Energy is also used to switch the direction of the domains in the iron core 50 times each second. This can be done easily in the iron, so energy losses are small.

The national grid

You may have seen a sign at the bottom of an electricity pylon saying 'Danger high voltage'. Power is transmitted around the country at voltages as high as 400 000 V. There is a very good reason for this – it saves a lot of energy. The following calculations explain why.

Figure 4 on the next page suggests two ways of transmitting 25 MW of power from a Yorkshire power station to the Midlands:
(a) The 25 000 V supply from the power station could be used to send 1000 A down the power cables.
(b) The voltage could be stepped up to 250 000 V and 100 A could be sent along the cables.
How much power would be wasted in heating the cables in each case, given that 200 km of cable has a resistance of 10 Ω?

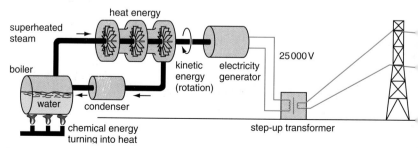

Figure 3 *How the power gets to your home. The diagram shows how electricity is generated at a power station, and how it is distributed around the country through the national grid*

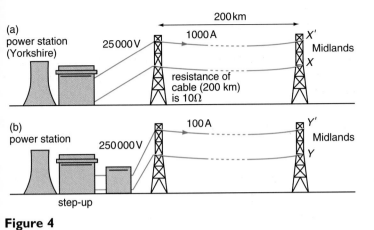

(a)
power station
(Yorkshire)

25 000 V

200 km

1000 A

X'
Midlands
X

resistance of
cable (200 km)
is 10Ω

(b)
power station

250 000 V

100 A

Y'
Midlands
Y

step-up

Figure 4

(a) Power lost = voltage drop along cable × current

$= IR \times I$

$= I^2R$

$= (1000)^2 \times 10$

$= 10\,000\,000$ W or 10 MW

(b) Power lost $= I^2R$

$= (100)^2 \times 10$

$= 100\,000$ W or 0.1 MW

We waste a lot less power in the second case. The power loss is proportional to the square of the current. Transmitting power at high voltages allows smaller currents to flow along our overhead power lines.

Homework Questions

1 This is about how a transformer could be used to melt a nail. You will need to use the data provided.

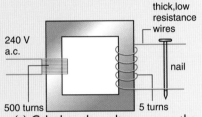

thick, low
resistance
wires

240 V
a.c.

nail

500 turns

5 turns

(a) Calculate the voltage across the nail.

- The nail has a resistance of 0.02 Ω.
- The melting point of the nail is 1540°C.
- The nail needs 10 J to warm it through 1°C.

(b) Why must the secondary circuit have thick wires?
(c) Calculate the current flowing in:
(i) the secondary circuit,
(ii) the primary circuit.
(d) Calculate the rate at which power is used in the secondary circuit to heat the nail.
(e) Estimate roughly how long it will take the nail to melt. Mention any assumptions or approximations that you make in this calculation.
(f) Explain how a transformer can be used to produce high currents for welding.

2 Explain why the electricity supply in your home is a.c. rather than d.c.

3 Use the data in Figure 4 to calculate the voltage across (i) the points XX' and (ii) YY'.

4 The data in the table below were obtained using samples of copper, aluminium and steel wires. Each wire was 100 m long and had a diameter of 2 mm. Use these data to explain why our overhead power cables are made out of aluminium with a steel core.

5 Overhead power cables have a cross-sectional area of about 1 cm².
(a) Discuss the advantages and disadvantages of using wires of greater area.
(b) Discuss how engineers decide the optimum diameter of a power cable.

Material	Resistance (Ω)	Force needed to break wire	Density in kg/m³	Cost of wire
Copper	2.2	320 N	8900	£5.60
Aluminium	3.2	160 N	2700	£1.60
Steel	127	1600 N	9000	£0.14

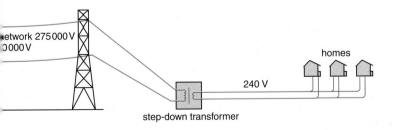

network 275 000 V
0000 V

homes

240 V

step-down transformer

SECTION J: Questions

1 Two students, Rajeeb and Emma have designed a new ammeter shown below. They have plotted a calibration graph to show the extension of the spring for a particular current.

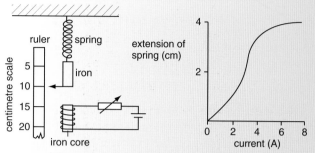

(a) Explain why their device can be used as an ammeter.

(b) Explain the shape of the graph in as much detail as you can.

(c) Here are some remarks that the students made about their ammeter. Evaluate their comments.

(i) *Rajeeb:* Our ammeter is not really any good for measuring currents above 4 A.

Emma: It would be better at measuring large currents if we used fewer turns on the solenoid.

(ii) *Rajeeb:* It does not matter which way the current flows, the spring still gets pulled down.

Emma: That's useful, we can use our ammeter to measure a.c.

2 You can use magnetic tapes to store information. These tapes can be used as computer memories or for recording music. The tape is made of plastic and is coated with very small magnetic particles. The direction of magnetisation of these particles can be changed by applying a strong magnetic field.

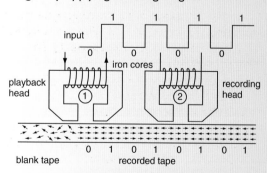

(a) In the diagram a series of pulses are sent into the recording head of a tape recorder. Explain how these produce the pattern of magnetism shown in the tape.

(b) Explain how the same tape could be used as a computer memory or for recording music.

(c) (i) When the tape is passed by the playback head, a voltage is induced in the coil. Explain why.

(ii) Draw a sketch to show the form of this induced voltage. Assume the tape moves at the same speed as it did when it was recording.

(d) To erase the tape, an erase head is used. The erase head is supplied with a very high frequency voltage (about 50 kHz). Explain why this high frequency is chosen.

3 The diagram below shows a coil connected to a sensitive meter. The meter is a 'centre zero' type. (This means that when no current is flowing the needle points to the centre of the scale.)

A girl performs two experiments.

First experiment

She pushes a magnet into the coil. A moment later, she removes the magnet. The meter needle deflects (moves away from zero) only when the magnet is moving.

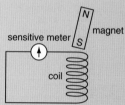

Second experiment

She brings a second coil close. She switches a current, supplied by a battery, on and off in this second coil. The needle deflects only for a very short time each time she switches on or off.

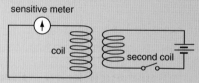

(a) In the first experiment:

(i) What is happening in the coil while the magnet is moving?

(ii) How does the deflection of the needle as the magnet is pushed towards the coil compare with the deflection of the needle as the magnet is pulled away?

(iii) Without changing any of the apparatus, how could she make the needle deflection as large as possible?

(b) In both experiments, what is happening in the space around the coil at the times when the needle is deflected?

(c) Two coils are wound around an iron core as shown. What, if anything, will you see on the meter if:

(i) a constant direct current is passed through coil X?

(ii) the constant direct current in coil X is switched

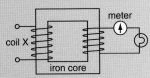

coil X

meter

iron core

on and then off again?

(iii) an alternating current of frequency 50 Hz is passed through coil X?

(d) The device in the diagram is a transformer. Name a household device which includes a transformer.

OCR (MEG)

4 The diagram shows a laboratory electromagnet, made from two iron cores and a length of wire. W and X are connected to a d.c. supply.

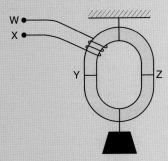

W
X

Y   Z

The number of turns of wire on the magnet is varied, and the largest weight that the magnet can support is shown in the table. For each measurement, the current remains at the same value of 2 A.

Number of turns in coil	5	10	15	20	25	30
Weight supported (N)	1.1		3.2	4.0	4.3	4.3

(a) What weight do you think can be supported when the magnet has 10 turns?

(b) Explain why the same load is supported by 25 or 30 turns.

(c) What happens if poor contact is made between the cores at Y and Z?

5 (a) Copy diagram (1). Then draw lines to represent the magnetic field between the two magnets.

(1)

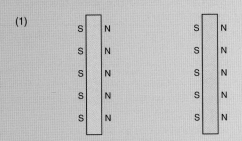

(b) Diagram (2) shows a wire that is at right-angles to the plane of the paper. The current in the wire flows up out of the paper. Copy the diagram and add lines to represent the magnetic field.

(2)

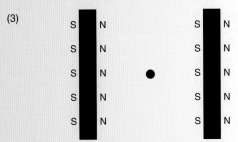

(c) In diagram (3) the wire has been placed between the poles of the magnet. Draw the field lines now.

(3)

S	N		S	N
S	N		S	N
S	N	●	S	N
S	N		S	N
S	N		S	N

(d) Which way will the wire move in diagram (3)?

(e) Diagram (4) shows a model motor.

(4)

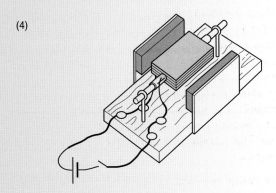

(i) Which position is the coil likely to stick in?

(ii) Explain why the coil rotates.

(iii) State and explain two changes that will make the coil turn faster.

6 In this question you are asked to investigate the cost of producing electricity by three different means. (The data for this question are given overleaf.) The methods are:

● a conventional coal-fired station
● a nuclear-powered station
● a tidal barrage.

Each scheme would be financed by borrowing money from a bank. The capital investment is to be repaid at an interest rate of 12% per annum.

(a) For the coal-fired station:

(i) Work out the annual interest payable.

(ii) Work out the total annual cost of the coal.

(iii) Work out the total annual cost of generating electricity.

(iv) What does it cost the station to produce 1 kWh of electricity?

(v) Explain why electricity companies will charge more than this per kWh.

	Coal-fired power station	Nuclear power station	Severn tidal barrage
Capital cost of buildings and plant, or barrage	£1200 million	£2500 million	£11 000 million
Running costs (maintenance and salaries) per annum	£90 million	£110 million	£40 million
Cost of coal	£50 per tonne	–	–
Waste disposal per annum	–	£40 million	–
Cost of reprocessing spent fuel	–	£150 000 per tonne	–
Coal/fuel used per year	4.5 million tonnes	800 tonnes	–
Maximum power output	2000 MW	2000 MW	7000 MW
Number of kWh produced per year	12 000 million	14 000 million	24 000 million

(b) Calculate the cost of generating 1 kWh of electricity by using (i) nuclear power, (ii) the tidal barrage.

(c) Which of the three methods runs its generators for the greatest time each year?

(d) Comment on the environmental impact of each scheme. Which has the greatest drawback: acid rain produced by coal burning, possible damages from nuclear fallout, or changing high tide levels to remove the habitat of thousands of waders and wild fowl?

(e) Producing electricity using the Severn Tidal Barrage seems the most expensive at the present time. If it were built now, would it still be the most expensive means of producing electricity in 20 years time? (Interest repayments will be the same but all other costs will have risen by about a factor of 2.)

(f) Which of the schemes would you choose? Justify your answer.

7 This question is about electromagnetism.
(a) Michael is investigating how a short length of copper wire can be made to move in a magnetic field. He uses this apparatus.

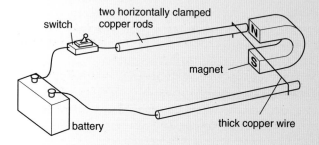

He places the magnet so that the wire is midway between the poles.
He writes down these observations.

We can only make the copper wire move along the rods if:
1) the switch is closed and
2) the poles of the magnet are above and below the wire, not on each side of it.

Explain these **two** observations. Use your ideas about electromagnetism.

(b) The diagram shows a model generator.

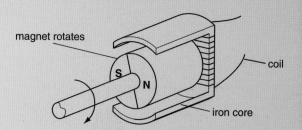

(i) What happens in the coil of wire when the magnet rotates?
(ii) Why does this happen?

(c) The ends of the coil are connected to a cathode ray oscilloscope (CRO). The diagram shows the trace on the screen as the magnet rotates.

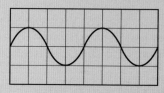

Draw new traces for each of the following changes using the same scale. (Assume the settings of the oscilloscope remain the same).
(i) The magnet rotates at the same speed but in the opposite direction.
(ii) The magnet rotates at the same speed, in the same direction, as the original, but the number of turns of the coil is doubled.
(iii) The magnet rotates at twice the speed, in the same direction, with the original number of turns of the coil.

(d) Explain why **iron** is used as the core in the model generator.

(e) The output from a power station generator is connected to a step-up transformer. The transformer is connected to transmission lines.

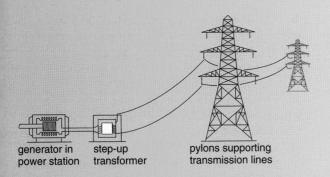

generator in power station | step-up transformer | pylons supporting transmission lines

Explain why a step-up transformer is needed. Use your ideas about power losses in transmission.

OCR

8 The waves from earthquakes are detected by instruments called seismometers. The diagram shows a simple seismometer.

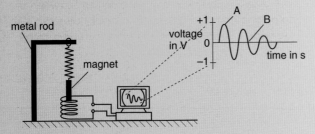

metal rod

magnet

It consists of a bar magnet suspended on a spring. The spring hangs from a metal rod that transmits vibrations from the Earth. A computer monitors the voltage across the coil. When there is an earthquake, the magnet moves in and out of the coil.

(i) Explain why a voltage is induced in the coil.
(ii) Why is the induced voltage alternating?
(iii) Describe the movement of the magnet when the induced voltage has its greatest value, at the point labelled A.
(iv) Describe the movement of the magnet when the induced voltage is zero, as at point B.
(v) Suggest TWO ways in which the seismometer could be made more sensitive, so that it can detect smaller earthquakes.

Edexcel

9 (a) When a coil rotates in a magnetic field, an alternating voltage is produced. Explain how the voltage is produced.

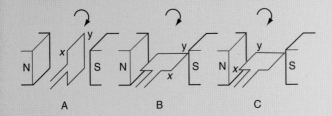

A   B   C

The diagrams **A B** and **C** show three positions of a coil as it rotates clockwise in a magnetic field produced by two poles.
The graph below shows how the voltage produced changes as the coil rotates.

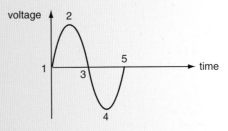

When the coil is in the position shown by diagram **A**, the output voltage is zero and is marked as 1 on the voltage-time graph.
State which point on the voltage-time graph corresponds to the coil position shown by
(i) diagram **B**,
(ii) diagram **C**.
(c) State **one** way of increasing the size of the voltage produced by **this** coil rotating in a magnetic field.
(d) The diagram shows a transformer connected to a 230 V a.c. supply. It is used to operate a 5V door bell.

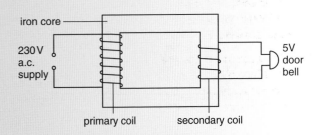

iron core

230V a.c. supply

primary coil   secondary coil

5V door bell

(i) Write down, **in words**, the equation connecting the number of turns in each coil to the voltages across them.
(ii) If the primary coil of the above transformer has 920 turns, calculate the number of turns required on the secondary coil so that the door bell operates at 5V.

WJEC

10 Anita's office is being updated. The electrician has arrived to wire in the new computers which have been imported and run off 115 V a.c. He uses a transformer to connect each computer to the 230 V a.c. ring main.
(a) (i) The secondary coil has 500 turns. Calculate the number of primary turns.
(ii) The transformer will only work with an a.c. supply and a soft iron core. Explain why.

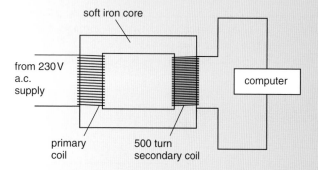

soft iron core

from 230 V
a.c.
supply

computer

primary
coil

500 turn
secondary coil

(b) The electrician connects the transformer to the ring main with a fuse and a switch.

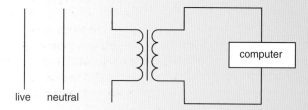

live   neutral

computer

Copy and complete the diagram above to show how he should do this.

(c) Each computer has a power of 460 W. The maximum safe current in the ring main is 30 A.
  (i) Write down the formula linking power, voltage and current.
  (ii) Calculate the current which each transformer draws from the ring main.
  (iii) State the maximum number of transformers the electrician should connect to the ring main.
  (iv) Explain why it would be unsafe to have a current of more than 30 A in the ring main.

OCR

11 A power station has four generators. Each generator produces 170 MW (1.7×10^8 W). The electricity is generated at 25 000 V.
  (a) (i) Calculate the current in one generator.
    (ii) The generator has hollow copper conductors. Water flows through them. Explain why this is necessary.

(b) The voltage is increased to 400 000 V before the electricity is fed into the national grid.
  (i) Describe how the voltage is increased.
  (ii) Explain why electricity is transmitted at high voltage.
(c) Electricity is transmitted along the national grid using a combination of overhead and underground cables. Suggest ONE advantage and ONE disadvantage of each method.
(d) Most of the electricity in the United Kingdom is generated from non-renewable sources. Some electricity is generated from moving water. Wind turbines also contribute to the electricity supply. Explain why these renewable sources can only provide a small proportion of the United Kingdom's electricity.

Edexcel

12 The diagram shows a long wire placed between the poles of a magnet. When a current I flows through the wire, a force acts on the wire causing it to move.

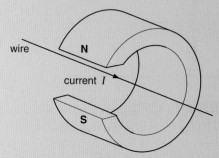

wire

N

current I

S

(a) Use Fleming's Left Hand Rule to find the direction of the force on the wire. Show the direction of the force **on the diagram** with an arrow labelled **F**.
(b) State what happens to the force on the wire when
  (i) the size of the current through the wire is increased,
  (ii) a weaker magnet is used,
  (iii) the direction of the current is reversed.
(c) Name **one** practical device which uses this effect.

WJEC

Control

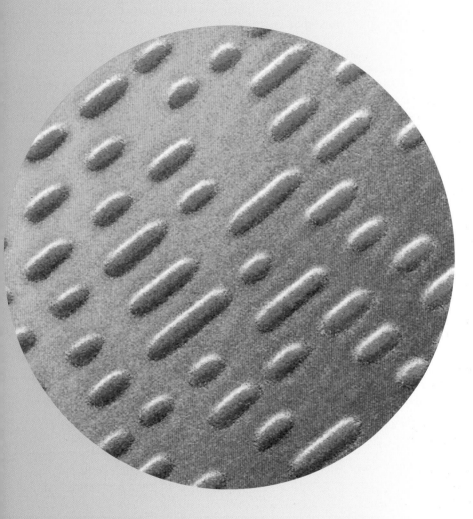

This coloured scanning electron micrograph (SEM) image shows the surface of an audio compact disc (CD). The CD is made of aluminium with a transparent plastic coating. The blue grooves represent tiny etchings made in the aluminium, corresponding to a digital signal. A laser is used to read this signal and convert it into music.

By the end of this section you should:

- be familiar with electronic devices such as diodes, LEDs, capacitors and transistors
- understand that most electronic systems have an input, a processor and an output
- know how amplifiers work
- understand logic gates and be familiar with the main types and their uses
- know some different ways in which data can be stored and retrieved

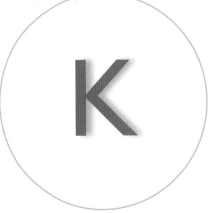

Light dependent resistor (LDR)

The electrical resistance of some materials depends on the brightness of the light around them. When it is dark the resistance of a piece of cadmium sulphide can be a few megaohms. In bright sunlight, the resistance drops to a few thousand ohms. Cadmium sulphide can be used to make a **light dependent resistor** (LDR).

Figure 1 shows how you can make a simple light meter using an LDR and an ammeter. When it is bright the resistance of the LDR is low and the reading on the ammeter is high. When it is dark the resistance of the LDR is high, so the current is low. Such a light meter can help a cricket umpire decide when it is too dark to carry on playing safely.

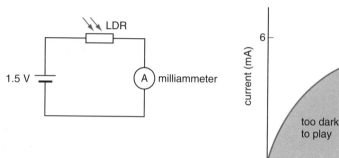

Figure 1 *A simple light meter*

Silicon diodes

A silicon diode allows current to pass through it in one direction only. Figure 2(a) shows the circuit symbol for the diode. Current flows easily from anode to cathode. However, current cannot flow the other way. When the anode is positive and the cathode negative, we say the diode is **forward biased**. The diode is **reverse biased** when the cathode is positive and the anode negative. Figure 2(b) shows how the current flowing through a diode varies with the applied voltage. Notice that once the voltage across the diode is about 0.7 V, the current increases very rapidly.

Figure 3 shows a diode in action. When it is forward biased the bulb is lit. There is about 0.7 V across the diode. This means that the voltage across the bulb is 6 V – 0.7 V = 5.3 V. When the diode is reverse biased no current flows. There is no voltage across the light bulb and so 6 V across the diode.

(a)

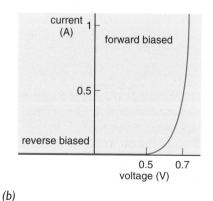

(b)

Figure 2

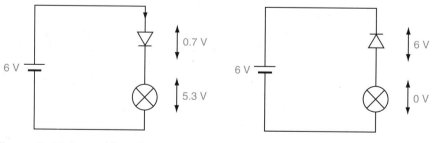

Figure 3 *(a) Forward biased*   *(b) Reverse biased*

Light-emitting diode (LED)

A **light-emitting diode** (**LED**) is a diode which gives out (emits) light when it is forward biased. Diodes can emit green, red or yellow light.

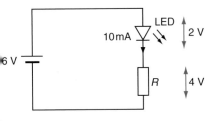

Figure 4

www

http://www.howstuffworks.
com/boolean.htm

When an LED is working, it usually has a voltage of about 2 V across it and a current of 10 mA flowing through it. An LED can easily be damaged if too large a current (50 mA) flows through it. So we protect an LED by putting a resistance in series with it.

Example. What value of resistor do you need for the circuit in Figure 4? The voltage across R must be 4 V (6 V – 2 V). The current flowing through R is

$$10 \text{ mA}, \quad \text{or} \quad \frac{10 \text{ A}}{1000} = 0.01 \text{ A}$$

$$R = \frac{V}{I}$$

$$= \frac{4 \text{ V}}{0.01 \text{ A}}$$

$$= 400 \text{ } \Omega$$

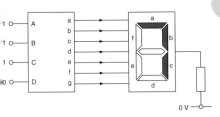

Figure 5 *Putting the binary code 0111 into the decoder displays the number 7, because the diodes a, b and c light up*

Displaying numbers

A common use of LEDs is to make a **7 segment display**. Here 7 LEDs are arranged to make a figure-of-eight pattern (Figure 5). Each LED can be switched on separately. Depending on which bars are lit, the display shows a different number. It is possible to display all the numbers from 0 to 9. You often see 7 segment displays on calculators and clocks.

To operate, a 7 segment display needs a **decoder**, which is an example of an **integrated circuit**, **IC**. This IC has the job of turning a binary number into a form which can be displayed by the diodes. Numbers are transmitted electronically in binary. The inputs DCBA can be in two possible 'states'. The voltage to them can be high, which we represent by '1'; or the voltage can be low, which is represented by '0'. The number going into the decoder is given by:

$$8 \times D + 4 \times C + 2 \times B + 1 \times A$$

Example. If D = 0, C = 1, D = 1, A = 1, the number (or code) 0111 means 7.

The decoder turns this into a suitable message to light the diodes. Outputs abc receive high voltages to light diodes abc. The other diodes receive low voltages, so they are off. This way the display shows the number 7.

Digital score boards, like this one at a cricket match, use an integrated circuit to decode electronic binary signals and display the numbers or letters as a visual, readable message

Binary codes

When we write the number 362, we mean: $(3 \times 100) + (6 \times 10) + (2 \times 1)$. So we are using powers of 10 to express numbers. The same number can also be written $(3 \times 10^2) + (6 \times 10^1) + (2 \times 10^0)$. We use numbers involving powers of ten, because we have ten digits on our two hands. However, computers can store numbers using either a high voltage level (1), or a low voltage level (0). So computers write numbers using powers of 2 or **binary**. The code going into the decoder was a binary number. The number 0111 means: $(0 \times 2^3) + (1 \times 2^2) + (1 \times 2^1) + (1 \times 2^0)$. This works out as: $4 + 2 + 1 = 7$.

Compact discs also use binary codes, to store information about music. Notches in the surface of the disc reflect a laser (Figure 6). Then a light-sensitive detector can pick up the information from the surface of the disc and turn it into an analogue signal (see unit G10). The analogue signal is then used to power loudspeakers and create the music we hear.

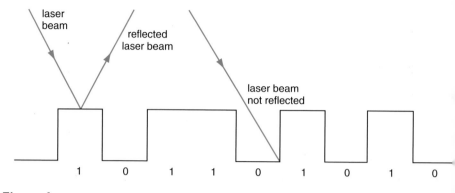

laser beam

reflected laser beam

laser beam not reflected

1   0   1   1   0   1   0   1   0

Figure 6

Homework Questions

1 Look carefully at the light meter in Figure 1.
(a) What is the resistance of the LDR when it is just too dark to play cricket safely?
(b) Sketch a graph to show how the resistance of the LDR depends on the brightness of the light falling on it.

2 (a) Which bulbs light in the circuits below?

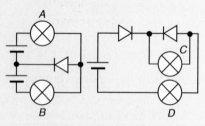

(b) Which bulbs light if you turn the batteries round?

3 The graph shows how the current through an LED varies with the applied voltage. The LED works normally when there is a current of 20 mA through it.

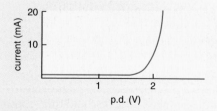

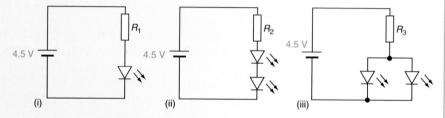

(i)   (ii)   (iii)

(a) What is the voltage across the diode when the current is 20 mA.
(b) For each of the circuits above choose a resistor which will make the diode(s) work correctly. You may only choose from the resistors given.
Values of available resistors (Ω): 33, 47, 56, 82, 100, 120, 150.

4 (a) This question refers to the diagram. Which diodes light for these inputs: (i) DCBA = 1001, (ii) DCBA = 0101?
(b) Why does no diode light for the input DCBA = 1100?

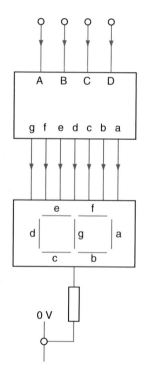

Rectification and Smoothing

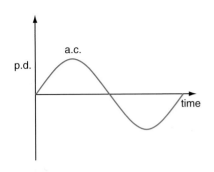

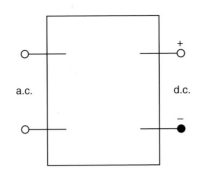

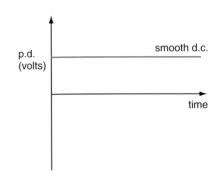

Figure I *Rectification*
(a) The voltage produced by the mains   *(b) The rectifier changes a.c. to d.c.*   *(c) The smoothed d.c. voltage*

The mains electricity supply produces alternating current (a.c.). Sometimes we want to turn this supply into a direct current (d.c.) supply. This process is called **rectification**. We also want to have a 'smooth' d.c. supply. This means that the d.c. supply must be constant (Figure 1).

Half-wave rectifiers

Figure 2 shows the simplest way of rectifying an a.c. supply, to produce d.c. for a resistor, in which a single diode is used. This is called **half-wave rectification**.

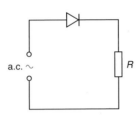

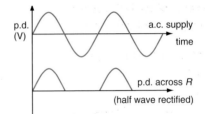

Figure 2 *Half-wave rectification*

The a.c. supply tries to drive current first one way, then the other, through the resistor. However, the diode only allows current to flow one way. Half of the time, current flows through the resistor. The other half of the time there is no current, because the diode is reverse biased. To make a smooth d.c. supply, we need to use a **capacitor**.

Some practical capacitors

Capacitors

A capacitor is like a rechargeable battery. It stores a small amount of charge and energy. This energy can be used to make a current flow, for a short time, through a resistance or a light bulb. The construction of capacitors is explained in Figure 3.

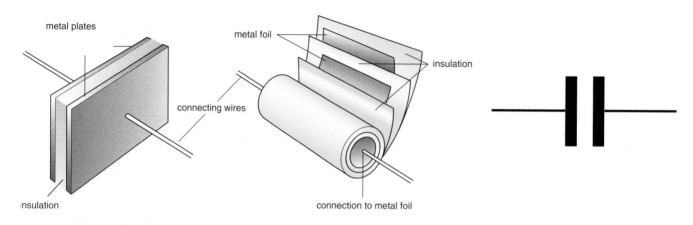

Figure 3

(a) The simplest form of capacitor is made from two metal plates, with insulation between them

(b) Practical capacitors are made like a swiss roll. Metal foil, separated by layers of insulation, is rolled up

(c) Circuit symbol for a capacitor

The size of a capacitor is measured in units called **farads**. A farad is a very large unit; so we usually use microfarads or μF to measure the size of a capacitor. 1 000 000 μF = 1 farad.

In Figure 4(a) the capacitor is charged by connecting it to the battery. When the switch is closed there is a quick pulse of current. This leaves one side of the capacitor with positive charge, and the other side with negative charge. Once the capacitor is charged, no more current passes through it.

In Figure 4(b) the capacitor is discharged by connecting it to a resistor and LED. Charge flows, until the positive charge has neutralised the negative charge. A large capacitor stores more charge than a smaller capacitor. This means that a large capacitor keeps the current going for a longer time. So the LED lights for longer. A large resistance also makes the current last longer. When R is big, I is small. So the capacitor loses its charge more slowly.

For a slow discharge, $R \times C$ must be large

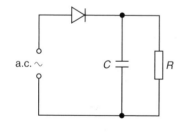

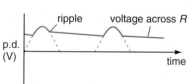

Figure 5 *Smoothing the voltage from an a.c. supply*

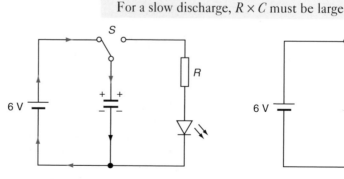

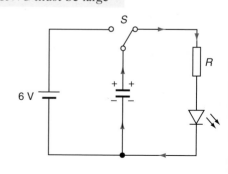

Figure 4

(a) Charging the capacitor

(b) Discharging the capacitor

Smoothing

Figure 5 shows how to smooth the voltage from an a.c. supply, using a large capacitor. Each time the a.c. supply reaches its maximum voltage, the capacitor gets charged up to this voltage. When the a.c. voltage drops, the voltage across the resistor stays roughly constant. This is because the capacitor acts like a battery to provide the extra current. Now the d.c. voltage shows only a small 'ripple'.

Increasing the current drawn from the supply makes the ripple worse. This is because the capacitor cannot supply enough charge. You can make the ripple less by using a large capacitor.

Resistor colour codes

To make identification easy, resistors are colour coded. This is how the code works. Each resistor has four coloured bands on it. The first two colours give the first two figures; for example (in Figure 6) brown then black means 10. The next band, red in this case, gives the number of zeros after the first two figures. So the value of this resistor is 10×100 i.e. 1000 Ω. The last band gives the 'tolerance' of the resistor; a gold band means the value is accurate to ±5%, a silver band accurate to ±10%; if the last band is missing the tolerance is ±20%.

Black 0, Brown 1, Red 2, Orange 3, Yellow 4,
Green 5, Blue 6, Purple 7, Grey 8, White 9.

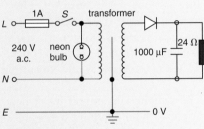

Figure 6

(a) red
red
brown
silver

(b) violet
green
orange

(c) blue
black
red
gold

Figure 6

Homework Questions

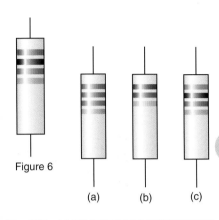

1 The circuit above shows a d.c. power supply which plugs into the mains.
(a) What does the transformer do?
(b) Why is the core of the transformer earthed?
(c) Why does the live wire have: (i) a switch, (ii) a fuse?
(d) Why is there a neon bulb?

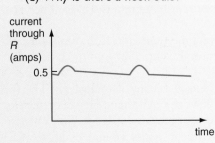

(e) The graph shows how the current through R changes with time. Copy the graph. Add to it two further graphs to show the current when these two separate changes are made: (i) $C = 2000$ μF, (ii) $R = 12$ Ω.

2 This diagram (right) shows a bridge rectifier. It produces a voltage which is 'full-wave rectified'.
(a) The arrows in the diagram show the current path when A is positive. Copy the diagram and show the current path when B is positive and A negative.
(b) Now explain the shape of the graph showing the voltage across R. Why is it called 'full-wave rectified'?
(c) Explain how a capacitor can be used to smooth this rectified voltage. Show on your diagram how the capacitor should be connected to the circuit.

3 (a) Draw diagrams (in colour) to represent these resistors with 5%

tolerance; 10 Ω; 32 Ω; 560 Ω; 2200 Ω; 4700 Ω; 82 kΩ; 2.7 MΩ.
(c) Why is it rare to discover a resistor whose third band is white?

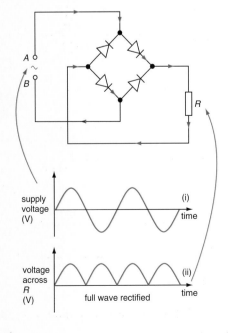

3 Transistors

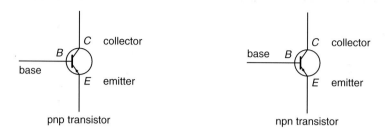

pnp transistor

npn transistor

Figure 1 *These are the circuit symbols for two types of transistor. The arrows show the direction of the current through the emitter*

The outside of a transistor is nothing special to look at. But the transistor is the key to all modern electronic circuits. It looks like a small piece of plastic or metal, with three long legs sticking out. These legs are connecting wires to the transistor's three terminals. These terminals are called the **base**, the **emitter** and the **collector**. Transistors are made out of specially manufactured germanium or silicon. Figure 1 shows the circuit symbols for two types of transistor.

Turning a transistor on and off

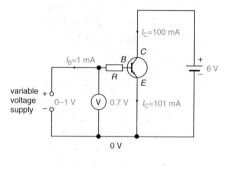

Figure 2 *A circuit showing how a transistor works*

Figure 2 shows a circuit which will help you to understand the action of a transistor. A 6 V battery has been connected across the collector and the emitter. The power supply connected between the base and the emitter can vary the voltage between 0 and 1 V. Table 1 shows how the voltage between the base and the emitter, V_{BE}, affects the currents going into and out of the transistor. The currents are called the base, collector and emitter currents (I_B, I_C and I_E).

When there is a voltage of about 0.7 V between base and emitter, the transistor is on. This means a current goes into the base and a current flows from collector to emitter. If the voltage (V_{BE}) is less than 0.7 V, the transistor is off. No current flows into or out of it.

The transistor is so useful because it can be switched on and off by a small change in base voltage. It is an electronic switch with no moving parts, so it does not wear out. In computers, transistors are switched on and off millions of times a second! That is why computers can calculate so quickly.

Controlling the transistor

Figure 3 shows one way to control the base current of a transistor. A variable resistor is connected between the base and the positive side of the battery. When the resistance is very high (1 MΩ) no current flows into the base. The lamp is off. When the resistance is made lower (1 kΩ) current flows into the base. Then the lamp is on.

The extra resistance, R_B, is there to protect the transistor. If the resistance of the variable resistor is made zero, a large current would flow into the base and cause damage.

A potential divider (Figure 4) can also be used to control a transistor. The two resistors are in series, so the same current flows through them. However, resistor X is five times bigger than resistor Y, so the voltage across X is five times bigger than the voltage across Y. There is a voltage of 5 V across AB and a voltage of 1 V across BC. The voltage at A is 6 V, at B, 1 V, and at C it is 0 V.

V_{BE} (V)	I_B (mA)	I_C (mA)	I_E (mA)
0	0	0	0
0.3	0	0	0
0.6	0	0	0
0.7	1	100	101

Table 1

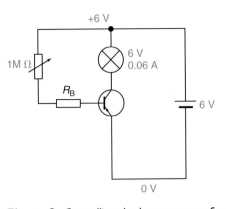

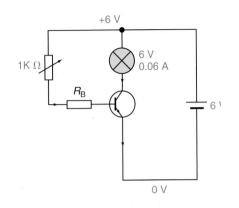

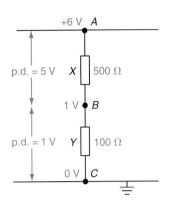

Figure 3 *Controlling the base current of a transistor*
(a) High resistance; current cannot flow into the base, so the lamp is off

(b) Low resistance; a small current flows into the base, so the lamp is on

Figure 4 *A potential divider*

Homework Questions

1 In this question you may assume that the voltmeters V_1 and V_2 have a very high resistance, so you can ignore any current which flows through them.

(a) What do the voltmeters read in the circuit below when:

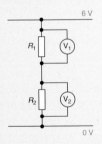

(i) $R_1 = 5$ kΩ; $R_2 = 10$ kΩ,
(ii) $R_1 = 2$ kΩ; $R_2 = 2$ kΩ,
(iii) $R_1 = 300$ Ω; $R_2 = 1500$ Ω?
(b) (i) What does V_1 read in the circuit below? (ii) What does V_2 read? (iii) What is the value of R_3?

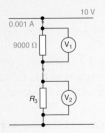

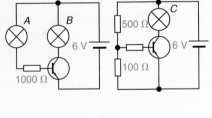

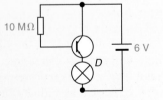

2 In the diagrams shown above, the transistors are similar to the transistor shown in Figure 3. The light bulbs need a current of about 100 mA (0.1 A) to make them light. Explain which of the bulbs will light in these diagrams.

3 This question is about the currents and voltages associated with the transistor circuit below. It looks complicated, but you just need to apply the normal rules about currents and voltages.

(a) Remembering that whatever current flows into a point must flow out, calculate I.

(b) Remembering that the voltage drops (or potential differences) round a circuit must add up to the battery voltage, calculate V_1 and V_2.

(c) Calculate the value of R_1.

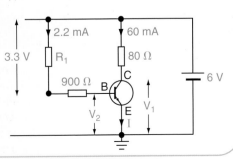

4 | Using Transistors

Electronic systems

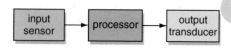

Figure 1

Most electronic systems can be divided into three major parts as shown in Figure 1:

- an input sensor or transducer
- a processor
- an output transducer.

A transducer is a device which changes one form of energy to another; a microphone changes sound energy to electrical energy, and a loudspeaker changes electrical energy to sound energy.

The input sensor detects changes to the surroundings, and turns them into electrical energy. Examples of input sensors and transducers include, thermistors, LDRs, microphones and pressure switches.

The processor is a circuit which decides which action to take. The processor might be relatively simple as in the circuits shown on this page, or the processor might be a computer controlling a complicated machine.

The output transducer turns electrical energy into another form. Examples of output transducers include buzzers, light bulbs, heaters, relays and motors.

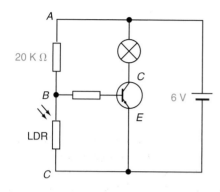

Figure 2 *Making a light come on in the dark*

Turning on a light in the dark

In daylight an LDR has a resistance of about 500 Ω. So when it is light the voltage across BC is very small (Figure 2). This is because the resistance of an LDR is much smaller than the 20 kΩ resistor. The voltage at B is close to zero; the transistor is switched off and the bulb is out.

When it is dark the resistance of the LDR becomes very high, about 1 MΩ (1 000 000 Ω). The voltage across the 20 kΩ resistor is small compared with the voltage across the LDR. The voltage at B is nearly 6 V; the transistor is switched on and the lamp lights.

An automatic tomato waterer

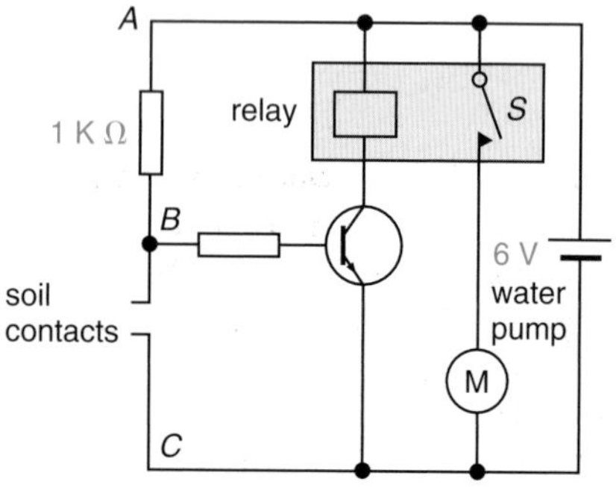

The circuit in Figure 3 makes sure your tomatoes get watered when you are away on holiday. The soil contacts are placed into the soil around the tomato plants. When the soil is wet it conducts electricity well. This means that there is a short circuit between the base and the emitter of the transistor. So the transistor is switched off. When the soil dries out the resistance between B and C becomes large. This makes the voltage at B rise and the transistor is switched on. Now the current flowing through the transistor energises the relay coil. The magnetic field from the coil makes the switch S close. This switches the pump on. We need a relay to switch on the pump because it uses a current of 2 A. This is a far larger current than can flow through the transistor.

Figure 3 *A tomato-watering system*

Controlling the temperature

This circuit might help you grow tomatoes in winter. The idea is to turn on a heater when your greenhouse gets too cold. The resistance of the thermistor changes as shown in the graph (Figure 4). The thermistor's resistance is highest when it is cold.

We can calculate what value the variable resistor must be set to, so that the heater is switched on when the temperature drops below freezing point (0°C) (Figure 4). From the graph you can see that the resistance of the thermistor is 700 Ω at 0°C. For the transistor to be switched on, the voltage drop across the thermistor needs to be 0.7 V. This means there must be 5.3 V (6.0 V – 0.7 V) across the variable resistor (Figure 5).

The same current goes through the resistor and the thermistor. (We ignore any small base current going into the transistor.)

So $I = \dfrac{V}{R} = \dfrac{\text{voltage across resistor}}{\text{resistance of } R} = \dfrac{\text{voltage across thermistor}}{\text{resistance of thermistor}}$

or $\qquad \dfrac{5.3 \text{ V}}{R} = \dfrac{0.7 \text{ V}}{700}$

So $\qquad R = 700 \ \Omega \times \dfrac{5.3}{0.7} = 5300 \ \Omega$

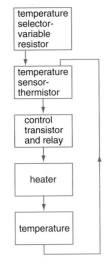

Figure 4 *The thermistor resistance changes with temperature*

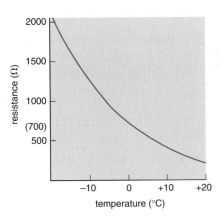

Figure 6 *Achieving control through negative feedback*

Adjusting R allows you to control the temperature of your greenhouse. This is an example of control in an electronic system being achieved through negative feedback. The temperature is selected by adjusting the variable resistor. The thermistor senses the temperature in the greenhouse, and the heater is controlled by the action of the transistor and relay. The heater switches on and off and the temperature oscillates around 0°C.

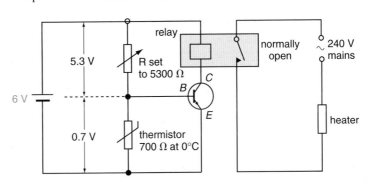

Figure 5

Homework Questions

1 Jamal has designed the circuit shown, so that his light bulb will come on in the dark. Has he got his circuit right? Explain your answer.

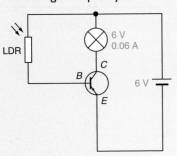

2 Look at the circuit in Figure 5. You have decided that you want the heater in the greenhouse to switch on when the temperature is 10°C.
(a) What is the resistance of the thermistor at this temperature?
(b) What is the voltage across the thermistor when the transistor is switched on?
(c) Therefore, what is the voltage across the variable resistor when the transistor is on?
(d) Now work out what value R must be set to, so that the heater comes on at a temperature of 10°C.

3 Design an electronic system to turn on a freezer motor when the temperature inside the freezer rises

above −10°C. In your system you might use a relay, a thermistor and variable resistor similar to those in Figure 5. Explain how your system works, using appropriate calculations.

4 Design an electronic system for a photographic dark room, to sound an alarm if the light intensity is too high.

5 For circuits in Figures 3 and 5, explain which parts form (i) the input sensor, (ii) the processor, (iii) the output transducer.

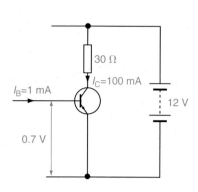

Figure 1

Current gain

In Figure 1 the voltage between the base and the emitter is 0.7 V. The current going into the base is 1 mA and the current going into the collector is 100 mA. So a small base current controls a much larger collector current. The **current gain** of this transistor is 100.

$$\text{current gain} = \frac{I_C}{I_B}$$

The gain varies for different transistors; it can be anywhere between 10 and 1000.

The transistor is very sensitive to changes in its base current. Figure 2 shows that I_C is proportional to I_B. So if we double the base current to 2 mA the collector current increases to 200 mA.

This behaviour of the transistor is very important. It allows us to build **amplifiers**. When a small alternating current goes into the base, a much larger alternating current flows into the collector (Figure 3).

Instead of the resistor in Figure 1, you can put in a loudspeaker or earphone. The amplifier in your stereo system uses lots of transistors. When you play a tape or CD, a small current goes into the base of a transistor. A much larger current flows through the loudspeaker. Now you can hear the music.

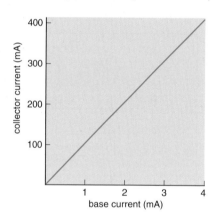

Figure 2 *The collector current is proportional to the base current*

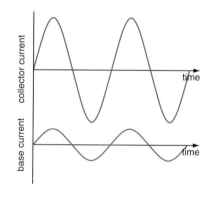

Figure 3

Making an amplifier

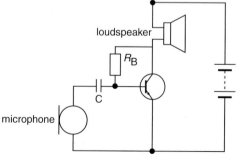

Figure 4 *A circuit for a simple amplifier*

Figure 4 shows how to make a simple amplifier. A microphone is used to pick up a speaker's voice. A loudspeaker relays what is said to an audience:

Big amplifiers are needed for large outdoor concerts.

- The base resistor R_B is there to allow a small current to go into the base. This switches the transistor on. We call this biasing the transistor.
- When someone speaks into the microphone, a small changing voltage is produced across it. This signal passes through the capacitor, and makes changes to the base current.
- The small changes to the base current are amplified by the transistor. The current is now large enough to drive the loudspeaker.
- It is important to have a capacitor in the circuit. Capacitors allow alternating currents through, but not direct currents. This means that the signal can get through to the transistor. Without the capacitor the biasing of the transistor would be upset. This is because a direct current would go from the base through the microphone. Now the base would be at the wrong voltage, and the transistor would not work properly.

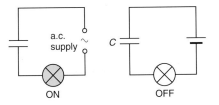

Figure 5 *A capacitor passes a.c. but not d.c.*

Homework Questions

1 Below you can see a transistor circuit driving a loudspeaker. An alternating current is going into the base (graph 1). Graph 2 shows how the base current controls the collector current.

(a) What is the current gain of the transistor?
(b) What are the maximum and minimum values of: (i) I_B, (ii) I_C?
(c) Sketch a graph to show how I_C varies with time.
(d) When I_B is 1 mA, how big is the current I_E?

2 Look again at the diagram in question 1.
(a) When the collector current I_C is 50 mA, what is the voltage across the loudspeaker?
(b) Now explain why the largest collector current which can flow through this circuit is 150 mA.
(c) A very large base current is now fed into the transistor (graph 3). The music now sounds odd. Can you explain why? This is called distortion.

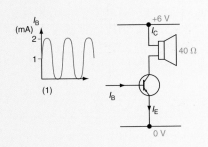

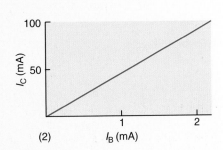

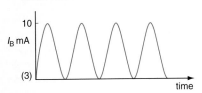

6 Logic Gates

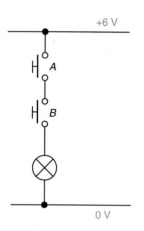

Figure I *A two-state system: the bulb is on or off*

State of switch		State of bulb
A	**B**	
open	open	OFF
closed	open	OFF
open	closed	OFF
closed	closed	ON

Table I

Two states: ON and OFF

Logic gates are widely used in computers and other electronic systems. They collect and display information.

A very simple example of a logic gate is shown in Figure 1. To turn the light bulb on, you have to press both switches. It is no good just pressing one of them. The behaviour of the circuit is summarised in Table 1. This simple circuit can collect information about your fingers! When two fingers press A and B the bulb lights.

Figure 2 shows a similar circuit which works with relays. This time the circuit collects information about voltages. The relay switches in the circuit are normally open. However, if the voltage at A is high (for example, above 3 V), the top switch is closed. So when A and B are both above 3 V the lamp switches on.

Truth tables

Truth tables show the behaviour of an electronic system in shorthand. A high voltage (above 3 V in our example) is defined as **logic state '1'**. A low voltage (below 3 V) is defined as **logic state '0'**.

You can describe the behaviour of the circuit in Figure 2 like this. When both A AND B are 1, Q is 1; otherwise Q is 0. Table 2 summarises this. We call this sort of table a **truth table**.

The circuit you have just been looking at makes an **AND-gate**. This gate was made with switches and relays. Logic gates are also made easily with transistors in **integrated circuits**. The advantages of integrated circuit logic gates are: they are cheap, small and can be switched millions of times each second. The circuit symbol for an AND-gate is shown in Table 2.

All integrated circuits need batteries to power them. We usually leave out connections to batteries in the circuit diagrams though. This helps to make the circuits easy to follow.

www

http://www.howstuffworks.com/boolean1.htm

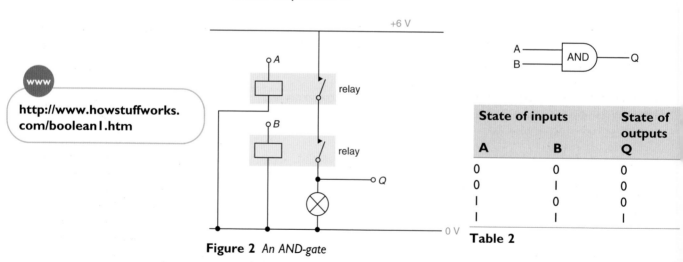

Figure 2 *An AND-gate*

State of inputs		State of outputs
A	**B**	**Q**
0	0	0
0	1	0
1	0	0
1	1	1

Table 2

298

More logic gates

- An **OR-gate** is shown below. When A OR B (OR both) is 1 then Q is 1 (Table 3).
- A **NOT-gate** is shown below. When A is NOT 1, Q is 1 (Table 4).
- A **NOR-gate** symbol and truth table are shown below. When neither A NOR B is 1, Q is 1 (Table 5).
- A **NAND-gate** symbol and truth table are shown below. When both A AND B are NOT 1, Q is 1 (Table 6).

State of inputs		State of outputs
A	B	Q
0	0	0
0	1	1
1	0	1
1	1	1

Table 3 *Circuit symbol and truth table for an OR-gate*

State of input A	State of output, Q
0	1
1	0

Table 4 *Circuit symbol and truth table for a NOT-gate*

Input A	Input B	Q
0	0	1
0	1	0
1	0	0
1	1	0

Table 5 *Circuit symbol and truth table for a NOR-gate*

Input A	Input B	Q
0	0	1
0	1	1
1	0	1
1	1	0

Table 6 *Circuit symbol and truth table for a NAND-gate*

Homework Questions

1 This question is about working out logic states. For example when A is 1, B is 0. What are the states of the points C and D?

2 The circuit below shows a security system for a car.
(a) Which switches have to be closed to turn on the starter motor?
(b) What happens if any other switch is closed?

3 Which single gate can be made from the AND-gate and the NOT-gate? Explain your answer.

4 Design these electronic systems using the gates in this unit:
(i) a 4 input AND-gate,
(ii) a 3 input NOR-gate.

5 Taking Figure 1 as an example, design an OR-gate using two switches and a bulb.

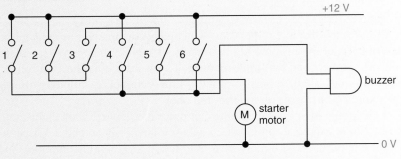

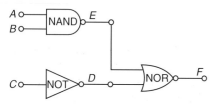

F gure I

A	B	C	D	E	F
0	0	0	1	1	0
0	0	1	0	1	0
0	1	0	1	1	0
1	0	0	1	1	0
0	1	1	0	1	0
1	0	1	0	1	0
1	1	0	1	0	0
1	1	1	0	0	1

Table I

An Apple Macintosh microcomputer contains about half a million NOR gates

Analysing logic systems

More complicated logic systems can be made by using a combination of gates. In Figure 1, how does the output F depend on the states of A, B and C? You can work out this problem by constructing a truth table (Table 1).

First you write out the columns A, B and C, working out all the possible combinations of states. The state of E can be worked out from the truth table of a NAND-gate. E is only 0 when A and B are both 1. D is 0 when C is 1; D is 1 when C is 0. You can now fill in the columns D and E. D and E are the inputs to the NOR-gate; F is the output. F is 1 when D and E are 0.

So this circuit makes a 3-input AND gate. When A AND B AND C are 1, F is 1. Otherwise F is 0.

The bistable

The **bistable** or **flip-flop** is the basis of electronic computer memories. A bistable can be made from two NOR gates, as shown in Figure 2. The sequence of diagrams shows how the bistable works. You should remember that the output (Q or $\bar{Q}$) of a NOR gate is only 1 when both inputs are 0. If either input (or both) is 1, the output is 0.

In diagram (a) the bistable is set with S = 1 and C = 0. Since S = 1, $\bar{Q}$ = 0; both inputs to the lower NOR gate are 0, so Q = 1.

In diagram (b), S has changed to 0. This does not affect Q or $\bar{Q}$. So Q = 1 still. However, in diagram (c) S = 0 and C = 1. This means that Q = 0 and $\bar{Q}$ = 1. The bistable has been cleared.

In diagram (d) C goes back to 0. This does not affect Q or $\bar{Q}$.

Notice that the bistable remembers which of S or C was *last* in the logic state 1. The output, Q, of the bistable has two states. Q is either 0 or 1. We say that the bistable remembers one **bit of information**. The word 'bit' is short for binary digit. Computers calculate only in terms of binary numbers. All binary numbers can be expressed in terms of noughts and ones.

The electronic memory for a home computer has about 2 500 000 bistables inside it. These can be accommodated on a few small silicon chips. When you turn your computer off, it forgets what is stored in its electronic memory. So to store information permanently, you must transfer it to a magnetic disc or tape.

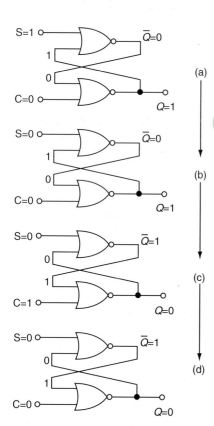

Figure 2 *This shows how a bistable changes from one state to another*

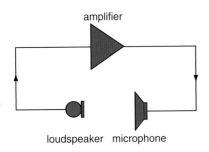

Figure 4 *Here is another example of positive feedback, but not as useful as a bistable. By placing a microphone close to a loudspeaker a loud pitched whine can be produced. The microphone picks up a small noise, which is amplified and emitted by the loudspeaker. The microphone picks this noise up and it is amplified again and so on*

An electronic latch

Bistables are often used in alarm systems. This is because they work as **electronic latches**. When the alarm has been triggered, the latch keeps the alarm on.

Figure 3 shows a circuit for a 'latched' burglar alarm. An infra-red beam of light falls onto an LDR. This keeps the LDR's resistance low. B is at a low voltage. Both inputs of NOR gate A are low. This makes $\bar{Q}$ high, and Q low, The buzzer is off.

If a burglar walks across the infra-red beam, the resistance of the LDR goes high for a moment. Now B goes high and $\bar{Q}$ goes low. Both inputs to NOR gate B are low and Q goes high. The buzzer sounds the alarm. But the alarm stays on because the bistable 'remembers' that the burglar was there.

This is a useful example of positive feedback in an electronic system.

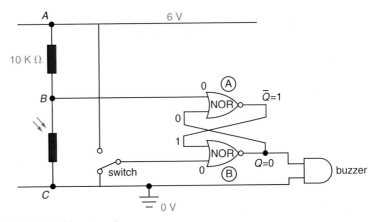

Figure 3 *A latched burglar alarm*

Homework Questions

1 (a) Why is an infra-red beam of light used in the burglar alarm?
(b) Explain how you can turn the burglar alarm off.
(c) Think of another way you could use an electronic latch.

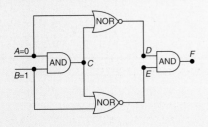

2 (a) In the diagram above, work out the logic state of the points C, D, E, F.
(b) When F is in logic state 1, what are the states of A and B?

3 The circuit on the right shows part of a security system for a car ferry.

S_1 closes when the bow doors are shut. S_2 opens when the passenger gangway is lifted. S_3 is an ignition switch on the bridge. Explain how the system works.

4 The diagram shows a bistable made from two NAND gates.
(a) Copy the diagram and write in the new logic states at S, R, Q and $\bar{Q}$, after S has been switched to low. Illustrate your answer with reference to the truth table for a NAND gate.

(b) Explain why this bistable triggers only when S or R are switched to low from high.

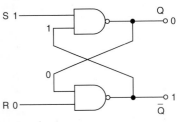

5 Design a three input AND gate, using only 2 gates.

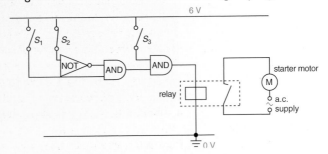

We are all used to taking measurements. We use a ruler to measure length, a thermometer to measure temperature, a watch to measure time, and voltmeters and ammeters in electrical experiments. We usually measure two or more things at once. For example, we might want to know how the temperature of a cup of tea changes with time; so you place a thermometer in the tea and record the temperature at 1 minute intervals. This is a very simple, manual way of **recording, or logging**, data. Nowadays we can use preprogrammed instruments to do the job for us. These instruments are called **data loggers**.

LogIT

LogIT is an example of a cheap and easy-to-use data logger. At the press of a button, LogIT can be started and it will record automatically from a variety of sensors. These sensors can record such variables as temperature, light intensity and voltage, so the experimenter can carry out a wide range of experiments. The data logger can record measurements every few milliseconds, or slow its rate down to one measurement every few hours for a long experiment where changes are very slow. So, not only does LogIT make it easier to do some experiments, but it enables you to measure changes that are too fast or too slow for normal laboratory work. LogIT can even measure *three* variables simultaneously. Finally when the experiment is finished, LogIT is connected to a computer system which is programmed to receive and analyse the data. The computer can then be instructed to tabulate the data or display it graphically.

http://www.dcpmicro.com/
sens.htm

Examples of use

- **Light output from a bulb**
  A bulb was pulsed on for about 1 second in a darkened room. Figure 1 shows the circuit used. LogIT recorded readings of light intensity and voltage across the bulb every 10 milliseconds (Figure 2).

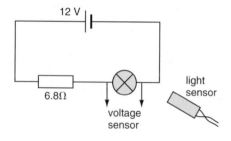

Figure 1

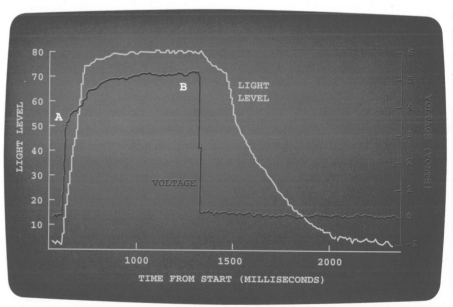

Figure 2

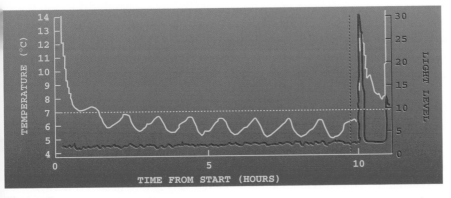

Figure 3

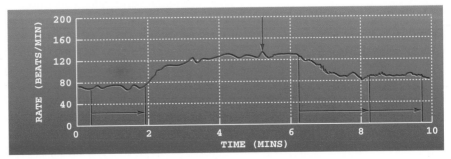

Figure 4

Peter carries LogIT to record his heart rate before, during and after he runs

- **Temperature inside Steve's fridge overnight**
  LogIT records temperature and light intensity every 5 minutes (Figure 3).
- **Cooling curves**
  This is a familiar experiment you can do yourself; LogIT can record temperatures of two beakers of water simultaneously (Figure 4). The results can be displayed immediately on a screen. Which beaker in Figure 4 is insulated?
- **How fit are you?**
  The graph in Figure 5 shows Peter's heart rate before, during and after a run. A sensor strapped to the body detects electrical pulses caused by the heart beating. The sensor then transmits these pulses, using radiowaves, to a receiver which is plugged into LogIT. Peter carries LogIT on his belt. On returning from the run the data can be displayed on a computer again.

Figure 5

Homework Questions

1 This question is about the light levels and voltage changes of the light bulb (Figure 2).
   (a) What is the voltage across the light bulb at times (i) A, (ii) B?
   (b) Use the answers to part (a), and the data in Figure 2, to calculate the voltage across the 6.8 Ω resistor at times (i) A, (ii) B.
   (c) Now deduce the current flowing through the circuit at each time (i) A, (ii) B.

   (d) Calculate the resistance of the bulb at times A and B. Explain why the changes occurred.
   (e) Describe how the light level changed immediately after the bulb was turned off. Account for these changes.

2 (a) Describe how the temperature changed in Steve's fridge overnight.
   (b) What happened after 10 hours?
   (c) The motor on Steve's fridge is rated at 100 W. Use the graph to

   calculate the cost of running his fridge overnight, given that 1 kWh costs 7p.

3 (a) How long did Peter run for?
   (b) What was his average heart rate (i) before, (ii) during, (iii) after, the run?
   (c) What was Judy's recovery time?

4 Design an experiment using LogIT to monitor a chemical reaction which involves a colour change in a liquid.

If you go into a music shop to buy a stereo system, it is possible to buy one that allows you to play records (or vinyl), tapes, compact discs (CDs) or Minidiscs. However, a lot of companies have stopped cutting records and concentrate on producing CDs. Whichever system you choose, information has been stored on record, tape, Minidisc or CD, which you retrieve when you listen to the music.

Vinyl discs

The photograph opposite shows a high powered magnification of the grooves which have been cut into a vinyl disc. When you play a record, a very small stylus tracks along the groove. The indentations along this groove make the stylus vibrate, up and down, or sideways. A transducer turns these vibrations into electrical pulses, which are amplified to make the loudspeaker vibrate. You then hear a reproduction of the original music.

A stylus following the grooves on a record

Magnetic tapes

Figure 1 shows the principles behind a tape recorder. The tape is made of thin plastic, coated with a special form of ferric oxide which can easily be magnetised. When a recording is made the microphone turns the sound into audio frequency electrical oscillations. These oscillations are amplified and fed into the recording head, which is rather like a small electromagnet. As the tape passes under the recording head it is magnetised. The information about the music which you are recording is then stored in the tape.

To play the music back, the tape is fed past the playback head. The process now goes into reverse. The magnetised tape induces currents in the coil in the playback. These currents are amplified to power the loudspeaker. Tape recorders have an erase head to wipe the tape clean, so that you can rerecord over material on a tape. A very high frequency current passes through the erase head, which jumbles up all the directions of magnetisation on the tape. The information about the music is lost. You can erase a tape for yourself using a magnet. Take a tape that you have recorded and move a magnet backwards and forwards past the exposed part. Play it back and listen to the effect. Make sure that you don't want whatever is on the tape first!

http://www.howstuffworks.com/analog-digital.htm

http://www.howstuffworks.com/boolean1.htm

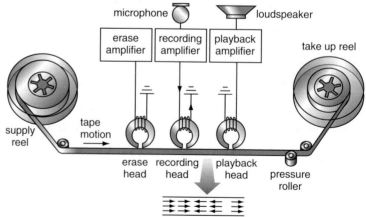

The different directions of magnetisation on the tape carry the information.

Figure 1 *Layout of a tape recorder*

Compact disc

http://www.ee.washington.
edu/conselec/CE/kuhn/
cdmulti/cdhome.htm

The photograph at the start of this section on electronics (page 285) shows an electron micrograph of a compact disc. The music is coded in a series of tiny notches. Laser light is bounced off these notches and decoded to play the music, (see page 288).

A compact disc is similar to the vinyl disc in that they are both **read only memories** (ROMs). The information is stored permanently, cannot be altered, and can only be read. Magnetic tape is an example of an erasable memory. A compact disc differs from vinyls and tapes in that the music is recorded in a digital code; vinyls and tapes produce analogue, or continuously changing, signals. Digital signals produce much clearer recordings, with less accidental 'noise', which happens during the recording of a tape or vinyl.

This magneto-optical drive is used to store computer data. It works through using a combination of a magnet and a laser. To write to the disc, both the magnet and the laser are used, while only the laser is required to read information from the disc. The drive uses a disc similar in size to a 3.5 inch floppy disc, but a magneto-optical disc can store much more data than a floppy disc

Computer memories

In 1975 computer programs were stored on punched cards or tapes, which were read very slowly into the computer. By 1980 programs for home computers were stored on magnetic tape which you used in tape recorders. In 1985 most home computers were beginning to use floppy discs, and now home computers have hard discs.

Magnetic discs work in a similar way to tape. However, they are far faster to use because the read head on the disc drive can reach any part of the disc very quickly.

Computers also store information in electronic memories, which are of two types: ROMs and RAMs. RAM stands for **Random Access Memory**; this is a read and write or erasable memory.

Homework Questions

1 (a) (i) What are the similarities and differences between vinyl discs, tapes and CDs?
(ii) Give one advantage and one disadvantage of each.
(b) Explain how a video tape stores information.
(c) Minidiscs and Minidisc players were introduced to the music market a few years ago. Explain briefly what each of these new products can offer.

2 The microphone and recording head on a tape recorder are examples of transducers.
(a) Explain what is meant by a transducer.
(b) Explain how these two transducers work.

3 (a) Which of the following devices use erasable memories, ROMs or both? CD player, tape recorder, washing machine, digital watch, cash point, book, calculator, electronic till.

(b) A video recorder uses both sorts of memory. Explain how each is used.

4 A book such as Physics Matters can now be stored on disc and downloaded into a computer.
(a) Give and explain three advantages of electronic books.
(b) Explain advantages of publishing books on paper as opposed to disc.

SECTION K: Questions

1 With the components connected as shown in diagram (1) the LED glows.

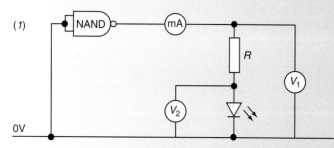

(1)

0V

(a) What gate could be used instead of the NAND gate?
(b) What is the purpose of the resistor R?
The voltmeters V_1 and V_2 have high resistances, so a negligible current passes through them. The readings on the voltmeters are: $V_1 = 3.8$ V, $V_2 = 2.0$ V. The milliammeter reads 10 mA.
(c) What is the resistance of R?
(d) The diode is now removed from the circuit and replaced by a light bulb labelled 3 V, 0.15 A. Explain why the bulb does not light.
(e) The bulb does light when a transistor is used as shown in diagram (2). Explain the action of this circuit.

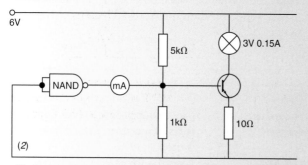

(2)

(f) A transistor cannot drive an electric motor by itself. Explain how you would modify diagram (2) so that an electric motor could be turned on and off by switching the inputs of the NAND gate from a high to a low voltage.

2 The graph shows how the resistance of a light dependent resistor (LDR) depends on the intensity of light falling on it.

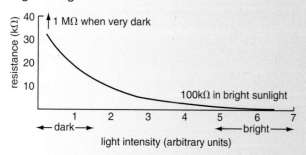

(a) Describe the action of the LDR.
(b) The milliammeter in the circuit below reads 1 mA.

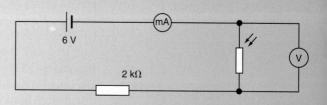

(i) Calculate the resistance of the LDR.
(ii) Use the graph to calculate the light intensity.
(c) The voltmeter across the LDR has a very high resistance. Estimate the reading on this voltmeter: (i) in bright sunlight, (ii) in very dark conditions.
(d) The truth table describes the operation of the diagram below it. Copy and complete the table.

LDR 1	LDR 2	Voltage states			Buzzer
		A	B	C	
light	light	1			OFF
light	dark				
dark	light				
dark	dark				

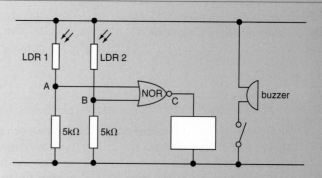

(e) Why is a relay needed to operate the buzzer?
(f) (i) Explain how this system could be used in a biscuit factory to reject any biscuits that are too long to fit into the packet.
(ii) How would you adapt the circuit to detect biscuits that are too short?

OCR (MEG)

3 (a) Explain how you would make a bistable using two NAND gates.
(b) The diagram shows a circuit with 5 NAND gates. The input receives a series of 1 Hz pulses which switch it from high to low. Describe the behaviour of the three lamps, X, Y, Z when the 'hold' lead is (i) kept low, (ii) kept high.
(c) Explain how this circuit can be used as a memory; it is called a **data latch**. What advantage does this circuit have over an ordinary bistable memory?

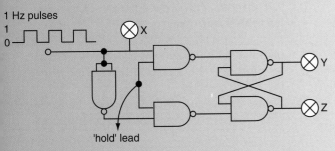

1 Hz pulses

'hold' lead

4 (a) Copy and complete the truth table for the circuit below.

A	B	C	D	E	F	G
0	0	1				
0	1	1				
1	0	1				
1	1	0				

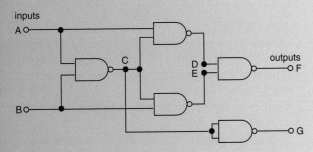

inputs

outputs

(b) What arithmetic function does this circuit carry out?

5 This circuit shows part of a car security lock system. The lock opens when the relay is switched on.

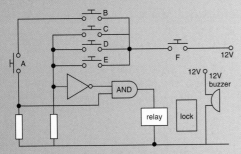

(a) Which switches must be pressed to open the lock?
(b) If the wrong switches are pressed the alarm sounds and *stays on*. Copy the diagram and add extra circuit components to make the alarm sound.

6 Mr Corrigan owns an amusement arcade. He is having some trouble with Tommy who is very rough with the pinball machines. So Mr Corrigan decides to fit anti-tilt devices to his pinball machines. When Tommy tips the machine, the power supply turns off. The circuit is shown.

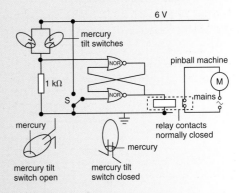

mercury tilt switches

pinball machine

mercury

relay contacts normally closed

mercury tilt switch open

mercury tilt switch closed

(a) Explain how the mercury tilt switches work.
(b) Why are there two mercury tilt switches?
(c) What do the two NOR gates do?
(d) Why are the relay contacts normally closed?
(e) Explain how the machine can be started again by putting another coin in.

7 (a) For the circuit below, calculate the input voltage to the NOT gate (the voltage across the thermistor) when the thermistor has a resistance of 500 Ω.

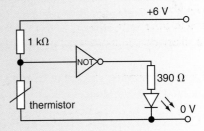

This graph shows the input/output voltage characteristics of the NOT gate used in this circuit.
(b) What is the output voltage of the NOT gate when

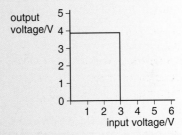

the thermistor has a resistance of 500 Ω?
(c) When the light-emitting diode is on there is a voltage of 1.8 V across it. Calculate the current through the 390 Ω resistor.
(d) Write down what the answers to parts (a) and (c) will be if the thermistor and the 1 kΩ resistor are interchanged.

OCR (MEG)

8 The circuit in the next diagram controls a motor.

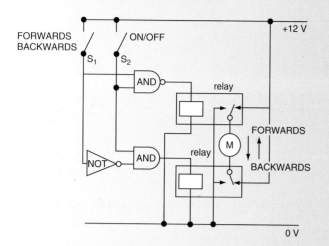

Explain, in as much detail as possible, how it works.

9 This question is about making a time control switch. When the switch is pressed and released, the capacitor gets charged up. For a while the voltage at B is high. The transistor is on and the bulb lights. However, the capacitor loses its charge through R. After a while the voltage at B drops. This makes the bulb go out.

(a) Explain where you might use this idea in your house.

(b) What changes could you make to the circuit to make the bulb light for longer?

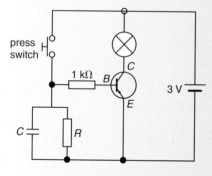

10 Bobby is testing a circuit which he would like to use to replace the battery in his radio. He connects a diode bridge to an a.c. supply. This provides d.c. in a resistor.

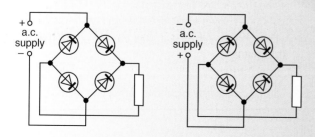

(a) The diagram shows the polarity of the supply voltage at different times.

Copy the diagrams and draw arrows to show the path taken by the current as it flows from one terminal of the a.c. supply, through the bridge to the other terminal.

(b) Bobby connects a CRO directly to the a.c. supply terminals. Here is the trace he sees on the screen.

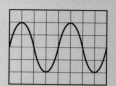

(i) The timebase is set at 5 ms/cm. Calculate the frequency of the supply.

Bobby now connects the CRO across the resistor. He does not change any of the settings of the CRO.

(ii) Draw the trace he sees on the CRO screen, using the same scale in the diagram above.

(c) Bobby uses a capacitor to smooth the d.c. current in the resistor.

(i) State how the capacitor should be connected into the circuit.

(ii) Draw the trace which Bobby sees on the CRO screen when he connects the capacitor, using the same diagram you have just completed.

OCR

11 Bobby constructs this circuit. He tells Joy that it has a memory. She wants to find out what this means.

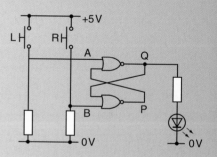

(a) Copy and complete the truth table for **one** NOR gate.

A	P	Q

(b) Joy starts off by pressing the switch labelled **R**.
  (i) Explain why **B** goes HIGH when she presses switch **R**.
  (ii) State and explain what happens to **Q** and **P** when she presses switch **R**.

(c) To her surprise, the LED remains on when Joy stops pressing **R**. This is because the circuit has a memory.
  (i) Explain why the LED remains on.
  (ii) State and explain what Joy should do to turn the LED off again.

OCR

12 It is dangerous for aircraft to take off or land when there is a strong wind across the runway. Neil's airport has installed this device to detect these dangerous cross winds.

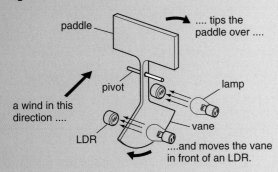

The lamps shine light onto the LDRs. Any cross wind pushes the vane between the lamp and one of the LDRs. Here is the circuit for **one** of the LDRs.

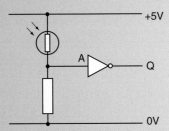

(a) Use the words HIGH or LOW to copy and complete the sentences.
  When there is no wind, there is lots of light on the LDR. It has a _____ resistance and the voltage at **A** is _____.
  In a strong wind, there is no light on the LDR. So it has a _____ resistance and the voltage at **A** is _____.

(b) The graph shows how the voltage at **A** changes during a day.

voltage at A	voltage at Q
less than 2.0 V	4.5 V
more than 2.0 V	0.5 V

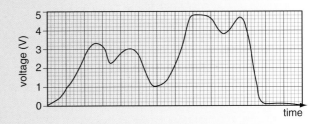

Sketch a copy of the graph and then show how the voltage at **Q** changes during the day. Use the data in the table.

(c) A logic gate **Z** combines the signals from the two sensors.

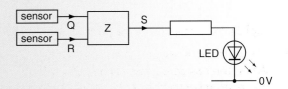

The LED must glow if the cross wind is dangerous. The output from each sensor is LOW when there is no wind.

(i) Copy and complete the table.

R	Q	S
LOW	LOW	
LOW	HIGH	
HIGH	LOW	
HIGH	HIGH	HIGH

(ii) Name the logic gate **Z**.

OCR

13 Anita uses a remote control to operate her compact disc (CD) player.
  The remote control uses a beam of infra-red light from an LED to operate the CD player.
  (a) The LED is turned on and off by a NOT gate.

(i) Copy and complete the table

A	Q	LED
	(HIGH or LOW)	(ON or OFF)
HIGH		
LOW		

(ii) Use words from this list to copy and complete the sentence.

electrical   **heat**   **kinetic**
light   **nuclear**

_____ energy from the NOT gate is transferred to _____ energy in the LED and _____ energy in the resistor.

(b) The graph shows the pattern of pulses emitted by the LED when a key is pressed on the remote control. Each key makes a different pattern.

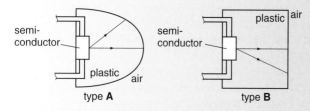

(i) This is a digital signal. How can you tell this from the graph?

(ii) Explain the advantage of using a digital signal.

(c) The semiconductor which emits the infra-red light is embedded in solid plastic. As the infra-red light passes from the plastic into the air it is refracted.

(i) What is meant by refraction?

(ii) The diagrams show rays of infra-red light in two different types of LED. Draw lines, on each diagram, to show the path of the light in the air.

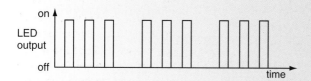

type **A**   type **B**

(iii) Copy and complete the sentence.
The remote control uses LED type _____ *because ...*

OCR

14 (a) All electronic systems have *input sensors*, *processors* and an *output device*. Explain the function of
(i) input sensors,
(ii) processors.

(b) The block diagram below shows an electronic system that can be used as a burglar alarm.

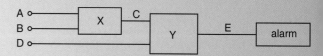

A, **B** and **D** are the inputs. The processor contains logic gates **X** and **Y**. The alarm is the output device. The truth table for the circuit is shown below.

A	B	C	D	E
0	0	0	0	0
0	1	1	0	0
1	0	1	0	0
1	1	1	0	0
0	0	0	1	0
0	1	1	1	1
1	0	1	1	1
1	1	1	1	1

(i) Use the truth table to identify the logic gates **X** and **Y**.

(ii) State an input, **A**, **B** or **D** which could be connected to a sensor in order to detect a burglar.

(iii) Name a suitable device which could be used as an input sensor.

WJEC

Radioactivity

The small nuclear reactor on board means this submarine can remain submerged in the ocean for many months without a need to refuel. It only surfaces to replenish food and other supplies, or for maintenance

By the end of this section you should:

- be familiar with the structure of an atom
- know the three types of radioactivity, and know the differences between them
- understand what is meant by radioactive decay
- know about nuclear fission and how it is used in nuclear power stations to produce electricity
- be aware of the dangers associated with radiation
- be familiar with the many useful ways in which radioactive materials are used

Atomic Structure

Aerial view of an atomic bomb exploding at a test site in Nevada, USA, illustrating the distinctive mushroom cloud these weapons produce. A complete ban on nuclear weapons testing in this manner was implemented in 1996 by the United Nations, after much concern over the increase in incidents of cancer in areas surrounding test sites. This picture shows how research into nuclear physics has led to some destructive ends, alongside more constructive ones

Particle	Mass*	Charge*
proton	1	1
neutron	1	0
electron	$\dfrac{1}{1840}$	−1

* by comparison with a proton's mass and change

Table 1

Neutrons, protons and electrons

Experiments done at the beginning of the twentieth century led to the nuclear model of the atom. We now believe that an atom has a very small nucleus, of diameter approximately 10^{-15}m. Inside the nucleus there are two types of particle, **protons** and **neutrons**. The protons and neutrons have approximately the same mass; a proton has a positive charge whereas the neutron is neutral. Outside the nucleus there are **electrons**, which orbit the nucleus at a distance of approximately 10^{-10} m. Electron orbits are not like planetary orbits; electrons can occupy a variety of positions. Electrons have very little mass, in comparison with neutrons or protons, and they carry a negative charge (see Table 1). Evidence for the existence of the nuclear atom is discussed in section L5.

A hydrogen atom has 1 proton and 1 electron; it is electrically neutral because the charges of the electron and proton cancel each other. A helium atom has 2 protons and 2 neutrons in its nucleus, and 2 electrons outside that. The helium atom is also neutral because it has the same number of electrons as it has protons; it has 4 times the mass of a hydrogen atom because it has 4 particles in the nucleus (see Figure 1 and Table 2). You should remember that nearly all of an atom's mass is in the nucleus.

element	hydrogen, H	helium, He	lithium, Li
number of electrons	1	2	3
number of protons	1	2	3
number of neutrons	0	2	4
number of particles in nucleus	1	4	7
mass relative to hydrogen	1	4	7

Table 2

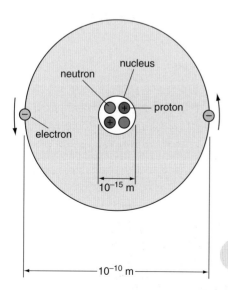

Figure 1 *The helium atom; this is not drawn to scale – the diameter of the nucleus is about 100 000 times smaller than that of the atom itself*

Ions

Atoms are electrically neutral since the number of protons balances exactly the number of electrons. However, it is possible either to add extra electrons to an atom, or to take them away. When an electron is added to an atom a **negative ion** is formed; when an electron is removed a **positive ion** is formed. Some examples are given in Table 3. The name ion is also used to describe charged molecules.

element	number of protons	number of electrons	total charge	ion
helium, He	2	1	+1	He$^+$
magnesium, Mg	12	10	+2	Mg^{2+}
chlorine, Cl	17	18	−1	Cl$^-$

Table 3

Proton and nucleon numbers

The number of protons in the nucleus of an atom determines what element it is. Hydrogen atoms have 1 proton, helium atoms 2 protons, uranium atoms 92 protons. The number of protons in the nucleus decides the number of electrons which are to be found surrounding the nucleus. The number of electrons determines the chemical properties of an atom. The number of protons in the nucleus is called the **proton** (or **atomic**) **number of the atom** (symbol Z). So the proton number of hydrogen is one, $Z = 1$.

The mass of an atom is decided by the number of neutrons and protons added together. Scientists call this number the **nucleon** (or **mass**) **number of an atom**. The name nucleon refers to either a proton or a neutron.

Proton number   =   number of protons
Nucleon number =   number of protons and neutrons

For example, an atom of carbon has 6 protons and 6 neutrons. So its proton number is 6, and its nucleon number is 12. To save time in describing carbon we can write it as $^{12}_{6}C$; the nucleon number appears on the left and above the symbol C, for carbon, and the proton number on the left and below.

Nucleon number 12   **C**
Proton number 6

You should remember that the symbols $^{12}_{6}C$ describe only the **nucleus** of a carbon atom.

Isotopes

Not all the atoms of a particular element have the same mass. For example, two carbon atoms might have nucleon numbers of 12 and 14. The nucleus of each atom has the same number of protons, 6, but one atom has 6 neutrons and the other 8 neutrons. Atoms of the same element (carbon in this case) which have different masses are called **isotopes**. These two isotopes of carbon can be written as carbon-12, $^{12}_{6}C$, and carbon-14, $^{14}_{6}C$.

The removal of a fuel element at the High Flux Isotope Reactor at Aok Ridge Laboratory (USA). The fuel element is submerged in water; the blue glow is due to radiation.

Homework Questions

1. (a) An oxygen atom has 8 protons, 8 neutrons, and 8 electrons. What is its:
   (i) proton number?
   (ii) nucleon number?
   (b) Why is the oxygen atom electrically neutral?

2. How many protons, neutrons and electrons are there in each of the following atoms?
   (a) $^{17}_{8}O$
   (b) $^{238}_{92}U$
   (c) $^{235}_{92}U$
   (d) $^{40}_{19}K$

3. Write a paragraph to describe the structure of an atom. In your essay, you ought to mention terms such as proton number, nucleon number and electrons.

4. (a) What are isotopes?
   (b) Why are isotopes difficult to separate by chemical methods?

5. Lead 209 and Lead 210 are isotopes of lead, and they both have the same proton number 82.
   (a) What do the numbers 209, 210 and 82 represent?
   (b) What do these two isotopes of lead have in common and how do they differ?

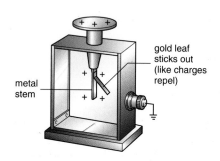

Figure 1
(a) Positively-charged electroscope

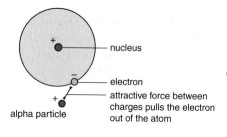

(b) Negative ions neutralise the electroscope

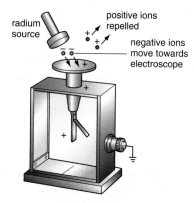

Figure 2

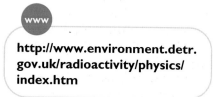

http://www.environment.detr.
gov.uk/radioactivity/physics/
index.htm

⚠Pupils under 16 may not handle
radioactive sources.

The nucleus of an atom is usually very stable; the atoms which we are made of have been around for thousands of millions of years. Atoms may lose or gain a few electrons during chemical reactions, but the nucleus does not change during such processes.

However, there are some atoms which have unstable nuclei which throw out particles to make the nucleus more stable. The first element discovered which emitted these particles was radium, and the name **radioactivity** was given to this process. There are three types of particle which can be released:

- **Alpha particles** are the nuclei of helium atoms, so they have a nucleon number of 4 and a proton number of 2. They have 2 positive charges since they are helium atoms stripped of their 2 electrons. When an alpha particle is emitted from a nucleus it causes the nucleus to change into another nucleus with a nucleon number 4 less and a proton number 2 less than the original one. It is usually only very heavy elements which emit alpha particles, for example:

$$\underset{\substack{\text{uranium}\\\text{nucleus}}}{^{238}_{92}\text{U}} \rightarrow \underset{\substack{\text{thorium}\\\text{nucleus}}}{^{234}_{90}\text{Th}} + \underset{\substack{\text{alpha particle}\\\text{(helium nucleus)}}}{^{4}_{2}\text{He}}$$

This is called **alpha decay**

- **Beta particles** are electrons. In a nucleus there are only protons and neutrons but a beta particle can be created and thrown out of a nucleus when a neutron turns into a proton and an electron. Since an electron has a very small mass, when it leaves a nucleus it does not alter the nucleon number of that nucleus. However, the electron carries away a negative charge so the removal of an electron increases the proton number of a nucleus by 1. For example, carbon-14 decays into nitrogen by emitting a beta particle.

$$\underset{\substack{\text{carbon}\\\text{nucleus}}}{^{14}_{6}\text{C}} \rightarrow \underset{\substack{\text{nitrogen}\\\text{nucleus}}}{^{14}_{7}\text{N}} + \underset{\substack{\text{beta}\\\text{particle}}}{^{0}_{-1}\text{e}}$$

This is called **beta decay**

- When some nuclei decay, by sending out an alpha or beta particle, they also give out a **gamma ray**. Gamma rays are electromagnetic waves, like radio waves or light. They carry away from the nucleus a lot of energy, so that the nucleus is left in a more stable state. Gamma rays have no mass or charge, so when one is emitted, there is no change to the nucleon or proton number of a nucleus (see Table 1).

	Particle lost from nucleus	Change in nucleon number	Change in proton number
alpha decay α	helium nucleus $^{4}_{2}\text{He}$	−4	−2
beta decay β	electron $^{0}_{-1}\text{e}$	0	+1
gamma decay γ	electromagnetic waves	0	0

Table 1

Ionisation

All three types of radiation (alpha, beta and gamma) cause **ionisation** and this is why we must be careful when we handle radioactive materials. The radiation makes ions in our bodies and these ions can then damage our body tissues (see page 325).

Your teacher can show the ionising effect of radium by holding some close to a charged gold leaf electroscope (Figure 1). The electroscope is initially charged positively so that the gold leaf is repelled from the metal stem. When a radium source is brought close to the electroscope, the leaf falls, showing that the electroscope has been discharged. The reason for this is that the alpha particles from the radium create ions in the air above the electroscope. This is because the charges on these particles pull some electrons out of air molecules (Figure 2). Both negative and positive ions are made; the positive ones are repelled from the electroscope, but the negative ones are attracted so that the charge on the electroscope is neutralised. It is important that you understand that it is not the charge of the alpha particles that discharges the electroscope, but the ions which they produce.

http://www.sciencenet.org.uk/database/Physics/Lists/radioactivity.html

Background radiation

There are a lot of rocks in the Earth which contain radioactive uranium, thorium and potassium, and so we are always exposed to some ionising particles. In addition the Sun emits lots of protons which can also create ions in our atmosphere. These two sources make up **background radiation**. Fortunately the level of background radiation is quite low and in most places it does not cause a serious health risk.

In some jobs, people are at a greater risk. X-rays used in hospitals also cause ionisation. Radiographers make sure that their exposure to X-rays is as small as possible. In nuclear power stations neutrons are produced in **nuclear reactors**. The damage caused by neutrons is a source of danger for workers in that industry.

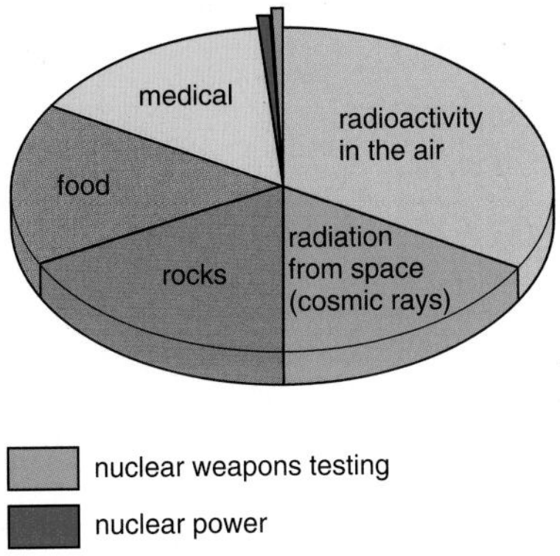

medical
radioactivity in the air
food
rocks
radiation from space (cosmic rays)

☐ nuclear weapons testing

☐ nuclear power

Figure 3 *Sources of radiation in Britain*

Homework Questions

1. Fill in the gaps in the following radioactive decay equations.
   (a) $^{3}H \rightarrow {}_{2}He + {}^{0}e$
   (b) $^{229}_{90}Th \rightarrow Ra + {}^{4}_{2}He$
   (c) $^{14}_{6}C \rightarrow ? + {}^{0}_{-1}e$
   (d) $^{209}_{82}Pb \rightarrow {}_{83}Bi + ?$
   (e) $^{225}_{89}Ac \rightarrow {}_{87}Fr + ?$

2. $^{238}_{92}U$ decays by emitting an alpha particle and two beta particles; which element is produced after those three decays?

3. Explain what effect losing a gamma ray has on a nucleus.

4. Explain carefully how a radioactive source which is emitting only alpha particles can discharge a negatively charged electroscope.

5. (a) What is background radiation and where does it come from?
   (b) Use the pie chart (Figure 3) to discuss whether the nuclear power industry in the UK is likely to cause a serious health hazard.

More on α, β and γ Radiation

Detecting particles

We make use of the ionising properties of α, β and γ- radiations to detect them. This is done using a **Geiger-Müller (GM) tube**. Figure 1 shows how such a tube works. A metal tube is filled with argon under low pressure; inside the tube there is a thin wire anode. A potential difference of about 450 V is applied between the inside and outside of the tube. When alpha, beta or gamma radiation enters the tube the argon atoms inside are ionised. These ions are then attracted to the electrodes in the tube so a small current flows. This current is then amplified and a counter can be used to count the number of particles entering the tube.

Ionising radiation can also be detected using photographic film. Radiation workers wear a badge with photographic film in it; checking the level of exposure on the film monitors radiation levels.

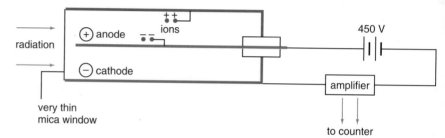

Figure 1 A Geiger-Müller tube

Cloud chambers

Another way of detecting radiation is to use a **cloud chamber** (Figure 2). The bottom of the cloud chamber is kept cold by placing some solid carbon dioxide ('dry ice') underneath the metal base plate. The inside of the chamber is filled with alcohol vapour. When a radioactive source is placed inside the cloud chamber, tracks are formed in the dense alcohol vapour. These white tracks can be seen clearly against the black bottom of the chamber. The alcohol molecules condense to leave a vapour trail in the region where ions have been produced by the passage of a particle. The tracks left by alpha particles are straight and thick; these show us that alpha particles are very strongly ionising. Beta particles do not ionise air so strongly, so their tracks are much thinner. Gamma rays leave nearly no track at all because they produce few ions in a given distance.

Properties of radiation

- Alpha particles travel about 5 cm through air and they are stopped by a sheet of paper (Figure 3). They ionise air very strongly. Alpha particles travel at speeds of about 10^7 m/s. This is more slowly than beta or gamma rays travel. They can be deflected by a very strong magnetic field, but the deflection is very small indeed because alpha particles are so massive.
- Beta particles can travel several metres through air and they will be stopped by a sheet of aluminium a few millimetres thick (Figure 3). They do not ionise air as strongly as alpha particles. Beta particles travel at speeds just less than the speed of light (3×10^8 m/s). Beta particles can be deflected quite easily by a magnetic field, because they are such light particles (see Figure 4).
- Gamma rays can only effectively be stopped by a very thick piece of lead (Figure 3). They are electromagnetic waves, so they travel at the speed of

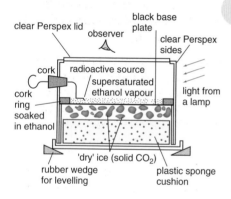

Cloud chamber tracks, shown in false colour. The green lines illustrate the straight paths of alpha particles. One of the alpha particles, coloured yellow, strikes a nitrogen nucleus and recoils. The nitrogen nucleus travels a short distance forward, and this is shown by the red line.

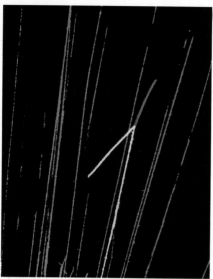

Figure 2 A cloud chamber

⚠ The source in a cloud chamber is so weak that pupils may use it under supervision.

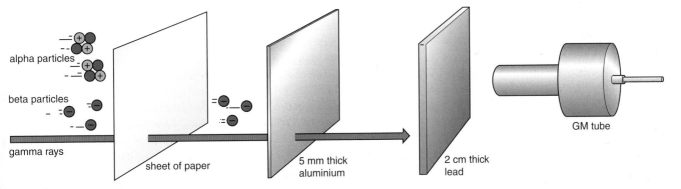

Figure 3

Radiation	Nature	Speed	Ionising power	Penetrating power	Deflection magnetic field
alpha α	helium nucleus	10^7 m/s	very strong	stopped by paper	very small indeed
beta β	electron	just less than 3×10^8 m/s	medium	stopped by aluminium	large
gamma γ	electro-magnetic waves	3×10^8 m/s	weak	stopped by thick lead	none

Table 1 *A summary of radiation properties*

Figure 4 *The deflection of beta particles by a magnetic field. Note that the deflection is not towards the poles of the magnet, but at right angles to them*

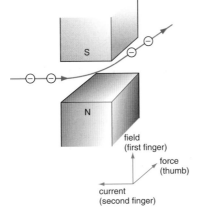

field (first finger)

force (thumb)

current (second finger)

if you are very keen you can check the direction of the deflection with Fleming's left hand rule

light. Gamma rays only ionise air very weakly, and they cannot be deflected by a magnetic field because they carry no charge.

Alpha particles will cause the most damage to your bodies if they get inside you; this could happen if you were to breathe in a radioactive gas such as radon. The alpha source in school is less dangerous because the source will not enter your body . You must keep well away from gamma sources since these rays can get right into the middle of your body and cause damage there. In all cases you will see your teacher take great care with sources, and handle them with tongs or special holders.

Homework Questions

1 Explain carefully how you could use a Geiger-Muller tube and some pieces of paper, aluminium and lead to show that radium emits alpha, beta and gamma radiations.

2 Which type of radiation is most dangerous to us?

3 A beta particle can be deflected by a magnetic field. Why can an alpha particle only be deflected a little and a gamma ray not at all?

4 (a) Why do gamma rays leave only very faint tracks in a cloud chamber?
(b) Explain why the red track produced by the nitrogen nucleus in the photograph opposite is stronger than the alpha particle tracks.

5 This question is about testing the thickness of a metal sheet. The metal sheet moves past a β-source and Geiger counter at a speed of 0.2 m/s.
(a) Plot a graph from the data below. Explain why the count rate changes over the first 50 s.
(b) Explain why the count rate drops and then rises again, after 50 s.

Count rate (s^{-1})	75	80	77	73	76	75	63	57	50	55	67	75	77
Time (s)	0	10	20	30	40	50	60	70	80	90	100	110	120

Throw	Number of coins left
0	1000
1	500
2	250
3	125
4	62
5	31
6	16
7	8
8	4
9	2
10	1

Table 1 *Coin tossing experiment*

Time (hour)	Number of nuclei left
0	1 000 000
1	500 000
2	250 000
3	125 000
4	62 500
5	31 250
6	15 620
7	7810
8	3900
9	1950
10	980

Table 2 *The number of nuclei left in a sample: half life 1 hour*

We know that the atoms of some radioactive materials decay by emitting alpha or beta particles from their nuclei. But it is not possible to predict when the nucleus of one particular atom will decay. It could be in the next second, or sometime next week, or not for a million years.

The radioactive decay of an atom is rather like tossing a coin. You cannot say with certainty that the next time you toss a coin it will fall heads up. However, if you throw a lot of coins you can start to predict how many of them will fall heads up. You can use this idea to help you understand how radioactive decay happens. You start off with a thousand coins, if any coin falls heads up then it has 'decayed' and you must take it out of the game. Table 1 shows the likely result (on average). Every time you throw a lot of coins about half of them will turn up heads.

Radioactive materials decay in the same way. If we start off with a million atoms then we find that after a period of time (say one hour), half of them have decayed. In the next hour we find that half of the remaining atoms have decayed, leaving us with a quarter of the original number (Table 2). The period of time taken for half the number of atoms to decay in a radioactive sample is called the **half life**, and it is given the symbol $t_{1/2}$. You can see that after 10 tosses of the coins, nearly all the coins have fallen heads up, and that after 10 half lives, nearly all of the nuclei have decayed.

Measurement of half life

If you look at Table 2 you can see that the number of nuclei that decayed in the first hour was 500 000, then in the next hour 250 000 and in the third hour 125 000. So as time passes not only does the number of nuclei left get smaller but so does the rate at which the nuclei decay. So by measuring the decay rate of a radioactive sample we can determine its half life.

Figure 1 shows how we can measure the half life of radon, which is a gas. (You are not allowed to use radioactive materials until you are over 16, so you cannot do this experiment yourself.) The gas is produced in a plastic bottle; we can give the bottle a squeeze and force some gas into a chamber which is fixed on to the end of a GM tube. The GM tube is attached to a ratemeter, which tells us the rate at which radon is decaying in the chamber. We measure the rate of decay on the ratemeter every 10 seconds and plot a graph of the count rate against time, Figure 2. We can see that the count rate halves every 50 seconds, so that is the half life of radon.

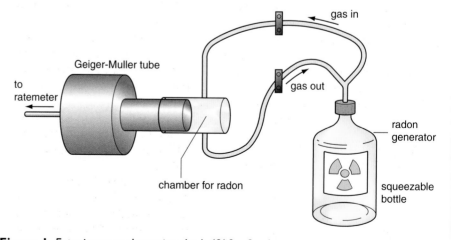

Figure 1 *Experiment to determine the half life of radon*

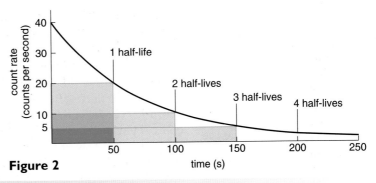

Figure 2

Dating archaeological remains

Carbon-14, $^{14}_{6}$C, is a radioactive isotope; it decays to nitrogen with a half life of about 5500 years. All living things (including you) have a lot of carbon in them, and a small fraction of this is carbon-14. When a tree dies, for example, the radioactive carbon decays and after 5500 years the fraction of carbon-14 in the dead tree will be half as much as you would find in a living tree. So by measuring the amount of carbon-14 in ancient relics, scientists can calculate their age.

Disposal of radioactive waste

Nuclear power stations produce radioactive waste materials, some of which have half lives of hundreds of years. These waste products are packaged up in concrete and steel containers and are buried deep underground or are dropped to the bottom of the sea. This is a controversial issue; some scientists tell us that radioactive wastes produce only a very low level of radiation, and that the storage containers will remain intact for a very long time. Others worry that these products will contaminate our environment and believe it is wrong to dump radioactive materials that could harm future generations.

Homework Questions

1 A GM tube is placed near to a radioactive source with a long half life. In three 10 second periods the following number of counts were recorded: 150, 157, 145. Why were the three counts different?

2 A radioactive material has a half life of 2 minutes. What does that mean? How much of the material will be left after 8 minutes?

3 The following results for the count rate of a radioactive source were

Counts per second	time (minutes)
100	0
59	1
34	2
20	3
12	4
7	5

recorded every minute. Plot a graph of the count rate (y-axis) against time (x-axis), and use the graph to work out the half life of the source.

4 Why does radioactive waste worry some people?

5 When doing an experiment to measure the half life of radon you will also detect some background radiation. How can you correct for this?

6 A radioisotope has a half-life of 8 hours. At 12 noon on 2 March a GM tube measures an activity of 2400 Bq.
(a) What will be the activity at 4.00 am on 3 March?
(b) At what time will an activity of approximately 75 Bq be measured?

7 The age of rocks can be estimated by measuring the ratio of the isotopes Potassium-40 and Argon-40. We assume that when the rock was formed it was molten, and that any Argon would have escaped. Thus at the rocks' formation there was no Argon. The half-life of Potassium-40 is 1.3×10^9 years, and it decays to Argon-40.
(a) Analysis of two rocks gives these potassium (K) to Argon (A) ratios:
Rock A $\frac{K}{A} = \frac{1}{1}$; Rock B $\frac{K}{A} = \frac{1}{7}$
Calculate the ages of the two rocks.
(b) Why would you not expect to find a K/A ratio of 1/15?

5 Inside the Nucleus

The particle accelerator at CERN near Geneva conducts experiments using sub-atomic particles moving close to the speed of light

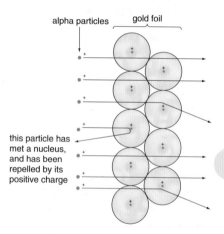

alpha particles   gold foil

this particle has met a nucleus, and has been repelled by its positive charge

Figure 1 *Most of the alpha particles pass straight through the gold foil or are deflected slightly. A very small number bounce back; this happens when an alpha particle makes a 'direct hit' on the nucleus.*

The nuclear model of the atom

You will already know about atoms. You have learned how Brownian motion helped us to discover them. We think of atoms as hard bouncy balls which exert a pressure by hitting the walls of their container. We now discuss the insides of atoms and the nucleus itself.

In 1909 Geiger and Marsden discovered a way of exploring the insides of atoms. They directed a beam of **alpha particles** at a thin sheet of gold foil. Alpha particles were known to be positively charged helium ions, He^{2+}, which were travelling very quickly. They had expected all of these energetic particles to pass straight through the thin foil. Much to their surprise they discovered that a very small number of them bounced back, although most of them travelled through the foil without any noticeable change of direction.

Rutherford produced a theory to explain these results; this is illustrated in Figure 1. He suggested that the atom is made up of a very small positively-charged **nucleus**, which is surrounded by **electrons** which are negatively-charged. His idea was that the electrons orbit around the nucleus in the same way that planets orbit around the Sun; now, however, we think electrons exist in a 'cloud' of positions not in one definite orbit. The gap between the nucleus and electrons is large; the diameter of the atom is about 100 000 times larger than the diameter of the nucleus itself. Because so much of the atom is empty space most of the alpha particles could pass through it without getting close to the nucleus. Some particles passed close to the nucleus and so the positive charges of the alpha particle and the nucleus repelled each other causing a small deflection. A small number of particles met the nucleus head on, these were turned back the way they came. The fact that only a very tiny fraction of the alpha particles bounced backwards tells us that the nucleus is very small indeed. Rutherford proposed that all the mass and positive charge of an atom are contained in the nucleus; the electrons outside the nucleus balance the charge of the protons. Rutherford did not appreciate that there are neutrons in the nucleus; these were not discovered until 1933.

Nuclear stability

Figure 2 shows a plot of the neutron number (the number of neutrons in a nucleus) against the proton number for all known *stable* nuclei. Other nuclei could be plotted on this chart, but such nuclei are unstable and they decay to more stable nuclei.

There are some points to notice about this curve.

- All nuclei with a proton number above 82 are unstable.
- Nuclei which lie above the curve are likely to decay by the emission of a β-particle.
- Heavy nuclei which lie below the curve are likely to decay by the emission of an α-particle.
- Lighter nuclei which lie below the curve are likely to decay by the emission of a positron (β⁺ particle).

So far you have only met β (or β⁻) decay. A β-particle is a fast moving electron. A positron is exactly the same mass as an electron, but it carries a positive charge; a positron is also known as a β⁺ particle.
Here is an example of positron decay:

$$^{40}_{19}K \rightarrow\ ^{40}_{18}A\ +\ ^{0}_{1}e$$

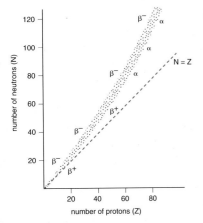

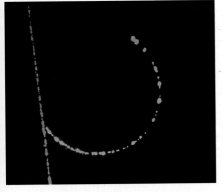

Figure 2

Cloud chamber photograph of a cosmic ray muon (green) knocking out an atomic electron (red). Muons belong to the family of elementary particles called leptons.

The structure of neutrons and protons

Over the last twenty years particle physicists have been looking for **fundamental particles**. A fundamental particle is one which cannot be broken down any further. Positrons and electrons are examples of fundamental particles, whereas protons and neutrons are not.

Experiments suggest that protons and neutrons are made up from two sorts of fundamental particles called **quarks**. Quarks are described as having different **flavours**. An 'up' quark has a charge of $+\frac{2}{3}$ e , and a 'down' quark $-\frac{1}{3}$ e. [e is the charge of an electron.] A proton is made of 2 up quarks and 1 down quark; a neutron consists of 1 up quark and 2 down quarks. β-decay occurs when a down quark changes its flavour to become an up quark (see Figure 3).

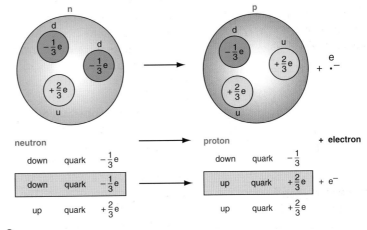

Figure 3

Homework Questions

1 (a) Explain carefully how Geiger and Marsden's experiment led us to believe that atoms had a small nucleus which carried all the positive charge of an atom and nearly all its mass.
(b) What was the 'Plum Pudding' model of an atom?

2 In Geiger and Marsden's original experiment about one out of every 10 000 alpha particles 'bounced back'. What effect would the following changes have had on that number?
(a) using a thicker gold foil.
(b) using alpha particles which travelled more slowly.
(c) using a copper foil of the same thickness.

3 Draw a diagram to illustrate how a quark changes its flavour when a nucleus decays by positron emission.

4 What is meant by a fundamental particle?

5 (Optional) Another sort of quark is the 'sideways' quark; it is rather more massive than an up or down quark, it has a charge of $-\frac{1}{3}$e. In addition the sideways quark has a new quantity called 'strangeness'. A family of particles called Baryons (heavy particles) is made by combining up, down and sideways quarks. The table below shows some Baryons which are formed by mixing *up to* 2 quarks of one flavour with another.
(a) Copy and complete the table below.
(b) Use the information above to comment on the mass and strangeness of particles.

Particle name	Symbol	Quarks	Charge	Strangeness	Relative mass
Proton	p	uud	+1	0	1.0
neutron	n		0	0	1.0
sigma⁺	Σ⁺	uus			1.27
sigma⁻	Σ⁻		−1	1	1.27
cascade	Ξ⁰	uss		2	1.40
cascade⁻	Ξ⁻		−1	2	1.40

6

Nuclear Fission

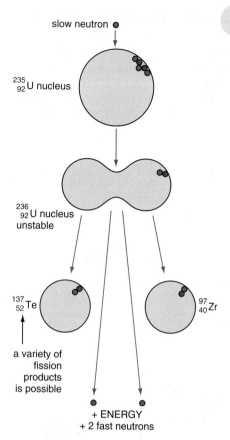

Figure 1 *The fission of a uranium-235 nucleus*

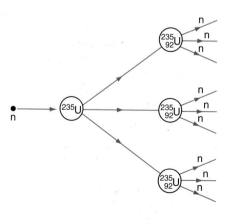

Figure 2 *A chain reaction in uranium-235*

Fission

You read in Section L2 that the nuclei of some large atoms were unstable and that to become more stable they lost an alpha or a beta particle. Some heavy nuclei, ^{235}U for example, may also increase their stability by **fission**. Figure 1 shows how this works. Unlike alpha or beta decay, which happens at random, the fission of a nucleus is usually caused by a neutron hitting it. The uranium nucleus absorbs this neutron and turns into a ^{236}U nucleus, which is so very unstable that it splits into two smaller nuclei. The nuclei which are left are very rarely identical; two or three energetic neutrons are also emitted. The remaining nuclei are usually radioactive and will decay by the emission of beta particles to form more stable nuclei.

The fission process releases a tremendous amount of energy. The fission of a nucleus provides about 40 times more energy than the release of an alpha particle from a nucleus. Fission is important because we can control the rate at which it happens, so that we can use the energy released to create electrical energy.

Once a nucleus has divided by fission, the neutrons which are emitted can strike other neighbouring nuclei and cause them to split as well. This chain reaction is shown in Figure 2. Depending on how we control this chain reaction we have two completely different uses for it. In a controlled chain reaction, on average only one neutron from each fission will strike another nucleus and cause it to divide. This is what we want to happen in a power station. In an uncontrolled chain reaction most of the neutrons from each fission strike other nuclei. This is how nuclear bombs are made. It is a frightening thought that a piece of pure uranium-235 the size of a tennis ball has enough stored energy to flatten a town.

Nuclear power stations

Figure 3 shows a gas-cooled **nuclear reactor**. The energy released by the fission processes in the uranium fuel rods produces a lot of heat. This heat is carried away by carbon dioxide gas which is pumped around the reactor. The hot gas then boils water to produce steam, which can be used to work the electrical generators.

- The **fuel rods** are made of uranium-238, 'enriched' with about 3% uranium-235. ^{238}U is the most common isotope of uranium, but it is only ^{235}U which will produce energy by fission.
- The fuel rods are embedded in graphite, which is called a **moderator**. The purpose of a moderator is to slow down neutrons which are produced in fission. A nucleus is split more easily by a slow-moving neutron. The fuel rods are long and thin so that neutrons can escape. Neutrons leave one rod and cause another nucleus to split in a neighbouring rod.
- The rate of production of energy in the reactor is carefully regulated by the **boron control rods**. Boron absorbs neutrons very well, so by lowering them the reaction can be slowed down. In the event of an emergency they are pushed right into the core of the reactor and the chain reaction stops completely.

Figure 1 shows a possible fission of a uranium nucleus, described by:

$$^{1}_{0}n + ^{235}_{92}U \rightarrow ^{137}_{52}Te + ^{97}_{40}Zr + 2^{1}_{0}n$$

The nucleon and proton numbers on each side balance. However, very accurate measurement shows that the mass on the left hand side of the equation is slightly more than the mass on the right hand side.

Isotope	Mass in u
$^{235}_{92}\text{U}$	235.048
$^{137}_{52}\text{Te}$	136.918
$^{97}_{40}\text{Zr}$	96.906
$^{1}_{0}\text{n}$	1.008

http://www.uilondon.org/
factsheets/index.htm

The table opposite shows the masses of the nuclei in atomic mass units, u. 1 u = 1.66×10^{-27} kg, which is 1/12 of the mass of a carbon atom.

Check that when ^{235}U undergoes this fission it loses a mass of 0.216 u. According to Einstein's Theory of Special Relativity, if mass disappears energy is created. The lost mass is turned into the kinetic energy of the fission fragments. The energy can be calculated using the equation $E = mc^2$, where E is the energy produced, m the lost mass, and c is the speed of light; $c = 3 \times 10^8$ m/s. The energy produced in this fission is:

$$E = mc^2$$
$$= 0.216 \times 1.66 \times 10^{-27} \text{ kg} \times (3 \times 10^8 \text{ m/s})^2 = 3.2 \times 10^{-11} \text{ J}$$

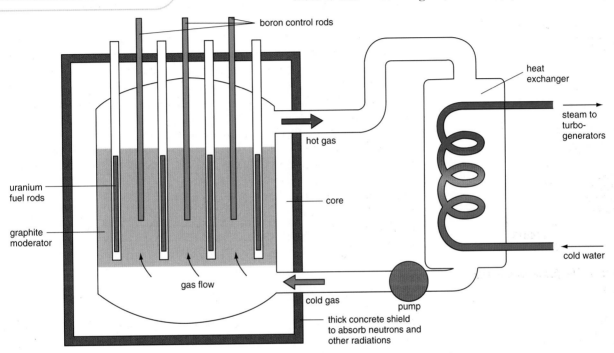

Figure 3 *A gas-cooled nuclear reactor*

Homework Questions

1 Explain what is meant by nuclear fission. In what way is fission (i) similar to (ii) different from radioactive decay?

2 What is a chain reaction? Explain how the chain reaction works in a nuclear bomb and in a nuclear power station.

3 The following questions are about the nuclear reactor shown in Figure 3.
(a) What is the purpose of the concrete shield surrounding the reactor?
(b) Why is carbon dioxide gas pumped through the reactor?
(c) Which isotope of uranium produces the energy in the fuel rods?
(d) Will the fuel rods last for ever?
(e) What is the purpose of the graphite moderator?
(f) What would you do if the reactor core suddenly got too hot?

4 This question is about producing energy inside the nuclear reactor core shown in Figure 3. This core has 1700 uranium fuel rods, each 1 m long with a diameter of 30 mm. Use the data provided to answer the following questions.
(a) How much ^{235}U is there in the core?
(b) What is the total amount of heat energy that this amount of ^{235}U can release?
(c) How long will this amount of nuclear fuel last for, if the core produces power continuously?

- Mass of one fuel rod is 14 kg
- 3% of the fuel is ^{235}U
- Power produced in the reactor core is 2400 MW
- 1 kg of ^{235}U produces 10^{14} J of heat energy
- There are 3×10^7 s in 1 year

7

The Hazards of Radiation

Measuring radiation

When scientists try to work out the effect on our bodies of a dose of radiation, they need to know how much energy each part of the body has absorbed. After all, the damage done to us will depend on the amount of energy which each kilogram of body tissue absorbs. The unit used to measure a **radiation dose** is the **gray** (symbol Gy). A dose of 1 Gy means that each kilogram of flesh absorbs 1 joule of energy.

$$1 \text{ Gy} = 1 \text{ J/kg}$$

Some radiations are more damaging than others, so scientists prefer to talk in terms of a **dose equivalent**, which is measured in **sieverts** (symbol Sv).

$$\text{dose equivalent (Sv)} = Q \times \text{dose (Gy)}$$

Q is a number that depends on the radiation, as shown in Table 1. Alpha particles are very strongly ionising and cause far more damage than a dose of beta or gamma radiation which carries the same energy. Usually the amounts of radiation that we are exposed to are very small. Most people receive about 1/1000 sievert each year, this is a **millisievert** (symbol 1 mSv).

Q	Type of radiation
1	beta particles/gamma rays
10	protons and neutrons
20	alpha particles

Table 1

Risk estimates

On 26 April 1986 there was an explosion in the Ukrainian nuclear reactor at Chernobyl, causing a large leakage of radiation. During May the **background count** in Britain increased causing us all to be exposed (on average) to an extra dose equivalent to 0.1 mSv. This is a small dose and no worse than going on holiday in Cornwall, where granite rock areas produce low amounts of radiation. However, estimates have been made to suggest that over the next 30 years, extra people will get cancer as a result of the Chernobyl disaster.

www

http://www.environment.detr.gov.uk/radioactivity/radon/index.htm

http://www.nea.fr/html/rp/chernobyl/chernobyl.html

View of the remains of the Chernobyl nuclear power station in the Ukraine. The core of the reactor overheated, resulting in an explosion that sent radioactive material into the atmoshpere. The effects of this, the worst nuclear accident to date, were felt across the whole of northern Europe.

Research suggests that for a population of 1000, about 12 fatal cancers will be caused by a dose equivalent of 1 Sv. In Britain, the population is about 50 million, so the number of deaths expected by a dose for all of us of 1 Sv would be:

$$\frac{12}{1000} \times 50\,000\,000 = 600\,000$$

However, the dose from Chernobyl was only 0.0001 Sv, so the estimated number of deaths from the Chernobyl disaster, in Britain over the next 30 years, is about $600\,000 \times 0.0001 = 60$.

How dangerous is radiation?

Radiation affects materials by ionising atoms and molecules. When an atom is ionised, electrons are removed or added to it. This means a chemical change has occurred. In our bodies such a chemical change could cause the production of a strong acid which will attack and destroy cells.

- **High doses** of radiation will kill you. There is only a 50 per cent chance of surviving a dose equivalent to 4 Sv. A 10 Sv dose equivalent would give you no chance of survival. Such high doses kill too many cells in the gut and bone marrow for your body to be able to work normally. You could be exposed to such doses in a nuclear war, and people died in Hiroshima and Nagasaki as a result of such doses.
- **Moderate doses** of radiation below 1 Sv will not kill you. Damage will be done to cells in your body, but not enough to be fatal. The body will be able to replace the dead cells and the chances are that you would then recover totally. However, a study of the survivors from Hiroshima and Nagasaki shows that there is an increased chance of dying from cancer some years after the radiation dose. Even so, you would only have a chance of about 1 in 100 of getting cancer from such levels of radiation.
- **Low doses** of radiation, below 10 mSv, are thought to have little effect on us. However, some people think that any exposure to radiation will increase your chances of getting cancer.

There can be no doubt that radiation doses can cause cancer or leukaemia (see Table 2). Uranium miners are exposed to radon gas, and girls who painted luminous watch dials were exposed to radium.

Source of radiation	Type of radiation	Number of people studied	Extra number of cancer deaths caused by radiation
uranium miners	alpha	3400	60
radium luminisers	alpha	800	50
medical treatment	alpha	4500	60
medical treatment	X-rays	14 000	25
Hiroshima bomb	gamma rays and neutrons	15 000	100
Nagasaki	gamma rays	7000	20

Table 2 *This table illustrates the connection between radiation and the increased chance of cancer*

Homework Questions

1 In Table 1, the value of Q for alpha radiation is 20. Why is it so high?
2 What does a sievert measure?
3 Summarise the effects of high, moderate and low doses of radiation on us.
4 Many modern watches do not have luminous dials. Instead they have small lights that turn on at the press of a switch. Explain why lights are safer.
5 Use the data in Table 2 to show that exposure to alpha radiation is more likely to cause cancer than exposure to gamma radiation or X-rays.
6 In a nuclear reactor disaster about 200 workers are exposed to a radiation dose equivalent to 2 Sv. Use the data in the text to estimate the number of them likely to die from cancer some time after the accident.

A view of Princeton University's Tokamak Fusion Test Reactor (TFTR). The THTR researches nuclear fusion, a process in which nuclei of deuterium combine, giving off immense amounts of energy. The temperature inside the TTFR is around 100 million degrees celcius.

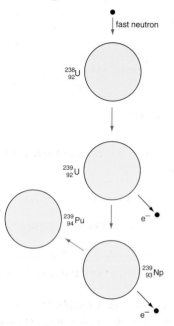

Figure I *Production of plutonium from uranium*

At the moment about 28% of our electricity is generated using nuclear power. Nearly all the rest is produced in coal-burning power stations. The government has not committed to build more nuclear power stations, but it seems likely that early next century more of our electricity will come from nuclear power.

The reason for the increased use of nuclear fuels is that our fossil fuels (coal, gas and oil) are running out; once they are gone we cannot replace them. In Britain we have saved up about 20 000 tonnes of uranium – how long will that last? At present we do not use our uranium very efficiently. Only 0.7 per cent of uranium is the fissionable ^{235}U, which produces energy in most reactors. However, in 1976 at Dounreay (Scotland) a new type of power station opened. This was a **fast breeder reactor**, which used a new fuel, **plutonium**.

Plutonium is an element which does not occur naturally, but is produced from uranium, as shown in Figure 1. Plutonium nuclei will release energy by fission, but the process is triggered by the nucleus absorbing a fast neutron (hence the name 'fast reactor'). By producing plutonium from uranium our stocks of nuclear fuel will last for a few hundred years.

Nuclear fusion

The energy which is produced inside our Sun comes from the fusing together of hydrogen nuclei. **Fusing** means melting together, which is a good description of the process. At the centre of the Sun the temperature is about 15 000 000 K; at these temperatures the nuclei of atoms are stripped of all their surrounding electrons, and they are moving very quickly indeed. Fusion involves two small nuclei colliding and sticking together to form a larger nucleus. As in the fission of a large nucleus, the fusion of two small nuclei releases a lot of energy (Figure 2).

At Culham in Oxfordshire, attempts are being made to get energy from nuclear fusion. This is an extremely difficult project; as you can imagine, producing conditions similar to the inside of a star is no easy matter! If this experiment is successful it might solve the problem of producing electricity for a long time to come.

The nuclear debate

Is nuclear power the way into the next century, or should we be looking to produce energy from natural sources such as wind and the tides? A lot of people are pressing for more nuclear power stations and others are strongly against them. This is an important issue and you should have your own ideas about it. Below

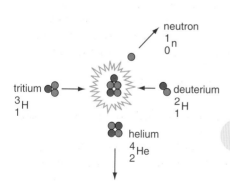

Figure 2 *The fusion of deuterium and tritium*

A lot of people are worried by the dumping of radioactive waste

Homework Questions

1 Why does the production of plutonium allow us to get more energy than we would if we used uranium as a nuclear fuel?

2 Fast reactors do not have moderators. Explain why.

3 What is nuclear fusion? Why is it much more difficult to control nuclear fusion than nuclear fission?

4 You have now read about nuclear energy. Write a paragraph to explain three advantages of using nuclear energy and three disadvantages. Do you think we should develop more nuclear power stations, concentrate on burning coal, or look for new sources of energy?

5 The Sun produces energy at a rate of 4×10^{26} W. Use Einstein's equation, $E = mc^2$, to calculate the mass which the Sun loses per second. If the Sun lives for 10^{10} years, how much mass does it lose in its lifetime? What percentage of its present mass is this?
$c = 3 \times 10^8$ m/s;
Sun's mass is 2×10^{30} kg;
1 year = 3×10^7 s

are listed some points that someone in favour of nuclear power might make, and also some points that could be made by someone against it.

Views of someone in favour of nuclear power stations

- Fossil fuels are running out, so nuclear power provides a convenient way of producing electricity.
- Nuclear power stations produce a very small level of radiation. The extra radiation is very little in comparison with the background radiation, and is not a health hazard.
- Coal-fired power stations put out more radiation into the atmosphere than nuclear-power stations, because coal is naturally radioactive. Burning coal also produces acid rain.
- Radioactive waste can be safely stored.
- The chances of a large nuclear accident in this country are very small. Our technology is far better than that of the Ukrainians, so an accident like Chernobyl could not happen here.
- Accidents happen anyway; nobody seems to worry about the number of deaths caused in road accidents. Is anybody suggesting banning cars?
- People do not understand radiation. That's why they are afraid of it.

Views of someone against nuclear power stations

- Fossil fuels are running out, so we should be looking to conserve energy. Research should be done to use wind and wave power.
- Nuclear power stations produce dangerous quantities of radioactive waste. The government has ordered Sellafield to stop discharging waste into the Irish Sea. Statistics show that children are more likely to die of leukaemia near Sellafield. Furthermore, workers at this plant have been accused of falsifying records, to cover up problems.
- Coal-fired power stations cause acid rain and produce radiation. They should be closed down as well.
- It is irresponsible to store radioactive wastes with long half-lives; it pollutes the environment for our grandchildren.
- The fact remains that a power station blew up in 1986, belching radioactive stuff all over Europe. We may have escaped lightly, but a lot of people in the Ukraine died as a result.
- Cars have got nothing to do with it.
- We *do* understand radiation. That's why we're afraid of it.

Radioactive materials have a great number of uses in medicine, industry and agriculture. People who work with radioactive materials must wear radiation badges which record the amount of radiation to which they are exposed.

Medicine

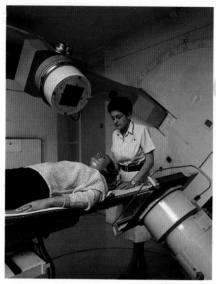

Gamma rays can be used to destroy cancer cells. This photograph shows a patient with Hodgkins disease (cancer of the lymph nodes) being treated by radiotherapy

- Radioactive **tracers** help doctors to examine the insides of our bodies. Iodine-131 is used to see if our thyroid glands are working properly. The thyroid is an important gland in the throat which controls the rate at which our bodies function. The thyroid gland absorbs iodine, so a dose of radioactive iodine (the tracer) is given to a patient. Doctors can then detect the radioactivity of the patient's throat, to see how well the patient's thyroid is working.
- Cobalt-60 emits very energetic gamma rays. These rays can damage our body cells, but they can also kill bacteria. Nowadays nearly all medical equipment such as syringes, dressings and surgeons' instruments is first packed into sealed plastic bags, and then they are exposed to intense gamma radiation. In this way all the bacteria are killed and so the equipment is sterilised.
- The same material, cobalt-60, is used in the treatment of cancers. Doctors direct a strong beam of radiation on to the cancerous tissue to kill the cancer cells. The treatment is very unpleasant and causes the patient to be very ill, but it is often successful in slowing down the growth or completely curing the cancer.

Industry

- Radioactive tracers may be used to detect leaks in underground pipes (Figure 1). The idea is very simple; the radioactive tracer is fed into the pipe and then a GM tube can be used above ground to detect an increase in radiation level and hence the leak. This saves time and money because the whole length of the pipe does not have to be dug up to find the leak.
- A radioisotope of iron is used in industry to estimate the wear on moving parts of machinery. For example, car companies want to know how long their piston rings last for. A piston ring which has radioactive iron in it is put into an engine and run for several days. At the end of the trial, the oil from the engine can be collected, and from the radioactivity of the oil the engineers can calculate how much of the piston ring has worn away.

Agriculture

To check the amount of radiation which workers in a nuclear power station are exposed to, they wear special radiation-sensitive badges, like the ones in this photograph. At the end of each month the sensitive film in the badges is developed and examined

- Tracers are used in agriculture too. Phosphates are vital to the growth of plants and are an important component of fertilisers. Radioactive phosphorous-32 is used as a tracer to show how well plants are absorbing phosphates.
- Gamma radiation is used to prolong the shelf-life of food. Gamma rays are very penetrating so this process can be used on pre-packaged or frozen foods. Gamma rays kill the bacteria in the food and so can eliminate the chance of food poisoning. However, the gamma rays will also kill some cells in the food itself and therefore can alter the taste considerably. This process is allowed in Britain but most of our irradiated food is imported.
- Gamma rays are also used to help produce new types of crops. Large doses of gamma rays will kill cells, but smaller doses can cause mutations to the cells,

which will change the nature of the crop. The seeds of crops are exposed to gamma radiation to encourage mutations. The new crops may show desirable qualities, like being stronger or producing a greater yield. These successful mutations can be kept and used in the fields.

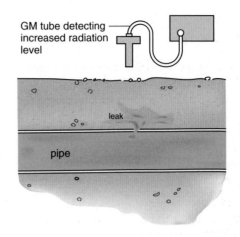

Figure 1 *How to find leaks in pipelines without digging*

Homework Questions

1. (a) What is a radioactive tracer?
   (b) Do radioactive tracers show any chemical differences from other isotopes of the same element?

2. The table below shows information about some radioactive isotopes.
   (a) You are a Medical Physicist working in a hospital. Advise the consultants which isotopes are suitable for the following tasks.
   (i) Checking for a blockage in a patient's lungs.
   (ii) Directing a strong dose of radiation deep into a patient to treat cancer.
   Explain in each case what apparatus you would use, explain why you have chosen a particular isotope and what safety precautions you would take to protect the doctors and the patient.
   (b) A company makes plastic sheeting by rolling it out between rollers. Two problems arise:
   (i) They need to check that the sheet is of uniform thickness.
   (ii) The sheet gets charged and needs to be discharged.
   Choose two isotopes to help solve these problems. Explain your choice and how the problems will be solved. What safety regulations will you enforce?

Isotope	Solid, liquid or gas at 20°C	Type of radiation	Half-life
Hydrogen-3	gas	beta	12 years
Cobalt-60	solid	gamma	5 years
Strontium-90	solid	beta	28 years
Xenon-133	gas	gamma	5 days
Terbium-160	solid	beta	72 days
Actinium-227	solid	alpha	22 years
Americium-241	solid	alpha	430 years

SECTION L: Questions

1 The brain can suffer from a particularly nasty cancer called a glioblastoma. This cancer penetrates the brain and cannot be cured by surgery. Instead the neurosurgeon gives the patient an injection which contains some boron. The boron is absorbed by the glioblastoma. Then the patient is irradiated with neutrons. The following reaction occurs:

$$^{10}_{5}B + ^{1}_{0}n \rightarrow ^{7}_{3}Li + ^{x}_{y}He$$

(a) Copy the equation and fill in the missing numbers x and y.
(b) The boron nucleus splits up to form lithium and helium. What is this process called? Explain why the lithium and helium nuclei move away from each other very quickly.
(c) Explain how this process can kill the glioblastoma.
(d) Why is this process dangerous for healthy patients?

2 An experiment to measure the half life of caesium-140 is done in a region where there is a high background count. The results of the experiment are shown in the table. Determine the half life of caesium-140 by plotting a suitable graph.

Count rate (counts/s)	Time (s)
68	0
52	30
40	60
32	90
24	120
20	150
16	180
14	210
12	240
8	270
10	300

3 The age of archaeological remains can be found using carbon dating. All living things contain small amounts of carbon-14; this is a radioactive isotope. The concentration of carbon-14 is the same for all living things. But when the creature (or plant) dies the carbon-14 decays. Its half life is about 5700 years. So after that time the concentration of carbon-14 has halved.

Cro-Magnon man is one of our ancestors. Five adult skeletons were found near Les Eyzies in France. A 1 g sample of charcoal from this site produced a radioactive count of 0.5 counts per minute. A modern sample of charcoal of the same mass produces a count rate of 32 counts per minute. Both counts were corrected for background radiation.

How long ago did Cro-Magnon man live?

4 Plutonium-241 is unstable and it decays by giving out an alpha particle. This is the start of a long decay series. By the emission of more alpha and beta particles, eventually a stable isotope of bismuth is made.

The table shows the decay series. Copy it and fill in the gaps.

Element	Symbol	Radioactive emission
Plutonium	$^{241}_{94}Pu$	α
Uranium	$^{237}_{92}U$	β
Neptunium	$^{?}_{?}Np$	α
Protactinium	$^{?}_{91}Pa$	β
Uranium	$^{233}_{?}U$	?
Thorium	$^{229}_{90}Th$	α
Radium	$^{?}_{?}Ra$	β
Actinium	$^{?}_{?}Ac$	?
Francium	$^{221}_{87}Fr$	?
Astatine	$^{217}_{85}At$	α
Bismuth	$^{?}_{?}Bi$	?
Polonium	$^{213}_{84}Po$	α
Lead	$^{?}_{?}Pb$	β
Bismuth	$^{209}_{83}Bi$	stable

5 A silver atom has a proton number of 47 and a nucleon number of 107. The atom is neutral.
(a) The atom contains protons and neutrons. How many of each does the atom have? Where are the protons and neutrons?
(b) What other particle does the atom have? How many of these particles are there?
(c) Why is the atom neutral?
(d) Silver-108 is another isotope of silver. Explain, with as much detail as possible, what this means.

6 This diagram shows a method which is used in factories to check the thickness of polythene being produced. In this case a long radioactive source is placed below the whole width of the polythene and a long Geiger-Muller tube is place above it.

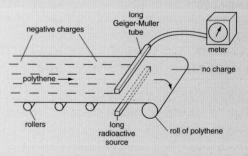

A Geiger-Muller tube is used for detecting radiation. The output pulses of current from the tube may go into a counter, an amplifier connected to a loudspeaker or a meter.

In this application, the reading on the meter can then be used as a measure of thickness of the polythene; the thicker the polythene, the lower the meter reading.

When the polythene passes over the rollers, effects of friction cause it to become negatively charged. The presence of the radioactive source enables the polythene to become discharged.

(a) It is suggested that because radioactive decay is random this method for checking thickness gives better results when the polythene is going through slowly.
(i) What is meant by *random*?
(ii) Why is the result likely to be more reliable when the polythene is going through slowly?
(b) Radiation from the radioactive source ionises the air. This produces many positive and negative ions from atoms in the air. Discuss how these ions are affected by the negative charge on the polythene and hence explain how the polythene becomes discharged.
(c) If sources of similar activity giving either α or β radiation were available, which one would be better for:
(i) measuring the thickness of the polythene,
(ii) discharging the roll? Explain your choice in each case.
(d) In view of the presence of the radioactive material, state any *two* suitable precautions which should be observed for the safety of workers in the factory.
(e) A buyer of polythene visits the factory and is alarmed by the use of radioactive sources in the method shown. He is concerned that the polythene may become radioactive.
(i) Why has he no real cause for concern?
(ii) Explain briefly an experimental check which you could make to show that there is no cause for concern.

Edexcel (ULEAC)

7   The equation below shows part of the reaction in a nuclear reactor.

$$^{235}_{92}U + ^{1}_{0}n \rightarrow ^{236}_{92}U$$

(a) Explain the significance of the numbers 235 and 92.
(b) $^{236}_{92}U$ atoms are unstable and disintegrate spontaneously into fragments, together with two or three fast-moving neutrons and a large amount of energy. What is this process called and what is the source of the energy?

(c) $^{235}_{92}U$ is much more likely to absorb slow-moving (thermal) neutrons than fast-moving neutrons. Describe how neutrons may be slowed down in the reactor core.
(d) Explain what is meant by a *chain reaction*.
(e) How is the rate of energy production in the reactor core controlled?
(f) The energy is produced in the form of heat in the reactor core. How is the heat removed from the core and how is it converted into electricity?
(g) When the fuel rods are withdrawn from the reactor core they are *radioactive*, containing *isotopes* with long *half lives*. Explain the terms in italics.
(h) Outline three precautions which must be taken to ensure safe operation of the reactor.

AQA (NEAB)

8   Iodine-131 is a *radioisotope*. This isotope is used as a *tracer* to investigate the working of patients' thyroid glands. The thyroid absorbs iodine and doctors can discover how well it is working by detecting *radioactive emissions*. Iodine-131 decays by emitting β and γ rays with a *half life* of 8 days.
(a) Explain the meaning of the phrases in italics.
(b) The table lists the proton number of some elements. Which element does $^{131}_{53}I$ decay to? Explain why this daughter element is safe for the patient.

Element	Proton number
Antimony (Sb)	51
Tellurium (Te)	52
Iodine (I)	53
Xenon (Xe)	54
Caesium (Cs)	55

(c) A patient receives a dose of 10 mg of iodine-131. After 24 days, what is the maximum mass of the isotope that can be left in her body?

Questions

9 Melanie wishes to investigate the nature of the radiations emitted by three different radioactive sources (see diagram). She placed each source 20 mm from the window of a Geiger-Muller tube. The table shows the count rate when different absorbers were placed between the window and the source. The background radiation was measured to be 24 counts per minute.

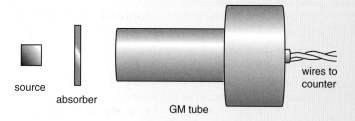

source
absorber
GM tube
wires to counter

Absorber	Count rate (counts per minute)		
	Source A	Source B	Source C
air	3127	890	4281
paper	3142	873	3752
1 mm of aluminium	3072	381	1215
10 mm of lead	1890	23	437
no source present	24		

(a) Which source is the most active?
(b) What effect did the paper have on the radiation from: (i) source A, (ii) source C?
(c) What effect did the lead have on the radiation from: (i) source B, (ii) source C?
(d) Use the data to reach a conclusion about the nature of the radiation from each of the sources.

10 Imagine that you are the Minister of State for the Environment, Countryside and Planning. The following report, produced by *Friends of the Earth* (FoE), has landed on your desk. Read it carefully; use the data in it to check the claims made and decide what action you are going to take. You may find the information about risk estimates in Section L, Unit 7, helpful.

Unacceptable radiation levels on the banks of the River Esk, West Cumbria

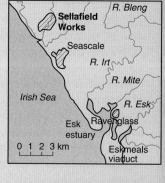

Scientists working on behalf of the FoE, have identified radioactive contamination on the banks of the River Esk. The contamination is due to radionucleides carried in the discharges from the nearby Sellafield reprocessing plant. Sellafield discharges low level radioactive waste through pipelines into the Irish Sea. Although these pipelines extend 2.1km into the sea, waste is washed back onto the shore.

Dose rates on the banks of the River Esk have been measured to be 0.4 μSv per hour. Thus a person working on or near the river for 40 hours a week is exposed to an unacceptably high dose. The Nuclear Radiation Protection Board's annual site specific limit is 0.5 mSv per year.

We make these recommendations:
- Further detailed radiological surveys should be carried out to assess the public's exposure to radiation in the area.
- The Minister should explain his failure to inform the public of the extent of contamination.
- All discharges from British Nuclear Fuels Limited at Sellafield should be stopped immediately.

11 A patient has internal bleeding from a blood vessel in her leg. A small quantity of the isotope ^{131}I is injected into her blood stream. A detector is used to find the internal bleeding. The diagram below shows the arrangement and the results of the test.

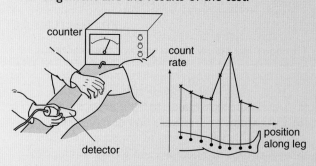

counter
count rate
detector
position along leg

(i) State the name of a suitable detector.
(ii) The radioactive isotope used for this purpose is a gamma emitter and not an alpha emitter. Why is a gamma emitter used?
(iii) How will the doctor tell from the results where internal bleeding is taking place?

(iv) The blood circulates once around the body in less than 15 minutes.
Describe the advantages and disadvantages of using an isotope having a half-life of 8 days rather than one with a half-life of 30 minutes.

Edexcel

12 A water pipeline is laid across the country. The pipes are buried deep underground. The water company uses radioactive sources to mark the route of the pipeline so that they can dig it up and repair it in the future.

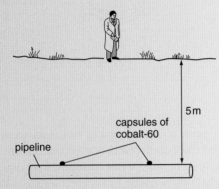

Capsules of radioactive cobalt-60 are attached to the pipe. The pipe is then buried 5 m underground. Cobalt-60 emits gamma radiation.

(a) Explain why an alpha- or beta-emitting source would not be useful for detecting buried pipes.

(b) Gamma rays are part of the electromagnetic spectrum.
(i) Name **two** parts of the electromagnetic spectrum which can be used for communication.
(ii) Name **two** parts of the electromagnetic spectrum which can cause cancer in people.
(iii) Name **two** parts of the electromagnetic spectrum which can be used to heat up food.

(c) Cobalt-60 has a half-life of 5 years.
When the pipe has just been laid, the activity at the surface just above the capsule is 120 Bq.
(i) Copy and complete this table for the activity at ground level.

time in years	activity in Bq
0	120
5	
10	
15	
20	
25	

(ii) Draw a graph to show how the activity at the surface changes over the next 25 years.

(iii) The source can be just detected if the activity at the surface is above 10 Bq. After how many years will the water company not be able to detect their pipes underground?

(d) Describe and explain **two** of the safety precautions which the people installing the cobalt-60 capsules need to take.

Edexcel

13 The equation below shows the nuclear reaction which takes place when a slow neutron interacts with a $^{235}_{92}U$ nucleus.

$$^{235}_{92}U + ^{1}_{0}n \rightarrow ^{146}_{57}La + ^{87}_{35}Br + 3^{1}_{0}X$$

(a) (i) state the name of the process which is taking place.
(ii) What is represented by X?
(iii) What is the difference between this type of nuclear reaction and the nuclear reaction which occurs in the Sun?

(b) This reaction is used in the nuclear generation of electrical energy. Describe ONE environmental problem associated with this type of electricity generation.

(c) (i) The mass loss in one nuclear reaction of this kind is 3.4×10^{-28} kg. The speed of light is 3.0×10^8 m/s. Calculate the energy released in the reaction.
(ii) The table gives the masses of the nuclei in atomic mass units (u). One atomic mass unit is 1.7×10^{-27} kg.

Particle	Mass (u)
$^{1}_{0}n$	1.01
$^{235}_{92}U$	235.04
$^{146}_{57}La$	145.90
$^{87}_{35}Br$	86.92
$^{1}_{0}X$	1.01

Use the data to confirm that the mass loss is 3.4×10^{-28} kg.

Edexcel

Questions

14 The diagram shows the variation in background radiation in England, Scotland and Wales.

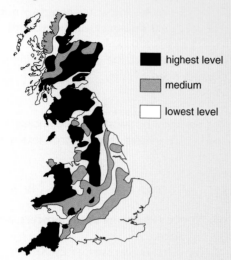

■	highest level
▨	medium
□	lowest level

(a) The background radiation is calculated by finding the average value of a large number of readings. Suggest why this method is used.

(b) The high levels of radiation in some parts of Britain are caused by radon gas escaping from underground rocks such as granite.

Radium-224 ($^{224}_{88}$Ra) decays to form radon-220 ($^{220}_{86}$Rn).

(i) What particle is emitted when radium-224 decays?

(ii) Radon-220 then decays to polonium by emitting an alpha particle.
Copy and complete the decay equation for radon-220.

$$^{220}_{86}\text{Rn} \rightarrow \text{Po} + \text{He}$$

(iii) The half-lives of these isotopes are given in the table.

Isotope	Half-life
radium-224	3.6 days
radon-220	52 seconds

A sample of radium-224 decays at the rate of 360 nuclei per second. The number of radon-220 nuclei is growing at less than 360 per second. Suggest a reason for this.

(iv) Radon-220 has a short half-life and it emits the least penetrative of the three main types of radioactive emission.
Explain why the presence of radon gas in buildings is a health hazard.

Edexcel

15 The diagram shows the piston in the cylinder of a car engine. When the car engine is running, the piston moves up and down inside the cylinder many times each second, which causes the cylinder wall to become worn.

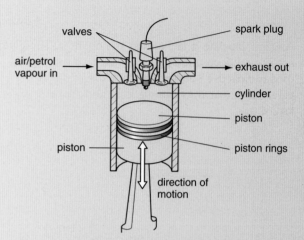

A car manufacturer wants to run tests to measure the wear of the cylinder wall due to the piston movement. A radioactive isotope of chromium with a short half-life is used.

(a) What are isotopes?

(b) Explain the term **half-life**.

(c) A very thin layer of the radioactive isotope is placed on the inside wall of the cylinder and the car engine run continuously. A detector is placed outside the cylinder to measure the count rate produced by the radioactive isotope.

   (i) Which type of emission from the radioactive isotope would be needed to reach the detector through the metal wall of the cylinder?

   (ii) State the name of a detector which could be used to measure the count rate produced by the radioactive isotope.

(d) The half-life of the emitter is 23 hours and the count rate taken at the start of the test was 600 counts/hour.

   (i) What would you expect the count rate to be after 46 hours?

   (ii) The count rate measured after 46 hours was actually 120 counts/hour. This was explained by assuming that part of the layer of radioactive isotope on the cylinder wall had been worn away. Calculate the fraction that had been worn away. State one assumption you have made in your calculation.

   (iii) Explain why the half-life of the radioactive isotope has to be short but not too short.

Edexcel

16 Evidence for the structure of the atom comes from alpha particle scattering. The diagram below represents alpha particles from a radioactive source being directed at thin gold foil.

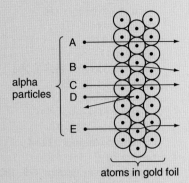

alpha particles

atoms in gold foil

(a) (i) Explain why particle **B** is deflected but particles **A** and **C** are not.
(ii) What does the deflection of particle **D** show about the charge on the nucleus?
Explain your answer.
(iii) Only a very small number of particles are deflected in the same way as particle **D**. What does this show about the structure of a gold atom?
(b) Suggest the likely result of an experiment using thick gold foil instead of thin gold foil.

OCR

Index